# The Health Care Case

# The Health Care Case

## The Supreme Court's Decision and Its Implications

EDITED BY NATHANIEL PERSILY,

GILLIAN E. METZGER

*and*

TREVOR W. MORRISON

# OXFORD

UNIVERSITY PRESS

Oxford University Press is a department of the University of Oxford.
It furthers the University's objective of excellence in research, scholarship,
and education by publishing worldwide.

Oxford   New York
Auckland   Cape Town   Dar es Salaam   Hong Kong   Karachi
Kuala Lumpur   Madrid   Melbourne   Mexico City   Nairobi
New Delhi   Shanghai   Taipei   Toronto

With offices in
Argentina   Austria   Brazil   Chile   Czech Republic   France   Greece
Guatemala   Hungary   Italy   Japan   Poland   Portugal   Singapore
South Korea   Switzerland   Thailand   Turkey   Ukraine   Vietnam

Oxford is a registered trademark of Oxford University Press
in the UK and certain other countries.

Published in the United States of America by
Oxford University Press
198 Madison Avenue, New York, NY 10016

Library of Congress Cataloging-in-Publication Data

The healthcare case : the Supreme Court's decision and its implications / Edited by
Nathaniel Persily, Gillian E. Metzger and Trevor W. Morrison.
pages cm.
Includes index.
ISBN 978-0-19-930105-8 (hardback ; alk. paper)—ISBN 978-0-19-930106-5 (pbk. : alk.
paper)   1. National Federation of Independent Business,—Trials, litigation, etc.   2. Sebelius,
Kathleen, 1948-,—Trials, litigation, etc.   3. Health insurance—Law and legislation—United
States.   4. Medical care—Finance—Law and legislation—United States.   5. Health care reform—
United States.   6. Health care reform—Economic aspects—United States. I. Persily, Nathaniel,
editor of compilation.   II. Metzger, Gillian E., 1965- editor of compilation.
III. Morrison, Trevor W., editor of compilation.
KF228.N34H43 2013
344.7302'2—dc23

*For my mother, Nancy Alfred Persily, M.P.H.*
*N. P.*

*For my father, Walter Paul Metzger,*
*and in memory of my mother, Loya Ferguson Metzger*
*G. E. M.*

*For my parents, Anne and Hugh Morrison*
*T. W. M.*

# CONTENTS

# ACKNOWLEDGMENTS

This book goes to press less than a year after the Supreme Court decision that inspired it. It could not have come together so quickly or well without the help of many people. For his support of the project and of a September 2012 conference where most of the authors presented early drafts of their chapters, we thank Dean David Schizer of Columbia Law School. Natalia Chavez, Rachel Jones, and Khamla Pradaxay provided expert administrative support in connection with the conference and many other aspects of our work. Columbia Law students Sara Chimene-Weiss, Evan Ezray, and Jack Mizerak provided excellent editing on several of the chapters, on very short notice. Our editors, David McBride and Sarah Rosenthal at Oxford and Sunoj Shankaran at Newgen, were terrific partners. Last, but far from least, Sara Mark, the executive director of the Center for Constitutional Governance at Columbia, was indispensable in a whole range of ways throughout this project. For her skillful and tireless efforts, we are truly thankful.

# CONTRIBUTORS

**Nathaniel Persily** is Charles Keller Beekman Professor of Law and Professor of Political Science, Columbia Law School.

**Gillian E. Metzger** is Stanley H. Fuld Professor of Law and Vice Dean, Columbia Law School.

**Trevor W. Morrison** is Liviu Librescu Professor of Law, Columbia Law School.

**Jonathan H. Adler** is Johan Verheij Memorial Professor of Law, Case Western Reserve School of Law.

**Samuel R. Bagenstos** is Professor of Law, Michigan Law School.

**Jack M. Balkin** is Knight Professor of Constitutional Law and the First Amendment, Yale Law School.

**Randy E. Barnett** is Carmack Professor of Legal Theory, Georgetown University Law Center.

**Andrea Louise Campbell** is Professor of Political Science, MIT.

**Richard A. Epstein** is Laurence A. Tisch Professor of Law, New York University; the Peter and Kirsten Bedford Senior Fellow, the Hoover Institution; James Parker Hall Distinguished Service Professor of Law, Emeritus and Senior Lecturer, the University of Chicago.

**Charles Fried** is Beneficial Professor of Law, Harvard Law School.

**Abbe R. Gluck** is Associate Professor of Law, Yale Law School.

**Michael J. Graetz** is Columbia Alumni Professor of Tax Law, Wilbur H. Friedman Professor of Tax Law, Columbia Law School, and Justus S. Hotchkiss Professor Emeritus at Yale Law School.

**Jamal Greene** is Professor of Law, Columbia Law School.

**Linda Greenhouse** is Senior Research Scholar in Law, Joseph Goldstein Lecturer in Law, Yale Law School.

**Timothy Stoltzfust Jost** is Robert L. Willett Family Professor of Law, Washington and Lee Law School.

**Andrew Koppelman** is John Paul Stevens Professor of Law, Northwestern Law School.

**Jerry L. Mashaw** is Sterling Professor of Law, Yale Law School.

**Sara Rosenbaum** is J. D. Harold and Jane Hirsh Professor, Health Law and Policy, George Washington University School of Public Health and Health Services.

**Theodore W. Ruger** is Professor of Law, University of Pennsylvania Law School.

**Neil S. Siegel** is Professor of Law and Political Science, Duke Law School.

**Ilya Somin** is Professor of Law, George Mason University Law School. He is the author of an amicus brief on behalf the Washington Legal Foundation and a group of constitutional law scholars in *NFIB v. Sebelius*, arguing that the mandate exceeded the scope of Congress's powers under the Necessary and Proper Clause because it was not "proper."

**Robert N. Weiner** is Partner, Arnold & Porter LLP. From 2010 to 2012, Mr. Weiner served as Associate Deputy Attorney General at the U.S. Department of Justice, where he oversaw the government's defense of the health care litigation.

**John Fabian Witt** is Allen H. Duffy Class of 1960 Professor of Law, Yale Law School.

# Introduction

*Nathaniel Persily, Gillian E. Metzger, and Trevor W. Morrison*

The U.S. Supreme Court's decision in the *Health Care Case, NFIB v. Sebelius*, surprised everyone. Some may have predicted that the core of the Patient Protection and Affordable Care Act (ACA) would survive judicial review, as it did. But no one foresaw the strange coalition of justices and rationales that would uphold some parts of the law, strike down others, and offer new interpretations to four different constitutional sources of federal power. This book presents reactions to the Court's surprising decision from several of the nation's top scholars in constitutional, administrative, and health law.

Because we tend to view a constitutional controversy through the lens of the decision that settles it, the Court's narrowly divided—and, at times, fractured—decision will, no doubt, become the basis on which legions of future law professors and students understand the case. Doing so, however, risks limiting the surprise of the case to the more traditional notion that some justices unexpectedly switched sides and bought arguments previously not thought to appeal to them. But in the *Health Care Case*, the surprise was more unfamiliar and went beyond common mistakes in judicial nose counting. From the political saga leading to the law's enactment, through the litigation in the lower courts, to the oral argument before the Supreme Court, and then to the day of the decision's release, the ACA's journey took unexpected turns.

At the beginning of the litigation, many observers were surprised that the arguments at the crux of the case were being taken seriously by anyone at all. Indeed, arguments that eventually won a majority of the Court, under the Commerce and Spending Clauses, were barely on the radar screen when the legislation was drafted. The legislative fight was brutal enough—itself filled with surprises, as the President's yearlong courtship of certain legislators proved fruitless and was further frustrated by an unexpected Senate election in Massachusetts. That election, in turn, led the House of Representatives to approve the earlier Senate version of the bill, which would have been filibustered if voted on anew. The President signed the bill into law on March 23, 2010, and seven minutes later, a coalition of Republican attorneys general filed a federal lawsuit in Pensacola, Florida.

The high partisan passions both preceding and succeeding the ACA vote should have served as an alert to the court battle that would follow. Yet the doctrinal arsenal for transferring those political complaints into constitutional challenges seemed especially inhospitable at the time. How could a massive regulation of the health care industry, which constitutes close to one-sixth of the national economy, not be a regulation of interstate commerce? How could it be that the requirement that all Americans buy health insurance—the so-called "individual mandate" provision, originally endorsed by none other than the conservative Heritage Foundation—violated some constitutional rule against federal regulation of "inaction"? Indeed, if such a prohibition existed, one would have expected to find it in the Bill of Rights, rather than structural provisions like the Interstate Commerce Clause. Such notions of "economic due process" hearken back to the long-since-disavowed days when the Court used its power to strike down key components of the New Deal, and so the challenges to the ACA did not focus on such claims. Yet in arguing instead for limits inherent in the grants of broad regulatory power to Congress, the challenges seemed, to many commentators at the outset of the litigation, to take on more than existing doctrine could bear.

When three federal district courts accepted the constitutional arguments previously considered far-fetched, however, these "off the wall" arguments now were decidedly "on the wall," to quote Yale Law School's Jack Balkin.[1] As the cases moved through other district courts and then through the courts of appeals, a real divide appeared among judges. The case began to look like other ideologically tinged cases, even if the "partisan" division among the judges who considered the ACA's constitutionality did not fall perfectly according to the party of the presidents who appointed them.

As the case reached the Supreme Court, the clear partisan divide over the ACA and the constitutional challenge to it was unmistakable. Republican officials at all levels of government lined up as amici urging the Court to strike the ACA down, while Democrats urged the Court to uphold it. Among the public, most aspects of the ACA were more popular among Democrats than Republicans, but even among Democrats only a minority (45 percent) supported the individual mandate, which only 19 percent of Republicans supported. As the Court prepared to hear the case, a majority of Americans wanted and expected the Court to strike down the individual mandate.

Adding to the drama of the case, the Supreme Court heard oral argument for three days at the end of March 2012. The first day was reserved for argument on the application of the Tax Anti-Injunction Act, namely whether that 1867 statute required the Court to wait to hear the case until a person paid the statutorily mandated tax and then sued for a refund. The second day featured what was thought to be the critical phase of the challenge, addressing whether the individual mandate was constitutional under the Commerce, Tax, and/or Necessary and Proper Clauses of the Constitution. The final day included argument on two issues: first, whether the ACA's expansion of Medicaid to additional uninsured Americans exceeded Congress's powers under the Spending Clause, and second, whether the individual mandate could be severed from some or all of the rest of the ACA such that striking it down would not require scuttling the whole law.

By most media accounts, the oral argument did not go favorably for the ACA's defenders. The Court seemed poised to strike down the law, especially the individual mandate. Most infamously, CNN's Jeffrey Toobin described the oral argument as "a train wreck for the Obama administration" (a comment he would later regret). "All of the predictions including mine that the justices would not have a problem with this law were wrong," he said.[2]

Although the coverage of the oral argument painted doom for the law, rumors about what was happening inside the Court in the months following the argument suggested the result might not be so dire. Liberal and conservative commentators appeared to try to lobby the Court, aware (or at least suspecting) that Chief Justice John Roberts may have wavered from an initial apparent inclination to strike down the law. Indeed, according to postdecision leaks, Chief Justice Roberts did, in fact, change his vote in order to uphold the individual mandate.

The Court released its decision on June 28, 2012. The decision was so fractured and confusing that several media organizations, in a rush to declare a winner in the most politically salient case since *Bush v. Gore*, misreported that the Court had struck down the ACA. Once the dust settled from those initial erroneous reports, however, a consensus emerged—both within and beyond the White House—that the Obama administration had "won." Yet after digesting the opinion, opponents of the ACA also found reasons for relief, if not celebration. The core constitutional argument challenging the individual mandate under the Commerce Clause had been vindicated by five members of the Court, and a majority had struck down part of the Medicaid expansion as exceeding Congress's power under the Spending Clause.

Because Chief Justice Roberts's controlling opinion is not joined in full by any other member of the Court, the holding on each of the salient questions in the case is difficult to tease out. On what was thought to be the bedrock issue in the case, Congress's power under the Commerce Clause or Necessary and Proper Clause to pass the individual mandate, the Chief Justice found the law to exceed Congress's powers. However, he also concluded that, when properly construed to avoid constitutional difficulty, the mandate was constitutional under Congress's tax power. This caused many on and off the Court to wonder why the Chief Justice's discussion of the Commerce Clause was even necessary, as well as whether that portion of the decision was dicta, despite Roberts's admonition to the contrary. Moreover, the Chief Justice's conclusion that the mandate fell within the tax power seemed at odds with his determination that it was not a tax for purposes of the Anti-Injunction Act, a necessary determination in order for the Court to be able to consider the constitutional challenge at all.

The surprises in the decision did not stop with the individual mandate, however. Perhaps most unexpectedly, the Chief Justice, joined by Justices Stephen Breyer and Elena Kagan, struck down part of the law's Medicaid expansion as exceeding Congress's power to spend. The expansion required states that accepted Medicaid funds to insure any individual under sixty-five earning up to 133 percent of the poverty line. Previously, states were required to cover only pregnant women and children aged six and under in households with incomes up to that level, and in general were obliged to cover relatively few childless adults. The Chief Justice's opinion held that Congress could not withhold all Medicaid funding from states that refused to expand their Medicaid programs, because that would cross a constitutional line from a legitimate spending condition to coercion. Rather, the Secretary of Health and Human Services could only refuse those states the additional money the ACA made available, not the entirety of their Medicaid funding.

Different justices agreed with different parts of the Chief's opinion and sometimes only in result. In a strongly worded and unsigned joint dissent, Justices Antonin Scalia, Anthony Kennedy, Clarence Thomas, and Samuel Alito all agreed that the mandate exceeded Congress's powers under the Commerce and Necessary and Proper Clauses. But they disagreed with the Chief Justice that the same provision was constitutional under the tax power. Moreover, they concluded that the Medicaid expansion was unconstitutional, in its entirety, under the Spending Clause. And given the critical role that the mandate and the Medicaid expansion played in the ACA, the joint dissent found that the entire law needed to fall.

Just as the joint dissent would have struck down the entire ACA, Justice Ruth Bader Ginsburg's partial concurrence and dissent, joined by Justice Sonia Sotomayor, would have upheld the law in its entirety. She would have upheld the law under the Commerce Clause as well as the Tax Clause, and in this she was joined by Justices Breyer, Sotomayor, and Kagan. But she and Justice Sotomayor were alone in upholding the entire Medicaid expansion under the Spending Clause. For them, the fact that the law authorized the Secretary of HHS to withdraw all Medicaid funds from states that refused to insure the additional population protected by the ACA did not make it so coercive as to place it beyond Congress's Spending Clause authority.

Reactions to the decision were, as expected, swift, vituperative, and varied. Chief Justice Roberts was considered a traitor by some and a statesman by others. Some saw his opinion as a short-term gift to liberals; others viewed it as a long-term promise to conservatives. As news leaked about his switch of position, the story shifted to the proper role of politics and public opinion in the Court's decision-making process. All the while, scholars debated the implications of the decision for constitutional law, the effective implementation of the ACA, and future regulatory regimes.

This book attempts to gather together selections from the scholarly debate on the Court's decision in the *Health Care Case*. It is divided into four parts. The first part presents general reactions to the decision and related litigation. The second part examines more deeply the specific lines of argument in the decision and the conflicting interpretations of the scope of federal power. The third part offers observations on the role of the Chief Justice in the case and what his opinion means for the Court as an institution. The fourth and final part features a discussion of the implications of the decision for health and regulatory policy.

Part I includes five perspectives on the meaning of the Court's *Health Care Decision*. Jack Balkin of Yale Law School argues that the Court reaffirmed the nation's social contract with its decision. Just as previous transformations in the administrative state, such as during the New Deal, required a judicial affirmation of their appropriate place in the constitutional regime, so too did the ACA. In Balkin's view, this case gave the necessary judicial stamp of approval to incorporating the ACA into the constitutional balance between governmental obligations and individual rights. Randy Barnett of Georgetown Law Center, one of the chief architects of the constitutional theory challenging the mandate, offers a different account of the decision. He sees victory for the challengers in Roberts's interpretation of the Commerce and Necessary and Proper Clauses. In his words, the litigation was about "saving the country from Obamacare and saving the Constitution for the country." The Court's decision, in his view, did the latter but not the former. Richard Epstein of New York University Law School largely agrees and finds that any faithful originalist approach to interpreting the relevant constitutional clauses would have rejected the ACA as a constitutional exercise of congressional power. In contrast, Charles Fried of Harvard Law School expresses his mystification that the constitutional arguments—especially the so-called "broccoli argument" often deployed to suggest the unconstitutionality of the mandate—were taken seriously. Finally, Robert Weiner of Arnold and Porter, who helped oversee the federal government's litigation strategy in the health care cases while at the Department of Justice, describes in detail the political context of the litigation and ultimate decision, as well as the potential precedential impact of the controlling opinion.

Part II focuses on the different lines of argument in the Court's decision. Jamal Greene of Columbia Law School looks to a part of the Constitution—the Due Process Clause—that did not rear its head in the litigation and asks, "Why not?"

He maintains that the argument that the health insurance mandate violated individual liberty under the Due Process Clause by forcing people to pay for insurance was just as plausible (or implausible) an argument as the Commerce Clause challenge. Both Andrew Koppelman of Northwestern Law School and Ilya Somin of George Mason Law School debate the meaning of the Necessary and Proper Clause for the case and the Court's decision. Koppelman finds the Chief Justice's interpretation of the clause unpersuasive and convoluted, while Somin defends Roberts' conclusion that the individual mandate was not "proper," even if it was "necessary." Gillian Metzger and Trevor Morrison of Columbia Law School delve into the interpretive stances and preferences underlying both the Chief Justice's opinion and that of the joint dissent. They describe the debate between the Chief and the dissent as between the doctrine of constitutional avoidance and a preference for clear statement rules. However, they maintain that the presumption of constitutionality that courts ordinarily employ when considering constitutional challenges to federal legislation provides the best reason to view the mandate as a proper exercise of Congress's tax power.

Part III focuses on the role played by the Chief Justice in the decision as a window on his leadership of the Court. Jonathan Adler of Case Western Law School argues that the decision is perfectly in line with Roberts's earlier opinions. It is minimalist, restrained, and exhibits Roberts's characteristic preference for saving constructions of statutes to avoid constitutional difficulties. Linda Greenhouse of Yale Law School and the *New York Times* asks the question, "Is it the Roberts Court?" In other words, does the decision in this case solidify Roberts's role as the leader of the Court and represent his clearest attempt to protect the Court as an institution? Neil Siegel of Duke Law School seeks in his chapter to analyze the Chief Justice's opinion on its own terms, and in that regard Siegel finds Roberts's analysis of the tax power persuasive, but not his treatment of the Commerce and Necessary and Proper Clauses. Nevertheless, Siegel accedes to the possibility that this balance struck by offering such different interpretations of the relevant clauses represented an act of judicial statesmanship.

Part IV discusses the doctrinal and policy implications of the Court's decision. Samuel Bagenstos of the University of Michigan Law School, Abbe Gluck of Yale Law School, and Ted Ruger of the University of Pennsylvania Law School all discuss the consequences of the decision for federalism. For Bagenstos, the Court's ruling concerning Medicaid funding will accelerate the trend toward "federalism by waiver," in which statutes prescribe broad rules for states but allow the executive branch to create exceptions when conditions warrant. The decision thus gives states new bargaining leverage to gain exemptions when statutes permit them. Gluck focuses on "federalism from federal statutes," and argues that congressional efforts to include states as implementers of federal laws is the way in which federalism is best advanced in the post-New-Deal era. She contends that the Court, in failing to recognize this, did a disservice to the federalism it was trying to serve, and that the opinion will increase national power by discouraging Congress from including state partners in the future. Ruger expands the discussion of federalism beyond the constitutional questions answered by the Court to the complex relationships the ACA creates for states and the federal government in the context of health policy. He argues that the ACA will require a great deal of rulemaking to iron out the proper roles of the federal and state governments in the statute's implementation, including but not limited to the now-neutered Medicaid provision and the optional state-based insurance exchanges mandated by the law.

The other chapters in Part IV examine the implications of the Court's decision for health policy, social insurance programs, and public opinion toward the Court. Michael Graetz of Columbia Law School and Jerry Mashaw of Yale Law School speculate about what the Court's concerns about individual mandates mean for other possible social insurance programs, both past and future. Timothy Jost of Washington and Lee Law School and Sara Rosenbaum of George Washington University likewise consider what the future may hold in the arena of health reform. For Rosenbaum, the Court's decision worsens implementation challenges facing the ACA, and reform of Medicaid will be needed in order to realize the statute's promise of health care for all Americans. For Jost, the jury is still out on the ACA's future. He describes ongoing litigation challenging the ACA on different constitutional grounds, as well as the possibility that a future administration might not enforce certain provisions of the law. One factor that may influence that future is the popularity of the ACA over time. Andrea Campbell of MIT and Nathaniel Persily of Columbia Law School look at the impact of the decision on the popularity of both the ACA and the Supreme Court. They find that the Court took a short-term hit in public opinion as a result of its decision, while the ACA emerged with greater favorability ratings from the public.

As this book goes to press, the Supreme Court has moved on to other controversies, such as affirmative action, same-sex marriage, and voting rights. As a result, both legal experts and the attentive public will now focus on those and other more immediately salient issues. Later observers may be tempted to consider the *Health Care Case* as simply the featured case of the 2011–2012 Term, akin to other "big" opinions released during each term's final days.

That view would be mistaken. The *Health Care Case* was not just another case, and it was not just another "big case" either. In so many ways, the decision and the litigation that led to it were unique. Arguments initially discredited as frivolous quickly became foundational, not simply to a political movement but also to a constitutional approach that garnered five votes on the Court. The political drama that characterized the passage of the legislation was later matched in the lower courts and the Supreme Court as they considered the constitutional challenges. The fractured resolution at the Court was one no one could have predicted, given the altering coalitions for the Commerce, Taxing, and Spending Clause interpretations in the decision.

Although the decision did not silence or even subdue the voices of active opponents to the new health care law, by and large the general public accepted the Court's resolution and moved on. A presidential campaign refocused attention away from the Court, and health care took its place among many other issues in the election occurring five months after the decision. As the public's preoccupation with the *Health Care Case* is gradually replaced by interest in other cases and political events, we hope the commentary offered in this book memorializes what legal scholars at the time were thinking about the Court, the decision, and its implications.

## Notes

1. Jack M. Balkin, *From Off the Wall to On the Wall: How the Mandate Challenge Went Mainstream*, THE ATLANTIC, June 4, 2012, available at http://www.theatlantic.com/national/archive/2012/06/from-off-the-wall-to-on-the-wall-how-the-mandate-challenge-went-mainstream/258040/.
2. Quoted in Dylan Byers, *CNN's Jeffrey Toobin: "I got it wrong"*, POLITICO, June 28, 2012, available at http://www.politico.com/blogs/media/2012/06/cnns-jeffrey-toobin-i-got-it-wrong-127605.html.

# REFLECTIONS ON THE
# SUPREME COURT'S DECISION

# CHAPTER 1

# The Court Affirms the Social Contract

*Jack M. Balkin*

In civics class we learn that federal courts decide whether laws passed by Congress and the state legislatures are constitutional. Therefore the federal courts are the guardians of our Constitution. That is certainly true, but it is not the whole story. In fact, the most important function of the federal courts is to legitimate state building by the political branches. That is the best way to understand what happened in the *Health Care Case*.[1] It also helps explain why Chief Justice John Roberts's opinion is written the way it is.

What is "state building?" Throughout our country's history, government has taken on many new functions. The early nineteenth-century American state actually didn't do very much more than national defense and customs collection. The executive branch was tiny. Over the years, the federal government took on more and more obligations, offering new protections and new services for its citizens. After the Civil War, Congress passed a series of civil rights laws, it created the Interstate Commerce Commission to regulate railroads, it passed an income tax, and early in the twentieth century it created a central bank. State building really took off after the New Deal, which established the modern administrative and regulatory state and added a host of labor and consumer protection regulations, investments in infrastructure, and Social Security. The national security state was born after World War II, and the 1960s brought new civil rights laws and new social welfare programs through the Great Society. At the turn of the twenty-first century, the federal government expanded its national security infrastructure even further, implementing vast new surveillance programs and strategies for dealing with terrorism—including detention of "enemy combatants" — that I collectively call the National Surveillance State.

Whenever the federal government expands its capabilities, it changes the nature of the social compact. Sometimes the changes are small, but sometimes, as in the New Deal or the civil rights era, the changes are big. And when the changes are big, courts are called on to legitimate the changes and ensure that they are consistent with our ancient Constitution. In this way, courts ratify significant revisions to the American social contract.

The words "legitimate" and "ratify," however, are ambiguous terms. Courts do not simply rubber-stamp what the political branches do. Rather, they set new ground rules. The government may do this as long as it doesn't do that. Legitimation is Janus-faced: it establishes what government can do by establishing what the government cannot do.

When the judiciary is staffed by people more or less allied with changes in governance, courts legitimate them fairly easily. But when the federal judiciary is staffed by people hostile to a new president's program, it often casts a skeptical eye on the innovations. Then there can be a protracted struggle over the terms of the new social contract—a struggle waged not only in the courts but also in the court of public opinion.

The most famous example of this is the constitutional struggle over the New Deal between 1933 and 1942. In the early 1930s the Supreme Court was dominated by conservative Republican judges who feared that the New Deal was out-of-control socialism inconsistent with our nation's basic charter. They struck down President Franklin D. Roosevelt's National Recovery Act[2] and other legislation protecting coal miners[3] and railroad employees.[4] Roosevelt responded with a new round of state building, sometimes called the Second New Deal. In 1937 Justice Owen Roberts joined the liberal justices in a pair of five-to-four decisions upholding a state minimum wage law[5] and the National Labor Relations Act,[6] thus ratifying key aspects of the Roosevelt program. Over the next few years, Roosevelt made nine new appointments to the Supreme Court, and this Court legitimated the New Deal regime in a series of landmark opinions.

Contrast this with the civil rights revolution and the Great Society. By 1962, the Warren Court was staffed with liberal Republicans and Democrats who generally supported Kennedy/Johnson liberalism. The justices upheld the Civil Rights Act of 1964[7] and the Voting Rights Act of 1965,[8] and precedents established during the New Deal ensured that Great Society programs would be constitutional. The real constitutional struggle begins in 1968, when Richard Nixon appointed four new conservative justices to the Court in his first term. These new justices accepted and ratified the changes of the 1960s, but also limited them in important ways. They made clear that the welfare state was constitutionally permissible but not constitutionally required, held that education was not a fundamental right,[9] limited the use of busing to achieve racial integration,[10] and halted the Warren Court's revolution in criminal procedure. The changes in the social contract were ratified, but on more conservative terms.

Flash forward to today. During his first term in office, President Barack Obama made health care his signature issue. The Patient Protection and Affordable Care Act of 2010 (ACA) made the most significant change to the American social contract since the Great Society programs of the 1960s. It realized the long-held dream of progressives of universal and affordable care for everyone in the United States.

By the time the ACA was passed, however, the nature of the party system had radically changed. The New Deal and the Great Society had support from liberal and moderate Republicans as well as Democrats. But by 2010, there were almost no moderate Republicans left. The ACA was passed solely with Democratic votes, and the two parties were at loggerheads over the nature of the social contract. The new radical Republican Party wanted to roll back important aspects of the social safety net—the Paul Ryan budget was a blueprint for this new dispensation. Conversely, Democrats wanted to complete their long struggle for basic rights of health care.

Not surprisingly, the Affordable Care Act was challenged in the courts almost as soon as it was passed. A change this big in the social contract needed ratification by the federal courts. That is what this litigation was always about, and everybody knew it.

The litigation strategy was complicated. Opponents knew that most of the Act was perfectly constitutional under long-standing precedents. They needed to find a weak spot in the law that, once overturned, would throw the entire Affordable Care Act into jeopardy. They hoped their challenge would work like Luke Skywalker's well-aimed shot that brought down the entire Death Star.

But the task was even more challenging than this. Most Republican politicians don't actually want to strip the federal government of most of the powers to regulate, tax, and spend that came with the New Deal. That is because Republican politicians want to use those powers to promote Republican policies, like income tax breaks for corporations, new business-friendly environmental regulations, limits on abortion, national tort reform, and partial privatization of Social Security (which, ironically, would require individuals to purchase securities and pension plans from private companies). What opponents wanted, in short, was a constitutional challenge so precise and so narrowly targeted that it would take out one and only one law—the Patient Protection and Affordable Care Act of 2010—while leaving everything else standing for the next Republican majority.

The opponents seized on the individual mandate to purchase insurance as their most likely target. Ironically, it was a Republican idea, offered in response to President Clinton's failed health care proposal. Nevertheless, the attack on the individual mandate captured an important theme in the radical Republican vision of the social contract: the government should not force some people to buy insurance that would effectively subsidize health care for others. Moreover, because federal laws normally don't use mandates directed at the general public, the challenge would just take out the mandate and leave virtually every other federal law in place.

The opponents also attacked the ACA's Medicaid expansion, which sought to bring subsidized health care to millions of poorer Americans. Once again, the challenge reflected unhappiness with income redistribution in the new regime. Expanding Medicaid to cover everyone up to 133 percent of the poverty line would unfairly divert federal tax dollars to the poor and shift money to states with more poor people.

If either the mandate challenge or the Medicaid challenge succeeded, opponents would then argue that the entire statute had to fall, because the Affordable Care Act had no severability clause. In this way, the opponents could wipe Obamacare off the books with a single stroke, something they could never have done through the ordinary political process.

The stage was now set for the Supreme Court to decide whether to ratify the Democratic changes to the social contract. Would the Court act like the old Court that struck down the National Recovery Act and minimum wage laws? Would it be like the Warren Court that happily ratified the civil rights revolution? Or would it be like the Nixon Court that accepted the 1960s but on more conservative terms?

Four justices of the Supreme Court—Anthony Kennedy, Antonin Scalia, Clarence Thomas, and Samuel Alito—swallowed the radical Republican strategy hook, line, and sinker. Having decided that the individual mandate and the Medicaid expansion were unconstitutional, they sought to leverage that conclusion to strike down the entire law, including features that had nothing to do with the individual mandate or the Medicaid expansion.

Chief Justice Roberts thought this a bridge too far. He joined with the four liberals to uphold the Affordable Care Act, thus placing the Supreme Court's stamp of approval on the most important piece of social welfare legislation since the 1960s. But he exacted a price for this legitimation.

Roberts held that the individual mandate could not be justified by Congress's power to regulate interstate commerce. If it was constitutional, it was only as a tax, which gave people a choice to purchase health insurance or pay a small penalty. As I have argued for many years, this is, in fact, the correct interpretation of what the mandate does.[11] Once this point is accepted, the argument for the mandate's constitutionality is straightforward, and Roberts quickly showed why this was true.

The crucial point, however, is that Roberts's reasoning captures the dual nature of judicial legitimation. He has said to Congress: "You may compel people to enter into commercial transactions like the insurance mandate, but you may not do so as a direct order under the commerce power. Instead, you must do it through the taxing power, always giving people the choice to pay a tax instead. And as long as you structure the mandate as a tax, the people's rights are protected because they always have the right to throw their elected representatives out of office if they don't like the tax." Roberts's opinion thus harks back to a basic source of legitimacy enshrined in the American Revolution: "No taxation without representation." The converse of this proposition, Roberts tells us, is that if you have been represented, and if you can punish your representatives for passing new taxes, your rights have been respected. This logic accepts the new social contract but redefines it in a way more palatable to conservatives.

Roberts then turned to the Medicaid extension. He argued that Congress may create new social programs that expand protection for the poor. But Congress may not tell states that they must accept the new programs or else lose all federal contributions to existing social programs of long standing. The federal government may, if it wants, totally fund the Medicaid extension out of its own pocket without any help from the states. It may abolish the old version of Medicaid and create a new version in its place identical to the expanded version. What it may not do, Roberts argued, is to leverage states' dependence on federal money in established social welfare programs to compel states to participate in new social welfare programs. There are various problems with this solution, and it will probably require years of litigation to clarify the rules going forward. But the important point is that, here again, Roberts is both legitimating and redefining the new social contract in a more conservative way.

Some have called Roberts's opinion statesmanlike, putting aside personal ideology to apply the law. Others have called it clever, handing conservatives an ideological victory while giving Democrats a policy result they like. My own view is that the Court as a whole performed the traditional function of federal judges in our constitutional system. The political branches sought to build out the American state and change the terms of the American social contract. The Court legitimated this result, but set new ground rules for politics going forward.

What does the decision mean in terms of constitutional doctrine? Much will depend on who wins the next several presidential elections. If the Republicans dominate American politics in the decades to come, Roberts's opinion will seem much more conservative than it does now, precisely because Roberts will be assisted by a series of new conservative Supreme Court appointments. They will remake the Constitution in their own image. If the Democrats continue to hold the presidency, the Supreme Court may regain a liberal majority for the first time since the late 1960s, and the Constitution will look appreciably different. But whoever wins, health care reform is here to stay. The social contract in America has forever changed. That is the lasting legacy of President Obama's efforts, and the lasting legacy of the Supreme Court's decision.

# Notes

1. NFIB v. Sebelius, 132 S. Ct. 2566 (2012).
2. Schechter Poultry Co. v. United States, 295 U.S. 495 (1935).
3. Carter v. Carter Coal Co., 298 U.S. 238 (1936).
4. R.R. Ret. Bd. v. Alton R.R. Co., 295 U.S. 330 (1935).
5. West Coast Hotel Co. v. Parrish, 300 U.S. 379 (1937).
6. Nat'l Labor Rel. Bd. v. Jones & Laughlin Steel Corp., 301 U.S. 1 (1937).
7. Heart of Atlanta Motel v. United States, 379 U.S. 241 (1964); Katzenbach v. McClung, 379 U.S. 294 (1964).
8. South Carolina v. Katzenbach, 383 U.S. 301 (1966); Katzenbach v. Morgan, 384 U.S. 641 (1966).
9. San Antonio Indep. Sch. Dist. v. Rodriguez, 411 U.S. 1 (1973).
10. Milliken v. Bradley, 418 U.S. 717 (1974).
11. Jack M. Balkin, *The Constitutionality of the Individual Mandate for Health Insurance*, 362 New Eng. J. Med. 482–483 (2010).

CHAPTER 2

# Who Won the Obamacare Case?

*Randy E. Barnett*

## 1. Introduction

The legal challenge to the Patient Protection and Affordable Care Act[1] (ACA)—commonly known as Obamacare[2]—which I advocated as a law professor[3] before representing the National Federation of Independent Business as one of its lawyers, was about two big things: saving the country from Obamacare and saving the Constitution for the country. To my great disappointment, we lost the first point in the Supreme Court's five-to-four ruling to uphold the health care law. But to my enormous relief, we won the second.

Before the decision, I figured it was all or nothing. If we lost on Obamacare, it would mean the government's (and law professors') reading of the Commerce and Necessary and Proper Clauses would prevail. If we won, it would be because our theories of the Commerce and Necessary and Proper Clauses had been affirmed by the Court. But, as it happened, although we did not succeed in invalidating Obamacare, our view of the Commerce and Necessary and Proper Clauses was affirmed by five justices. And the reasons advanced by the government, by most law professors, and by the four liberal justices in Justice Ginsburg's concurring opinion for upholding the ACA, were rejected.

So the question, "Who won the case?" is actually a complicated one to answer, as it depends as much on what might have been decided as opposed to what actually was. It depends on what you think the constitutional law baseline was before the decision. And it depends on how much you think constitutional law doctrine matters. In this essay, I examine these issues.

## 2. Economic Mandates Are Unconstitutional

This battle for the Constitution was forced upon defenders of limited government by Congress in 2010, when the Democrats in Congress insisted in the health care bill that it was constitutional to require all Americans to purchase insurance or pay a fine as a regulation of interstate commerce. This claim of power was literally and legally unprecedented.[4] In the findings of the ACA, lawmakers argued that this mandate was justified by the Constitution's Commerce and Necessary and Proper Clauses.[5] Had we not contested this power grab, Congress's regulatory powers would have been rendered limitless. They are not.

On that point, we prevailed completely. Indeed, the case has put us ahead of where we were before Obamacare. Five justices of the Supreme Court have now definitively ruled that the Commerce Clause, Necessary and Proper Clause, and spending power have limits; that the mandate to purchase private health insurance, as well as the threat to withhold Medicaid funding unless states agree to expand their coverage, exceeded these limits; and that the Court will enforce these limits. This was huge.

On the Commerce Clause, Chief Justice John G. Roberts Jr. and four dissenting justices accepted all of our side's arguments about why the insurance mandate exceeded Congress's power. "The individual mandate cannot be upheld as an exercise of Congress's power under the Commerce Clause," Roberts wrote. "That Clause authorizes Congress to regulate interstate commerce, not to order individuals to engage in it."[6]

Roberts adopted this view for the precise reason we advanced: granting Congress this power would gravely limit the liberties of the people. As he put it: "Allowing Congress to justify federal regulation by pointing to the effect of inaction on commerce would bring countless decisions an individual could *potentially* make within the scope of federal regulation, and—under the Government's theory—empower Congress to make those decisions for him."[7]

Regarding the Necessary and Proper Clause, supporters of the health care overhaul had invoked the power of Congress "to make all laws which shall be necessary and proper for carrying into execution the foregoing powers," seeing it as a constitutional carte blanche to adopt any means to facilitate the regulation of insurance companies that did not violate an express constitutional prohibition. Roberts squarely rejected this argument: "Even if the individual mandate is 'necessary' to the Act's insurance reforms, such an expansion of federal power is not a 'proper' means for making those reforms effective."[8] Tellingly, he did not rest this finding of impropriety on any express prohibition in the Constitution, but on the threat of this invocation of power to undermine the enumerated powers scheme that is the federalist "spirit of the Constitution."

> [W]e have also carried out our responsibility to declare unconstitutional those laws that undermine the structure of government established by the Constitution. Such laws, which are not "consist[ent]" with the letter and spirit of the constitution," McCulloch ... are not "proper [means] for

carrying into Execution" Congress's enumerated powers. Rather, they are, "in the words of The Federalist, 'merely acts of usurpation' which 'deserve to be treated as such.'" Printz v. United States...(alterations omitted) (quoting The Federalist No. 33, at 204 (A. Hamilton)).[9]

From this, the Chief Justice concluded: "Applying these principles, the individual mandate cannot be sustained under the Necessary and Proper Clause as an essential component of the insurance reforms."[10]

Tellingly, the Chief Justice soundly rejected the reasoning that, for two years, had been offered by the government and academic defenders of the insurance mandate:

> Indeed, the Government's logic would justify a mandatory purchase to solve almost any problem. To consider a different example in the health care market, many Americans do not eat a balanced diet. That group makes up a larger percentage of the total population than those without health insurance. The failure of that group to have a healthy diet increases health care costs, to a greater extent than the failure of the uninsured to purchase insurance. Those increased costs are borne in part by other Americans who must pay more, just as the uninsured shift costs to the insured. Congress addressed the insurance problem by ordering everyone to buy insurance. Under the Government's theory, Congress could address the diet problem by ordering everyone to buy vegetables.[11]

He then continued:

> People, for reasons of their own, often fail to do things that would be good for them or good for society. Those failures—joined with the similar failures of others—can readily have a substantial effect on interstate commerce. Under the Government's logic, that authorizes Congress to use its commerce power to compel citizens to act as the Government would have them act.
>
> That is not the country the Framers of our Constitution envisioned.... Congress already enjoys vast power to regulate much of what we do. Accepting the Government's theory would give Congress the same license to regulate what we do not do, *fundamentally changing the relation between the citizen and the Federal Government.*[12]

For these reasons, the Court held that economic mandates are unconstitutional under both the Commerce and Necessary and Proper Clauses.

As for the spending power, while the Court has previously invalidated stat-utes that exceeded the Commerce Clause, not since the New Deal had it rejected a law for exceeding the spending power of Congress—until *NFIB v. Sebelius*. The Court invalidated the part of the Affordable Care Act that empowered the Department of Health and Human Services to coerce the states by withholding Medicaid funding for existing programs unless the states accepted new coverage requirements.[13]

All of this represents a fundamental departure from how most law professors viewed constitutional law before this decision. Under the holding of *NFIB*, eco-nomic mandates are unconstitutional.

## 3. The Reasoning of Chief Justice Roberts's Opinion Is the Holding of the Case

And, yes, Chief Justice Roberts's ruling that economic mandates are unconsti-tutional based on his analysis of the scope of the Commerce and Necessary and Proper Clauses was the holding of the Court. In Part IIIC of his opinion, which was joined without dissent by the four liberal justices, the Chief Justice writes: "The Court today *holds* that our Constitution protects us from federal regulation under the Commerce Clause so long as we abstain from the regulated activity."[14] Why the liberals concurred in this holding is a matter of the same sort of specula-tion that attends the Chief Justice's reported switch in time to save Obamacare. But vote for it they did.

Of course, we will now hear hyperformalist accounts of the holding-dictum distinction from those who are normally against formalism. They will tell us that the courts cannot dictate the holding of the case by what they say. But, however true this may be, that is not all that establishes the rule of this case.

Contrary to the assertion that Chief Justice Roberts did not need to reach the Commerce Clause issue, *on his reasoning*, which he controls, he clearly did. He not only held that the penalty could be justified as a tax; he also held that this was only so under a "saving construction" that eliminated the legal requirement to buy health insurance, and replaced it with an option to buy insurance or pay the tax.

> While the individual mandate clearly aims to induce the purchase of health insurance, it need not be read to declare that failing to do so is unlawful. Neither the Act nor any other law attaches negative legal con-sequences to not buying health insurance, beyond requiring a payment to the IRS. The Government agrees with that reading, confirming that if

someone chooses to pay rather than obtain health insurance, they have fully complied with the law.[15]

The fifth vote to uphold most of the Affordable Care Act rested upon this rationale every bit as much as Justice Powell's fifth vote in *Bakke* rested on "diversity."[16] As Roberts himself wrote, "Without deciding the Commerce Clause question, I would find no basis to adopt such a saving construction [of the penalty]."[17] The fact that the four dissenting conservative justices failed to formally join Chief Justice Roberts's opinion (or even mention it) does not entail that his reasoning is mere dictum. If it did, then his ruling that conditioning all Medicaid funding on the states accepting Obamacare's expansion of the program was unconstitutional would also be dictum.[18] After all, it was formally joined by just two other justices, rather than by a majority. Yet no one denies its legal effect.

But in addition to the "formalist" justifications for this being the holding, we have the "realist" fact that five justices embraced the entirety of our Commerce and Necessary and Proper Clause arguments. Critics can dismiss this as emanating from the leaderless Tea Party all they like.[19] But it is now embraced by "the rule of five." And even if the Tea Party played a role, we have long been told that this is how the living Constitution—by which is meant the Supreme Court's doctrine— evolves in response to social movements. So, unless it is "living constitutionalism for me, but not for thee," if the outcome of this case was indeed impelled by popular constitutionalism, this would make it more, not less, legitimate on living constitutionalist grounds.

## 4. The Court Did Not Uphold the Individual Mandate under the Tax Power

So, if we prevailed on all our arguments about economic mandates, how could Obamacare be upheld? Some have claimed that the Chief Justice upheld the power to impose economic mandates under the tax power, and thus rendered the Commerce and Necessary and Proper Clause parts of his analysis superfluous and without practical effect. As Justice Alito once responded, however, this is "not true."

Chief Justice Roberts, I noted above, upheld Obamacare by rewriting the law's "individual responsibility requirement" so that it was no longer a *mandate* but merely an *option*: get insurance or pay a mild "tax" penalty. Contrary to the statute, he ruled that anyone who did not have to pay the penalty would have no legal duty to get insurance. "The Federal Government does not have the power to order people to buy health insurance. Section 5000A would therefore be unconstitutional if read as a command."[20] Moreover, "the statute reads more naturally as a command to buy insurance than as a tax."[21]

Therefore, it is *because he does away with the mandate* by means of a "saving construction" that Roberts finds the *"penalty"* to be constitutional as a tax. Apparently, this is a difficult legal distinction to grasp, but one that matters nonetheless. In Obamacare, the mandate was called an "individual responsibility requirement." To "save" the rest of Obamacare, the Chief Justice essentially deleted the "requirement" part. So the mandate qua mandate is gone. What is left is a tax. What is the difference?

- Under Obamacare as enacted, all Americans (who were not exempted) had to buy health insurance. Under the Supreme Court's ruling, no American has to buy health insurance, though some Americans will pay a tax if they do not.
- Under Obamacare as enacted, millions of Americans who did not have to pay the penalty because they don't pay any or enough income taxes were still required by law to get insurance or be a lawbreaker.[22] Under the Supreme Court's revision, they don't.
- Under Obamacare as enacted, those Americans who paid the penalty but did not get health insurance were still outlaws because they disobeyed the "requirement." Under the Supreme Court's ruling, if you pay the tax, you're cool with the feds.[23]

Chief Justice John Roberts justified his recharacterization of the "penalty" in Obamacare as a tax on the ground that the amount involved is so small as not to be coercive. It merely provided an "incentive," like how Cash for Clunkers provided a $5,000 incentive to trade in an old car. Millions kept their old cars and effectively lost $5,000. In *New York v. United States*, he reasoned, "we interpreted the statute to impose only 'a series of incentives' for the State to take responsibility for its waste. We then sustained the charge paid to the Federal Government as an exercise of the taxing power. We see no insurmountable obstacle to a similar approach here."[24]

The Court's opinion implied that, if this "tax" was so high as to coerce compliance, it would then be an unconstitutional penalty. "[W]e need not here decide the precise point at which an exaction becomes so punitive that the taxing power does not authorize it. It remains true, however, that the 'power to tax is not the power to destroy while this Court sits.'"[25] Those who think that this criterion is judicially unenforceable said the same thing about the *Dole* "coercion" test, which Chief Justice Roberts and four justices applied to the Medicaid requirements being imposed on the states. As he did with the individual mandate, Roberts rewrote the statute to eliminate this coercive penalty.[26]

But this is not what is most important about converting the individual insurance mandate to a tax on the failure to buy insurance: *under the Court's ruling, Congress is not free in the future to supplement the monetary penalty or tax with additional fines or jail time.* Had the argument that the mandate was a constitutional regulation of interstate commerce under the Commerce Clause been accepted, future Congresses could jack up the amount of the penalty, and add prison time to boot.

Many believed that this would be inevitable because the penalties in the ACA are too low to effectively compel the performance of those who would be willing to violate the legal requirement to purchase insurance. Now, in the absence of any mandate, thousands, if not millions, will opt to pay the tax rather than buy insurance, and Congress will be barred from increasing the penalty as it would have had the four liberal justices' view prevailed. Ultimately, this could reinforce the need to repeal Obamacare.

For those who may still not see the difference between the legal theory we defeated and that which was adopted by Chief Justice Roberts, imagine that all the federal drug laws were enforced by the nonpunitive tax he allowed rather than as Commerce Clause regulations, which is how the prohibitions of the Controlled Substances Act are now justified. Under this shift of powers, we would have to open the jails and release tens of thousands of prisoners. And Americans could now use intoxicating substances without fear of violating any federal law, provided they were willing to pay a small noncoercive federal tax on their activity. Such is the difference between the Commerce Clause power Congress claimed under the Affordable Care Act, and the new limited tax power the Chief Justice has allowed it to exercise.

## 5. The Bad Doctrine That Roberts Made

Roberts's decision made bad law in two respects. First, he claimed the power to rewrite a law by giving it a "saving construction" to uphold it, after he admitted that this was not the best reading of what the law actually said.[27] This was bad because the statute that will now be implemented was not the law that was written by Congress, but was instead a law written by one justice. The statute that is now being enforced did not command the assent of both houses of Congress and agreement by the President.

The principal constraint on the tax power is political and, for political reasons, Congress could not enact the penalty as a tax. Now, the Court has enacted a law that the political process could not, which undermines the political process itself. Moreover, under this approach, Congress may now enact laws with the expectation that the Court will fix any constitutional problems the laws may have, reducing any incentive Congress has to address constitutional issues itself.

Second, the Chief Justice allowed that Congress may impose an unprecedented tax on inactivity. Had he upheld *the mandate* under the tax power (as some claim he did) this would have been little different than upholding it under the Commerce Clause, though the remedy would be limited to a punitive fine, rather than imprisonment. However, in holding the mandate unconstitutional under any power, but allowing the "penalty" to stand as a tax, Roberts did so only because the amount of the penalty was low enough to preserve the tax payer's "choice" to obey or pay. On his reasoning, even a punitive fine would be unconstitutional *under the tax power*.

Moreover, Congress always had the power to tax persons solely because of their status—which is called a "direct" tax—provided the tax was apportioned equally among the states.[28] Now, as a result of this ruling, Congress has the unprecedented and dangerous power to tax inactivity without apportioning the incidence of such a tax equally among the states. But this new power to tax is limited to nonpunitive taxes that preserve the option of not acting as Congress desires.

On the other hand, while these maneuvers made constitutional law worse, as was noted above, Roberts's opinion also made the constitutional law implementing the Commerce Clause, Necessary and Proper Clause, and spending power better in more important ways. Together with the four conservative dissenters, Roberts provided a fifth vote for the propositions that the powers of Congress were limited by Article I of the Constitution; that the Supreme Court would enforce these limits; that the individual insurance mandate exceeded the powers of Congress under the Commerce Clause; that compulsion to engage in commerce was "improper" under the Necessary and Proper Clause; and that Congress could not use its spending power to coerce states into vastly expanding the Medicaid program by withholding existing funding. These are all positions that a majority of law professors had denied and argued against; but in the Obamacare case, all were adopted by five justices.

## 6. Conclusion: Does the Doctrine Matter?

In the end, realistically, how much does this improvement in constitutional doctrine really matter? Does not *NFIB* really mean that the Supreme Court will uphold a federal law by hook or by crook? Would it ever adhere to this doctrine if it really made a difference in a big case? Although the answers to these questions require speculating about the future, to see why doctrine matters, let me offer the following thought experiment.

Suppose that Congress were now to amend the ACA to impose a criminal sanction on the failure to purchase health insurance, or decide to greatly increase the "tax" on the status of failing to have health insurance. Would law professors dismiss a constitutional challenge to these measures as "frivolous"? I doubt it. How would lower courts likely rule? I think it is obvious that many more district court judges would invalidate these enactments than those who ruled favorably on the previous ACA challenges, and their rulings would likely be upheld by their circuit courts of appeals. Would the Supreme Court even grant certiorari on such a ruling? I doubt it. Such is the significance of the holding of *NFIB*.

Doctrine certainly constrained us in our challenge to Obamacare. We might have liked to contest the insurance company regulations as outside the bounds of the original meaning of the Commerce Clause. But we were definitively foreclosed from such an argument by *U.S. v South-Eastern Underwriters*.[29]

Of course a change in the justices could negate the importance of the *NFIB* decision, but that could happen with any doctrine. And this is as possible with an additional conservative justice as it is with an additional progressive justice. Supreme Court doctrine is always "living." But ask any litigant whether doctrine matters so long as it survives, and I believe the answer will tell you that the doctrine established by the *NFIB* decision matters too.

I have heard some claim that, because the Court has only barred economic mandates, which Congress had never before adopted and which it was unlikely to adopt in the future, this ruling is of only marginal significance. Yet, as I insisted for two years in the face of claims that a ruling invalidating the Obamacare would undermine the entire edifice of federal programs, all such a ruling would have done was bar the Congress from using economic mandates. Here is how I usually closed my speeches on the implications of invalidating the ACA: "Should the Supreme Court decide that Congress may not commandeer the people in this way, such a doctrine would only affect one law: the ACA. Because Congress has never done anything like this before, the Supreme Court does not need to strike down any previous mandate."[30]

The true scope of our legal victory is measured by the constitutional theories we prevented from being adopted by the Supreme Court. While our failure to prevent the egregious Affordable Care Act from taking effect remains a bitter disappointment, this should not be allowed to detract from what we accomplished.

- We fought this case to deny the federal government the power to compel that citizens engage in economic activity. On this we won.
- We fought this case to prevent the Court from adopting the argument that Congress may adopt any means, not expressly prohibited, when it is regulating the national economy. On this we won.

- We fought this case to prevent an end run around the limits on the Commerce and Necessary and Proper Clauses by using the tax power instead. On this we won a partial, but significant, victory.
- We fought this case to establish that conditions on federal spending, which constitute compulsion on states, are unconstitutional, as was stated by Chief Justice Rehnquist in dictum in *South Dakota v. Dole*. On this we also won.

In sum, we prevailed in preserving the enumerated powers scheme of Article I, Section 8 as a protection of liberty. As the Chief Justice wrote:

> Today, the restrictions on government power foremost in many Americans' minds are likely to be affirmative prohibitions, such as contained in the Bill of Rights. These affirmative prohibitions come into play, however, only where the Government possesses authority to act in the first place. If no enumerated power authorizes Congress to pass a certain law, that law may not be enacted, even if it would not violate any of the express prohibitions in the Bill of Rights or elsewhere in the Constitution....
>
> The Federal Government has expanded dramatically over the past two centuries, but it still must show that a constitutional grant of power authorizes each of its actions.... Our respect for Congress's policy judgments thus can never extend so far as to disavow restraints on federal power that the Constitution carefully constructed.... And there can be no question that it is the responsibility of this Court to enforce the limits on federal power by striking down acts of Congress that transgress those limits.[31]

This is what we fought to preserve. Only time will tell who *really* won the Obamacare case. But the same can be said of any constitutional case.

# Notes

1. Patient Protection and Affordable Care Act, Pub. L. No. 111–148, § 1501, 124 Stat. 119 (2010) (codified as amended in scattered sections of 26 and 42 U.S.C.).
2. See, e.g., I LIKE OBAMACARE, http://www.barackobama.com/i-like-obamacare/ (last visited Nov. 30, 2012).
3. See, e.g., Randy E. Barnett, *Commandeering the People: Why the Individual Health Insurance Mandate Is Unconstitutional*, 5 NYU J.L. & LIBERTY 581 (2010).
4. See NFIB v. Sebelius, 132 S. Ct. 2566, 2586 (Roberts, C.J.) ("Congress has never attempted to rely on that power to compel individuals not engaged in commerce to purchase an unwanted product").

5. See 42 U.S.C. § 18091 (2010) ("The individual responsibility requirement provided for in this section…is commercial and economic in nature, and substantially affects interstate commerce, as a result of the effects described in paragraph (2)").

6. *NFIB*, 132 S. Ct. at 2608.

7. *Id.* at 2587 (Roberts, C.J.).

8. *Id.* at 2592.

9. *Id.*

10. *Id.*

11. *Id.* at 2588 (citations omitted).

12. *Id.* at 2589 (emphasis added). *Compare* Barnett, *supra* note 3, at 583 ("A newfound congressional power to impose economic mandates to facilitate the regulation of interstate commerce would *fundamentally alter the relationship of citizen and state* by unconstitutionally commandeering the people" [emphasis added]).

13. See *NFIB*, 132 S. Ct. at 2607 ("[W]e determine…that §1396c is unconstitutional when applied to withdraw existing Medicaid funds from States that decline to comply with the expansion").

14. *Id.* at 2599 (emphasis added).

15. *Id.* at 2596–2597.

16. See Regents of CA v. Bakke, 438 U.S. 265, 314 (1978) ("the interest of diversity is compelling in the context of a university's admissions program)."

17. *NFIB*, 132 S. Ct. at 2601.

18. See *id.* at 2607 ("[W]e determine…that § 1396c is unconstitutional when applied to withdraw existing Medicaid funds from States that decline to comply with the expansion").

19. See, e.g., Charles Fried, The June Surprises: Balls, Strikes, and the Fog of War, in this volume (making five disparaging connections between the conservative justices and the Tea Party) ("Justice Kennedy's question in oral argument, faintly echoed in the Chief's opinion, should be dismissed as mindless Tea Party rhetoric").

20. *NFIB*, 132 S. Ct. at 2601.

21. *Id.* at 2600.

22. See *id.* at 2597 ("Indeed, it is estimated that four million people each year will choose to pay the IRS rather than buy insurance").

23. *Id.* ("Congress did not think it was creating four million outlaws").

24. *Id.*

25. *Id.* at 2600 (quoting Oklahoma Tax Comm'n v. TX Co., 336 U.S. 342, 364 (1949) (quoting Panhandle Oil Co. v. MS *ex rel.* Knox, 277 U.S. 218, 223 (1928) (Holmes, J., dissenting)).

26. See *id.* at 2607 ("[W]e determine…that § 1396c is unconstitutional when applied to withdraw existing Medicaid funds from States that decline to comply with the expansion").

27. *Id.* at 2600 ("the statute reads more naturally as a command to buy insurance than as a tax").

28. See U.S. CONST. art. I, § 9 ("No capitation, or other direct, tax shall be laid, unless in proportion to the census or enumeration herein before directed to be taken").

29. United States v. Se. Underwriters, 322 U.S. 533 (1944).

30. See Randy E. Barnett, *Turning Citizens into Subjects: Why the Health Insurance Mandate is Unconstitutional*, 62 MERCER L. REV. 608, 617 (2011).

31. *NFIB*, 132 S. Ct. at 2577, 2579–2580.

CHAPTER 3

# A Most Improbable 1787 Constitution

A (MOSTLY) ORIGINALIST CRITIQUE OF THE
CONSTITUTIONALITY OF THE ACA

*Richard A. Epstein*

## 1. Introduction: Our Two Constitutions

The United States has had two Constitutions over the past 225 years. The first Constitution, which featured limited government and strong property rights, was crafted in 1787, after which it was duly ratified in a set of state conventions. The second was crafted during the New Deal era by a set of Supreme Court decisions that inverted the old order by allowing large government administrative agencies to operate freely in a regime of weak property rights. The second Constitution grants the federal government powers of taxation and regulation that are far greater than those in the 1787 Constitution. The force of this second Constitution, on both the liberal and conservative justices, was on full display in *National Federation of Independent Business v. Sebelius* (*NFIB*),[1] which sustained the individual mandate found in the Patient Protection and Affordable Care Act (ACA).[2] Debate in the case blurred the lines between the two Constitutions by making it appear at critical junctures that the original Constitution supported this bold new initiative.

I can understand, even acquiesce in, the pragmatic claim that the decisions of the New Deal period, most notably *Wickard v. Filburn*,[3] ceded all control over economic regulation to the national government. Accordingly, any effort to carve off some sliver of the ACA—the individual mandate—through the action/inaction distinction must fail. What I find unacceptable and incomprehensible, however, is the dogged insistence that the ACA is defensible under an originalist approach that featured strong property rights and limited government. The 1787 Constitution was intended to cure the defects of the Articles of Confederation, including the lack of *federal* powers over taxation and commerce. Evidence of this intention comes only at a high level of abstraction, for there is little by way of direct and useful historical evidence as to the precise decisions made on most key decisions. The originalist approach here does not claim to have some magical constitutional bullet that resolves all these questions, but relies largely on textual evidence internal to the Constitution to defend its conclusions, which I think are, in any event, more reliable guides to interpretation than any appeal to scattered external texts. In some cases, there are explications of these constitutional provisions given after the fact, which must be taken into account. But these too should be regarded not as evidence of original intention in any strong sense, but as the best views, often articulated by people with particular agendas, of how particular clauses should be interpreted. They have to be read with respect and caution at the same time. Putting this whole package together, the one clear point about the Constitution is, whatever its internal uncertainties, that it was not intended to provide the framework of the New Deal state with its emphasis on public participation and administrative expertise, and on the substantive guarantees of Franklin Roosevelt's Second Bill of Rights.[4] This transformation has not been pretty, for in my view it rests on a serious misinterpretation, an artificial truncation of constitutional text, and a deep misunderstanding of the political theory embraced by the framers. The devotees of small government were on *all* sides of the original constitutional debates, and they did not, and could not, have drafted the Constitution that emerged in the tumultuous years of the New Deal.[5]

## 2. The Constitutional Moment: Of Taxation and the Commerce Power

The drafters of the Constitution sought to achieve two ends: to remedy the defects of the Articles of Confederation without creating an overpowering central government that would reduce the status of the states to bit players in the constitutional scheme. Two provisions of Article I, Section 8 give voice to those dual concerns in its treatment of the federal powers to tax and to regulate commerce. I take them up in order.

### A. TAXATION

The constitutional text of Article I, Section 8, Clause 1 reads in full:

> The Congress shall have Power To lay and collect Taxes, Duties, Imposts and Excises, to pay the Debts and provide for the common Defence and general Welfare of the United States; but all Duties, Imposts and Excises shall be uniform throughout the United States.

This particular provision did not receive an authoritative judicial interpretation until 1936.[6] But its basic structure rests on a close reading of the text, which specifies three enumerated ends for which taxes may be used: the debt, the common defense, and the general welfare of the United States. Alexander Hamilton's Report on Manufactures took an expansive view of the phrase, "general welfare," noting that it must extend beyond the first two clauses.[7] In contrast, James Madison gave a narrow reading to the clause, by explicitly hearkening back to similar language in Article III of the Articles of Confederation, which states: "The objects of the Union among the States, as described in article third, are 'their common defense, security of their liberties, and mutual and general welfare.'"[8] This linkage led Madison to tie the power to tax to the other enumerated powers of Article I, Section 8.[9] Justice Joseph Story's extensive *Commentaries* on the provision elaborates on the controversy by noting that the three listed objects of taxation (debt, common defense, and general welfare of the United States) are not independent powers, but ancillary to the power to tax. Story noted that the words *"in order"* must be inserted between "Excises," and "to pay the Debts" and so on, in order to preserve the principle of enumerated powers.[10]

Second, these three ends—debts, common defense, and general welfare—must be understood with reference to the key phrase that follows them, "of the United States," which Hamilton dropped in his Report on Manufactures. The Congress of the United States has no power to pay the debts of individuals or of the states. That ability to pay the debts of the United States is critical for allowing the United States to borrow to fund capital projects, as allowed in Article I, Section 8, Clause 2. That power is critical, for otherwise there is no way to finance the long-term capital projects that are needed to build up an army and a navy, and to make the long-term expenditures needed to carry out the other enumerated powers.

Similarly, the common defense in this case is that of the United States, not that of individual states, which are dealt with elsewhere.[11] The common defense of the United States, however, applies to all threats of foreign invasion, wherever they may take place, and all overseas adventures. What makes the defense "common" is the absence of explicit transfer payments, initiated by the United States, from one group of individuals to another. From the *ex ante* perspective, therefore, all states benefit from this national power. From the *ex post* perspective, it is likely that individual expenditures will tend to "even out" over time. Nothing in the subsequent history of the United States from the War of 1812, to the Civil War, to the war in Iraq falsifies that insight.

"[G]eneral Welfare of the United States" should be read in parallel fashion. It is intended to produce public goods, that is, those goods that if provided to one individual cannot be excluded from the other. The clause lets the United States overcome the collective action and free-rider problems, well discussed by the late economist Mancur Olson.[12] But in practice, few, if any, public goods are supplied in equal measure and with equal value to all members of the public. As with the common defense, however, it would be wrong, indeed constitutionally perverse, to insist that all public goods must meet an exacting standard of equality of access or value for all citizens of the United States. A public street or a lamppost will rarely generate uniform benefits or burdens, given that some people like to be located near to, and others farther from, either. These variations in the incidence of public goods are fit for political deliberation, not constitutional limitation under either the taxing power or eminent domain power, with its "public use" limitation.[13] Nonetheless, any sensible definition of public goods *does* mean that any outright transfer payment of wealth from one group of citizens to another (which even Hamilton did not consider) does *not* count as taxation for the general welfare of the United States.

The simple explanation is that public goods involve nonexclusive goods that when supplied to one person must to a greater or lesser degree be supplied to another, while transfer payments result in the private ownership of property or wealth that is indistinguishable from any private good acquired in any other fashion. The key benefit of prohibition against transfer payments is that it increases the odds that all exertions of the powers to tax (and to take) will result in Pareto improvements where no one is left worse off afterwards than before. The distribution of the gains from the provision of standard nonexcludable public goods is a difficult subject, although in principle the use of a pro rata rule tends to equalize gains across persons. But transfer payments, even with their supposed "indirect benefits," virtually never create Pareto improvements, but instead facilitate the factional fights that Madison warned against in Federalist Number 10. A cash transfer from one set of corporate shareholders to another is never for the benefit of the corporation itself for the simple reason that private investors will not put money up if they know that it is subject to expropriation. The Constitution is intended to get states to invest in the same type of governance found in a corporate venture. Since the powers under the Constitution are greater than those under the Articles, the need for an explicit counterweight against these transfers is, if anything, more important in the new legal order than it was in the old.

The limited scope of the spending power is consistent, moreover, with the constitutional treatment of the phrase "all Duties, Imposts and Excises shall be uniform throughout the United States." Uniformity is not sustainable with respect to taxes that are based on income from earnings and investment where the tax base requires the inclusion of multiple transactions for which it is not possible in practice to have a uniform rate. But uniformity is possible with the duties, imposts, and excises, all of which operate solely in connection with discrete transactions in goods that have a clear monetary value. That geographical uniformity is yet another way to prevent disguised transfer payments among the states, by limiting the ability of states to manipulate rates sensitive to the value of the products subject to the tax.[14] As Story put it: "It was to cut off all undue preferences of one state over another in the regulation of subjects affecting their common interests. Unless duties, imposts, and excises were uniform, the grossest and most oppressive inequalities, vitally affecting the pursuits and employments of the people of different states, might exist."[15]

The full force of the constitutional scheme is also evident by looking at the treatment of direct taxes found in Article I, Section 9, Clause 4:

> No Capitation, or other direct, Tax shall be laid, unless in Proportion to the Census or enumeration herein before directed to be taken.

As the text makes evident, these direct taxes include capitation taxes, or poll or head taxes, as well as taxes that are levied on the ownership of land, as distinct from taxes on earned and investment income.[16] The apportionment here was intended to equalize the burden of the taxes across states lines, so that each state has to pay a direct tax in direct proportion to population regardless of wealth, so that large poor states need to pay more than smaller rich ones. Any imposition of direct taxes is *regressive* toward wealth, which is one reason why these taxes are not routinely imposed. The tight restrictions on direct taxation found in Article I, Section 9 make it hard to remove the parallel restraints on taxation consciously included in Article I, Section 8. The two neighboring clauses should receive complementary interpretations. The broader reading given to direct taxes in *Pollock v. Farmer's Loan & Trust Co.*[17] may have been overruled by the Sixteenth Amendment,[18] but that does nothing to influence the interpretation of Article I, Section 8, Clause 1, which remains as it was. My reading of these taxing provisions allows for the achievement of every goal sought by the replacement of the Articles of Confederation, for it precludes no form of taxation intended to provide public goods, as opposed to transfer payments, which were from the outset not the responsibility of the United States under the original constitutional scheme.

## B. COMMERCE

The interpretation of the Commerce Clause was equally contentious in the debate over the constitutionality of the ACA. Article I, Section 8, Clause 3 reads:

> The Congress shall have Power ... To regulate Commerce with foreign Nations, and among the several States, and with the Indian tribes.

Like all clauses, this one bristles with interpretive difficulties, but none that go to the constitutionality of the ACA. For example, Story was a great champion of the view that federal powers were often *exclusive* of the states. That position is possible to maintain, for example, on his reading of the spending power: even if the national government could only tax and spend for its three enumerated purposes, the states still retained the power to tax for their own separate purposes. But that principle fails with respect to the commerce power, on which Story was at his worst. His arguments in favor of this strong form of exclusivity seem weak because he does not explain why the "full power to regulate a particular subject implies the whole power, and leaves no *residuum*."[19] That logic appears to make it improper to apply the state common law, or the modern Uniform Commercial Code, to interstate sales—a position that no one has ever held. Story tries to save his position by defining commerce narrowly, by excluding from its province those powers that he finds are "entirely distinct in their nature from that to regulate commerce."[20] These include the extensive police powers of the states, which include "inspection laws, health laws, laws regulating turnpikes, roads, and ferries, all of which, when exercised by a state, are legitimate, arising from the general powers belonging to it, unless so far as they *conflict* with the powers delegated to congress."[21] The claim unravels with Story's "unless" clause, for all sorts of decisions on turnpikes, roads, and ferries, at the very least, could be subject to concurrent powers, at which point the Supremacy Clause makes preemption the focal point of analysis. But even with that major concession to reality, Story's formulation *does* leave exclusively within the control of the states such key activities as agriculture, mining, and manufacture. That residuum of state powers position makes perfect sense because it is wholly implausible to think that the state ratification conventions would have ceded powers to the federal government on anything like the scale of the Supreme Court's New Deal decisions.

On two other questions, however, Story may be closer to the mark. The first asks whether the Commerce Clause gives the federal government the power to regulate internal activities within the state, most notably agriculture, manufacture, and mining. The second asks whether the admitted power to regulate commerce gives Congress the power to *block* the shipment of any and all goods through the arteries of interstate commerce, a power that could be waived only for those states that comply with certain directives from the national government, relating to the internal activities within the states. From a cautious originalist perspective, the correct answers to these questions are no and no.

Start with the basics of the grand bargain that led to the formation of the United States Constitution: limited delegated powers that were intended to let the national government function without destroying the autonomy of the states, which cannot survive if the national government can regulate any and all economic issues that remain, indisputably, within the province of the state governments. That relationship is well captured in James Madison's famous observation in Federalist Number 45:

> The powers delegated by the proposed Constitution to the federal gov-ernment are few and defined. Those which are to remain in the State governments are numerous and indefinite. The former will be exercised principally on external objects, as war, peace, negotiation, and foreign commerce; with which last the power of taxation will, for the most part, be connected. The powers reserved to the several States will extend to all the objects which, in the ordinary course of affairs, concern the lives, liberties, and properties of the people, and the internal order, improve-ment, and prosperity of the State.[22]

Note that in this passage Madison refers only to *foreign* commerce, which hardly suggests that the regulation of commerce among the several states was meant to be the juggernaut that it became. It is also worth recalling that Hamilton in Federalist Number 11 thought of an unregulated common market at home, even as he was happy to propose protectionist barriers from abroad. It is every bit as telling that for Hamilton that succinct point on the distribution of federal and state powers is, of course, in line with the general deliberations that surrounded the replacement of the Articles of Confederation with the Constitution. Joseph Story put the point forcefully in his *Commentaries*, portions of which look as though they are lifted nearly verbatim from Chief Justice Marshall's oft-misread decision in *Gibbons v. Ogden*.[23] In Story's view, the Commerce Clause was a linchpin for the union. Thus at the outset of his discussion on the topic he reminds his reader: "The oppressed and degraded state of commerce, previ-ous to the adoption of the constitution, can scarcely be forgotten."[24] But it is instructive again that his main concern, like Hamilton's was with the ability of the United States to maintain a united front against foreign powers when "our disunited efforts to counteract their restrictions were rendered impotent by a want of combination."[25] There are dangerous shades of a protectionist policy at work in Story's confident declaration, but for our purposes, it is clear that he sees no parallel issue with respect to domestic commerce where those foreign forces have no role to play whatsoever. Now the threat is state disruption of interstate commerce, a very different question.

Once he is finished with his statement of purpose, Story gives a definition of regulation that simply says that the power to regulate is the power "to pre-scribe the rule, by which commerce is to be governed."[26] The question is what can be made of these broad declarations. Nothing much, it turns out, when they are placed in context. Story, like John Marshall in *Gibbons*, takes a view of commerce that is tied to all forms of business intercourse among the states. The narrow sense, by modern standards, that he attributes to this view is caught by two considerations. First, he writes that "Inspection laws are not, strictly speaking, regulations of commerce, though they may have a remote and considerable influence on commerce."[27] The reason is clear enough: these laws act on their subject "before it becomes an article of commerce." [28] If inspection laws exert their influence prior to interstate commerce, the manufacture, agriculture, or mining that generates the goods that are provided in interstate or foreign commerce precedes them as well—a point that Story took for granted, following *Gibbons*. Second, he reads the term "commerce" in Article I, Section 8, Clause 3 *in pari materia* with the word in Article I, Section 9, Clause 5, which provides, "No Preference shall be given by any Regulation of Commerce or Revenue to the Ports of one State over those of another: nor shall Vessels bound to, or from, one State be obliged to enter, clear, or pay Duties in another." The use of the term "commerce" in this clause is perfectly consistent with its use in the Commerce Clause proper in Article I, Section 8, Clause 3. Indeed the term "regulation of commerce" shows the closeness of connection between the two clauses.

These propositions make it possible to address the first of the two questions, which is whether the power to regulate commerce among the states carries with it the power to regulate agriculture, manufacture, and mining within each individual state. From his long discussion of the definition of commerce, it is clear that Story, following Marshall, does not include any of these activities under the clause, but concentrates on explaining why navigation into the interior of the states is subject to federal power.

It is harder to reach a definitive conclusion on the question of whether Congress's power to regulate commerce among the states gives it carte blanche to prohibit any or all interstate activities. Hamilton in Federalist Number 11 favors both a strong unified federal government to deal with foreign nations, *and* an open and unregulated common market on the domestic front.[29] On the former he writes: "By prohibitory regulations, extending, at the same time, throughout the States, we may oblige foreign countries to bid against each other, for the privileges of our markets."[30] But he switches gears with respect to domestic commerce: "An unrestrained intercourse between the States themselves will advance the trade of each by an interchange of their respective productions, not only for the supply of reciprocal wants at home, but for exportation to foreign markets."[31]

Story takes the same position. He does not discuss the prohibition of commerce in the short portions of his *Commentaries* that deal properly with commerce among the several states, where the terms "agriculture," "manufacture," and "mining" are not used at all.[32] But those activities surge to the fore when he asks in connection with foreign commerce "whether congress have a constitutional authority to apply the power to regulate commerce for the purpose of encouraging and protecting domestic manufactures."[33] On foreign commerce, Story ultimately follows Hamilton's protectionist line by insisting that any want of power at the federal level to encourage domestic manufacture "would secure the most complete triumph over us by foreign nations."[34] But on domestic commerce, he follows Hamilton's lead by asking "whether, under the pretence of an exercise of the power to regulate commerce, congress may in fact impose duties for objects wholly distinct from commerce." And further, "whether a power, exclusively for the regulation of commerce, is a power for the regulation of manufactures?"[35] And again, "Are not commerce and manufactures as distinct, as commerce and agriculture?"[36] He then follows this line to its conclusion:

> It is true, that commerce and manufacturers are, or may be, intimately connected with each other. A regulation of one may injuriously or beneficially affect the other. But that is not the point of the controversy. It is, whether congress has a right to regulate that, which is not committed to it, under a power, which is committed to it, simply because there is, or may be an intimate connexion between the powers. If this were admitted, the enumeration of the powers of congress would be wholly unnecessary and nugatory. Agriculture, colonies, capital, machinery, the wages of labour, the profits of stock, the rents of land, the punctual performance of contracts, and the diffusion of knowledge would all be within the scope of the power; for all of them bear an intimate relation to commerce. The result would be, that the powers of congress would embrace the widest extent of legislative functions, to the utter demolition of all constitutional boundaries between the state and national governments.[37]

What is striking about this argument is that Story never suggests that this argument fails to carry the day for the regulation of commerce among the several states, once foreign nations drop out of the equation. His silence echoes Hamilton in Federalist Number 11. All states need a free trade zone to profit in both domestic and foreign markets. Indeed, Story's protectionist instincts have in principle no application to American exports, which is consistent with Article I, Section 9, Clause 5's bald statement that "No tax or Duty shall be laid on Articles exported from any State." In this context, the Congress surely could not shut down by regulation the very export activities that it could not tax. And if it cannot through regulation shut down *all* foreign commerce, it cannot shut down all commerce among the several states, at least absent some strong justification in some particular case. That last qualification opens up difficult questions as to what counts as a "legitimate cause" that would allow the selective limitation on the export of certain goods, such as military weapons to foreign nations. But in principle there is no escape from trying to sort out this middle ground, for neither of the two extremes—that Congress can abolish the export of nothing or everything—is tenable. Indeed, any justifications for limiting trade apply more powerfully to exports to foreign nations than to cross-border trade among the states. It is not credible therefore to think that Congress in 1840 constitutionally could have passed a general law that prohibited the shipment of all cotton produced with slave labor in interstate commerce in an effort to drive slavery out of the South. This interpretive approach supports the outcome in *Hammer v. Dagenhart*,[38] which perceived the threat to enumerated powers in a federal statute that prohibited the shipment in interstate commerce of goods made by firms that used child labor somewhere in their factories, even goods that were themselves not shipped into interstate commerce.

## 3. Originalism Revised

The legal materials on both taxation and regulation thus reveal a picture of the Founding period that is at massive variance with the modern New Deal state. The transformation of constitutional visions relied on two related strategies. The first involves ingenious textual arguments that are unfaithful to the Founding period, and in some instances unfaithful to the original text. The second invokes supposedly functional reasons, often tied to the complexity of modern society, to justify a change in constitutional approach. This section addresses the first of these problems. The next section takes on the second.

### A. TAXING AND SPENDING

The modern analysis of the power to tax and spend rips the words "general welfare" out of their constitutional context in line with Hamilton's reading. The initial judicial sally in this area was the Court's decision in *United States v. Butler*,[39] which by a six-to-three vote struck down a complex scheme under the 1933 Agricultural Adjustment Act to "stabilize" prices by taxing those farmers with excess production. Justice Owen Roberts purported to adopt Hamilton's broader view, but the decision itself resonated more with Madison's position that the taxing power should not allow end runs around the limitations found in the other enumerated powers, including the Commerce Clause, as it was interpreted before the 1937 transformation. But once the shackles were removed from the Commerce Clause, the question remained whether Madison's approach could still survive. On that issue, we are faced with what is best termed a kind of second-best constitutionalism. Before 1937, a narrow reading of the Commerce Clause was in harmony with a narrow reading of the spending power. Once the commerce power is expanded, the Court faces a stark choice. It can keep to the narrow reading of the spending power on grounds of fidelity to text. Or it can preserve the parallelism between the two clauses by expanding the scope of the spending power, as in *Helvering v. Davis*,[40] where a five-to-four majority of the Supreme Court took the second course when it upheld a program of "Federal Old-Age Benefits" under Title II of the Social Security Act, citing *Butler* but ignoring its implications. In defending his broad reading of the clause, Justice Cardozo noted that

> Congress may spend money in aid of the "general welfare." U.S. Const., art. I, § 8; United States v. Butler, 297 U.S. 1, 65.... The conception of the spending power advocated by Hamilton and strongly reinforced by Story has prevailed over that of Madison, which has not been lacking in adherents. Yet difficulties are left when the power is conceded. The line must still be drawn between one welfare and another, between particular and general. Where this shall be placed cannot be known through a formula in advance of the event. There is a middle ground or certainly a penumbra in which discretion is at large. The discretion, however, is not confided to the courts. The discretion belongs to Congress, unless the choice is clearly wrong, a display of arbitrary power, not an exercise of judgment.... Nor is the concept of the general welfare static. Needs that were narrow or parochial a century ago may be interwoven in our day with the well-being of the nation.[41]

Note that the full text of Article I, Section 8, Clause 1 is not quoted, and that the words "general welfare" are no longer read in parallel with the payment of the public debt and the provision of the common defense. The words "of the United States" also recede from view. *Butler* struck down an elaborate scheme for tax and transfer that had short-circuited the then-applicable limits on the Commerce Clause. Yet *Davis* ignored the impact that the newly expansive, and in my view wholly indefensible,[42] reading of the Commerce Clause in *NLRB v. Jones & Laughlin Steel*,[43] decided shortly before *Davis*, had on the connection between the two clauses, making it hard to tell whether Cardozo thought his decision was correct on originalist grounds or a compensating adjustment to the expanded power of the Commerce Clause. Cardozo's opinion contains the usual quota of waffly words: he notes that no "formula" can resolve the issue, that the principle has its own "penumbras," that the concept is not "static," and that we are not bound by a "narrow" or "parochial" view of the subject. He thus reduces judicial review over Spending Clause issues to a flabby rational basis standard under which just about every program passes muster. But nothing precludes the continued application of the original conception of general welfare that would stop these transfer payments cold. The threats that transfer payments pose to social welfare are as great in 1937 as they were in 1787. In both eras, it is best to seek out Pareto improvements instead.

That same jurisprudential mishmash dominates Chief Justice John Roberts's opinion in *NFIB*, which also rips the words "general welfare" out of context. His opening salvo on the clause states: "Put simply, Congress may tax and spend."[44] He makes no effort to explicate the other words contained in the clause. His expansive reading is in fact shared by all the justices of the Supreme Court, conservative and liberal alike.[45] At this point, the only debate is on the arid question of how broad is broad. With the individual mandate, Chief Justice Roberts struggles to demonstrate that the statutory penalty could be recast as a tax. But he never asks whether the set of direct and indirect taxes, duties, imposts, and excises, can attach to pure inactivity unrelated to earned or investment income, or to their person or the ownership property. The federal government has never taxed the failure (if that term is correct) to engage in a particular type of transaction, for the simple reason that every person at any given time is *not* engaged in thousands of activities that could expose him to taxes from all sides. The Chief Justice argues that Congress cannot regulate such inactivity under the Commerce Clause.[46] It is ludicrous to conclude in the next breath that it can do an end run around that limitation by resorting to the taxing power. The logic of evasion here is exactly the same as it was in *Butler*, with only one critical difference. Today's broad commerce power leaves many fewer activities outside the spending power. But so long as inactivity is out from the one, it should be out from both.

## B. COMMERCE

Similar techniques of constitutional interpretation fueled the expansion of the scope of the commerce power. Here is one example among many. In his public defense of the expansive interpretation of the commerce power after Solicitor General Donald Verrilli's argument before the Supreme Court, Professor Akhil Amar writes, ostensibly in textualist mode:

Question: What are the limits of congressional power?
A. The limits are those found in the Constitution itself, of course—its text, its history, and its structure as glossed by subsequent practice and precedent. The Constitution expressly gives Congress the power to "Regulate commerce … among the several states." Here, we have a genuine *regulation*—both the micro-mandate/penalty/tax and the larger regulatory regime of which it is an integral part. We have *commerce* under any reading of the word. Insurance is a purely commercial or

economic question about who pays whom. And we have an underlying problem that is truly "*among the several states.*" The problem of health care creates spillover costs that cross state lines, problems that result in some states in effect imposing costs on other states or bearing costs that properly belong to other states.[47]

The first point to note is the three dots in the middle and the period at the end of the sentence. The full clause refers to a trio of powers: "with foreign Nations, and among the several States, and with the Indian tribes." Insert the ellipsis in the expression and it becomes easier—not correct, but easier—to campaign for a broader definition of commerce that in turn embraces the ACA structure because no longer must the definition of commerce mesh as well with either foreign or Indian commerce. "Congress shall have the power to regulate health care insurance with foreign nations, among the several States, and with the Indian tribes." Not really. Indeed, as an originalist matter it is surely incorrect to claim that all insurance falls under the Commerce Clause given that much of it involves local transactions that do not involve parties in two or more states. This in turn explains why insurance contracts were subject to regulation only at the state level under the 1869 decision in *Paul v. Virginia*,[48] which survived until overruled by the 1944 post–New Deal decision in *United States v. South-Eastern Underwriting.*[49]

Likewise, the ACA does nothing to address negative spillovers between states, except perhaps to create them. Pointing to these supposed spillovers among states fails to meet Story's point that any intimate connections between manufacture and commerce do not make the former amenable to regulation as a part of the latter, or as a target of regulations themselves directed to interstate transactions. But in this instance, virtually none of the key provisions of the ACA are directed to these interstate spillovers, unlike, for example, the provision of the Clean Air Act that regulates pollution originating in state A only to cause harm in state B.[50] Indeed there are no interstate spillovers if medical services are accurately priced, so it is hard to imagine the ills that the ACA is intended to counteract. Indeed, the major redistributions worked by the ACA are only among individuals, such as community rating systems that require younger people to subsidize older ones in part through the mandate. Nothing in the ACA addresses any negative interstate externality. Indeed it is more likely that the ACA *creates* these negative spillovers from states with high percentages of younger people to those with greater percentages of older ones.

In other cases, isolated passages are quoted without placing them in their historical or functional context. Thus Professor Jack Balkin offers a "living" originalist defense of *Wickard* as "a fairly easy case," which requires some federal solution.[51] He does not start with Madison's observation in Federalist Number 45, quoted above, that "[t]he powers delegated by the proposed Constitution to the federal government, are few and defined."[52] Instead he prefers to start with a well-known speech that James Wilson delivered to the Pennsylvania ratifying convention in November 1787:

> Whatever object of government is confined in its operation and effects within the bounds of a particular state should be considered as belonging to the government of that state; whatever object of government extends in its operation or effects beyond the bounds of a particular state should be considered as belonging to the government of the United States. But though this principle be sound and satisfactory, its application to particular cases would be accompanied with much difficulty; because in its application, room must be allowed for great discretionary latitude of construction of the principle. In order to lessen or remove the difficulty arising from discretionary construction on this subject, an enumeration of particular instances, in which the application of the principle ought to take place, has been attempted with much industry and care.[53]

In interpreting this passage, Balkin asserts that, read as a whole, "the purpose of the enumeration was not to *displace* the principle, but to *enact* it."[54] In order to make this argument credible, he claims (contrary to Amar) that the word "commerce" "had strongly social overtones. To have commerce with someone meant to exchange things or ideas with them, converse with them, or interact with them."[55] As a matter of English grammar, no person has ever "had commerce" (unlike tea) with any one else, to use Balkin's infelicitous phrase. Nor is there the slightest shred of contemporary evidence that gives the term "commerce" so broad a reading—one that is utterly inconsistent with both Marshall's and Story's view of the matter.

Even if we put the textual point aside, moreover, there is nothing about the enumeration that leads to a *Wickard*-like rendition of the Commerce Clause. Wilson writes on the explicit premise that these matters fall to *either* the states *or* the federal government, in line with Story's exaggerated insistence that the federal government has exclusive power of matters delegated to it under the Commerce Clause. *Wickard*, and all the modern cases, are decided on the premise that there are *concurrent* state and federal powers in any and all cases, which is not Wilson's message at all. The simple point is that the enumeration offers the concrete path for the application of the general principle, as inferred from the constitutional text and *Gibbons v. Ogden*, and not from an interpretation that guts the enumeration altogether, just as Story stressed. No statement from the Founding period supports Balkin's novel reading of the term "commerce," or the clause as a whole.

Unfortunately, it is easy to find too many instances where the conscious manipulation of key text is used to obscure the originalist understanding of the Commerce Clause. Professor Max Farrand's Records of the Constitution contains this observation of the new Constitution offered at the national convention:

> That the Legislature of the United States ought to possess the legislative Rights vested in Congress by the Confederation; and moreover to legislate in all Cases for the general Interests of the Union, and also in those Cases to which the States are separately incompetent, or in which the Harmony of the United States may be interrupted.[56]

There is no doubt that in this instance, he is referring to the breakdown that takes place at the center on the key question of the federal powers to tax, spend, and regulate commerce. But his remark is only a general reference to "the legislature," without reference to any particular constitutional provision, which was of course one of the well-known defects of the Articles of Confederation. Nonetheless the last phrase referring to situations in which states are "separately incompetent" gave Justice Ruth Bader Ginsburg the opening to make this breathtaking transformation of the original passage. In her view, "States cannot resolve the problem of the uninsured on their own,"[57] because interstate competition will lower the level of payments offered to those in need. She then concludes in originalist mode that the framers were well aware of the problem by taking out the words "the legislature" and substituting the italicized phrase:

> *The Framers' solution was the Commerce Clause, which, as they perceived it, granted Congress the authority to enact economic legislation* "in all Cases for the general Interests of the Union, and also in those Cases to which the States are separately incompetent."[58]

Wow. The words "Commerce Clause," let alone the modern sounding phrase "enact economic legislation," are not to be found anywhere near this passage in the original text. Their interpolation here completely distorts the textual meaning to secure this massive expansion of federal power. No one contests that there are some "Cases to which the States are separately incompetent." But there are multiple enumerated powers that satisfy this description without expanding the Commerce Clause beyond recognition.

Justice Ginsburg's liberties with the text are not an isolated incident. That same pattern of selective inclusion of earlier text mars key Supreme Court decisions from an earlier period. Thus in *United States v. Darby*,[59] the Court upheld the provision of the Fair Labor Standards Act that regulated the wages and terms of employment in manufacturing and other local positions. In so doing, it overruled *Hammer v. Dagenhart*,[60] by concluding that Congress "is free to exclude from the commerce articles whose use in the states for which they are destined it may conceive to be injurious to the public health, morals or welfare, even though the state has not sought to regulate their use."[61] Pure historical fantasy. The concerns of the improper extension of federal power are removed. Nor does Justice Stone mention a prior sentence from *Gibbons* that says that the federal power "is the power to regulate; that is, to prescribe the rule by which commerce is to be governed."[62] That domain for Marshall, and for Story following him, was limited to these cross-border transactions and explicitly excluded the local transactions that Stone subjects to its control. *Darby* expunges all those references and their associated constitutional restraints.

The same pattern was exhibited in *United States v. Wrightwood Dairy*.[63] In *Gibbons*, Chief Justice Marshall had written: "Comprehensive as the word 'among' is, it may very properly be *restricted* to that commerce which concerns more States than one."[64] *Wrightwood Dairy* manages to deflect that meaning in two steps. First it states, "The power of Congress over interstate commerce is plenary and complete in itself, may be exercised to its utmost extent, and acknowledges no limitations other than are prescribed in the Constitution."[65] All references to the "specified objects" for which it can be used are suppressed from the sentence in *Gibbons* that begins: "If, as has always been understood, the sovereignty of Congress, though limited to specified objects, is plenary as to those objects ...." *Darby* then turns the sense of *Gibbons* upside down by stating that commerce "*extends* to those activities intrastate which so affect interstate commerce."[66] Professor Laurence Tribe in his treatise introduces a variation on this theme: "Congress could legislate with respect to all 'commerce which concerns more states than one.'"[67] "Restrict" and "extend" are opposites. "With respect to" conceals the obvious limitations on federal power. Yet such gross mischaracterizations were a key element of the New Deal jurisprudence.

Not to be outdone, in *Wickard v. Filburn* Justice Jackson wrote as if the law were emerging from a dark intellectual age that inexplicably followed the death of Chief Justice Marshall. "At the beginning Chief Justice Marshall described the Federal commerce power with a breadth never yet exceeded," he says,[68] citing to *Gibbons v. Ogden*.[69] Later on he adds that it was now necessary "to bring about a *return* to the principles first enunciated by Chief Justice Marshall in *Gibbons v. Ogden*."[70]

To do so, Justice Jackson relied on a truncated version of the *Shreveport Rate Case* that held, wrongly in my view, that the power to regulate transportation between two states allowed the federal government to regulate as well a local transportation run that was in direct competition with the interstate line.[71] Lest there be any doubt on the issue, look closely at the textual makeover. The key quotation from the Hughes opinion in the *Shreveport Rate Case* is the following:

> *[Congress's] authority, extending to these interstate carriers as instruments of interstate commerce, necessarily embraces the right to control their opera-tions in all* matters having such a close and substantial relation to inter-state traffic that the control is essential or appropriate to the security of that traffic, to the efficiency of the interstate service, and to the main-tenance of conditions under which interstate commerce may be con-ducted upon fair terms and without molestation or hindrance.[72]

Justice Jackson excised the italicized words from the *Wickard* quotation. In their place was an introductory sentence penned by Justice Jackson that began, "The opinion of Mr. Justice Hughes found federal intervention constitutionally authorized because of …"[73] He then sets off the rest of the quotation beginning with "matters." If that truncated rendition were correct, no one could explain what the shouting was about in the earlier cases. Justice Hughes inserted the ital-icized words, "extending to these interstate carriers as instruments of interstate commerce,"[74] for the sole and explicit purpose of explaining how the *Shreveport Rate Case* coexisted with *United States v. E.C. Knight*,[75] an unquestioned author-ity at the time, and one that accepted the hard-edged distinction between com-merce and manufacture. Naughty is the kindest word that comes to mind for these self-conscious elisions. No precedent, however carefully written, can escape such merciless redaction. The question that remains is whether the game is worth the candle.

## 4. Why Expand?

The implicit subtext behind the rise of the New Deal Constitution was that only a unified response by the national government could meet the challenges posed by a modern economy, most specifically by the Great Depression of the 1930s. The Depression had no single cause. But it is possible to list at least some of the factors that contributed to the dramatic economic slowdown. The persistent deflation during that period meant that debts had to be repaid in more expensive dollars than the original loans, leading to high default levels. The high taxes intro-duced by Hoover's Revenue Act of 1932 stifled investment.[76] The Smoot-Hawley Tariff Act of 1930 wrought substantial damage to international trade.[77]

The constitutional transformation of the New Deal did nothing to combat deflation, lower taxes, or restore international trade. Instead its massive central-ization of power in the federal government facilitated the creation of cartels and the institution of unprecedented transfer programs, both of which compounded the overall problem.[78] The New Deal champions believed that the older system of federalism had failed because it could not cope with the destructive race to the bottom when the states have sole power over the vital sectors of manufacturing, agriculture, and mining. The point was put very forcefully by Solicitor General John W. Davis in his argument in *Hammer v. Dagenhart*[79] when he insisted that no state would enact the desired child labor law, with a minimum age of fourteen, so long as its rivals were prepared to make do with a lower one, with a minimum age of twelve.[80] Justice Cardozo echoed this reasoning in *Helvering v. Davis*, by insisting that state unemployment insurance programs had to founder not only for a lack of local resources, but because

> states and local governments are at times reluctant to increase so heavily the burden of taxation to be borne by their residents for fear of placing themselves in a position of economic disadvantage as compared with neighbors or competitors. We have seen this in our study of the problem of unemployment compensation. A system of old age pensions has special dangers of its own if put in force in one state and rejected in another. The existence of such a system is a bait to the needy and dependent elsewhere, encouraging them to migrate and seek a haven of repose. Only a power that is national can serve the interests of all.[81]

Professor Amar's familiar argument that the ACA addresses "spillover costs that cross state lines" again points toward a national solution to cope with a problem of nationwide dimensions. The implicit premise in this argument is that competition among states on matters of regulation and taxation is a social curse, not a social benefit. It is instructive in this regard to contrast this gloomy prognosis with the view of Justice Brandeis in *New State Ice Co. v. Liebmann*:[82] "It is one of the happy incidents of the federal system that a single courageous state may, if its citizens choose, serve as a laboratory; and try novel social and economic experiments *without risk to the rest of the country*."[83] The phrase that I italicized offers an implicit denial that all local experiments have the negative externalities on other states imagined by the champions of extensive federal power. Instead, the pre-1937 Justice Brandeis maintains that competition among the states allows for the experimentation and innovation often missing in a heavily centralized system, which makes it much more difficult to undo mistakes adopted by faulty legislation policy at the federal level.

On this point, it would be Pollyannaish to deny the risks inherent in a strong form of federalism. Experimentation in local racial segregation is not something to be praised. Nor should local governments be allowed to use their zoning and permitting powers to exploit landowners who cannot take their land elsewhere to escape oppressive local regulation. But the correction for these ills is not massive centralization of control over policy in the Congress. It is to use, as the Fourteenth Amendment uses, the power of the United States Congress to *prevent* local governments from exploiting their own citizens by repressive or confiscatory regulations. Under the post–Civil War constitutional scheme, the federal government does not have the power to initiate state policies, but it can check those that are most abusive of individual rights.

The progressive worldview that drives the centralization of power starts from the assumption that stronger protective legislation, higher unemployment benefits, and greater mandatory health care is superior to state systems that stint on supplying these commodities. More is better. But that view begs the key question of whether stronger child labor laws, more unemployment insurance, and more comprehensive health care benefits are good things, not bad things. All social endeavors pose two kinds of error: too much regulation and too little regulation. Seen from this perspective, the comparative strength of the New Deal vision is far from clear. There was, even in 1918, much to be said against a restrictive child labor law, which could keep off the market those children whose labor could help improve the welfare of a well-functioning family, and drive young children into the black market, prostitution, begging, and worse.[84] Unemployment benefits that last too long, including those that run for ninety-nine weeks under federal law, can induce productive individuals to stay outside the workforce while imposing unduly heavy burdens on those who continue to work. The ACA mandates huge and expensive minimum benefit packages; it requires a compression in rates so that younger people are forced to subsidize older persons. Indeed the ACA is so complex that it is impossible to know whether, or if so how, it corrects the supposed sin of negative spillovers between states, when its major effect is to create massive cross-subsidies between different groups of individuals within the various states.[85]

The clear lesson from all this is that certain key features of political life are not contingent on changes in technology. The dangers of monopoly and of faction are as real today as they were in 1787. They urgently require sensible institutional responses today as they did then. On this view, the exit rights that private individuals have from states, although highly imperfect, should be viewed in a positive light, as an all-purpose, if indirect, way of limiting the excessive size of government by forcing state sovereigns to compete with each other for their loyalty.[86] The only way that this system can work is if there are strong limitations on what the national government can do, and that is only possible if the Constitution controls the powers of taxation and regulation at the center, as the founders tried to do.

But it was not to be. Over and over, we are told that national problems require national solutions. Judge Silberman has written: "The right to be free from federal regulation is not absolute, and yields to the imperative that Congress be free to forge national solutions to national problems, no matter how local—or seemingly passive—their individual origins."[87] And so they do. But the correct national solutions cannot be provided by Congress, which is itself the national problem whose excesses need to be constrained. The national solution that is needed necessarily operates at the constitutional level. It is one that by strict constitutional order cabins the discretion of Congress so that it cannot fall prey to the powerful political forces that seek short-term gain in factional warfare, which in turn produces systematic losses to the nation as a whole. This problem is so large and so persistent that there is no single set of remedies, whether dealing with structure or with individual rights, capable of meeting these threats.

The great intellectual vice behind the New Deal is that it forgot the lessons about the dangers of concentrated government power that the founders had profoundly grasped. By removing the fetters on the national government, the courts have paved the way for Congress to institutionalize stagnation and decline. This nation cannot thrive on its joint policies of expanding regulation and taxation. Regulation stifles growth. Taxation loads an ever-larger set of transfer payments onto a smaller base. That is a one-two punch that is hard to avoid, and even harder to contain so long as the justices on the Supreme Court are oblivious to the national perils that lurk in their unthinking deference to Congress on key matters of taxation and regulation. Congress is the problem, not the solution.

## Acknowledgments

My thanks to Michael McConnell for correcting some serious errors in an earlier draft of this essay, and to Jordana Haviv, Peter Horn, and Joshua Stanton, NYU Law School class of 2014, for their valuable research assistance.

## Notes

1. 132 S. Ct. 2566 (2012).
2. Pub. L. No. 111-148, 124 Stat. 119 (2010) (codified as amended in scattered sections of 26 and 42 U.S.C.).
3. 317 U.S. 111 (1942).
4. For the speech, see President Franklin D. Roosevelt, 1944 State of the Union Address (Jan. 11, 1944), *available at* http://www.presidency.ucsb.edu/ws/index.php?pid=16518.
5. See HERBERT J. STORING, WHAT THE ANTIFEDERALISTS WERE FOR: THE POLITICAL THOUGHT OF THE OPPONENTS OF THE CONSTITUTION (Murray Dry ed., 1981).
6. See, e.g., Helvering v. Davis, 301 U.S. 619 (1937); United States v. Butler, 297 U.S. 1 (1936) (purporting to adopt Hamilton's broad definition of the spending power, but nonetheless striking down provisions of the Agricultural Adjustment Act).
7. ALEXANDER HAMILTON, REPORT ON MANUFACTURES, 192 (Henry Cabot Lodge ed., Federal ed., G.P. Putnam's Sons 1904) (1791), *available at* http://oll.libertyfund.org/index.php?option=com_staticxt&staticfile=show.php?title=1712&Itemid=99999999.
8. THE FEDERALIST No. 41 (James Madison).

9. *Id.*

10. 2 JOSEPH STORY, COMMENTARIES ON THE CONSTITUTION OF THE UNITED STATES, § 905 (Boston, Hilliard, Gray & Co. 1833) [hereinafter STORY, *Commentaries*] (stressing that a tax that is not laid for any of these purposes "would be unconstitutional, as an excess of its legislative authority").

11. U.S. CONST. art I, § 10, cl. 3 (no state power to engage in war "unless actually invaded, or in such imminent Danger as will not admit of delay"); *id.* art. IV, § 4 (protecting "Republican Form of government" against "Invasion" and "domestic Violence").

12. MANCUR OLSON, THE LOGIC OF COLLECTIVE ACTION: PUBLIC GOODS AND THE THEORY OF GROUPS (1965).

13. U.S. CONST. amend. V.

14. See, e.g., The Head Money Cases, 112 U.S. 580 (1884).

15. STORY, *Commentaries, supra* note 10, § 974.

16. For an early account, see *id.* §§ 952–953.

17. Pollock v. Farmer's Loan & Trust Co., 158 U.S. 601 (1895), vacating 157 U.S. 429 (1895).

18. U.S. CONST. amend. XVI ("The Congress shall have power to lay and collect taxes on incomes, from whatever source derived, without apportionment among the several States, and without regard to any census or enumeration").

19. STORY, *Commentaries, supra* note 10, § 1063.

20. *Id.* § 1066.

21. *Id.* (emphasis added).

22. THE FEDERALIST NO. 45, at 328 (James Madison) (Benjamin Fletcher Wright ed., 1961).

23. 22 U.S. 1 (1824).

24. STORY, *Commentaries, supra* note 10, § 1054.

25. *Id.*

26. *Id.* § 1057. The phrase is lifted literally from *Gibbons,* 22 U.S. at 196.

27. *Id.* § 1014. The parallel passage in *Gibbons* can be found at 22 U.S. at 203.

28. *Id.* § 1014.

29. THE FEDERALIST NO. 11 (Alexander Hamilton) (Benjamin Fletcher Wright ed., 1961).

30. *Id.* at 137.

31. *Id.* at 140–141.

32. STORY, *Commentaries, supra* note 10, §§ 1063–1064, 1071.

33. *Id.* § 1073.

34. *Id.* § 1080.

35. *Id.* § 1075.

36. *Id.*

37. *Id.*

38. 247 U.S. 251 (1918).

39. 297 U.S. 1 (1936).

40. 301 U.S. 619 (1937).

41. *Id.* at 640–641.

42. For discussion, see Richard A. Epstein, *The Proper Scope of the Commerce Power,* 73 VA. L. REV. 1387, 1443–1447 (1987). Note that the three courts that passed on the issue all struck down the NLRA. *Id.* at 1446 n.197.

43. 301 U.S. 1 (1937).

44. NFIB v. Sebelius, 132 S. Ct. 2566, 2579 (2012).

45. See *id.* at 2606; *id.* at 2636 (Ginsburg, J., concurring in part, concurring in judgment in part, and dissenting in part).

46. *Id.* at 2585–2590.

47. Akhil Reed Amar, *How To Defend Obamacare—A Commentary by Akhil Reed Amar '84,* YALE LAW SCHOOL NEWS, Mar. 29, 2012, http://www.law.yale.edu/news/15229.htm. For a longer, but equally unpersuasive defense of Obamacare, see Akhil Amar, *The Lawfulness*

*of Health Care Reform* (Yale Law Sch. Pub. Law Working Paper No. 228, 2011), *available at* http://papers.ssrn.com/sol3/papers.cfm?abstract_id=1856506.

48. 75 U.S. 168 (1868).

49. 322 U.S. 533 (1944).

50. 42 U.S.C. § 7426 (2006).

51. See JACK M. BALKIN, LIVING ORIGINALISM 164 (2011).

52. THE FEDERALIST No. 45, at 328 (James Madison) (Benjamin Fletcher Wright ed., 1961).

53. James Wilson, Speech to the Pennsylvania Ratification Convention (Dec. 1, 1789), *in* 2 THE DEBATES IN THE SEVERAL STATE CONVENTIONS ON THE ADOPTION OF THE FEDERAL CONSTITUTION AS RECOMMENDED BY THE GENERAL CONVENTION AT PHILADELPHIA 424–425 (Jonathan Elliot ed., 2d ed. 1836) (*quoted in* BALKIN, *supra* note 51, at 143, 145, in two separate places), *available at* http://oll.libertyfund.org/index.php?option=com_ staticxt&staticfile=show.php%3Ftitle=1906&layout=html.

54. BALKIN, *supra* note 51, at 145.

55. *Id.* at 140.

56. Proceedings of Tuesday July 17, 1787, *in* 2 RECORDS OF THE FEDERAL CONVENTION OF 1787, para. 8, pp. 131–132 (Max Farrand ed. 1966), *available at* http://oll.libertyfund.org/index.php?option=com_staticxt&staticfile=show.php%3Ftitle=1786&Itemid=99999999.

57. NFIB v. Sebelius, 132 S. Ct. 2566, 2612 (2012) (Ginsburg, J., concurring in part, concurring in judgment in part, and dissenting in part).

58. *Id.* at 2615 (quoting 2 RECORDS OF THE FEDERAL CONVENTION OF 1787, *supra* note 54, at 131–132).

59. 312 U.S. 100 (1941).

60. 247 U.S. 251 (1918).

61. *Darby,* 312 U.S. at 114.

62. 22 U.S. 1, 196 (1824).

63. 315 U.S. 110 (1942).

64. *Gibbons,* 22 U.S. at 194 (emphasis added).

65. *Wrightwood Dairy,* 315 U.S. at 119. The original quotation is in *Gibbons,* 22 U.S. at 197.

66. *Id.*

67. LAURENCE H. TRIBE, AMERICAN CONSTITUTIONAL LAW 808 (2d ed. 1988) (quoting *Gibbons,* 22 U.S. at 194).

68. 317 U.S. 111, 120 (1942).

69. 22 U.S. at 194–195.

70. *Wickard,* 317 U.S. at 122 (emphasis added).

71. The Shreveport Rate Cases, 234 U.S. 342 (1914).

72. *Id.* at 351 (emphasis added).

73. *Wickard,* 317 U.S. at 123.

74. 234 U.S. at 351.

75. 156 U.S. 1 (1895).

76. Revenue Act of 1932, ch. 209, 47 Stat. 169 (top tax rates were raised from 25 to 63 percent).

77. Smoot-Hawley Tariff Act of 1930, Pub. L. No. 71-361, 49 Stat. 590 (codified as amended in scattered sections of 19 U.S.C. ch. 4).

78. For this theme, see MICHAEL S. GREVE, THE UPSIDE-DOWN CONSTITUTION (2012); Richard A. Epstein, *The Cartelization of Commerce,* 22 HARV. J.L. & PUB. POL'Y 209 (1998).

79. 247 U.S. 251 (1918).

80. Davis stated: "[I]f one State desired to limit the employment of children, it was met with the objection that its manufacturers could not compete with manufacturers of a neighboring State which imposed no such limitation. The shipment of goods in interstate commerce by the latter, therefore, operates to deter the former from enacting laws it would otherwise enact for the protection of its own children." Transcript of Oral Argument, 247 U.S. at 251 (No. 704), *available at* http://tlc-patch.tourolaw.edu/patch/Hammer/.

81. Helvering v. Davis, 301 U.S. 619, 644 (1937) (internal citations omitted).

82. 285 U.S. 262 (1932).

83. *Id.* at 311 (emphasis added).

84. For a modern version of the argument, see BENJAMIN POWELL, No Sweat: How Sweatshops Improve Lives and Economic Growth (forthcoming 2013).

85. For a detailed account of the above, see Richard A. Epstein & Paula M. Stannard, *Constitutional Ratemaking and the Affordable Care Act: A New Source of Vulnerability*, 38 AM. J.L. & MED. 243 (2012).

86. See Richard A. Epstein, *Exit Rights Under Federalism*, 55 L. & CONTEMP. PROBS. 147 (1992); Richard A. Epstein, *Exit Rights and Insurance Regulation: From Federalism to Takings*, 7 GEO. MASON L. REV. 293 (1999).

87. Seven-Sky v. Holder, 661 F.3d 1, 20 (D.C. Cir. 2011) (Silberman, J.) (citing Heart of Atlanta Motel, Inc. v. United States, 379 U.S. 241, 258–259 (1964)), *abrogated by* NFIB v. Sebelius, 132 S. Ct. 2566, 2651 (2012).

# CHAPTER 4

# The June Surprises

## BALLS, STRIKES, AND THE FOG OF WAR

*Charles Fried*

Chief Justice Roberts, in his confirmation hearing, famously analogized the role of the judge to an umpire, calling balls and strikes.[1] Many of those relieved at the outcome of the litigation about the Patient Protection and Affordable Care Act (ACA),[2] think the Chief Justice called a ball a strike, a strike a ball, but at the end of the day at least the batter was safe on base.[3] Though a dwindling number of Court watchers thought the mandate in the ACA might survive, the actual outcome of the case came as a surprise—a bag of surprises, indeed—to almost everyone. Few had predicted that Chief Justice Roberts would be the only one of the Republican-appointed justices to vote with what the media call the liberal four to carry the mandate over the top. Even fewer thought this would be on the ground that the mandate could be and thus must be justified as an exercise of Congress's taxing power. Among constitutional experts the attack on the Medicaid expansion seemed even more ill-grounded than the Commerce Clause attack on the mandate. And most surprising of all, no one would have predicted that the Medicaid expansion would fail by a vote of seven to two, with Justices Breyer and Kagan joining the Republican majority. Finally, even though the Chief Justice's lead opinion rejected the Commerce Clause basis for the mandate in the same terms as his four Republican colleagues, those four did not join, or even so much as mention their Chief's opinion on this issue, but instead published a highly unusual (though not entirely unprecedented) joint opinion that—whatever its motivation[4]—had the appearance of a deliberate repudiation, not of the opinion but of its author. It is these four surprises that are the subject of this essay. In setting the stage for these surprises, I am afraid I must go over some ground that constitutional scholars would by now have plowed into a veritable dust bowl of commentary, but the lesson I draw may be a different one from the many that are being drawn from the unexpected dénouement of this most important case.[5]

## 1. Background

I was thoroughly engaged in the case, though not as a partisan so much as a constitutional scholar. I had written about it; testified to the Senate Judiciary Committee;[6] in three different fora debated Randy Barnett (the owner if not the inventor of the broccoli argument); was the counsel of record in an amicus brief for 104 health law professors; and in October 2010, in an interview on Greta Van Susteren's Fox TV program, offered to eat my hat on camera if the Court struck the ACA down.[7] As I testified to the Senate, I have doubts that the ACA is good policy and am pretty sure that it will not improve the medical situation or the wallet of well-insured, upper-middle-class, well-connected persons like me. But like most students of constitutional law I found the argument that it violated the Constitution bordered on the frivolous. After all, since 1937 the Court had not come even close to invalidating on Commerce Clause grounds a statute that was without question one of economic regulation. (The 2000 and 1995 *Morrison*[8] and *Lopez*[9] cases prove the point, because penalizing beating up a girlfriend or carrying a gun near a school—contrasted to offering meals at Ollie's Barbecue—could not without a very long stretch be characterized as economic regulation.)

The Commerce Clause argument seemed so bad, that neither the district court decisions by Judge Vinson in Florida[10] and Judge Hudson in Virginia[11]— written in extravagant terms that seemed to be dictated by right-wing talk radio—nor the fact that all the major Republican candidates for the presidential nomination competed to outdo each other in condemning particularly the mandate, nor even the polls showing that the public had been decisively turned against the mandate, had much moved me. But then a decision in the Eleventh Circuit upholding Judge Vinson[12] and the skillful advocacy of Paul Clement shook my confidence—even after remarkable opinions by Judges Sutton[13] and Silberman[14] upholding the ACA. Very briefly, the argument that never before had Congress included as a premise for regulation of commerce a requirement that individuals engage in commerce (the broccoli argument), seemed both wrong and irrelevant. After all in the signal case of *Wickard v. Filburn*[15] the Court had held that "the stimulation of commerce is a use of the regulatory function quite as definitely as prohibitions or restrictions thereon." And even as far back as *Gibbons v. Ogden*[16] Chief Justice Marshall had written that the clause empowered Congress to lay down the rule by which commerce (not persons in commerce) could be regulated. And the ACA clearly did that. At any rate it was easily demonstrated that an overwhelming portion of the adult population was already as much engaged in the commerce of the health care system as was the wheat farmer in *Wickard*.[17] And finally, the energy behind the broccoli argument was about personal liberty, and no litigant ventured that the mandate violated the liberty clause of the Fifth Amendment (which having the identical scope as the liberty clause of the Fourteenth would have made a scheme like that of Massachusetts unconstitutional). Only Justice Thomas, who has consistently proclaimed a pre–New Deal conception of the Commerce Clause, was likely to vote to strike the ACA down on that ground. Especially after Judges Sutton's and Silberman's opinions—two conservative stalwarts—the guessing in the halls of legal academe favored at least a six-to-three if not an eight-to-one vote upholding the ACA, with the Chief Justice writing. Justice Kennedy, it was thought, would once again break ranks, and the Chief, unwilling to yield the opinion leftward, would join and write.

The end of March brought the three days of oral argument, and the betting odds changed dramatically.[18] The questions by the four Republican-appointed justices were uniformly hostile. Justice Kennedy, the hoped-for swing vote, early on asked: "I understand we must presume laws are constitutional, but, even so, when you are changing the relation of the individual to the government in this, what we can stipulate is, I think, a unique way, do you not have heavy burden of justification to show authorization under the Constitution?"[19]—a question straight out of the Tea Party playbook. That "fundamental" change was worked seventy-five years before by the Social Security Act and fifty years before with Medicare. And Justice Scalia seemed more to bait and mock the Solicitor General than to probe the strengths of his arguments. The betting odds changed precipitously. Such hope as there was for the mandate reposed now—precariously—on the Chief, and on some small "c" conservative instinct he might retain in the name of tradition and restraint. As for the argument that the mandate might be justified as a tax—for if it had been frankly a tax, like the Social Security or Medicare taxes, then only Justice Thomas would touch it—it was argued by the Solicitor General almost as an afterthought. After all, Congress had for political reasons studiously avoided calling it a tax. And if it was a tax, maybe the whole dispute was premature because the Tax Injunction Act required waiting until the tax was due before it could be challenged. (And then there was the obscure, almost antiquarian question whether it was a "direct tax" constitutionally permissible only if apportioned among the states—a provision that the income tax avoided only by virtue of the Sixteenth Amendment specifically authorizing it.)

Then on June 27 came the decision. As a touch of comic irony, CNN—violating the rule of "read on" and eager to be the very first with a news story available to all—reported that the Court had struck down the Act by a vote of five to four,[20] apparently reading only so far as section 2 of the Court's syllabus summarizing the decision. Five justices voted that neither the Commerce Clause nor the Necessary and Proper Clause of Article 1, Section 8 authorized the mandate; five justices—four from the dissent on the previous issue, plus the Chief Justice, again writing—that the mandate nevertheless was authorized by the Article 1, Section 8 taxing power and that the Tax Injunction Act did not deprive the Court of jurisdiction to rule on the point until after the tax was due (in 2013). And finally seven justices voted that the threatened denial of all federal Medicaid funds to states that would not join in the significant expansion of Medicaid eligibility was so coercive as to constitute a form of duress that violated the states' sovereignty and dignity, as announced in cases such as *New York v. U.S.*[21] and *Printz*.[22] The Chief Justice and the four justices of the joint opinion diverged on the Medicaid expansion only to the extent that for the Chief Justice the supposed unconstitutional coercion of the cutoff invalidated only the cutoff, so that a state that refused to expand Medicaid eligibility could nonetheless continue to participate and receive federal funds at the preexpansion level. As the joint opinion notes, this was a solution the government proposed "in two cursory sentences at the very end of its brief."[23] The joint opinion bridles at this suggestion, and in the only passage in which the joint opinion deigns to refer to the Chief Justice by name,[24] rejects the government's and the Chief's conclusion and invalidates the Medicaid expansion altogether, for participating as well as nonparticipating states. Justices Breyer and Kagan did not dissent from the Chief's opinion on this point, so that if one draws the appropriate Venn diagram of the opinions, the Chief's resolution on this point controls—although Justices Breyer and Kagan might arguably have produced the same result by joining Justice Ginsburg's dissenting opinion rejecting the coercion argument altogether. Here were the surprises listed at the outset of this essay.

On the commerce power, the Chief's opinion, while calm and methodical, is a veritable cascade of non sequiturs and solecisms. Many of these will have been noted by others and by Justice Ginsburg's equally calm and methodical dissent. It is nonetheless worthwhile, in confronting the surprises to which this essay is addressed, to touch on a few of the chief's bad arguments. The foremost among these echoes the heart of the Tea Party–inspired detestation of this Act: the claim that if Congress can regulate individuals by requiring them to engage in commerce, then "that is not the country the Framers of our Constitution envisioned. James Madison explained that the Commerce Clause was 'an addition which few oppose and from which no apprehensions are entertained.'"[25] Professor Randy Barnett, the champion of the broccoli argument, made this semihysteric and invalid point in his testimony to the Senate Judiciary Committee, declaiming that if the defense of the mandate is valid, then we are all no longer "citizens but subjects."[26] As I have indicated, Justice Kennedy early in the argument of the case, picking up the Tea Party banner with this silly slogan emblazoned on it, asked whether, technicalities aside—I suppose technicalities such as the taxing power—upholding the mandate worked a fundamental change in the relationship of the citizen to the government. The Solicitor General, with superhuman restraint, let this pass, when he might have answered "Perhaps, Justice Kennedy, but that is a change worked seventy-five years ago by Social Security and fifty years ago by Medicare." And of course the slogan ignores the fact that the mandate was first proposed by the conservative Heritage Foundation (whose amicus brief in this case trying to explain this fact away is almost comical in its tergiversations)[27] and might well have been a feature in an analogous scheme proposed by President George W. Bush partially to privatize Social Security.

The Chief commits a similar constitutional solecism by harping on the supposed unprecedented nature of the mandate as somehow a symptom of its invalidity. (He does acknowledge that, of course, "there is a first time for everything.")[28] But the novelty of a Commerce Clause scheme proves nothing—though it does deprive a scheme of the safe harbor of an existing all-fours precedent. As economic circumstances change and economic projects and opportunities are devised to respond to them, regulation will necessarily take on new forms: new kinds of regulatory commissions and other mechanisms, including public/private and state collaborations, changing configurations of prohibition, requirement, and incentive, the use of private causes of action, court enforcement by government agents or adjudication in the first instance by regulatory bodies. Novelty is a matter of degree and description. Whether the requirement that certain categories of persons purchase health insurance coverage from commercial vendors is indeed a novel requirement has been the subject of considerable ingenious debate, with various analogies offered and refuted along the way. But the very scholasticism of this debate shows how irrelevant the sobriquet "novel" is to the question of validity. Doubtless any number of regulatory schemes when first proposed had some element of novelty about them, but the proper question has always been thought to be whether the scheme is indeed a regulation of interstate *commerce*. It is the failing grade on this, the only relevant question, that doomed—and to my mind properly—the Gun Free School Zone Act and the private cause of action under the Violence Against Women Act (VAWA). That the provision of health care and the modalities of payment for it are interstate commerce has never been doubted. That should have been the end of the story, which is why until only a couple of years ago the mandate (like the similar proposal of the Heritage Foundation) were debated only in policy, not constitutional terms.

Particularly eye-catching is the Chief's fallacious refutation of the Necessary and Proper argument, which admits Chief Justice Marshall's expansive reading of the word "necessary" in *McCulloch v. Maryland*, but rests instead on the word "proper."[29] Once again the Chief Justice acknowledged that the mandate was "necessary" in Chief Justice Marshall's sense of convenient or adapted to the fulfillment of the regulatory purpose of making health insurance widely available without consideration of medical history or lifetime caps.[30] Indeed, the mandate is much closer to being necessary to the success of the regulatory scheme even in the more restrictive sense urged by counsel of Maryland in *McCulloch v. Maryland* than many subsequent invocations of the clause. For this reason the Chief Justice fell to arguing that though necessary to the regulatory scheme, the mandate was not proper. But certainly since the New Deal and thus for the last seventy-five years of jurisprudence under the clause—consider its invocation in relation to legislation under Section 5 of the Fourteenth Amendment—the conception has been that propriety is a matter of not contravening some distinct constitutional prohibition or principle. Put another way, questions of the power of Congress under Article I, Section 8 or any of the other power-conferring provisions of the Constitution (e.g., Article II, Section 2, Article III, Section 1) have been conceptualized as questions about how far the granted power extends; if the assertion of power is neither comprehended in the explicit grant nor necessary to such a power, then the grant runs out. If the purported reach is too long a stretch, as in the VAWA, then the grant is not necessary and the power has run out. The *propriety* of the reach has been thought to be a question of whether the claim bumps up against an explicit or implicit constitutional barrier. So "necessary" extends the reach of a grant, but not beyond plausibility when, as in VAWA, it runs out. And "proper" is an affirmative block to any means of exercising a granted power contrary to constitutional command. Thus Congress's compelled contribution to its mushroom-marketing scheme in *U.S. v. United Foods*[31] may have been marginally necessary to that silly scheme, but it was improper because it bumped up against the explicit command of the First Amendment.

That is not how the Chief Justice interpreted the propriety term. He first posited a constitutional limit to the otherwise necessary reach of the granted power and then argued that the mandate was improper (though undoubtedly necessary) because it exceeded that limit.[32] The purported limit was not any distinct constitutional prohibition, but the very notion that the extension of congressional power just went too far. But this is double counting. Why did the mandate go too far? Because it reached into a domain in which otherwise only the police power of the states would be available. But that is true of most commercial regulations under the Necessary and Proper Clause—for instance, various congressionally mandated regulations of the terms of private employment, as in wages and hours regulation. After all, that is just the standard effect of the Supremacy Clause and preemption. So to avoid this double counting or question-begging use of the impropriety notion, there has to be something particularly wrong about this necessary extension, and not just that it was an extension. And here the Chief Justice reached for the notion that the extension was improper not because it extended into a domain where otherwise only the states might regulate, but because there was something particularly inappropriate about this reach, and that was found in the notion that the regulation of medical systems and practice was a particular and traditional realm of state responsibility. (This kind of argument was invoked, particularly by Justice Kennedy, in both *Lopez*[33] and *Morrison*.[34]) Now this is a very imprecise and untethered notion, but as applied in this case it is just wrong. One need only consider the massive intrusion of federal regulation represented by Medicare, Medicaid (both to be sure under the Spending Clause, but so what?), and the FDA to recognize how pervasive is the federal presence in the regulation of medical services. So it is one of the dangerous loose ends left dangling in this case that we have here a newly open-ended limit in terms of propriety to otherwise necessary features of congressional regulation. Nor can *New York v. U.S.*[35] or *Printz*[36] be invoked to impose such a constitutional limit (said to be implicit in the Tenth Amendment), as those cases rested on the improper "commandeering" of state authority, but the only commandeering going on here is of individual citizens (or, if you will, "subjects") to whom this argument had never before been applied.

Of course, the real shadow of impropriety on everyone's mind but studiously omitted from the argument and justifications is the supposed intrusion on *individual liberty* implicated in Congress's scheme: the offense to liberty in requiring someone to enter the market and buy something from a nongovernmental purveyor. It is bewildering why it would be a greater offense to the liberty of the "subject" to compel someone to enter an equivalent or even more coercive and comprehensive scheme in which the benefit is supplied by the government and paid for by taxes. (Is it some kind of objectionable compelled association?) This is why Justice Kennedy's question in oral argument,[37] faintly echoed in the Chief's opinion, should be dismissed as mindless Tea Party rhetoric. The Tea Party, of course, views many government schemes as similarly offensive to liberty and perhaps hopes at some point to see those annulled too. But the argument was not made because it would have had to be made under the Liberty Clause of the Fifth Amendment, and this would have carried over to the similar clause in the Fourteenth and therefore rendered any such scheme enacted by a state, as in Massachusetts, similarly invalid.

But after marching, puffing, and wheezing, up this mountain of fallacy, it is astonishing to read the Chief's account of why the Court must nonetheless in spite of the Tax Injunction Act ("no suit for the purpose of restraining the assessment or collection of any tax shall be maintained in any court by and person")[38] uphold the mandate under Congress's Article I taxing powers, a conclusion with which the Chief's four Republican colleagues vehemently and convincingly disagreed, and the four Democrats with little comment and evident relief were prepared to join.[39] The Chief correctly and canonically set out the Court's traditional doctrine, by which if Congress designates a measure a tax it must for constitutional purposes be taken as one, even if on an ordinary view it would seem more like a penalty for violation of a regulatory requirement.[40] The mandate and the associated charge for failure to comply with it might be taken as a tax on a course of conduct: not obtaining health insurance though eligible to do so. Note that here to make this out a tax the incident has to fall on inactivity, but that the five ruled it was a fatal defect only when Congress's regulatory Commerce Clause power is invoked. That the tax acted as an incentive to engage in the desired conduct was deemed not to be fatal. Taxes quite often are used as incentives. Consider the case of heavy taxes on cigarettes. And once again such incentives operate to discourage activity, not inactivity. And the amount of the "tax" was not so great that it did not leave its targets a realistic option not to comply—once again, a line depending very much on a matter of degree, although the possibility that many would exercise the tax option was quite realistic. (Under a similar scheme in Massachusetts significant numbers choose to forgo insurance and pay the "tax.") But the cases on which the Chief relied—on gambling, on machine guns, on certain narcotic substances[41]—were all cases in which the Court indulged Congress's designation as a tax of what to the ordinary eye may have seemed like a penalty for violating a prohibition. In the case of the mandate exactly the opposite was the case: Congress had deliberately and on evident political grounds declined to designate the mandate and the consequences for noncompliance a tax, even though it had assigned certain administrative aspects of the monetary exaction to the Internal Revenue Service and lodged some of the provisions in the Internal Revenue Code.

A further difficulty with this maneuver was the Tax Injunction Act (TIA): the Court in order to avoid the politically intolerable result of postponing decision for a couple of years and until after the election had to find a way of ruling that the mandate was a tax for the purpose of its being a valid exercise of Congress's constitutional taxing power but not a tax for the application of the TIA. This was an exercise in interpretive jujitsu—more reminiscent, in the words of Justice Rehnquist (as he then was) in another context, not of the work of "jurists like Hale, Holmes and Hughes, but escape artists like Houdini"[42]—a maneuver in which the four other justices concurred with little comment and on which the four dissenters poured scorn. The chief makes the delicate but correct general point that what is a tax for constitutional purposes need not be one for the purposes of the TIA, the former being in the ultimate control of the Court's duty to "say what the law is," the latter a matter of Congress's free intent. But this truism does not do the job. The Court is not compelled to accept for constitutional purposes whatever Congress calls a tax, while Congress certainly may specify the coverage of its own enactments like the TIA. The trouble is that in this case the Court is calling a tax what Congress would not, and there is therefore no indication of its intention as to the application of the TIA to the mandate, which it declined to call a tax.

But the Commerce Clause activity/inactivity argument is so artificial and strained that at the end of the day it may not be very constraining, easily gotten around by skillful drafting. The Medicaid expansion invalidation, however, has potential for cutting a broad swath through many programs hitherto seen as unassailable under the rubric of cooperative federalism. The Medicaid expansion provision, which required states to cover under their Medicaid programs persons whose income did not exceed 133 percent of the poverty line, was an integral part of the ACA, because only in this way could the near universal coverage be achieved for persons too poor to purchase insurance even on a subsidized market. Initially the federal government would pay the full cost of this expansion, but after 2016 its contribution would decrease to some 90 percent.

There are innumerable programs in which the federal government invites the states to participate, funding all or part of the cost of the program. This device is crucial for two reasons. First, in some of them there is no or a contestable constitutional power granted to Congress to concern itself with a subject apart from its grant to "spend … for the general welfare"—education being one of the earliest such programs. Second, even if a modern view of the extent of federal regulatory power under the Commerce Clause might now grant such regulatory power to Congress over a particular subject matter, after the decisions in *New York v. United States*[43] and *Printz*,[44] it would seem Congress could not enlist unwilling state participation in a regulatory scheme even though it could regulate the scheme directly itself. The pre-1937 decision of *United States v. Butler* affirmed a long-standing interpretation to the effect that Article I, Section 8 conferred an authority to tax and spend for the general welfare not tied to any other power enumerated in the Constitution, but went on to strike down the use of that power in Roosevelt's Agricultural Adjustment Act because it invaded the states' supposed exclusive authority over agricultural, manufacturing, and mining.[45] The latter part of that decision was abandoned in *Steward Machine Co. v. Davis*.[46] In *South Dakota v. Dole*, the Court declined to invoke the anticommandeering principle to preclude conditioning the provision of federal highway funds to any state that did not enact a twenty-one-year-old drinking age.[47] Only Justice O'Connor would have required that the condition on the funding be directly related to the activity for which the funding was granted[48]—on this view Congress might condition highway funds by provisions detailing how those highway funds must be expended (e.g., requiring certain safety features in the construction of the highways) but not attach more remote conditions, like the drinking age. Chief Justice Rehnquist went no further than to note that the consequence of noncompliance was a mere 5 percent reduction in the funds available.[49] In *South Carolina v. Baker*, however, the Court, with only Justice O'Connor dissenting, approved a provision denying tax exempt status to any state securities not issued in prescribed, traceable, nonbearer form.[50] And in the Solomon Amendment, Congress imposed a complete cutoff of all federal funding to any university if it denied equal access to military recruiters.[51] The Court in *Rumsfeld v. Forum for Academic and Institutional Rights, Inc.* did not reach the draconic aspect of this provision, ruling that Congress was entitled to command such access directly, even if no funding at all was involved.[52]

In the Medicaid expansion portion of the decision the Chief Justice ruled that the provision cutting off all federal Medicaid funds to a state that did not participate in the expansion was unduly coercive and therefore amounted to a violation of the anticommandeering principle of *New York*[53] and *Printz.*[54] The Chief Justice treated this as analogous to an unconscionable provision in a contract or to imposition of a contract by duress, because the complete cutoff would work a drastic deprivation on nonacquiescent states, many of whose citizens depended on the old Medicaid provision and the noncompliant could only continue these accustomed benefits at unbearable cost to its own treasury. The decision is problematic on many scores. It is worth noting that although the modern Court had twice—in *Lopez*[55] and *Morrison*[56]—ruled that a federal program exceeded the power of Congress under the Commerce Clause, it has not since *Butler* struck down or limited a Spending or Taxing Clause program. The invocation of *Butler* as if it were still good law[57] is particularly remarkable, because it suggests that pre-1937 decisions and principles, long believed discredited and abandoned, might once again be invoked to limit Congress's powers.

In straight contract cases the argument is regularly rejected when franchisees object to contractually allowable franchise termination or alteration, pleading their large prior investments in the franchise. Or imagine a commercial tenant who has a lease in commercial premises in which he has invested heavily and where he has lots of goodwill (e.g., a neighborhood restaurant). The lease is terminable after five years on sixty days' notice and the lessor insists on a greatly increased rent. I submit that the tenant's complaint that this constituted duress would get nowhere. The analogy of states to hapless consumers as in some stretchy unconscionability cases[58] is obviously inapposite.

There is little reassurance in the Chief Justice's citation to the language in *Dole* that emphasizes that the fund cutoff in that case was a mere 5 percent, and of federal highway funds at that[59]—not a 100 percent of a massive budget item like Medicaid. The Chief Justice quotes *Steward Machine*, the first case overruling the restrictions in *Butler*: while "[we] did not attempt to 'fix the outermost line' where persuasion gives way to coercion.... [It is] 'enough for present purposes that wherever the line may be, this statute is within it.'"[60] That may be good enough to say that a provision, as in *Steward*, is valid. The use of that offhand rhetoric to invalidate an act of Congress is deeply disturbing. It leaves open the suggestion that federal funding programs in transportation, education, public safety, and many other domains exist on a kind of ratchet: once a state has accepted them and its citizens have grown accustomed to them, they may not be amended or discontinued. An analogous argument under the Takings Clause was rejected in *Bowen v. Public Agencies Opposed to Social Security Entrapment.*[61] Here indeed is a provision that nods in the direction of the Tea Party program of the "constitution in exile," whose ambition it is to unravel the fabric of the post-1937 welfare administrative state. What was truly astonishing was that two such accomplished administrative law scholars as Justices Breyer[62] and Kagan joined this opinion, making this most mischievous argument a seven-to-two decision of the Court.

## 2. The Mysteries

The main mystery is why five members of the Court should have signed on to the weak and untethered broccoli argument. Cynical commentators charge this up simply to partisan politics: the Republican justices wanted to hand President Obama a signal defeat to a cherished but unpopular program, four months before the election, and incidentally dispensing Mitt Romney from the trouble of proposing an alternative to a statute he had pledged to repeal. This was another *Bush v. Gore,*[63] a naked intrusion into electoral politics. Never mind that *Bush v. Gore* was on the merits (not the remedy) a seven-to-two decision, reacting in part to the Supreme Court of Florida's blatant disregard of a previous unanimous order of the Supreme Court in *Bush v. Palm Beach County Canvassing Bd.*[64] It is a challenge, but I choose to believe that the justices were sincerely trying to do their job, calling—in the Chief Justice's words—balls and strikes. They just got it terribly wrong. Why? Because they are human beings, with emotions and susceptibilities. In this case I believe they were carried away on a tide of hostility to a measure that looked like it might be the prelude to a major expansion of federal power, so that there just had to be something wrong with it. And the activity/inactivity line of the broccoli argument, by dint of constant repetition, looked like that might be what it was.

I have been a judge, and I am aware that one way one goes about deciding a difficult, disturbing case is to start with a feel, a gut reaction that there is something terrible wrong here. And now the intellectual and professional task is to try to locate what it is. A vague discomfort in the abdomen turns out to be an enlarged liver pressing on the descending aorta, and so on. This is a perfectly correct, perhaps inevitable way to proceed, but it demands discipline and questioning self-doubt. The seemingly eligible diagnosis must be subject to relentless skeptical probing, and the possibility must be entertained that the pain in the abdomen is just gas, so that what started seeming to be something dire turns out to be nothing at all. This is a very good Court, with able, conscientious judges—none more so than the Chief—and that is how every day they do their work. This time the discipline failed them—it happens. Perhaps their distaste for the scheme, perhaps Justice Kennedy's libertarian instincts (here entirely out of place), perhaps the intense partisanship prevailing in the city in which they work, perhaps the approach of the end of the term and the shortness of time, the close and heated media scrutiny and expectations for the case threw them off. It happens. It did not happen to Judges Lawrence Silberman or Jeffrey Sutton, whose instincts and predilections are very similar to those of the five. To the five it must have seemed like a time for boldness, a chance to strike a signal blow for liberty, for limited government. The atmosphere in the courtroom, the tenor of the questioning, the unusual fixed gaze of the media for three days. It may just have overwhelmed them.

Now let us move to the mystery of Chief Justice Roberts's march up one side of the mountain and then down again on the other. I hold him to be a supremely intelligent and disciplined man, whose ambitions are for his Court and the honor of his role as Chief Justice. I think he was terribly torn: between the exhilaration of the moment, the intoxicating, raging exhilaration of his colleagues ( I would exempt Justice Thomas from this: he only followed what he had been saying for more than a decade—and as usual he said it calmly, without rancor) and a nagging sense that something was not quite right. In the end that led him to the precarious logic of the Taxing Clause—all the more valid-seeming because precarious and implausible.

Principles of strategy, the balance of forces, from a great distance seem as if they might decide a battle, but generals thrust into the fog of war, the choking smoke of exploding shells, gruesome death on all sides, act almost at random, and the outcome is unpredictable. One thinks of the battle descriptions in *War and Peace* and in *The Charterhouse of Parma*; the participants in the battle rush about, perform feats of bravery or not, sometimes don't know who they are shooting at and only afterwards when the smoke clears do they (or the generals) know who won the battle, how and why. That was Roberts's situation in this case.

The cynics tell a different story, rather two different stories, stories of calculation and cowardice. In both stories the Chief is moved by a desire to save the reputation of the Court, and his own place in it, from an accusation of naked partisanship. To some his decision to uphold the statute on Taxing Clause grounds is a case of cold feet. To others it was an act of supreme cunning: the Tea Party broccoli argument prevails, but the Court cannot be blamed for the practical outcome. And the potentially far more destructive Spending Clause ruling is left to lie about like Justice Jackson's loaded weapon, available to wreak havoc on federal welfare programs. Finally, the Chief saves up (maybe acquires) some capital as an independent, principled jurist to spend on the upcoming affirmative action and Defense of Marriage Act cases.

I don't believe it. I just see a serious man torn and groping to find his way. Consider the quite strained argument about why it was justified to rule on the broccoli argument at all, once the Chief had decided that the ACA could be sustained under the taxing power. If an important federal statute can be sustained on one ground, it seems gratuitous to go on to demonstrate why it would fail on another, novel, highly controverted and fraught ground; one that attracts a powerful dissent. The Chief's explanation is that the justification under the taxing power was an interpretive stretch, given Congress's assiduous avoidance of the tax label, but that nevertheless it was appropriate to stretch so as to honor the principles of judicial restraint and deference to a coordinate branch. I believe him. There is a Frankfurterian, Jacksonian (Robert Jackson), even Rehnquistian legacy to which Roberts is an heir, that is extremely reluctant to strike down congressional economic regulation. But this autobiographical note does not explain why, having granted the ACA this deference and saved it as an exercise of the taxing power, he went ahead and made up a Court of five justices for the Commerce Clause argument that, once he had ruled the statute was valid as a tax, was no longer relevant to any work the Court properly had before it. To be sure, the dissenters, having rejected the tax argument, had every reason to go on to make the broccoli argument on the Commerce Clause, but Roberts had none. It is as if, having crossed the tax bridge, he was casting a wistful glance backwards to the dramatic argument he could have, but did not in principle, feel entitled to make. Again, the account of Roberts as judicial Machiavelli would have this as a shrewd way for him to have it both ways. I tend to see it not as a calculated maneuver but as the understandable impulse to lay bare one's thinking, and if along the way this allows him to show that his heart really does beat in the right part of his chest, perhaps that was a temptation too hard to resist.

There is another, more dramatic indication that something unusual and untoward happened: the joint opinion of Justices Scalia, Kennedy, Thomas, and Alito, making the broccoli argument in terms—tone and rhetoric apart—hardly distinguishable from the Chief's opinion on that count. First, the jointness: the usual protocol going back to the days of the Marshall Court has a single designated author for an opinion—majority, concurring, or dissent—which others join. (In earlier times and in England there was a practice of seriatim individual announcement, but not so now.) So it was in *Marbury v. Madison*, in *Brown v. Board of Education*, in *Lopez* and *Morrison*.[65] In signal cases the Chief will generally assign the opinion to himself. Historians, digging through the papers of former justices and justices themselves delivering lectures on the functioning of the Court, explain how these opinions are circulated to the chambers in draft, other justices signaling their willingness to join, though sometimes they will condition that agreement on the author's agreeing to changes. Though often robbing opinions of a certain individual flair, the practice has the great virtue of offering the world—and particularly the bar and lower-court judges—a carefully negotiated, crafted, and therefore perhaps more stable and reliable statement of the law.

Then there is the joint opinion. It is a very rare phenomenon. The justices designate each of themselves as joint authors. Famous examples are the joint opinion of all nine justices in *Cooper v. Aaron*, proclaiming the supremacy as law of the Supreme Court's desegregation cases;[66] the joint opinion of Justices O'Connor, Kennedy, and Souter in *Planned Parenthood of Southeastern PA v. Casey*, affirming the commitment of these three justices to the what they termed "the central holding" of *Roe v. Wade*;[67] and the joint opinion of Justices Stevens and O'Connor in *McConnell v. Federal Election Comm'n*, upholding the most important features of the 2002 Bipartisan Campaign Finance Reform Act (McCain-Feingold).[68] Formally a joint opinion has no greater weight than an opinion by a single justice joined by others, but obviously the justices designating themselves as joint authors are seeking to make some special point. In *Casey* it was that a change in personnel since the 1974 decision and appointments by two Republican presidents who had proclaimed their disagreement with *Roe* had not undermined the validity of that decision. In *McConnell* perhaps the joint opinion was intended to emphasize the support from two separate wings of the Court for campaign finance reform. And the point in *Cooper*, in the face of concerted attacks on the authority of the Court, was obvious.

But here? One anodyne explanation is that the Chief may have switched sides and his tax ruling came as a surprise, leaving the four dissenters little time until the end of the term and forcing them to parcel out the different parts of the very lengthy (sixty-five pages as against the fifty-nine pages of the Chief's opinion announcing the opinion of the Court) opinion. That won't do. It is entirely possible—indeed the internal evidence of the Chief's opinion points that way—that the Chief in this important case had assigned the opinion to himself, written his broccoli analysis as the opinion of the Court, and then some time later became persuaded that the tax argument is possible and that, if possible, it was his duty to embrace it. But then the four dissenters could have joined the Chief's broccoli opinion with which they were in virtually complete agreement, as well as Medicaid extension opinion, leaving them only to explain in dissent why they rejected the tax argument and therefore why, with the mandate gone, they would strike down the whole ACA, from which they thought the mandate was not severable.

And why joint? As I have shown, this is done only to make a special point. It may be a failure of imagination on my part, but I can think of no special institutional point being made and so am left concluding that the four wished to signal their utter condemnation of the Chief's retreat from what they thought of as the path of righteousness. The jointness signals, if nothing else, the personal, individual commitment to the opinion, but there is no other grounds for such a personal gesture than a sense of personal betrayal. That this is a gesture of contempt and repudiation shows up also in the fact that the four do not advert to the Chief's opinion, although the largest part of what they write is in complete agreement with the largest part of what he writes.

If I am right about that, perhaps we can reconstruct what happened from this internal evidence. The Chief voted initially to strike down the mandate and assigned to himself the opinion doing so. He may or may not have agreed that the mandate was inseparable from the rest of the ACA, although he at least thought the Medicaid extension provision was unconstitutional (as applied to states unwilling to go along with it). And then he thought again. And the Frankfurterian in him could not allow him to ignore the tax argument in order to condemn the mandate. This left his four colleagues high and dry—and, because this was the signal piece of legislation it was, with a feeling not just of disappointment, not just with disagreement, but with a sense of betrayal in the heat of battle. The atmosphere was fraught, and the end of the term was near. Perhaps there was not time, inclination, or energy for the Chief to reconsider his conclusion under the Taxing Clause. Similarly, this may account for his reluctance to withdraw his now gratuitous Commerce Clause portion of his opinion—or even just to say that had he not felt compelled to uphold the mandate under the tax power he would have agreed with the four on the Commerce Clause.

In the end, the Chief comes out the winner: not because he made the best arguments or even consistently adhered to his own principles, but because it is evident that in this most fraught, pressured, and political of cases, he tried to do the right thing and was willing to pay the price in the esteem of those with whom he was in closest political, doctrinal, and temperamental agreement.

By way of coda, I must address the mystery of Justices Breyer and Kagan joining the Chief's most mischievous ruling that the Medicaid expansion provision could not be imposed on unwilling states by threatening a total cutoff of federal Medicaid funds. The cynical suggestion that this was a kind of payoff to the Chief for saving the mandate borders on the paranoid. And yet one can imagine that as June 28 approached these emotionally and mentally exhausted justices just lacked the energy to pick up the cudgels once again to deal further blows to the already bloodied Chief. And in those last fraught days Justices Breyer and Kagan might have been concerned to save as much of the expansion as possible by joining the Chief's opinion, which would have preserved existing Medicaid participation for states unwilling to accept the expanded coverage. The joint opinion would have invalidated the expansion altogether. As I have noted, the present less radical invalidation result might have been achieved by joining Justice Ginsburg's dissent, but less emphatically.

# Notes

1. See Charles Fried, *Balls and Strikes*, 61 EMORY L.J. 641 (2012).
2. NFIB v. Sebelius, 132 S. Ct. 2566 (2012).
3. Ball 1 incorrectly called a strike, strike 1 incorrectly called a ball, balls 3 and 4 correctly called balls, strike 2 incorrectly called a ball: batter walks.
4. Adam Liptak, *After Ruling, Roberts Makes a Getaway from the Scorn*, N.Y. TIMES, July 2, 2012, *available at* http://www.nytimes.com/2012/07/03/us/politics/scorn-and-withering-scor n-for-chief-justice-roberts.html.
5. Although the blogosphere has been awash in rumors, gossip, and conjectures about what "really" happened, this chapter is based entirely on public, internal evidence. As Justice Scalia has said, most of those who purport to have inside information don't, and of those who might, their very speaking condemns them as unreliable because willing dishonorably to break confidences. See *Justice Scalia Disputes Accuracy of "Leak,"* NPR MORNING EDITION, July 25, 2012, *available at* http://www.npr.org/2012/07/25/157319766/justice-scalia-disp utes-accuracy-of-leak.
6. *Hearing on the Constitutionality of the Affordable Care Act Before the S. Comm. on the Judiciary*, 112th Cong. (2011) (statement of Charles Fried, Beneficial Professor of Law, Harvard Law School), *available at* http://www.judiciary.senate.gov/pdf/11-02-02%20Fried%20 Testimony.pdf.
7. See David Bernstein, *Should Charles Fried Eat His Kangaroo Skin Hat?* THE VOLOKH CONSPIRACY (July 8, 2012, 9:39 PM), http://www.volokh.com/2012/07/08/should-cha rles-fried-eat-his-kangaroo-skin-hat/. Technically, the Court did sustain the broccoli argument, though it upheld the mandate, so perhaps I may be liable, but then as I explain below that ruling was dictum. I have located a bakery that for $300 would be willing to make a perfect replica of the hat—which I had long ago given to my daughter-in-law on whom it looks much better (photos on request)—so that Greta and invited guests could join me in the feast.
8. U.S. v. Morrison, 529 U.S. 598 (2000). Full disclosure: I was cocounsel for *Morrison* in the Supreme Court.
9. U.S. v. Lopez, 514 U.S. 549 (1995).
10. Florida *ex rel.* Bondi v. U.S. Dep't of Health & Human Servs., 780 F. Supp. 2d 1256 (N.D. Fla. 2011), *aff'd in part, rev'd in part*, 648 F.3d 1235 (11th Cir. 2011), *aff'd in part, rev'd in part sub nom. NFIB*, 132 S. Ct. 2566 (2012).
11. Virginia *ex rel.* Cuccinelli v. Sebelius, 702 F. Supp. 2d 598 (E.D. Va. 2010), *rev'd*, 656 F.3d 253 (4th Cir. 2011), *cert. denied*, No. 11-420 (June 29, 2012).
12. Florida *ex rel.* Bondi v. U.S. Dep't of Health & Human Servs., 648 F.3d 1235 (11th Cir. 2011), *aff'd in part, rev'd in part sub nom. NFIB*, 132 S. Ct. 2566 (2012).
13. Thomas More Law Ctr. v. Obama, 651 F.3d 529 (6th Cir. 2011) (Sutton, J., concurring), *cert. denied*, No. 11-117 (June 29, 2012).
14. Seven-Sky v. Holder, 661 F.3d 1 (D.C. Cir. 2011), *cert. denied*, No. 11-679 (June 29, 2012).
15. 317 U.S. 11 (1942).
16. 22 U.S. 1 (1824).
17. *Wickard*, 317 U.S. 11.
18. INTRADE, THE U.S. SUPREME COURT TO RULE INDIVIDUAL MANDATE UNCONSTITUTIONAL BEFORE MIDNIGHT ET 31 DEC 2013, http://www.intrade.com/v4/markets/contract/? contractId=745354 (depicting graph that shows changes in betting odds in the time period before the Supreme Court's decision).
19. Transcript of Oral Argument at 12, *NFIB*, 132 S. Ct. 2566.
20. *Mandate Struck Down*, CNN, June 28, 2012, *available at* http://www.slate.com/blogs/ browbeat/2012/06/28/aca_mandate_struck_down_cnn_and_fox_misreport_the_ historic_decision_.html.

21. 505 U.S. 144 (1992).

22. 521 U.S. 898 (1997).

23. NFIB v. Sebelius, 132 S. Ct. 2566, 2667 (2012) (Scalia, Kennedy, Alito, Thomas, JJ., dissenting).

24. *Id.* at 2666.

25. *Id.* at 2589.

26. *Hearing on the Constitutionality of the Affordable Care Act Before the S. Comm. on the Judiciary,* 112th Cong. (2011) (statement of Randy E. Barnett, Carmack Waterhouse Professor of Legal Theory, Georgetown University Law Center).

27. Brief for The Heritage Foundation et al. as Amici Curiae Supporting Respondents, *NFIB,* 132 S. Ct. 2566 (No. 11-398), 2012 WL 484070.

28. *NFIB,* 132 S. Ct. at 2586.

29. *Id.* at 2591–2593.

30. *Id.*

31. 533 U.S. 405 (2001).

32. *NFIB,* 132 S. Ct. at 2591–2593.

33. 514 U.S. 549.

34. 529 U.S. 598.

35. 505 U.S. 144.

36. 521 U.S. 898.

37. Transcript of Oral Argument at 12, *NFIB,* 132 S. Ct. 2566.

38. 28 U.S.C. § 1341 (2006).

39. *NFIB,* 132 S. Ct. at 2593–2600.

40. *Id.*

41. *Id.*

42. United Steelworkers of America, AFL-CIO-CLC v. Weber, 443 U.S. 193, 222 (1979) (Rehnquist, J., dissenting).

43. 505 U.S. 144.

44. 521 U.S. 898.

45. 297 U.S. 1 (1936).

46. 301 U.S. 548 (1937).

47. 483 U.S. 203 (1987).

48. *Id.* at 212–218.

49. *Id.* at 211.

50. 485 U.S. 505 (1988).

51. Rumsfeld v. Forum for Academic and Institutional Rights, Inc., 547 U.S. 47 (2006).

52. *Id.*

53. 505 U.S. 144.

54. 521 U.S. 898.

55. 514 U.S. 549.

56. 529 U.S. 598.

57. *NFIB,* 132 S. Ct. at 2599.

58. See, e.g., Williams v. Walker-Thomas Furniture, Co., 350 F.2d 445 (D.C. Cir. 1965).

59. 483 U.S. at 211.

60. *NFIB,* 132 S. Ct. at 2606.

61. 477 U.S. 41 (1986).

62. It is particularly remarkable because during the oral argument Justice Breyer remarked that of course the federal government would never have to nor choose to impose this severe provision. Like Justice Breyer's observations in other cases regarding the limits of the Commerce Clause, this appeal to real-world possibilities to cut off recourse to extreme hypotheticals such as forcing people to buy broccoli or a particular make of car, would suggest that such far-fetched possibilities should be ignored in judging the constitutional validity of statutes.

63. 531 U.S. 98 (2000).

64. 531 U.S. 70 (2000). Full disclosure, I was counsel of record in that case for the Florida House of Representatives urging the prevailing result. See Charles Fried, *An Unreasonable Reaction to a Reasonable Decision, in* BUSH VERSUS GORE (Bruce Ackerman ed., 2002).

65. 1 Cranch 137, 176 (1803); 347 U.S. 483 (1954); 514 U.S. 549; 529 U.S. 598.

66. 358 U.S. 1 (1958).

67. 505 U.S. 833 (1992).

68. 540 U.S. 93 (2003).

CHAPTER 5

# Much Ado

THE POTENTIAL IMPACT OF THE SUPREME COURT
DECISION UPHOLDING THE AFFORDABLE CARE ACT

*Robert N. Weiner*

In the lead-up to the Supreme Court's decision in *National Federation of Independent Business v. Sebelius* (*NFIB*)[1] on the constitutionality of the Affordable Care Act (ACA), many commentators dubbed it the case of the century.[2] The public awareness of the case was extraordinary, and the partisan blaze surrounding it blurred legal distinctions and obscured the limitations that the government built into its arguments. Notwithstanding the hype, the legal ruling upholding the individual mandate—though critical to the fate of health care reform—turned out to be largely inconsequential in the evolution of constitutional law.

If the precedential force of the decision is limited, however, the partisan forces that produced it could dramatically affect constitutional jurisprudence. Or perhaps not. It is too early to know for sure. It is not too early, though, to identify the factors that could determine that result.

## 1. The Political History of a Legal Battle

On March 23, 2010, Congress enacted the ACA without a single Republican vote.[3] The new law was the signature legislative accomplishment of the Obama administration—the comprehensive health care reform that had eluded Democrats for more than sixty years. The victory was all the more dramatic because, just two months before, the bill was given up for dead when Republican Scott Brown won the special election to succeed the late Senator Edward Kennedy. The changeover deprived Democrats of the sixtieth vote they needed in the Senate to defeat a Republican filibuster.[4] The legislative maneuvering that overcame this setback left Republican legislators livid. With near unanimity, they vowed repeal.[5] One Republican congressman threatened to "meet the federal government at the state line to keep them from mandating this bill upon us."[6] The Republican leadership was only slightly more temperate. The Speaker of the House proclaimed that the new law portended "Armageddon" and would "ruin our country."[7] The Senate minority leader disparaged the result as "the culmination of a year-long quest by a partisan majority to force its will on the public over bipartisan opposition."[8] Partisan rancor ran so high that Democrats received threats of violence, and Republicans accused Democrats of "fanning the flames" by blaming them.[9]

The partisan legislative dispute spilled immediately into the courts. Seven minutes after the President signed the bill, the Republican attorney general of Florida, along with eleven other Republican state attorneys general and the Democratic attorney general of Louisiana, filed suit.[10] Four of the Republican attorneys general proceeded despite objections by their Democratic governors.[11] Virginia's Republican attorney general filed separately.[12]

Bypassing the federal courthouse only blocks from his Tallahassee office, the Florida attorney general sued more than 200 miles away in Pensacola.[13] That jurisdiction had no connection to the case. What it did have was a federal district court with only three judges, all conservatives appointed by Republican presidents.[14] This forum shopping, while legal, highlighted the partisan tinge of the case.

As the suit proceeded, seven more states joined, three represented by their Republican attorneys general, as well as four by Republican governors who signed on over the objections of their Democratic attorneys general, the customary decision-makers regarding state litigation.[15] In January 2011, four more Republican attorneys general and one Republican governor joined the litigation. The Court did not ask, and the states did not explain why—nine months after the suit was filed and six months after the Court's deadline for joining new parties—they suddenly realized that they, too, had been injured. Only one explanation is plausible—the change in the leadership of each of the seven states from Democratic to Republican in the November 2010 elections. Indeed, just two weeks after the elections, Tim Pawlenty, then vice-chair of the Republican Governors Association, urged "[n]ewly elected Republican governors" to join the lawsuit.[16]

In the meantime, a rush of other litigation by conservative advocacy groups, fundamentalist religious organizations, and Republican officials advanced through the federal courts.[17] In the Florida litigation, Republican officials representing twenty-six states were joined by a small business trade association linked closely with the Republican Party[18] plus a local Republican official from Washington state and other individuals. Florida became the lead case and the one that the Supreme Court decided.[19]

Although the party affiliation of the president who appointed a judge is an inadequate proxy for the judge's outlook in a specific case, the district courts that reached the merits of the ACA challenges divided precisely along that fault line. Republican appointees in Florida, Virginia, and Pennsylvania invalidated the law.[20] Democratic appointees in Michigan, Virginia, and the District of Columbia upheld it.[21] The decisions on the merits in the courts of appeals continued to reflect this partisan division, with notable exceptions. In particular, two of the leading conservative intellectuals on the bench broke from the partisan orthodoxy and upheld the law,[22] while one Democratic appointee voted to strike it down.[23]

Party politics and the judicial process grew increasingly entangled as the unconstitutionality of the individual mandate in the ACA became, in essence, the official position of the Republican Party.[24] The partisan commandeering of the constitutional argument against the individual mandate was nearly seamless, even though key Republicans, including presidential candidates Mitt Romney and Newt Gingrich, had previously supported such a provision.[25] The lineup of amici in the lower courts, and ultimately in the Supreme Court, also reflected the partisan rift. Citing their oath to uphold the Constitution, forty-three Republican senators told the Supreme Court that the individual mandate undermined the federal system,[26] even though ten of these signatories—bound by the same oath—had sponsored legislation containing such a mandate.[27] The Republican Speaker of the House, two additional Republican-led states, the Republican Governors Public Policy Committee, and five Republican former Justice Department officials also filed briefs advocating that the ACA be struck down.[28] Urging that the statute be upheld were the Democratic leadership of the House and Senate, thirteen Democratic-led states and territories and the District of Columbia, and one Democratic governor.[29] And, as if to punctuate the issue, the Republican-controlled House of Representatives voted more than thirty times to repeal, defund, or undercut the ACA while the litigation was pending.[30]

The Supreme Court heard argument over three days in March 2012, and the Court's questioning prompted another wave of partisan dispute. Democrats, including the President, invoked comparisons to the reactionary Court that blocked New Deal reforms.[31] Republicans accused Democrats of trying to intimidate the Court.[32] Raising the temperature even more as the Court took the bench on the last day of the term, June 28, 2012, to announce its decision, the presidential campaign was well under way. The ACA, and the role of the Supreme Court, were pervasive features of the political debates.

Although the ideological and partisan bonfires surrounding the litigation may have cooled somewhat since then, this political history remains critical to decoding the decision and predicting its effect. Partisanship is in the DNA of the case, marking its birth, its progress through the lower courts, and its turn before the Supreme Court. As shown below, with regard to central legal issues, the legal indeterminacy of the opinion that emerged may elevate the significance of this extralegal factor in setting the course of constitutional jurisprudence.

## 2. The Legal Issues in Dispute

The central goal of the ACA—reducing the number of people without health insurance—is relatively uncontroversial, as are many provisions of the law.[33] The means it employs, however, are the subject of vehement dispute as a matter of politics and policy. Like many such disputes, this one has mutated into litigation, particularly with regard to the requirement that individuals have a minimum level of health insurance.

Presumably in anticipation of the constitutional challenges, Congress made statutory findings demonstrating that the minimum coverage provision addresses significant issues arising in and substantially affecting interstate commerce. Specifically, Congress found that the minimum coverage requirement "regulates activity that is commercial and economic in nature: economic and financial decisions about how and when health care is paid for, and when health insurance is purchased."[34] Congress found further that the requirement is essential for other reforms in the ACA to work, in particular, guaranteed issue and community rating.[35] Without the individual mandate, Congress determined, individuals guaranteed coverage under the Act could wait until they became ill to buy a policy. That "adverse selection" would push premiums up,[36] which in turn would lead more people to wait until they were sick to purchase insurance, causing a "death spiral" in the insurance industry. In addition, Congress found that uninsured individuals still receive health care, but often cannot pay for it. The cost of such uncompensated health care for those without insurance—$43 billion in 2008—falls on others in the health care market, adding $1,000 to the annual insurance premiums of a typical family.[27] Based on these factors, Congress concluded that the failure to obtain health insurance substantially affects interstate commerce.[38]

The plaintiffs in the NFIB case disputed the finding that the ACA regulates how people pay for health care. Not buying health insurance, they argued, is inactivity, and inactivity is not "commerce" subject to Congressional regulation.[39] To hold otherwise, the challengers claimed, would obliterate all limits on federal regulation.[40] They contended further that even if the mandate was essential to the other insurance reforms in the ACA, the Necessary and Proper Clause could not validate it because it is beyond the purview of federal authority.[41]

The government's response to the Commerce Clause challenge largely tracked the congressional findings. But the government added a wrinkle to the argument. Individuals who fail to obtain health insurance, the government contended, shift not only medical costs, but also insurance risk. Those who have insurance bear the risk—which their premiums reflect—that the uninsured will incur medical expenses beyond their ability to pay. This argument, it appears, was drowned out by the political din. But the same was not true of the government's alternative argument—that the minimum coverage provision was independently justified as an exercise of Congress's taxing power.[42] If there were any doubt regarding the applicability of the taxing power, the government argued, the Court had a duty to resolve that doubt in favor of the constitutionality of the statute. In other words, because the minimum coverage provision *could* be interpreted as an exercise of the taxing power, it *had* to be interpreted in that manner.[43]

## 3. Jigsaw Jurisprudence: Assessing the Impact of the ACA Decision

By a vote of five to four, the Supreme Court upheld the constitutionality of the minimum coverage provision under the taxing power. Justices Ginsburg, Breyer, Sotomayor, and Kagan joined the opinion of the Chief Justice on this issue.

With regard to the Commerce Clause, the Chief Justice, in a portion of his opinion joined by no other justice, said that the minimum coverage provision is beyond Congress's commerce powers, and cannot be salvaged by the Necessary and Proper Clause. Justices Scalia, Kennedy, Thomas, and Kennedy jointly penned a dissent drawing the same conclusion. Justice Ginsburg, joined by Justices Breyer, Sotomayor, and Kagan, would have upheld the provision under the Commerce Clause and the Necessary and Proper Clause. To assess the potential impact of the *NFIB* decision, it is necessary to extract from the shifting majorities and intersecting opinions what the Court held and did not hold on each of the issues described above. The task is not straightforward.

### A. THE COMMERCE CLAUSE AND THE NECESSARY AND PROPER CLAUSE

Because the Chief Justice and the four justices on the joint dissent agreed that the individual mandate exceeded Congress's commerce powers, some commentators have treated that conclusion as the holding of the Court.[44] It is not. As a matter of law, the various pronouncements of the justices regarding the constitutionality of the ACA under the Commerce Clause have no precedential value, for several reasons.

First, the opinion of the Chief Justice upholding the ACA based on the taxing power was a majority opinion that spoke for the Court and resolved the challenge to the individual mandate. Whether Congress had any other source of constitutional power to enact the mandate does not affect the outcome. The mandate would be constitutional either way. Although the Chief Justice offered a halfhearted rationale for discussing the Commerce Clause, it does not alter this fundamental fact.[45] There is thus a good argument that even if the Chief Justice's discussion of the Commerce Clause had been on behalf of the Court, it would still be dicta.[46]

Second, whether or not they agreed with the Chief Justice's rationale, the four justices on the joint dissent did not join that part (or any part) of the Chief Justice's opinion. Thus, there was no majority opinion regarding the constitutionality of the minimum coverage provision under the Commerce Clause.[47] Tallying the votes on the issue does not yield a binding precedent. As the Court held in Marks v. United States, "When a fragmented Court decides a case and no single rationale explaining the result enjoys the assent of five Justices, the holding of the Court may be viewed as that position taken by those Members who concurred in the judgments on the narrowest grounds."[48] Here, a single rationale— the ruling on the taxing power—did enjoy the assent of five justices. That ruling does explain the result. And the signatories of the joint dissent did not concur in the judgment.[49] In sum, the only authoritative ruling of the Court regarding the individual mandate is that it is constitutional as an exercise of Congress's constitutional authority to "lay and collect Taxes."

Determining the legal impact of the spray of opinions in NFIB, however, does not end the inquiry. Whether their views are precedential or not, the practical reality is that five justices believed the individual mandate exceeded Congress's powers under the Commerce Clause. It is a fair assumption that judges in the lower courts can count. Their tally of the votes in the case could well influence, if not dictate, their conclusions regarding any similar mandates that come before them.

Even on such a practical assessment, however, the Commerce Clause theories articulated by the Chief Justice and the dissenters are unlikely, in and of themselves, to alter the course of the law. First, both opinions reaffirmed existing Commerce Clause jurisprudence. Both cited Wickard v. Filburn[50] as the "most far reaching example of Commerce Clause authority over intrastate activity,"[51] or as "the ne plus ultra of expansive Commerce Clause jurisprudence."[52] But neither opinion purported to redraw the boundary set in Wickard. Rather, they characterized the ACA as falling outside it.[53]

Similarly, the Chief Justice's opinion reaffirmed existing precedent under the Necessary and Proper Clause and reiterated Congress's broad discretion in choosing how to effectuate its enumerated powers.[54] The problem, the Chief Justice found, was that the individual mandate did not effectuate Congress's enumerated powers, but rather extended them, exceeding the boundaries set in those cases.[55]

Second, both opinions emphasized the novelty of the individual mandate. The Chief Justice observed that "Congress has never attempted to rely on [the commerce] power to compel individuals not engaged in commerce to purchase an unwanted product."[56] The joint dissent deemed the mandate "unprecedented,"[57] and noted, "The relevant history is not that Congress has achieved wide and wonderful results through the proper exercise of its assigned powers in the past, but that it has never before used the Commerce Clause to compel entry into commerce."[58] Two points follow from these observations. One, if the ACA is truly unprecedented, then the *NFIB* decision should jeopardize no statutes currently on the books. And two, if the mandate is indeed novel, then for more than 220 years Congress accomplished, or at least tried to accomplish, its "wide and wonderful results" without deploying such a provision. Particularly given that the Court has now provided a road map to avoid constitutional infirmity by proceeding under the taxing power, Congress should have little reason to enact any provision remotely akin to a mandate under the Commerce Clause.

Third, on the optimistic assumption that over the long term, there is a judicial inclination toward coherence, the unworkability—both conceptually and practically—of the Commerce Clause standard articulated by the Chief Justice and the joint dissenters also should blunt its impact on the development of the law. The predicate of the Chief Justice's analysis was that "[t]he power to *regulate* commerce presupposes the existence of commercial activity to be regulated."[59] The Chief Justice conceded that "[t]o an economist, perhaps, there is no difference between activity and inactivity; both have measurable economic effects on commerce."[60] "But the distinction between doing something and doing nothing would not have been lost on the Framers."[61] In application, however, the line between "regulating commerce" and "requiring commerce," or between "activity" and "inactivity," blurs into incoherence. If, for example, General Motors set aside $100 million as a self-insurance reserve for tort cases, that undertaking would clearly be "economic activity."[62] If an individual without health insurance established a "medical expenses account" into which she deposited part of her salary every pay period to cover potential medical costs, is that not "economic activity," too? What aspect of the definition of economic activity supports a workable distinction between the two examples?

The line between regulating and requiring commerce is obscure in other respects as well. A prohibition on discriminating in providing accommodations is a mandate to treat people equally, and in particular, to engage in commerce with them.[63] To argue that a motel owner can avoid the mandate by not operating a motel—in other words, by giving up his livelihood—hardly frames a realistic choice.[64]

Further, it is foreseeable that the Court could confront cases in which this type of limitation would impair the federal government's ability to fulfill basic responsibilities. If, for example, the federal government were to quarantine an individual with a virulent, communicable disease, that would be an exercise of the commerce power—potentially in the absence of commerce, or, indeed, activity.[65] In the face of a pandemic, courts are not likely to deny the federal government authority essential to protecting the public safety. It is easy to conceive of other circumstances where some type of mandate is the best, if not the only, way to deal with a safety problem that individual states cannot solve on their own.[66]

In addition to the difficulties courts would encounter in attempting to draw these lines, they would also struggle to make sense of the temporal distinctions in the Chief Justice's opinion—the bar on regulating individuals *before* they (inevitably) enter the market for health care. The Court's earlier forays into temporal standards under the Commerce Clause did not fare well. At various points, the Court held that Congress could not regulate manufacturing, mining, or production because those activities preceded the entry of goods into interstate commerce, which did not occur until they were sold.[67] Until this case, such categorical approaches had been discarded as rigid and unworkable.[68]

Apart from the conceptual problems, the practical difficulties of such a temporal approach are legion. The Court's analysis suggests that Congress could require those who are in the health care market to have insurance. But if an individual enters the health care market, is she in it forever? If an errant and remote use of medical services does not permanently enlist the individual in the market, how long does she need to go without using medical services before she is no longer a participant?[69] And what constitutes entry into the market? Making an appointment with a doctor? Forming the intent to see a doctor? Knowing she is ill and should see a doctor? Further, once someone enters the market, could the government impose a retroactive penalty for not having health care previously? If so, how far back could the penalty reach?

The entanglements are likewise impassable if the analysis focuses on the timing of entry into the "insurance market." If an individual has health insurance for the first half of the year and then drops it, is she still a participant in the market for insurance? For what period? Judge Sutton recognized the analytical muddle produced by making Congress's constitutional authority dependent on the timing of an individual's activity:

> [T]he promise offered by the action/inaction dichotomy—of establishing a principled and categorical limit on the commerce power—seems unlikely to deliver in practice. Level of generality is destiny in interpretive disputes, and it remains unclear at what level plaintiffs mean to pitch their action/inaction line of constitutional authority or indeed whether a workable level exists. Does this test apply to individuals who have purchased medical insurance before? Those individuals

have not been inactive in any sense of the word when it comes to the medical-insurance market, yet plaintiffs say that Congress may not regulate them.[70]

Indeed, the logic of applying these temporal standards to health insurance is particularly problematic, for reasons the government discussed but the Court largely ignored. Whether or not an individual has participated in the market for health care by obtaining medical services within some specified time frame, she, like everyone else, is perpetually *at risk* of needing such services and of incurring catastrophic medical expenses. There are only two ways to deal with this risk: obtaining insurance from a third party, or not obtaining such insurance and attempting to pay out of pocket.[71] An individual who forgoes insurance, but cannot pay the ruinous medical expenses that arise in an emergency, will still receive treatment. The cost of that uncompensated care is shifted to others in the market. Those other market participants, in other words, bear the risk of those shifted costs. Whether or not one calls the uninsured individual's choice "self-insurance," the fact remains that she has not covered her risk of incurring medical expenses beyond her ability to pay. The insured end up shouldering some portion of that risk. They are, in effect, her excess carriers, and, according to congressional findings, the "reinsurance" they provide adds $1,000 to the typical family's annual health insurance premiums.[72] In sum, when the commodity at issue is insurance for a risk—in particular, a universal risk—barring regulation until that risk has been realized is not logical. With regard to health insurance, such a bar insulates free riders from paying for benefits they receive.

The Chief Justice's analysis of the Necessary and Proper Clause is no easier to unravel. The thesis was that even if the mandate is "necessary" to the ACA's entirely appropriate regulation of the interstate insurance market, it is not "proper" because it extends the reach of the federal government "beyond the natural limit of its authority and draw[s] within its regulatory scope those who otherwise would be outside of it."[73] But if a particular piece of legislation were already within the scope of Congress's enumerated power, there would be no need to invoke the Necessary and Proper Clause. Thus, what the Chief Justice appears to be saying is that, whether necessary or not, this particular provision simply strays uncomfortably far beyond the commerce power. The Court's comfort level does not provide a workable standard.

Standing alone, the abstruseness and impracticality of the Commerce Clause standards in the Chief Justice's opinion will not necessarily deflect judges from the effort to decipher and apply them. After all, lower courts must follow even illogical and unwieldy tests if Supreme Court precedent so requires. At least to some degree, the doctrine of *stare decisis* constrains even the Court itself from ignoring its own binding precedents. But, as noted, *NFIB* is not binding precedent on this issue. Moreover, the indistinct boundaries between mandates and prohibitions may leave room for constitutional avoidance. And the decision may provide the raw material for an argument that the individual mandate in the ACA presented unique, nonreplicable circumstances. Should all these escape routes be blocked, the taxing power rationale affords courts a haven from the tribulations of this Commerce Clause theory.

It is in this respect that the partisan dimensions of the ACA litigation may affect the attractiveness of these avoidance strategies. Professor Jack Balkin, in explaining why the constitutional theories advanced against the ACA went from "off the wall to on the wall" so quickly, noted that "the single most important factor ... was strong support by the Republican Party, including its politicians, its affiliated lawyers, and its affiliated media. The unconstitutionality of the mandate quickly became virtually the official position of the Republican Party."[74] If this analysis is correct, then it may be that a much hoped-for decrease in partisan toxicity at some point after the 2012 presidential election will loosen the moorings of the Commerce Clause theory espoused by the Chief Justice and the joint dissenters.

This result is by no means inevitable, or perhaps even probable. The elusiveness of the Commerce Clause analysis in the Chief Justice's opinion and the joint dissent could instead give courts a blank slate, affording the flexibility to narrow the Commerce Clause in almost any manner they choose. Further, requiring a rigorous, separate inquiry under the Necessary and Proper Clause as to whether a provision is "proper" potentially could hand courts a roving commission to second-guess Congress's judgments on how to accomplish its policy goals. But the partisan profile of the case could tighten the constraints of logic, workability, and decorum and impede the courts from moving in this direction. Deservedly, the Chief Justice has received much credit for calming the partisan tumult surrounding the ACA case and keeping the Court from becoming the focus of the presidential election campaign.[75] Nonetheless, he erased neither the perception nor the reality that the case was a partisan crusade, an exercise of politics by other means. The division on the Court regarding the Commerce Clause still tracked party lines, and Justice Scalia's performance in particular during the oral argument left a partisan aftertaste.[76] It is not necessary to question the legitimacy of the decision to recognize that the political glare of the case may divert some judges from the tortuous Commerce Clause road marked by the Republican appointees, particularly given the availability of off-ramps to avoid it.

The lineup of votes on the Commerce Clause issues, however, might also be important as a signal of an emerging antiregulatory jingoism on the Court. The four dissenting justices advocated a sweeping and radical position—invalidation of the entire 2,700-page statute, from abstinence education[77] to workplace accommodation of nursing mothers[78] to an excise tax on tanning salons.[79] That result would have precipitated untold chaos as to the significant portions of the ACA already in effect, for example, terminating small business tax credits on which many taxpayers have relied;[80] rescinding changes in Medicare payment rates already implemented in processing systems that handle 100 million claims a month; reopening the Medicare donut hole;[81] and nullifying audit provisions included in Medicaid contracts.[82] Beyond this startling position, the joint dissenters argued that the individual mandate could not be sustained under the Necessary and Proper Clause because it was not the "only practicable way" of implementing the insurance reforms.[83] That approach would have overruled *McCulloch v. Maryland*,[84] which for 193 years has stood for the proposition that the clause did not impose a standard of necessity.[85] Of course, a dissent by definition reflects views that did not prevail. But the Chief Justice, who supplied the fifth vote to uphold the Act, is scarcely a reliable supporter of federal regulation.

If there is such a swing to antiregulatory zealotry, the partisan cast of the litigation may yet be relevant in predicting the durability of that trend. Professor Balkin's thesis that achieving the status of partisan orthodoxy greatly enhances the persuasiveness of an argument to the Court, suggests the possible corollary that when (or if) the partisan passions subside, the justices caught up in the moment may revert to a more mainstream approach.[86] If so, then the more extreme positions of the joint dissenters may reflect not a galvanic shift, but rather a more temporary surrender to the fervor of a highly partisan debate.

Any effort at prediction, however, must recognize the prospect that a prospective nominee's views regarding the constitutional debate on the ACA could become a litmus test. A Democratic president will look for signs, if not overt reassurance, that the candidate rejects the position of the Republican-appointed justices in *NFIB*. A Republican president will seek just the opposite. The reelection of President Obama and the makeup of the Senate during his term thus may have more impact on Commerce Clause jurisprudence than any other factors.[87]

## B. THE TAXING POWER

In contrast with the fragmented opinions on the Commerce Clause, the portion of the Chief Justice's opinion upholding the mandate under the taxing power did command five votes. Therefore, it is binding legal precedent.

The first issue the Court considered in its discussion of the taxing power was whether the minimum coverage provision actually imposed a "mandate" to obtain insurance. The Court noted that the most natural reading of Section 5000A is as a mandate. The provision states in one subsection that individuals "shall" maintain health insurance, and in a separate subsection, specifies the penalty for being uninsured. But, because the Court's duty is to adopt any reasonable construction of the statute that preserves its unconstitutionality, the question, the Court found, "is not whether [construing the provision as a tax] is the most natural interpretation of the mandate, but only whether it is a 'fairly possible' one."[88]

In answering that question, the Court noted at the outset that, "[u]nder the mandate, if an individual does not maintain health insurance, the only consequence is that he must make an additional payment to the IRS when he pays his taxes."[89] On that basis, the government had argued that the mandate merely "establish[es] a condition—not owning health insurance—that triggers a tax— the required payment to the IRS."[90] The Court was persuaded that the provision need not be read "as a legal command to buy insurance."[91] Rather, the Court held, it "makes going without insurance just another thing the Government taxes, like buying gasoline or earning income."[92]

The Court observed that the "exaction the Affordable Care Act imposes on those without health insurance looks like a tax in many respects."[93] It is paid to the Treasury by taxpayers when they file their returns. It does not apply to individuals who earn too little to file returns. It is calculated based on familiar tax concepts. It appears in the Internal Revenue Code, and the IRS enforces it. And it has "the essential feature of any tax: it produces at least some revenue for the Government."[94] Although the statute called the payment a "penalty," the Court found that the label did not control in the face of operational factors inconsistent with a punitive function. First, the amount due is less than the price of insurance and by law, could never be more.[95] Second, there is no *scienter* requirement.[96] And third, the IRS collects the payment.[97] Plainly, the provision was intended to affect individual conduct, but, in the Court's view, "taxes that seek to influence conduct are nothing new.… That § 5000A seeks to shape decisions about whether to buy health insurance does not mean that it cannot be a valid exercise of the taxing power."[98] The issue, the Court held, was whether the penalty provision imposed punishment. Particularly absent negative legal consequences beyond the payment itself for failing to obtain insurance, the Court found that the provision was not punitive.

Finally, the Court addressed the objection that "[i]f it is troubling to interpret the Commerce Clause as authorizing Congress to regulate those who abstain from commerce, perhaps it should be similarly troubling to permit Congress to impose a tax for not doing something."[99] The Court cited three factors that allayed this concern. First, "the Constitution does not guarantee that individuals may avoid taxation through inactivity,"[100] and "Congress's use of the Taxing Clause to encourage buying something … is not new."[101] Second, the Court can strike down any unduly punitive exaction. And third, Congress's authority "under the taxing power is limited to requiring an individual to pay money into the Federal Treasury, no more."[102] By contrast, the government could bring the full weight of its authority to bear—including the criminal laws—to enforce a mandate under the Commerce Clause.

A factor upon which the Court did not rely provides a reason to believe that this holding, too—even though it is a binding precedent—is unlikely to influence significantly the design of future regulatory legislation. The Court has previously been comfortable with the elasticity of Congress's taxing power because of the powerful political check on it. That check reflects an axiom of American politics—people do not like to pay taxes.[103]

It is no response that the Court has encouraged congressional subterfuge by disregarding how Congress labels an exaction. The reason the label Congress uses cannot evade the political check is found in a second commonsense axiom—people generally know when they have to pay money.[104] A regulation, or even a corporate tax, may exact a cost—by raising the price of a good or service—that is less obvious to many individuals. But when an imposition falls directly on an individual, it is unlikely to escape attention—particularly when individuals must pay it every April 15 with their annual income tax returns. The penalty in the minimum coverage provision illustrates the point. It did not slip by unnoticed. Republican opponents of the ACA relentlessly characterized the minimum coverage provision as a tax during congressional debates.[105] And polls have consistently showed that the individual mandate is unpopular.[106]

It is possible that Congress could accomplish objectives in the future without raising political hackles, by providing tax incentives, rather than by imposing penalties. But this is nothing new. The Internal Revenue Code is saturated with such incentives, including, for example, the mortgage interest deduction encouraging home ownership and the favorable tax treatment of retirement plans to encourage saving, among many others.[107] Nothing in the *NFIB* case expanded congressional authority in this area.

In sum, the Court's ruling on the taxing power did not open some cavernous loophole allowing an unprecedented expansion of federal authority. The taxing power is a safety valve should Congress wish to fashion some other mandate applicable to individuals. But Congress is unlikely to use it extensively. The political cost of invoking the tax power, not to mention the political consequences of adopting another mandate, are significant deterrents.

## 4. Conclusion

*NFIB* may be the case of the century, but the unanswered question is whether that is because the issues the decision treat arise only once every hundred years, or because it marks a new epoch, when a revanchist and antiregulatory ideology gained a committed cadre of converts on the Court. The first answer is more likely. The second, however, remains a possibility.

# Notes

1. 132 S. Ct. 2566 (2012).
2. See, e.g., Jeffrey Toobin, *More than Health Insurance*, THE NEW YORKER BLOG (Mar. 27, 2010), http://www.newyorker.com/online/blogs/comment/2012/03/health-care-supreme-court.html; Mark A. Hall, *Supreme Court Argument on the ACA—A Clash of Two World Views*, 366 NEW ENG. J. MED. 1462, 1462 (2012) ("Constitutional lawyers consider this to be the Court's most important case since *Bush v. Gore*, but for health policy it's the case of the century").
3. See HEALTH REFORM VOTES: CONGRESSIONAL ROLL CALL VOTES ON SIGNIFICANT HEALTH REFORM LEGISLATION, http://www.healthreformvotes.org/ (last visited Nov. 28, 2012).
4. See Vincent L. Frakes, *Partisanship and (Un)compromise: A Study of the Patient Protection and Affordable Care Act*, Essay, 49 HARV. J. ON LEGIS. 135, 139 (2012) ("Sen. Brown's election changed the entire playing field of the healthcare debate because the Democrats could no longer end any filibuster by a party-line vote, thus casting into doubt their ability to pass a final bill resulting from a conference committee").
5. See, e.g., David Weigel, *Repeal Pledge Becomes GOP Litmus Test*, WASH. INDEP. (Mar. 29, 2010, 10:54 AM), http://washingtonindependent.com/80749/repeal-pledge-becomes-gop-litmus-test.
6. Lee Fang, *Extreme Right Wing of GOP Leads Health Reform Repeal Effort, Pledges to Repeal "The Whole Thing,"* THINK PROGRESS (Mar. 23, 2010, 9:55 AM), http://thinkprogress.org/politics/2010/03/23/88084/repeal-whole-thing/ (quoting Congressman Zack Wamp).
7. Sam Tanenhaus, *The Familiar Comforts of Conspiracies*, N.Y. TIMES, Mar. 31, 2010, *available at* http://www.nytimes.com/2010/04/04/movies/04theories.html? pagewanted=all (quoting Speaker John Boehner).
8. David M. Herszenhorn, *Senate Preparing to Take Up Reconciliation Bill*, N.Y. TIMES, Mar. 22, 2010, *available at* http://prescriptions.blogs.nytimes.com/2010/03/22/senate-preparing-to-take-up-reconciliation-bill/ (quoting Senate Minority Leader Mitch McConnell).
9. Shailagh Murray, *Congress Approves "Fixes" to Health-Care Law*, WASH. POST, Mar. 26, 2010, *available at* http://www.washingtonpost.com/wp-dyn/content/article/ 2010/03/25/ AR2010032500006.html (quoting Congressman Eric Cantor).
10. See Complaint, Florida *ex rel.* Bondi v. U.S. Dep't of Health & Human Servs., 780 F. Supp. 2d 1307 (N.D. Fla. 2010) (No. 3:10-cv-00091).
11. See Kevin Sack, *In Partisan Battle, Clashes over Health Lawsuits*, N.Y. TIMES, Mar. 27, 2010, *available at* http://www.nytimes.com/2010/03/28/us/politics/28govs.html. In addition, three of the Republican attorneys general were candidates for governor in their state. See GOP Governors Blast Health Care Takeover, REPUBLICAN GOVERNORS ASS'N, http://www.rga.org/homepage/gop-governors-blast-health-care-takeover/ (last visited Nov. 28, 2012).
12. See Complaint for Declaratory and Injunctive Relief, Virginia *ex rel.* Cuccinelli v. Sebelius, 702 F. Supp. 2d 598 (E.D. Va. 2010) (No. 3:10-cv-00188).
13. Robert Weiner, *Chutzpah: Politics and the Health Care Cases*, ACS BLOG (Jun. 6, 2012), http://www.acslaw.org/acsblog/chutzpah-politics-and-the-health-care-cases.
14. See *Current judges: United States District Court for the Northern District of Florida*, WIKIPEDIA, http://en.wikipedia.org/wiki/United_States_District_Court_for_the_Northern_ District_of_Florida (last visited Nov. 28, 2012); JEFFREY TOOBIN, THE OATH: THE OBAMA WHITE HOUSE AND THE SUPREME COURT, Chapter 21 (2012) ("Choosing his forum with care, McCollum filed the lawsuit in Pensacola, which had some of the most conservative judges in the country").
15. See Plaintiffs' Motion for Leave to File Second Amended Complaint Joining Additional Plaintiff States and Memorandum in Support, Florida *ex rel.* Bondi v. U.S. Dep't of Health & Human Servs., 780 F. Supp. 2d 1307 (N.D. Fla. 2011) (No. 3:10-cv-00091).

16. Tim Pawlenty, Op-Ed., *Repealing Obamacare, State by State*, U-T SAN DIEGO, Nov. 18, 2010, *available at* http://www.utsandiego.com/news/2010/nov/18/repealing-obmacare-state-by-state/.

17. Filings and rulings in twenty-six of the cases are available on the website of the Department of Justice. See U.S. DEP'T OF JUSTICE, DEFENDING THE AFFORDABLE CARE ACT, http://justice.gov/healthcare/ (last visited Nov. 28, 2012).

18. In 2012, of the $462,793 that the National Federation of Independent Business PAC contributed to federal candidates, 98 percent went to Republicans. See OPEN SECRETS: NATIONAL FEDERATION OF INDEPENDENT BUSINESS SUMMARY FOR 2012 ELECTION CYCLE, http://opensecrets.org/pacs/lookup2.php?strID=C00101105 (last visited Nov. 29, 2012).

19. *NFIB*, 132 S. Ct. at 2566; see also Harris Meyer, Op-Ed., *Why Do the Uninsured Want to Stay Uninsured? They Won't Say*, THE HEALTH CARE BLOG (Jun. 1, 2010), http://thehealthcare blog.com/blog/2010/06/01/why-do-the-uninsured-want-to-stay-uninsured-they-won%E 2%80%99t-say/.

20. See Florida *ex rel.* Bondi v. U.S. Dep't of Health & Human Servs., 780 F. Supp. 2d 1256 (N.D. Fla. 2011), *aff'd in part, rev'd in part*, 648 F.3d 1235 (11th Cir. 2011), *aff'd in part, rev'd in part sub nom. NFIB*, 132 S. Ct. 2566 (2012); Goudy-Bachman v. U.S. Dep't of Health & Human Servs., 764 F. Supp. 2d 684 (M.D. Pa. 2011); Virginia *ex rel.* Cuccinelli v. Sebelius, 702 F. Supp. 2d 598 (E.D. Va. 2010), *rev'd*, 656 F.3d 253 (4th Cir. 2011), *cert. denied*, 133 S. Ct. 59 (2012). Other courts dismissed cases on jurisdictional grounds, with no apparent partisan divide. *E.g.*, Peterson v. United States, 774 F. Supp. 2d 418 (D.N.H. 2011); Calvey v. Obama, 792 F. Supp. 2d 1262 (W.D. Okla. 2011); N.J. Physicians, Inc. v. Obama, 757 F. Supp. 2d 502 (D.N.J. 2010), *aff'd*, 653 F.3d 234 (3d Cir. 2011); Bryant v. Holder, 809 F. Supp. 2d 563 (S.D. Miss. 2011); Baldwin v. Sebelius, No. 10-CV-1033, 2010 WL 3418436 (S.D. Cal. Aug. 27, 2010), *aff'd*, 654 F.3d 877 (9th Cir. 2011).

21. See Thomas More Law Ctr. v. Obama, 720 F. Supp. 2d 882 (E.D. Mich. 2010), *aff'd*, 651 F.3d 529 (6th Cir. 2011), *cert. denied*, 133 S. Ct. 61 (2012); Liberty Univ., Inc. v. Geithner, 753 F. Supp. 2d 611 (W.D. Va. 2010), *vacated*, 671 F.3d 391 (4th Cir. 2011), *cert. denied*, 133 S. Ct. 60 (2012), *rehearing granted and order vacated*, 133 S. Ct. 679 (2012); Mead v. Holder, 766 F. Supp. 2d 16 (D.D.C. 2011), *aff'd sub nom.* Seven-Sky v. Holder, 661 F.3d 1 (D.C. Cir. 2011), *cert. denied*, 133 S. Ct. 63 (2012).

22. *Seven-Sky*, 661 F.3d at 1 (Silberman, J.); *Thomas More Legal Ctr.*, 651 F.3d at 549 (Sutton, J., concurring in part).

23. *Florida ex rel. Bondi*, 648 F.3d at 1235 (Hull, J.).

24. See, e.g., Jack Balkin, *Teaching Materials for NFIB v. Sebelius*, BALKINIZATION (Jul. 17, 2012), http://balkin.blogspot.com/2012/07/teaching-materials-for-nfib-v-sebelius.html; Karl Rove, Op-Ed., *The GOP's Health-Care Offensive Has Just Begun*, WALL ST. J., Jan. 20, 2011, *available at* http://online.wsj.com/article/ SB10001424052748704590704576091922171175748. html; Kevin Sack, *Suit on Health Care Bill Appears Likely to Advance*, N.Y. TIMES, Sept. 14, 2010, *available at* http://www.nytimes.com/2010/09/15/health/policy/15health.html.

25. See Brief of Health Care Policy History Scholars as Amici Curiae in Support of Petitioners at 26–32, *NFIB*, 132 S. Ct. 2566 (No. 11–398) [hereinafter NFIB Brief of Health Care Scholars].

26. Brief of Members of the United States Senate as Amici Curiae in Support of Respondents on the Minimum Coverage Provision Issue at 2, 4, *NFIB*, 132 S. Ct. 2566 (No. 11-398).

27. See NFIB Brief of Health Care Scholars, *supra* note 25, at 32 n.6 (identifying Republican senators opposing the constitutionality of the individual mandate, who previously sponsored legislation with such a mandate).

28. These briefs are available at the ACA LITIGATION BLOG, http://acalitigationblog.blogspot. com/2011/10/hhs-v-florida-no-11–398.html (last visited Nov. 29, 2012).

29. *Id.*

30. *House Approves ObamaCare Repeal in First Vote Since Supreme Court Ruling*, FOXNEWS.COM (Jul. 11, 2012), http://www.foxnews.com/politics/2012/07/11/house-approves-obamaca re-repeal-in-first-vote-since-court-ruling/.

31. See, e.g., David Nakamura, *Obama "Confident" Supreme Court Will Uphold Health Care Law*, WASH. POST, Apr. 2, 2012, *available at* http://www.washingtonpost.com/politics/obama-remains-confident-supreme-court-will-uphold-health-care-law/2012/04/02/gIQA9HI-OrS_story.html.

32. See, e.g., Kathleen Parker, *The Public Trial of John Roberts*, WASH. POST, May 22, 2012, *available at* http://www.washingtonpost.com/opinions/democrats-put-john-roberts-on-trial/2012/05/22/gIQAijq8iU_story.html; Jeffrey Rosen, *Are Liberals Trying to Intimidate John Roberts?* THE NEW REPUBLIC, May 28, 2012, *available at* http://www.tnr.com/article/politics/103656/obamacare-affordable-care-act-critics-response; Dahlia Lithwick, *The Scales of Intimidation*, SLATE (Jun. 11, 2012, 8:13 AM), http://www.slate.com/articles/news_and_politics/jurisprudence/2012/06/do_the_justices_feel_intimidated_by_the_media_s_scrutiny_of_their_decisions_and_conduct_.html.

33. See, e.g., Steve Benen, *Boehner Takes Credit for Democratic Health Care Advances*, WASH. MONTHLY, Apr. 30, 2010, *available at* http://www.washingtonmonthly.com/archives/individual/2010_04/023581.php (quoting Speaker of the House John Boehner on the Republican origins of various provisions of the ACA); Barak Richman, *On the Constitutionality of Health Care Reform*, 71 N.C. MED. J. 232, 232 (2010). Although the "individual mandate" became controversial, it originated as a conservative proposal backed by Republican legislators. See NFIB Brief of Health Care Scholars, *supra* note 25, at 25–32 (providing detailed history of the individual mandate).

34. 42 U.S.C. § 18091(2)(A).

35. *Id.* § 18091(2)(I).

36. *Id.*

37. *Id.* § 18091(2)(F).

38. *Id.* § 18091(1).

39. See Brief for State Respondents on the Minimum Coverage Provision at 15–24, *NFIB*, 132 S. Ct. 2566 (No. 11-398)

40. *Id.* at 36.

41. *Id.* at 33–34.

42. United States v. Butler, 297 U.S. 1, 66 (1935) ("the power of Congress to authorize expenditure of public moneys for public purposes is not limited by the direct grants of legislative power found in the Constitution").

43. See Brief for Petitioners at 62–63, *NFIB*, 132 S. Ct. 2566 (No. 11-398).

44. See, e.g., Drew Singer & Terry Baynes, *Analysis: Legal Eagles Redefine Winners, Losers*, REUTERS, Jul. 3, 2012, *available at* http://www.reuters.com/article/2012/07/03/us-usa-healthcare-court-idUSBRE8621A520120703; Veta T. Richardson, *Justice Roberts and the Commerce Clause: Did He Open a New Path for an Activist Congress?* FORBES, Jul. 5, 2012, *available at* http://www.forbes.com/sites/frederickallen/2012/07/US/justice-roberts-and-the-commerce-clause-did-he-open-a-new-path-for-an-activist-congress/.

45. See *NFIB*, 132 S. Ct. at 2600–2601. See Gillian Metzger, *Something for Everyone*, SCOTUSBLOG (Jun. 28, 2012, 5:08 PM), http://www.scotusblog.com/2012/06/something-for-everyone/ (observing that the Chief Justice reached the commerce power issue only through "some analytic fudging—Justice Ginsburg is right that the Court should not rule on the commerce power if upholding the mandate as a tax").

46. "A dictum is an assertion in a court's opinion of a proposition of law which does not explain why the court's judgment goes in favor of the winner. If the court's judgment and the reasoning which supports it would remain unchanged, regardless of the proposition in question, that proposition plays no role in explaining why the judgment goes for the winner. It is superfluous to the decision and is dictum." Pierre N. Leval, *Judging under the Constitution: Dicta about Dicta*, 81 N.Y.U. L. REV. 1249, 1256 (2006).

47. See Linda Greenhouse, *A Justice in Chief*, N.Y. TIMES, Jun. 28, 2012, *available at* http://opinionator.blogs.nytimes.com/2012/06/28/a-justice-in-chief/ (noting that the discussion of the taxing power was "the only portion of the Chief Justice's opinion labeled 'opinion of the court'").

48. 430 U.S. 188, 193 (1977) (internal quotation marks omitted) (citation omitted). Although there is split in the circuits as to whether dissenting opinions are included the *Marks* analysis, for the reasons noted above, this issue should not matter here. Nonetheless, one commentator argues that *NFIB* did provide a ruling of the Court on the Commerce Clause because the Chief Justice's opinion on the taxing power, in which Justices Ginsburg, Breyer, Sotomayor, and Kagan joined, stated, "*The Court today holds* that our Constitution protects us from federal regulation under the Commerce Clause so long as we abstain from the regulated activity." *NFIB*, 132 S. Ct. at 2599. See also John Elwood, *What Did the Court "Hold" About the Commerce Clause and Medicaid?* THE VOLOKH CONSPIRACY (Jul. 2, 2012, 11:28 AM), http://www.volokh.com/2012/07/02/ what-did-the-court-hold-abou t-the-commerce-clause-and-medicaid/. The notion that this offhand statement overruled *Marks v. United States* is far-fetched, particularly given that the justices concurring in this portion of the Chief Justice's opinion specifically disputed the appropriateness of reaching the Commerce Clause issue. See *NFIB*, 132 S. Ct. at 2627 (Ginsburg, J., concurring in part, concurring in judgment in part, and dissenting in part).

49. The Chief Justice's treatment of the Necessary and Proper Clause has even less claim to precedential force, as the dissenting justices, while reaching the same conclusion, did not apply the same standard. See Steven D. Schwinn, *Chief Justice Roberts's Necessary and Proper Clause*, CONSTITUTIONAL LAW PROF BLOG (Jul. 2, 2012), http://lawprofessors.typepad. com/conlaw/2012/07/chief-justice-robertss-necessary-and-proper-clause.html.

50. 317 U.S. 111 (1942).

51. 132 S. Ct. at 2588 (quoting United States v. Lopez, 514 U.S. 549, 560 (1995)).

52. *Id.* at 2643 (Scalia, Kennedy, Alito, Thomas, JJ., dissenting).

53. See Jonathan H. Adler & Nathaniel Stewart, *Positive Steps, Silver Linings*, NAT'L REV. ONLINE (Jul. 12, 2012, 4:00 AM), http://www.nationalreview.com/articles/309154/positive-steps -silver-linings-jonathan-h-adler ("Since a mandate to make purchases from a private company was unprecedented, the case did not require the Court to revisit its earlier Commerce Clause decisions").

54. *NFIB*, 132 S. Ct. at 2591.

55. *Id.*

56. *Id.* at 2586.

57. *Id.* at 2647.

58. *Id.* at 2649.

59. *Id.* at 2572. It is difficult to see why the classic definition of "regulate" in *Gibbons v. Ogden*, 22 U.S. 1, 196 (1824), "to prescribe the rule by which commerce is to be governed," presupposes that commerce is already in progress, rather than expected.

60. *Id.* at 2589. See Richard Posner, *Supreme Court Year in Review: The Commerce Clause was Clearly Enough to Uphold the Affordable Care Act*, SLATE (Jun. 28, 2012, 5:38 PM), http://www.slate. com/ articles/news_and_politics/the_breakfast_table/features/2012/_supreme_court_ year_in_review/affordable_care_act_upheld_why_the_commerce_clause_should_ have_been_enough.html ("Congress' regulatory power under the Commerce Clause is not limited to direct control of an interstate transaction; it includes the regulation of activities that affect an interstate industry, with 'activities' including inactivity").

61. *NFIB*, 132 S. Ct. at 2589. This proposition is questionable, given that in the 1790s, Congress—including numerous framers—mandated that shipowners provide medical insurance for their sailors, that sailors purchase hospital insurance, and that all able-bodied men purchase firearms. See Einer Elhauge, *If Health Insurance Mandates Are Unconstitutional, Why Did the Founding Fathers Back Them?* THE NEW REPUBLIC, Apr. 13, 2012, *available at* http://www.tnr.com/article/politics/102620/ individual-mandate-history-affordabl e-care-act. See also Laurence Tribe, *Chief Justice Roberts Comes into His Own and Saves the Court While Preventing a Constitutional Debacle*, SCOTUSBlog (Jun. 28, 2012, 3:41 PM), http://www.scotusblog.com/2012/06/chief-justice-roberts-comes-into-his-own-and-save s-the-court-while-preventing-a-constitutional-debacle/.

62. Neil Siegel, *Free Riding on Benevolence: Collective Action Federalism and the Minimum Coverage Provision*, 75 L. & CONTEMP. PROBS. 29, 52 (2012)

63. See Heart of Atl. Motel, Inc. v. United States, 379 U.S. 241 (1964) (upholding Civil Rights Act of 1964 under the Commerce Clause).

64. Posner, *supra* note 60. On the same theory, one could argue that individuals could avoid the mandate by choosing not to earn income, because those who make too little to file a tax return are exempt from the penalty, 26 U.S.C. § 5000A(b), and as the Court found, the penalty is the only legal consequence of not purchasing insurance. *NFIB*, 132 S. Ct. at 2574.

65. For 125 years, the Court has recognized congressional authority under the Commerce Clause to act in such circumstances. See Morgan's S.S. Co. v. La. Bd. of Health, 118 U.S. 455, 464 (1886) (noting congressional power to undertake "a general system of quarantine").

66. For example, consider the following hypothetical: Scientific evidence establishes that under certain weather conditions, particulates from the use of home fireplaces cause children to die from respiratory problems, often far from the site of emission and across state lines. It is not practical to predict when and where the weather conditions that concentrate the particulates will occur. But a $10 chimney filter eliminates the problem. Congress therefore requires anyone with a working fireplace to obtain a chimney filter or pay a penalty. Having a chimney is not "activity" under any common meaning of the word, nor is using a fireplace economic conduct. A constitutional rule that barred legislation to prevent these interstate harms to children would make no sense. See Neil Siegel, *Free Riding on Benevolence: Collective Action Federalism and the Minimum Coverage Provision, supra* note 62.

67. See, e.g., Carter v. Carter Coal Co., 298 U.S. 238, 304 (1936) ("Mining brings the subject matter of commerce into existence. Commerce disposes of it"); United States v. E.C. Knight Co., 156 U.S. 1, 12 (1895) ("Commerce succeeds to manufacture, and is not a part of it").

68. See United States v. Lopez, 514 U.S. 549, 554 (1995); *id.* at 569 (Kennedy, J., concurring) (noting the demise of categorical approaches under the Commerce Clause); see *Wickard*, 317 U.S. at 120 ("Questions of the power of Congress are not to be decided by reference to any formula which would give controlling force to nomenclature").

69. *Cf.* Gillian Metzger, *supra* note 45 ("The Court maintained that obtaining health care once or twice was not enough to make an individual permanently active in the health-care market. But it's hard to see why Congress couldn't require that individuals pay for the health care they obtain through health insurance or pay a penalty, or why Congress couldn't impose the mandate on individuals who use health care above a minimum threshold").

70. Thomas More Law Ctr. v. Obama, 651 F.3d 529 (6th Cir. 2011), *cert. denied*, 133 S. Ct. 61 (2012) (overruled in part by *NFIB*).

71. Judge Sutton made a similar point: "No one is inactive when deciding how to pay for health care, as self-insurance and private insurance are two forms of action for addressing the same risk. Each requires affirmative choices; one is no less active than the other; and both affect commerce." 651 F.3d at 561. See *id.* ("If done responsibly, [self-insurance] requires more action (affirmatively saving money on a regular basis and managing the assets over time) than the latter (writing a check once or twice a year or never writing one at all if the employer withholds the premiums)").

72. *Id.* at 2585.

73. *Id.*

74. Jack Balkin, *From Off the Wall to On the Wall: How the Mandate Challenge Went Mainstream*, THE ATLANTIC, Jun. 4, 2012, *available at* http://www.theatlantic.com/national/archive/2012/06/from-off-the-wall-to-on-the-wall-how-the-mandate-challenge-went-mainstream/258040/; TOOBIN, THE OATH, *supra* note 14, at Chapter 21 ("For two decades, the constitutionality of the individual mandate had never been questioned. But in just a few months, its illegality under the commerce clause became an article of faith within the Republican Party").

75. Greenhouse, *supra* note 47; Brad Joondeph, *A Marbury for Our Time*, ACA LITIGATION BLOG (Jun. 28, 2012), http://acalitigationblog.blogspot.com/2012/06/marbury-for-our-time.html;

Posner, *supra* note 60 (ruling striking down the ACA "would give President Obama an opening to run against the Supreme Court. It would confirm the widespread opinion of the 'Roberts Court' as being the conservative mirror image of the Warren Court. It would be bad for the court").

76. See TOOBIN, *supra* note 14, at Chapter 22 (discussing Justice Scalia's denigration of Congress and political commentary during the argument).

77. 42 U.S.C. § 710.

78. 29 U.S.C. § 207.

79. 26 U.S.C. § 5000B.

80. 26 U.S.C. § 45R.

81. 42 U.S.C.A. § 1395l.

82. 42 U.S.C. § 1396a(a)(42).

83. *NFIB*, 132 S. Ct. at 2647.

84. 4 Wheat 316 (1819).

85. Just as far-reaching was the standard the joint dissent advocated for determining whether federal grant conditions are coercive—focusing on the temptation created by the size of the grants the federal government offers. *NFIB*, 132 S. Ct. at 2661; see Andrew Koppelman, *Uninsured Still Being Screwed*, SALON (Jul. 2, 2012, 6:14 PM), http://www.salon.com/2012/07/02/uninsured_still_suffer ("The Scalia group suggested that a federal program becomes unconstitutional just by being big"). On that approach, the conditions of every large federal-state grant program potentially would have been unenforceable.

86. *Cf.* John Fabian Witt, *The Secret History of the Chief Justice's Obamacare Decision*, BALKINIZATION (Jun. 29, 2012), http://balkin.blogspot.com/2012/06/secret-history-of-chief-justices.html ("as the four Republican-appointed dissenters in the case make clear, the difference between constitutional law and partisanship is a razor's edge").

87. See Laurence Tribe, *The Chief Justice Comes into His Own and Saves the Court from a Constitutional Debacle*, *supra* note 61 ("With future Supreme Court offices occupied by appointees of a President Romney, today's limited holding could become the muse for another, perhaps more successful, wave of attacks on federal power").

88. 132 S. Ct. at 2573 (quoting *Crowell v. Benson*, 285 U.S. 22, 62 (1932)).

89. 132 S. Ct. at 2593–2594.

90. *Id.* at 2594.

91. *Id.*

92. *Id.*

93. *Id.*

94. *Id.* at 2594.

95. *Id.* at 2595–2596.

96. *Id.* at 2596.

97. *Id.*

98. *Id.*

99. *Id.* at 2599.

100. *Id.*

101. *Id.*

102. *Id.* at 2600.

103. See, e.g., *McCulloch*, 17 U.S. at 428 ("In imposing a tax, the legislature acts upon its constituents. This is, in general, a sufficient security against erroneous and oppressive taxation").

104. Akhil Amar, *The Lawfulness of Health-Care Reform* (Yale Law Sch. Pub. Law Working Paper No. 228, Jun. 1, 2011) ("surely members of the American electorate understand, when they are obliged to pay extra taxes to the I.R.S. if they refuse to procure proper health insurance, that they are being taxed; and that they are being taxed by Congress and the President; and that if they do not like these taxes (howsoever labeled), that they are free to vote the bums out and vote for a new set of bums—er, lawmakers").

105. See, e.g., News Conference, Republican Members of the House of Representatives Hold a News Conference on Health Care and IRS (Mar. 18, 2010) (transcript available from Roll

Call, Inc.) (Rep. Dave Camp: "individual mandate tax"); Press Release, Sen. Mike Crapo, Senate Halts Debate on Health Care with Crapo Motion Pending (Dec. 10, 2009), *available at* http://www.crapo.senate.gov/media/newsreleases/release_full.cfm?id=320602 ("excise tax … for individuals who fail to purchase insurance"); 156 Cong. Rec. 1917 (Mar. 21, 2010) (statement of Rep. Mark Kirk) ( "Individual Mandate Tax"); 155 Cong. Rec. 12,768 (Dec. 9, 2009) (statement of Sen. Chuck Grassley) (provision "can be called a penalty, but it is a tax"); 155 Cong. Rec. 11,454 (Nov. 18, 2009) (statement of Sen. John McCain) ($4 billion in "[t]axes on individuals who fail to maintain government-approved health insurance coverage"); 155 Cong. Rec. 12,576 (Nov. 6, 2009) (statement of Rep. Trent Franks) ( "penalty tax").

106. Henry J. Kaiser Family Found., Kaiser Public Opinion (Mar. 2012), *available at* www.kff.org/healthreform/upload/8296.pdf ("while the law as a whole has never gained majority support, many of its component parts—from the relatively narrow to the core and comprehensive—have been consistently popular over the past two years, with the glaring exception of the individual mandate").

107. Joint Comm. on Taxation, 111th Cong., Estimates of Federal Tax Expenditures for Fiscal Years 2010–2014 (Comm. Print 2d Sess. 2010); see also Leonard Burman, Christopher Geissler, & Eric Toder, *How Big are Total Individual Income Tax Expenditures, and Who Benefits from Them?* 98 Am. Econ. Rev. 79 (2008).

# LINES OF ARGUMENT

Commerce, Taxing and Spending, Necessary
and Proper, and Due Process

CHAPTER 6

# The Missing Due Process Argument

*Jamal Greene*

Opponents and supporters of the Patient Protection and Affordable Care Act (ACA) have agreed on very little, but one thing all sides seem to accept is that the Due Process Clause does not prevent Congress from requiring Americans to purchase health insurance. That consensus is surprising, or at least it should be. It is true that a substantive due process argument implicating "ordinary commercial transactions"[1] is at first blush obstructed by an understanding, foundational to modern American constitutional law, that "economic due process" is governed by a deferential, even abdicative, test of minimum rationality.[2] Contrary intimations tend to be shot down in a single breath: *Lochner*.[3]

But there are at least two reasons to think that the specter of *Lochner* should not have deterred opponents of the ACA from pushing a substantive due process argument. First, as section 1 discusses below, the ACA's opponents unabashedly pursued an argument grounded in limitations on Congress's Article I powers that respectable constitutional scholars on both sides of the political aisle deemed weak, even frivolous, at the start of the litigation.[4] Second, as section 2 explains, there are obvious differences between a law restricting the hours of bakers and one requiring the purchase of health insurance. The former is a limitation and the latter a command; the former implicates hours and conditions of employment, the latter the timing of health care expenditures. Any competent lawyer could make a case that these are constitutionally relevant differences. And yet none of the several elite lawyers representing the challengers pursued a due process argument.

This chapter suggests, in section 3, three broad and interrelated explanations for the relative absence of due process arguments from the litigation and the political discourse attending it. The first is psycho-political, the second politico-cultural, and the third socio-legal. First, an argument that the ACA's minimum essential coverage provision ("the individual mandate") violated the Due Process Clause would doom both the ACA's mandate and the similar mandate signed into law by Mitt Romney when he was governor of Massachusetts. The argument would therefore place the ACA's opponents—and their funders—in the uncomfortable position of arguing against the constitutionality of Romney's signal policy achievement.

Second, the competent due process argument referenced above would be difficult to advance without relying on the line of cases protecting fundamental decision autonomy and exemplified by *Roe v. Wade*[5] and *Planned Parenthood of Southeastern Pennsylvania v. Casey*.[6] Reliance on these cases would threaten to rend the fragile coalition between certain libertarian elements of the Tea Party and the mainstream Republican Party, who are united against federal regulatory power but divided on social and cultural issues. The ACA litigation was one prong in a unified political, legal, and cultural attack on "Obamacare" that engaged and relied upon the support of the Republican establishment. Article I arguments are consistent with that support in a way that due process arguments are not.

Third, and at least as significantly, *Lochner* is not an ordinary precedent. It is anticanonical, which means that it is invoked less for the logic of its reasoning than for the ethical propositions the case represents. This feature of *Lochner* gives it outsized significance and distorts doctrinal argument. The "law sense" of an American lawyer tells her to avoid certain due process arguments that might otherwise seem persuasive. It is not merely that, with Justice Scalia and Justice Thomas predisposed to reject substantive due process arguments, it would have been difficult to count to five votes. It is also that the optics of economic due process are so unappealing that even to advance the argument in the alternative would have fatally undermined the credibility of the attorneys and their clients.

To be clear, the case against a substantive due process holding is considerably stronger than the case in favor. The point, though, is that such a holding was at least as doctrinally plausible at the start of the *Health Care Case* as the Commerce Clause argument that succeeded at the Supreme Court.

## 1.

Health care is expensive and the need for it is unpredictable. This is why rational people often purchase health insurance. Doing so enables individuals effectively to amortize the cost of health care over a longer period of time. State and federal laws distort individual incentives to purchase health insurance by requiring health care providers to offer emergency medical care to those who are sick or injured regardless of their ability to pay. Those laws (and the laudable social norms that produce them) have the effect of discouraging young and healthy people from purchasing health insurance because it is likely that their most costly health care needs are those emergency needs that the law requires providers to meet. The unrecompensed cost of that care is passed on to taxpayers who fund public hospitals and clinics and to those who hold insurance policies, in the form of higher costs of care and therefore higher premiums. The refusal or inability of an individual to purchase health insurance until he needs it also creates an adverse selection problem that insurance companies have often solved by denying coverage or charging higher premiums to those with preexisting conditions likely to increase the cost of care.

For both moral and economic reasons, the ACA sought to vastly expand the number of Americans covered by health insurance policies. The government presumably could have done so by creating a "single-payer" government health insurance plan funded by tax revenues. Instead, with President Obama's blessing, Congress implemented a two-step approach. The first step, the guaranteed issue and community-rating provisions of the ACA, largely prohibit insurance companies from discriminating in coverage or in cost of premiums on the basis of preexisting conditions. Standing alone, these provisions disable insurance companies from responding to the adverse selection problem referenced above. The most obvious way—perhaps the only way—for an insurance company to remain profitable if not permitted to discriminate on the basis of preexisting conditions is if those who rationally choose to forgo health insurance are instead required to purchase it, in effect helping to fund the care provided to those with preexisting conditions. The crucial second step, the minimum essential coverage provision, therefore "mandates" that most Americans not covered by an employer-based plan or by Medicare or Medicaid purchase insurance on the private market.[7]

The purposes and mutually dependent structure of these provisions should have decided the question of whether the ACA exceeded Congress's Article I powers. But those very same purposes and structure likewise should have given some hope to those who would challenge the ACA as a violation of the Due Process Clause of the Fifth Amendment.

As to Article I powers, there were at the time of enactment three reasonably straightforward arguments, each sufficient in itself, in favor of congressional authority to enact the individual mandate. First, the Commerce Clause grants Congress the power, among other things, to regulate activities that substantially affect interstate commerce.[8] Self-financing of health care is, incontrovertibly, such an activity. ACA opponents variously argued that a requirement to purchase health insurance is not "regulation" of interstate commerce because it forces consumers into a market rather than setting terms and conditions of a preexisting one; that failing to purchase health insurance is not an "activity"; and that, even if it is an activity, any holding that permits Congress to enact a purchase mandate would grant Congress unlimited power.

As to the first argument, limiting "regulate" as used in Article I to preexisting markets is a novel limitation on the commerce power and a curious one at that.

It would suggest that federal rules designed to stimulate interstate commerce or promote innovation must rest on constitutional provisions other than the Commerce Clause. And as to the second argument, both acts and omissions have important consequences for interstate commerce, and it is difficult to understand the basis, absent some countervailing individual right, for permitting Congress to regulate one but not the other. Characterizing laws as addressing either activities or nonactivities is also a matter of semantics; thus, a law prohibiting assaults may be recharacterized as a law requiring nonassaultive behavior. This reality makes any constitutional doctrine that rests on this distinction unmanageable, not to mention, again, invented for this litigation.

The argument that the government's defense of the individual mandate presupposes a limitless Congress is either false or irrelevant. If by the claim one means that the individual mandate is inconsistent with *any* limitation on federal power, then it is false. That argument would imply that *United States v. Lopez*[9] and *United States v. Morrison*,[10] each of which limited congressional power to *economic* activity, are incompatible with the government's position. It is difficult to see why that follows: a prohibition on gun possession in school zones or the provision of a federal cause of action for claims of gender-based violence would remain unconstitutional on the government's theory, as would a *mandate* to possess guns in school zones or to litigate gender-based violence claims in federal court.

The claim, then, must instead be that if Congress may enact a health insurance purchase mandate, then it may enact *any* purchase mandate. This is what Justice Ginsburg labeled "the broccoli horrible."[11] Unlike the first slippery-slope argument, this one applies not to congressional power on the whole but to limits internal to a particular form of congressional power. The claim, then, is akin to saying that Congress may not prevent bank robbery because it would imply that Congress could prevent bank loans. *Gibbons v. Ogden*[12] offers a complete refutation of that line of reasoning. The commerce power, Chief Justice Marshall wrote,

> is complete in itself, may be exercised to its utmost extent, and acknowledges no limitations, other than are prescribed in the constitution....
> The wisdom and discretion of Congress, their identity with the people, and the influence which their constituents possess at elections, are, in this, as in many other instances, ... the sole restraints on which they have relied, to secure them from its abuse.[13]

Congress is not limited for the sake of limits; rather it is limited to federal domains of regulation, such as interstate commerce. Within those domains, its power is limited by independent constitutional checks, such as the Due Process Clause, and by the political process.

The second Article I argument rests distinctly on the Necessary and Proper Clause. The individual mandate, like the Bank of the United States long before it,[14] was enacted not as an end in itself but as a means to other ends. As refined by subsequent cases, most recently *United States v. Comstock*,[15] measures enacted pursuant to Congress's power under the Necessary and Proper Clause are constitutionally valid when they are "rationally related to the implementation of a constitutionally enumerated power."[16] The "implementation" to which the individual mandate is rationally, indeed intimately, related is the prohibition on preexisting condition discrimination embodied within the guaranteed issue and community-rating provisions of the ACA. Opponents have not argued that either provision in itself exceeds Congress's power under the Commerce Clause; regulating the availability and pricing of insurance policies plainly addresses an activity that substantially affects interstate commerce.

Chief Justice Roberts discussed this argument in his opinion, dismissing it on the ground that a means that could not be enacted under the Commerce Clause standing alone was "improper" and so could not be enacted under the Necessary and Proper Clause.[17] This is a plausible understanding of the constitutional structure and even of Chief Justice Marshall's opinion in *McCulloch v. Maryland*,[18] but notice that it would make the Necessary and Proper Clause entirely declaratory of powers Congress already had. Recent cases, including *Comstock*, have implicitly rejected this proposition,[19] which if true makes it difficult to understand, for example, why Justice Scalia felt the need to write a concurring opinion in *Gonzales v. Raich*.[20] There, he wrote that federal power to regulate activities that substantially affect interstate commerce "cannot come from the Commerce Clause alone" but rather "derives from the Necessary and Proper Clause."[21] As with the Commerce Clause argument, Chief Justice Roberts's Necessary and Proper Clause argument is, if not inexplicable, at least novel.

The final Article I power on which Congress could have relied in enacting the individual mandate is, as we all know by now, the taxing power. The validity of encouraging individuals to purchase health insurance through negative tax incentives is ably explained in Chief Justice Roberts's opinion, and I do not linger on it here. The only note worth pausing to consider is the fact that the joint dissent does not contest the proposition that the kind of tax incentive described in the Chief Justice's opinion would be constitutionally valid. The dissent also raises but does not dispute the proposition (discussed in the Chief Justice's opinion) that such a tax is not a "direct" tax that must be levied in proportion to state population. The dissent's lone point of contention, rather, is that the individual mandate is not, as a factual matter, such a tax incentive. The dissenters were prepared to effect the most significant invalidation of a federal law since *Dred Scott* solely on the ground that a "requirement" to purchase health insurance administered solely through the tax code, with no coercive enforcement mechanism, means-tested, collected by the Internal Revenue Service, and capped at the average cost of a health insurance plan could not reasonably be construed as a "tax."

The purpose of this discussion has not been to demonstrate that the joint dissenters were wrong to vote to invalidate the individual mandate, or that the Chief Justice was wrong in arguing that it exceeded Congress's power under the Commerce Clause or the Necessary and Proper Clause. The Court is free under some circumstances to embrace novel constructions of the Constitution.[22] Nor do I suggest that the advocates in any sense acted improperly in advancing the arguments I have just criticized: how could they have in light of the results obtained? The point of this section has been simply to suggest that it would have been unreasonable to describe the individual mandate as beyond Congress's Article I powers solely on the basis of precedent that existed at the time of its enactment. As the next section shows, the same cannot be said of the validity of the mandate under the Due Process Clause.

## 2.

The preenforcement challenges to the ACA that won the race to the Supreme Court were a pair of consolidated cases out of Florida. One was brought by twenty-six states challenging the Medicaid expansion component of the law. The other, a challenge by the National Federation of Independent Business (NFIB) and two individual plaintiffs, contested the constitutionality of the individual mandate. NFIB's original complaint challenged the mandate as, among other things, a violation of the Due Process Clause of the Fifth Amendment.[23] The district court rejected this claim on the merits, and the plaintiffs abandoned it on appeal.

The due process claim was not well argued in the briefing before the district court, and Judge Vinson dismissed it without significant discussion. The brief begins with a useful legal conclusion, but it does not lead the reader to that conclusion through any argumentation. The plaintiffs described the asserted liberty interest as the "recognized ... freedom to eschew entering into a contract, to direct matters concerning dependent children, and to make decisions regarding the acquisition and use of medical services."[24] The plaintiffs sensibly cited to *Washington v. Glucksberg*,[25] *Cruzan v. Director, Missouri Department of Health*,[26] *Meyer v. Nebraska*,[27] and *Pierce v. Society of Sisters*[28] in support of these interests. But they offered no further reasoning on this point other than to say that *West Coast Hotel v. Parrish* and other decisions repudiating the *Lochner* era "recognize that the *terms* on which entities and individuals may contract are subject to regulation in appropriate circumstances, but do not speak to the question of whether Congress can *compel* Americans to buy something in the first instance."[29]

The district court's opinion on the due process claim is only slightly more illuminating. Without reference to the argument just discussed, Judge Vinson wrote, referring to *Lochner*, that "this claim would have found Constitutional support in the Supreme Court's decisions in the years prior to the New Deal legislation of the mid-1930s, when the Due Process Clause was interpreted to reach economic rights and liberties."[30] In response to the plaintiffs' description of the liberty interest at stake, the district court wrote:

> There is, to be sure, a liberty interest in the freedom to be left alone by the government. We all treasure the freedom to make our own life decisions, including what to buy with respect to medical services. Is that a "fundamental right"? The Supreme Court has not indicated that it is—at least not yet. That is the current state of the law, and it is not a district court's place to expand upon that law.[31]

If section 1 is correct, then expanding upon existing law is precisely what the district court was quite willing to do with respect to limitations inherent in the Commerce Clause. And the tantalizing addendum "at least not yet" could easily have been viewed as an invitation to the plaintiffs to pursue their due process claim up the ladder to the Supreme Court, but the plaintiffs abandoned the claim on appeal.[32]

In fact, the plaintiffs were right that no prior precedent of the Court, including *Lochner*, foreclosed a due process claim in this case. *Lochner* of course invalidated a New York law setting maximum work hours for bakers. It did not concern a purchase mandate, which is more akin to a law requiring that bakers work a certain minimum number of hours. As the plaintiffs recognized, *West Coast Hotel* and its progeny have little to say about that very different kind of law.

A more apt precedent, raised in the government's brief but not in the district court opinion, is *Jacobson v. Massachusetts*,[33] which in the same term as *Lochner* upheld a compulsory smallpox vaccination program as a valid exercise of the state's police power. A forced vaccination implicates bodily integrity and so is arguably more intrusive than a forced insurance purchase, and yet the Court upheld it in an era in which it was not shy about invoking substantive due process. *Jacobson* is not a good precedent for opponents of the ACA, but it is readily distinguishable. First, the police power rationale approved in *Jacobson* rested on an imminent public health crisis that is plausibly a more significant state interest than the interest in preventing cost shifting in the health insurance market. It is also more narrowly tailored, since vaccination is a uniquely effective response to the spread of a fatal communicable disease, whereas a single-payer system would obviate the need for the individual mandate. Second, *Jacobson* was decided during an era in which, notwithstanding *Lochner*, forcing women to bear and beget

children, forbidding couples from using contraceptives, and compulsory sterilization of the mentally retarded were constitutionally unobjectionable. No substantive due process case implicating decisional autonomy may satisfactorily be
analyzed without confronting *Griswold v. Connecticut*[34] and subsequent modern
case law.

Analysis of that case law does not end with the observation that the individual mandate regulates a commercial transaction (or its absence). The repudiation of economic due process is a rejection of the proposition that the freedom
to enter into contracts is itself constitutionally exalted. It does not mean that due
process protections cannot attach to purely economic interests. Thus, punitive
damage awards are subject to constitutional scrutiny on substantive due process grounds.[35] Nor does the rejection of economic due process mean that the
government may deprive individuals of fundamental rights so long as it does
so through regulation of a contract. *Carey v. Population Services International*,[36]
which invalidated a New York law restricting sales of contraceptives to minors,
makes that clear, as does *Buckley v. Valeo*, which invalidated limits on election
expenditures on First Amendment grounds.[37] The most charitable question to
ask from the perspective of the ACA plaintiffs is not whether individuals have
a fundamental right to refrain from purchasing health insurance but rather
whether they have a fundamental right to control the timing and nature of the
health care they receive.

In fact, it is the government's argument in favor of the constitutionality of the
ACA that clarifies why this question may be appropriate. The individual mandate,
and the ACA more generally, is designed to respond to an adverse selection problem. Young and healthy individuals with limited resources would otherwise rationally choose to save their money and purchase insurance only when it is needed
(or, in the absence of the ACA, to rely on public largesse to finance emergency
medical care). The individual mandate responds to the adverse selection problem
in part by introducing a moral hazard: those forced to obtain insurance are more
likely to obtain preventive medical care than they would if they could choose
whether to pay for it.[38] The government's ultimate objective in enacting this law is
not simply to regulate the timing of medical payments; it is also to influence the
decisions people make about when and how to receive health care.

Imagine, for example, if the government required every American to pay into
a fund to cover the future costs of their own abortion services but exempted
those currently engaged in any form of family planning. Certainly one could
make a colorable argument that such a law would work a serious violation of personal autonomy. The ACA differs in obvious ways from this hypothetical law, but
deciding whether those differences are constitutionally relevant requires a bit of
work. Many more people will need serious medical care than will need abortion services, but due process questions are often evaluated from the perspective

of those (often exceptional) individuals who seek to exercise the right. As the joint opinion stated in *Planned Parenthood of Southeastern Pennsylvania v. Casey*, "The proper focus of constitutional inquiry is the group for whom the law is a restriction, not the group for whom the law is irrelevant."[39] A woman's decision whether to have an abortion is specifically protected under the Constitution, but so too are countless other decisions one might make regarding one's medical care.[40] The hypothetical law just described infringes on abortion rights no more than the individual mandate infringes on the right to make other kinds of medical decisions. Finally, this hypothetical abortion-funding law requires the government to inquire into family planning, which feels Orwellian, but the ACA requires the government to inquire into planning for health care (i.e., to determine whether you must pay the tax penalty). Indeed, the government insists that failing to purchase health insurance represents a decision to self-insure. Insurance is nothing if not planning.

Just as section 1 does not aim to demonstrate that Article I arguments against the individual mandate are somehow improper, this section has not suggested (nor do I believe) that a substantive due process argument is or should be a winner. It cannot be that any regulation that seeks to influence a decision or set of decisions in which individuals have a constitutionally protected autonomy interest is unconstitutional. Indeed, this is not even true in the abortion context.[41] But given the ambitious Article I arguments the plaintiffs pushed to within a hair's breadth of success, it is surprising that they found a no more ambitious due process argument unworthy of appellate briefing. The next section considers why.

## 3.

The most straightforward reason why the skilled lawyers who represented the plaintiffs in the *Health Care Case* chose to pursue Article I rather than due process arguments is that, whatever their abstract merits, Article I arguments had a greater likelihood of success. The outcome of the cases attests to the good sense of that judgment. My interest, then, is not in *whether* but *why* it was sensible. I suggest three reasons, the first two of which are speculative and only the last of which resonates with conventional legal argumentation. First, Mitt Romney's role in enacting an individual mandate in Massachusetts complicated the lines of attack both for the particular plaintiffs who reached the Supreme Court and for opponents of the ACA more broadly. Second, quite apart from Romney, the need for a substantive due process argument to rely on abortion rights precedents lessened its appeal among many opponents of the ACA. Third, *Lochner* does much more work in constitutional case law than its holding would suggest; its anticanonicity enables it to distort ordinary doctrinal arguments. I discuss each in turn.

The individual mandate provision Romney signed into law in Massachusetts was the model for the federal provision. The Article I arguments against the federal law do not apply to states, which have presumptively valid general police powers. But it has been assumed that the Fifth Amendment's Due Process Clause, which applies to the federal government, has the same scope as its Fourteenth Amendment analog, which applies to the states. A successful substantive due process argument would therefore imply the constitutional invalidity of Romney's Massachusetts plan.

This result would produce some awkwardness. The Florida plaintiffs' lawyers, David Rivkin and Lee Casey of BakerHostetler, served on Romney's justice advisory committee throughout the primary season. The NFIB, which brought the individual mandate challenge that reached the Supreme Court, is partly funded by the Claude R. Lambe Charitable Foundation, a philanthropic outfit controlled by Charles G. Koch. David Koch, Charles's brother and business partner, is a longtime Romney supporter who has hosted multiple big-ticket fund-raisers for Romney at his Hamptons home. Charles and David's brother, Bill, along with his energy companies Oxbow Carbon and Huron Carbon, donated $2 million to Romney's super PAC, Restore Our Future.

The conspiratorial reader is already a step ahead of me, but I need go no further. I need not assume, and I am in no position to declare, any conscious desire by the ACA litigants or their attorneys to further Romney's political aspirations through their litigation choices. Voluminous psychological research on motivated cognition suggests, however, that even in the absence of any conscious reflection, their assessments of the merits of the due process argument are not likely to be indifferent to the effect of that argument on Romney's signature legislative achievement. The ACA litigation (and in particular the choice to abandon the due process argument on appeal) was nearly simultaneous with the Republican primary race, in which Romney's biggest challenge was defending his health care plan against charges that it was identical to President Obama's. The litigation choice to avoid due process arguments was essential to the credibility of that defense even if it was not "caused" by Romney's particular circumstances.

Relatedly, that choice also aligned the interests of social conservatives and libertarians within the Republican Party. The Tea Party movement that galvanized the party during President Obama's first term was, as Emily Ekins reports, "unified on the role of government ... regarding economics and business" but "roughly split in half about the government promoting a particular set of values."[42] The Article I argument embeds a libertarian argument within a general anti-Washington, antiregulatory stance that gibes with a conservative political agenda of long standing. It does not threaten state and local control over personal decision-making, which would please many libertarians but would be anathema to social conservatives who oppose abortion rights.

This divide is perhaps symbolized by the battle between the Koch brothers and the Cato Institute. Charles and David Koch are cofounders of Americans for Prosperity, which is among the Tea Party movement's most significant logistical and financial supporters. In March 2012 the Kochs sued Cato to attempt to wrest control of its governing shareholder group.[43] Edward Crane, the former Cato president who resigned the post as part of a settlement, described the suit as "an effort by the Kochs to turn the Cato Institute into some sort of auxiliary for the G.O.P."[44] Whether or not Crane's characterization is accurate, it highlights the fact that the interests of libertarians and mainstream Republicans are often in tension. Cato filed a brief in support of John Geddes Lawrence's right to engage in sodomy in *Lawrence v. Texas*, it supported Angel Raich's right to grow medical marijuana in *Gonzales v. Raich*, and it opposed the Federal Marriage Amendment. Cato scholars have divided on abortion rights. All of these positions are nonstarters among many social conservatives. The Article I argument postponed the battle for the soul of the Republican Party that a due process argument would have invited.

All of which is not to say, again, that these political and cultural considerations standing alone "caused" the litigants and their attorneys to pursue Article I arguments. It is to say, rather, that these considerations, whether consciously or not, plausibly informed or reinforced a more conventional legal conclusion that the due process argument was not viable. I turn now to that conclusion, which is sufficient by itself but which nonetheless requires us to extend our thinking beyond legal doctrine narrowly conceived.

The uniform legal intuition that *Lochner* posed an obstacle to due process arguments against the individual mandate cannot be dismissed simply by noting that *Lochner* involved different facts and different legal theories. *Lochner* is what I and others have called an anticanonical decision.[45] It is one of a small number of decisions—along with *Plessy v. Ferguson*,[46] *Dred Scott v. Sandford*,[47] and perhaps *Korematsu v. United States*[48]—that are consistently cited to refute the propositions for which they stand. Crucial to the anticanonicity of a judicial decision is its susceptibility to citation across the political and ideological spectrum. We all agree that *Dred Scott*, *Plessy*, and *Lochner* are wrong, but our agreement is incompletely theorized.[49] Many conservatives cite *Dred Scott* for its support of substantive due process, while many liberals cite it for its support of originalism. Many conservatives cite *Plessy* for its lack of colorblindness, while many liberals cite it for its inattention to the social meaning of race-conscious decisions. Many conservatives cite *Lochner* for its use of substantive due process, while many liberals cite it for its support of liberty of contract. These criticisms stand in significant tension with each other, but their coexistence helps to sustain, indeed to enlarge, these decisions within our constitutional discourse.

The prospect that a substantive due process argument would require *Lochner* to be distinguished therefore had an *in terrorem* effect on the ACA litigation, which any U.S.-trained lawyer would have internalized. A peek at the Supreme Court oral argument in the *Health Care Case* helps to make the point. At several points the ACA litigants were pushed to say why their argument did not implicate *Lochner*. Solicitor General Donald Verrilli said that "to embark on the kind of analysis that [the ACA opponents] suggest the Court ought to embark on is to import *Lochner*-style substantive due process."[50] Chief Justice Roberts, puzzling through the implications of the government's argument, said "it would be going back to *Lochner* if we were put in the position of saying, no, you can use your commerce power to regulate insurance, but you can't use your commerce power to regulate this market in other ways."[51] Finally, Justice Sotomayor put to Paul Clement, representing the challengers to the mandate, whether he was advancing "a *Lochner* era argument that only the States can [require the purchase of insurance] even though it affects commerce."[52]

Notice that, in a case in which a due process argument had long since been abandoned, Verrilli, the Chief Justice, and Justice Sotomayor each invoked *Lochner*, and each invoked it for a different substantive point. For Verrilli, *Lochner* stood for economic due process; for Chief Justice Roberts it stood for inappropriate judicial line-drawing with respect to Congress's powers; and for Justice Sotomayor it stood for inherent limitations on federal power. In the mind of the American lawyer and judge, *Lochner* stands for all of these things and more, even though it is not on its face a case about federal power.

A lawyer charged with resurrecting *Lochner* stands accused of urging judicial activism. The defense to such a charge must be wholesale rather than retail; neat doctrinal distinctions are not sufficient. That reality is even more palpable for those who, like NFIB lawyer Randy Barnett, are on record in support of the reasoning in *Lochner* itself.[53] A substantive due process argument against the individual mandate rather plainly would not have garnered five votes on the Court that decided the *Health Care Case*: both Justice Scalia and Justice Thomas reject substantive due process conceptually. But more significantly, even raising the argument would have struck a blow to the credibility of the ACA opponents' case, making their Article I arguments appear all the more to be wolves in sheep's clothing.

Had the ACA opponents chosen to litigate a due process claim, instead of spending their briefing space and argument time describing why insurance mandates are like broccoli mandates, the lawyers would have spent it explaining why insurance mandates are not like maximum hours laws for bakers. Their supporters and funders would have had to explain why Mitt Romney was worthy of support even though his most significant policy achievement is unconstitutional. And they might have had to say why forcing an individual to buy insurance is a greater infringement on her liberty than forcing her to bear or beget a child or denying her the right to marry the partner of her choice. Under the circumstances, it is easy to see why a due process claim never got its day in court.

# Acknowledgment

A more detailed version of this chapter's argument appears in Jamal Greene, *What the New Deal Settled*, 15 U. Pa. J. Const. L. 265 (2012).

# Notes

1. United States v. Carolene Products, 304 U.S. 144, 152 (1938).
2. See *id.*; Williamson v. Lee Optical, 348 U.S. 483, 488 (1955).
3. Lochner v. New York, 198 U.S. 45 (1905).
4. See, e.g., Akhil Reed Amar, Op-Ed., *Constitutional Showdown: A Florida Judge Distorted the Law in Striking Down Healthcare Reform*, L.A. TIMES, Feb. 6, 2011, at 25; Ezra Klein, *Reagan's Solicitor General: "Health Care Is Interstate Commerce. Is This Regulation of It? Yes. End of Story*," WONKBLOG (Mar. 28, 2012, 1:09 PM), http://www.washingtonpost.com/blogs/ezra-klein/post/reagans-solicitor-general-health-care-is-interstate-commerce-is-this-a-regulation-of-it-yes-end-of-story/2011/08/25/gIQAmaQigS_blog; Andrew Koppelman, *Bad News for Mail Robbers: The Obvious Constitutionality of Health Care Reform*, 121 YALE L.J. Online 1 (2011).
5. 410 U.S. 113 (1973).
6. 505 U.S. 833 (1992).
7. As the reader likely knows by now, the Court construed the minimum essential coverage provision as a negative financial incentive rather than as a regulatory mandate.
8. See United States v. Lopez, 514 U.S. 549, 558–559 (1995).
9. *Id.*
10. 529 U.S. 598 (2000).
11. NFIB v. Sebelius, 132 S. Ct. 2566, 2624 (2012) (Ginsburg, J., concurring in part, concurring in the judgment, and dissenting in part).
12. 22 U.S. 1 (1824).
13. *Id.* at 196–197; see also United States v. Darby, 312 U.S. 100, 114 (1941).
14. See McCulloch v. Maryland, 17 U.S. 316 (1819).
15. 130 S. Ct. 1949 (2010).
16. *Id.* at 1956.
17. *NFIB*, 132 S. Ct. at 2592 (opinion of Roberts, C.J.).
18. 17 U.S. 316.
19. See *Comstock*, 130 S. Ct. at 1956–1957; Sabri v. United States, 541 U.S. 600, 605–606 (2004). The Chief Justice suggested without elaboration that compelling an individual to purchase insurance constitutes a "great substantive and independent power" that may not be authorized by the Necessary and Proper Clause. *NFIB*, 132 S. Ct. at 2591. The notion that the power to require people to purchase health insurance is a "great substantive and independent" power but that the power to imprison people (indeed beyond their criminal sentence), see *Comstock*, is not such a power nearly carries its own refutation. In any event, that proposition seems to require significantly more argumentation to justify invalidation of a federal statute.
20. 545 U.S. 1, 34 (2005) (Scalia, J., concurring in the judgment).
21. *Id.*
22. Whether the ACA litigation presented such a circumstance is another matter. See City of Boerne v. Flores, 521 U.S. 507, 536 (1997) ("When the political branches of the Government act against the background of a judicial interpretation of the Constitution already issued, it must be understood that in later cases and controversies the Court will treat its precedents with the respect due them under settled principles, including *stare decisis*, and contrary expectations must be disappointed").

23. Only eleven of the twenty-two federal court challenges to the individual mandate even raised a substantive due process claim.

24. Plaintiffs' Memorandum in Opposition to Defendants' Motion to Dismiss at 62, Florida *ex rel.* McCollum v. U.S. Dep't of Health & Human Servs., 716 F. Supp. 2d 1120 (N.D. Fla. 2010) (No. 3:10-cv-91).

25. 521 U.S. 702 (1997) (declining to recognize a right to assisted suicide but reaffirming the right to refuse unwanted medical treatment).

26. 497 U.S. 261 (1990) (strongly implying a personal right to refuse unwanted medical treatment).

27. 262 U.S. 390 (1923) (recognizing a right to direct the education of one's child).

28. 268 U.S. 510 (1925) (recognizing a right to school choice).

29. *Id.* at 64.

30. *Florida* ex rel. *McCollum*, 716 F. Supp. 2d at 1161.

31. *Id.* at 1162.

32. Even the government's brief in support of its motion to dismiss did not argue that the claim was foreclosed by prior precedent, only that it had not yet been recognized: "While acknowledging the fundamental rights to make 'personal decisions relating to marriage, procreation, contraception, family relationships, child rearing, and education,' the Court has never extended the concept to the purchase of health insurance." Memorandum in Support of Defendants' Motion to Dismiss at 53, *Florida* ex rel. *McCollum*, 716 F. Supp. 2d 1120 (No. 3:10-cv-91) (internal citations omitted).

33. 197 U.S. 11 (1905).

34. 381 U.S. 479 (1965).

35. See BMW of N. Am. v. Gore, 517 U.S. 559 (1996).

36. 431 U.S. 678 (1976).

37. 424 U.S. 1 (1976).

38. They are also, hypothetically, more likely to engage in risky behavior.

39. 505 U.S. 833, 894 (1992).

40. See Cruzan v. Dir., Mo. Dep't of Health, 497 U.S. 261, 269–270 (1990).

41. See *Casey*, 505 U.S. 833 (upholding informed consent and parental consent provisions of Pennsylvania's abortion law).

42. Emily McClintock Ekins, *The Character and Economic Morality of the Tea Party Movement*, Am. Pol. Sci. Assoc. Annual Meeting Paper No. 27 (Sept. 5, 2011), *available at* http://ssrn.com/abstract=1902394.

43. Charles Koch is a cofounder of the Cato Institute.

44. Eric Lichtblau, *Cato Institute Is Caught in Rift Over Its Direction*, N.Y. TIMES, Mar. 6, 2012, *available at* http://www.nytimes.com/2012/03/06/us/cato-institute-and-koch-in-rift-over-independence.html?pagewanted=all&_r=0.

45. See Jamal Greene, *The Anticanon*, 125 HARV. L. REV. 379 (2011).

46. 163 U.S. 537 (1896).

47. 16 U.S. (19 How.) 393 (1857).

48. 323 U.S. 214 (1944).

49. See Greene, *supra* note 45, at 460–461.

50. Transcript of Oral Argument at 30, Florida v. Dep't of Health & Human Servs., 132 S. Ct. 604 (2012), *sub nom. NFIB*, 132 S. Ct. 2566 (No. 11-398).

51. *Id.* at 39.

52. *Id.* at 66–67.

53. See RANDY E. BARNETT, RESTORING THE LOST CONSTITUTION: THE PRESUMPTION OF LIBERTY 211–223 (2004).

CHAPTER 7

# "Necessary," "Proper," and Health Care Reform

*Andrew Koppelman*

The Necessary and Proper Clause of Article I, Section 8[1] was always a major obstacle to the constitutional case against the Patient Protection and Affordable Care Act's[2] individual mandate to carry health insurance. Under settled law at the time that the ACA was enacted, the mandate was obviously constitutional.

Here is the argument in four sentences. Insurance is part of commerce among the several states. Congress can regulate it. Therefore, Congress can prohibit health insurers from discriminating on the basis of preexisting conditions. Under the Necessary and Proper Clause, Congress gets to decide what means it may employ to make that regulation effective.

The first three sentences are uncontroversial. The fourth sentence is the point of attack. How was it to be answered?

In *NFIB v. Sebelius* (*NFIB*), Chief Justice John Roberts thought the law exceeded Congress's commerce power, but his solution to the Necessary and Proper problem was cryptic. The mandate was not authorized by the Necessary and Proper Clause because it involved a "great substantive and independent power."[3] He did not explain how one could tell what constituted such a power. This limitation was worked out in more detail by amici (nonparty "friends" of the court), and Roberts may have been gesturing toward their argument. This chapter will look to the antecedents of Roberts's argument to try to make better sense of what he said. This strategy will fail. There is no way to make this argument look good.[4] It is a placeholder for a raw intuition that being required to enter into a contract is an extraordinary burden.

## 1. The Mandate

The ACA's so-called individual mandate, which required nearly everyone to purchase health insurance, is in practice a penalty or a tax—as it turned out, it matters a lot what you call it—that must be paid by those who fail to carry a minimum level of health insurance coverage.[5] It was the focus of challenges to the law. A central purpose of the ACA was to extend insurance to people with preexisting medical conditions,[6] whom insurers had become very efficient at keeping off their rolls. (This group includes not only sick people, but anyone likely to file an expensive medical claim, such as women of childbearing age.) But the rule against discriminating against those people, standing alone, would mean that healthy people could wait until they got sick to buy insurance. Because insurance pools rely on cross-subsidization of sick people by healthy participants, that would bankrupt the entire individual insurance market. Massachusetts, acting a few years before the federal law, had combined its guarantee of coverage with an individual mandate, but seven other states tried to protect people with preexisting conditions without mandating coverage for everyone. The results in those states ranged from huge premium increases to the complete collapse of the market. In New York, for example, the individual market dropped from 752,000 covered persons in 1994 to 34,000 in 2009.[7]

The American health care system before President Obama's election was fundamentally broken. About 15 percent of Americans had no health insurance in 2008, and the number was growing. About three-quarters of those people worked, more than half of them full-time. Coverage had eroded slightly for employees in the top two-fifths of earners, but more than 90 percent of them remained covered. The middle fifth had gone from 5 percent to 12.4 percent uninsured since 1980. The next-to-bottom fifth went from less than 10 percent to 21.9 percent uninsured, and the bottom fifth more than doubled, from 18 percent to 37.4 percent uninsured.[8]

The uninsured suffer avoidable illnesses, receive less preventive care, are diagnosed when their illnesses are more advanced, and once diagnosed receive less therapeutic care. The Institute of Medicine estimates that having health insurance would reduce their mortality rates by 10 to 25 percent.[9] For example, women without insurance are nearly 50 percent more likely to die of breast cancer, because their tumors are not diagnosed at an early stage.[10] Estimates of deaths from lack of health insurance vary wildly, but range as high as 45,000.[11] Those who don't die are in worse health, and sometimes are financially ruined by medical expenses.[12]

Obama's strategy was to expand coverage for the uninsured while delicately navigating around any interference with existing insurance arrangements. The ACA is complex, and it would take a book to adequately describe it.[13] Here I'll just focus on the problem of preexisting conditions.

How many Americans have preexisting medical conditions? Here, too, estimates vary wildly, ranging from 20 percent to 66 percent of the adult population. (The uninsured report fewer such conditions, because their problems are likely to be undetected.) In the first quarter of 2010, 19 percent of applicants in the individual market were denied enrollment, and a quarter of insurers had denial rates of 40 percent or more.[14]

The health reform statute responds to this problem in two ways. The guaranteed issue requirement bars denying coverage to those with preexisting conditions. The community-rating requirement prohibits insurers from charging dramatically higher rates to people based on their medical history.[15] The law also bans "rescission," the practice of cancelling an insurance policy after the policyholder becomes sick.

Under the ACA, beginning in 2014, every citizen and legal immigrant—with some exceptions for hardship and religious objections—must have minimal health insurance or pay a penalty. The annual penalty rises until 2016. After that the amount can vary with family size and income level, but the maximum a family is required to pay is the annual premium cost for a minimally adequate insurance plan, 2.5 percent of income, or $2,085 (the latter subject to cost-of-living adjustments).[16]

The problem could have been addressed in other ways. Obama thought, during his first presidential campaign, that people go without insurance because they can't afford it, and there's some evidence that he was right. The ACA's subsidies would have reduced the number of uninsured even without the mandate. The mandate's inclusion in the law was assured by a Congressional Budget Office report indicating that eliminating it would raise the uninsured population in 2019 by 16 million, with insurance rates rising by 15 to 20 percent for those who bought insurance individually.[17] Congress could have automatically enrolled individuals as a default with the ability to opt out, or imposed limited open-enrollment periods with penalties for late enrollment. An analysis of these options found that none of them could cover more than two-thirds as many of the uninsured as the ACA, none saves as much money, and all of them involve higher insurance costs.[18]

There were also other ways of paying for expanded coverage. One option was to tax citizens directly, as is done with Social Security and Medicare. Another was to mandate that businesses provide the services to those who cannot afford to pay and pass on the cost to their customers who can; that was once done voluntarily by insurers and hospitals, before competitive pressures made them stop, and it happens now when emergency rooms are required to treat indigent patients (though those hospitals are also quite willing to dun uninsured patients for thousands of dollars). Tax incentives could also have been provided for the purchase of insurance. Employers could have been required to provide insurance (though this discourages new hiring, is hard on small businesses, and is no help to the unemployed). The ACA's mandate was just another technique for financing broad coverage, adopted, despite its unpopularity, because all the other options had proven politically impossible or practically inadequate.

You may not like the mandate. It may not have been worth the political cost, and it nearly killed the whole law. But without it, millions more people would be uninsured. If you abandon the mandate, you probably abandon near-universal health care.

## 2. McCulloch

So now let's take up the key question: given that Congress has the power to try to get health insurance to those with preexisting conditions, is the mandate a permissible means of accomplishing that? The challengers never seriously questioned Congress's power to forbid insurers from turning away sick people. Instead, they argued that the mandate was an improper means for carrying out this purpose. In making that claim, they had to navigate around nearly two centuries of settled law.

The list of congressional powers in Article I ends with an authorization to "make all Laws which shall be necessary and proper" to carry out its responsibilities.[19] The interpretation of the Necessary and Proper Clause was settled in 1819 by Chief Justice John Marshall in *McCulloch v. Maryland*.[20] The central question in *McCulloch* was whether Congress had the power to charter the Bank of the United States, the precursor of today's Federal Reserve Bank. The Constitution does not enumerate any power to create corporations. The state of Maryland, which was trying to tax the Bank, argued that the "necessary and proper" language permitted Congress only to choose means that were *absolutely* necessary to carry out its powers. The same view was taken by Thomas Jefferson, who feared a government possessing "a boundless field of power, no longer susceptible of any definition."[21] (As we have already seen, the mandate would be authorized even under this narrower reading of the clause.)

Marshall rejected this reading, which, he thought, would make the government "incompetent to its great objects."[22] The federal government must collect and spend revenue throughout the United States, and so must quickly transfer funds across hundreds of miles. "Is that construction of the constitution to be preferred which would render these operations hazardous, difficult, and expensive?"[23] Without implied powers, Marshall argued, Congress's power "to establish post offices" could not entail the ability to punish mail robbers and might not even entail the power to carry letters from one post office to another. "It may be said with some plausibility that the right to carry the mail, and to punish those who rob it, is not indispensably necessary to the establishment of a post office and post road."[24] He concluded that Congress could choose any convenient means for carrying out its enumerated powers. So Congress is powerful—perhaps frighteningly powerful. But what Marshall said about the taxing power is true of the other powers as well:

> The only security against the abuse of this power is found in the structure of the Government itself. In imposing a tax, the legislature acts upon its constituents. This is, in general, a sufficient security against erroneous and oppressive taxation.[25]

The political accountability that Marshall emphasizes here is another reason why it makes sense to give Congress a choice of means. Opponents of the mandate sometimes suggest that it is reprehensible that Congress allowed political considerations to shape the law and eliminate options such as a single-payer system. But taking account of politics is Congress's job. The various possible means for addressing any problem are likely to affect different people differently, and those who are going to suffer if one or the other choice is made should have the opportunity to have that taken into account. That's democracy.

Marshall also wrote—and this is the passage upon which Roberts relied—that incorporation was "not, like the power of making war, or levying taxes, or of regulating commerce, a great substantive and independent power, which cannot be implied as incidental to other powers."[26] Instead, incorporation "must be considered as a means not less usual, not of higher dignity, not more requiring a particular specification than other means."[27] Accordingly, "No sufficient reason is, therefore, perceived, why it may not pass as incidental to those powers which are expressly given, if it be a direct mode of executing them."[28]

*McCulloch* has since been read to say that Congress has a broad choice of means. The distinction between a "great substantive and independent power" and lesser powers, on the other hand, was ignored until the ACA case. That language is only quoted in two nineteenth-century Supreme Court cases between *McCulloch* and *NFIB*, both upholding congressional power.[29]

The basic rule of *McCulloch* was reaffirmed by the Court as recently as May 2010 in *United States v. Comstock*.[30] The Court upheld a law authorizing civil commitment of mentally ill sexual predators who remain dangerous after completing their federal prison sentences—an appropriate federal role, Congress found, because no state may be willing to take custody. (The Court did not address the obvious individual rights issue, which was litigated separately.) In deciding whether Congress is appropriately exercising its powers under the Necessary and Proper Clause, the Court declared, the question is "whether the statute constitutes a means that is rationally related to the implementation of a constitutionally enumerated power."[31] Thus, for example, even though the

Constitution mentions no federal crimes other than counterfeiting, treason, and piracy, Congress has broad authority, pursuant to a number of its enumerated powers, to enact criminal statutes.

The Necessary and Proper Clause is a significant source of Congress's powers under the Commerce Clause. This is in large part because for many years the Court has held a constricted understanding of commerce among the several states as including only trade and navigation, when it is better understood as encompassing all problems that the states are separately incompetent to address. The Constitution was adopted specifically in order to give Congress power adequate to address the nation's problems. That is its fundamental and overriding purpose. A situation in which neither the states nor the federal government could solve the country's problems was what we had under the Articles of Confederation. The Commerce Clause is appropriately read in pursuance of that purpose.

The Court has accommodated the modern state by stretching the meaning of this narrow understanding of commerce and proliferating legal fictions, producing bizarrely formalistic law. An understanding of commerce limited to trade constrains the federal government with no regard for the reasons why federal regulation might be necessary, and thus pointlessly casts doubt on laws governing civil rights, workplace safety, sanitary food, drug safety, and employee rights.[32] The Necessary and Proper Clause provides a way out of this box. Thus, for example:

> The power of Congress over interstate commerce is not confined to the regulation of commerce among the states. It extends to those activities intrastate which so affect interstate commerce or the exercise of the power of Congress over it as to make regulation of them appropriate means to the attainment of a legitimate end, the exercise of the granted power of Congress to regulate interstate commerce. See McCulloch.[33]

This interdependence of the commerce power and the Necessary and Proper Clause was emphasized by the challengers to the ACA, most prominently by their leading theorist, Randy Barnett.[34] But even if such interdependence is established, it shows only that limits on Congress's power must include some corresponding limit on the Necessary and Proper Clause. There were already such limits, most notably in United States v. Lopez[35] and United States v. Morrison.[36] Those cases were not concerned at all about limiting Congress's choice of means, but rather aimed at the more fundamental structural goal of preserving the distinction "between what is truly national and what is truly local."[37] It could not plausibly be claimed that the ACA transgressed the limits laid down in those cases.

# 3. Roberts

Roberts thought that the mandate exceeded the commerce power, even augmented by the Necessary and Proper Clause. He argued that a law, even if it is necessary, is not "proper" if permitting it would "undermine the structure of government established by the Constitution."[38] Quoting *McCulloch*, he declared that the Necessary and Proper Clause did not authorize the use of any "'great substantive and independent power' of the sort at issue here."[39]

Two earlier cases had held that a law, even if "necessary," may not be "proper." In *Printz v. United States*,[40] the Court said that "[w]hen a 'La[w] ... for carrying into Execution' the Commerce Clause violates the principle of state sovereignty reflected in ... various constitutional provisions ... [,] it is not a 'La[w] ... *proper* for carrying into Execution the Commerce Clause.'"[41] The law invalidated in *Printz*, requiring state and local law enforcement officers to conduct background checks on prospective handgun purchasers, was clearly "useful" or "convenient" to carrying into execution Congress's power to regulate commerce in handguns. *Printz's* holding relied in part on the concept of "state sovereignty" embedded in the Tenth Amendment, but it emphasized that "[w]hat destroys the dissent's Necessary and Proper Clause argument ... is not the Tenth Amendment but the Necessary and Proper Clause itself."[42] In *Alden v. Maine*,[43] the Court concluded that states enjoy a constitutionally protected immunity from being sued for violating federal law, an immunity that applies in state court as well as federal court. *Alden* held that the Necessary and Proper Clause does not give Congress "the incidental authority to subject the States to private suits as a means of achieving objectives otherwise within the scope of the enumerated powers," because such authority is not "proper."[44]

These cases show that "proper" is a limit on Congress's choice of means. But they relied on state sovereignty, which was not at issue in *NFIB*. As Justice Ginsburg observed, these cases all held that Congress had the power to act on individuals, but not on states. The mandate, of course, only acts on individuals.[45] There is an analogous limitation on laws that can be "proper" as applied to individuals. That limitation is a familiar one: individual rights. A violation of those rights is improper and unconstitutional even if it is rationally related to a legitimate congressional goal. But no one claimed that the mandate violated individual rights. That concession should have been the end of the claim that it was not "proper."

Roberts, however, revived the long-dormant distinction between a "great substantive and independent power" and lesser powers. Ginsburg complained that Roberts provided no clue as to how to operationalize that distinction:

> How is a judge to decide, when ruling on the constitutionality of a federal statute, whether Congress employed an "independent power," or

merely a "derivative" one? Whether the power used is "substantive," or just "incidental"? The instruction THE CHIEF JUSTICE, in effect, provides lower courts: You will know it when you see it.[46]

Roberts assumed without argument that the mandate is some enormous new power. Ginsburg pointed out that there have been mandates in the U.S. Code since the founding—to purchase firearms in anticipation of service in the militia, register for the draft, file a tax return, report for jury duty, and exchange gold coin for paper currency.[47] (She didn't mention a 1798 requirement that sailors have health insurance.)[48] Roberts responded that each of these is "based on constitutional provisions other than the Commerce Clause."[49] But how can something be a great substantive and independent power in relation to one provision but not another? Roberts might respond that some powers inherently imply the capacity to impose mandates: the requirement of jury service has from time immemorial been part of the operation of courts, for example. But this won't work for all the mandates in question. The requirement, under the Emergency Banking Relief Act of 1933, that all persons "pay and deliver to the Treasurer of the United States any or all gold coin, gold bullion, and gold certificates"[50] owned by them, and accept paper money in exchange, cannot be inferred from the power to coin money.

The distinction that Ginsburg finds so mysterious is drawn, without acknowledgment, from an attack on the mandate developed by Gary Lawson and David Kopel.[51] They argued, on the basis of a new interpretation of the historical evidence, developed by Robert Natelson, that the Necessary and Proper Clause incorporates norms from eighteenth-century agency law, administrative law, and corporate law, and that the mandate (and perhaps much else in the U.S. Code, though they are coy about this) violates those norms. The clause, as Lawson and Kopel understand it, tightly limits the scope of implied powers to those that are less important less "worthy" or "dignified"—than the principal powers to which they are subsidiary.

Lawson and Kopel are the most coherent defenders of the distinction Roberts was trying to draw. Moreover, Kopel claimed, after the *NFIB* decision came down, that the Court had adopted the limits he and his coauthors had advocated.[52] Their work offers the most promising avenue for clarifying Roberts's cryptic dictum.[53] They argue that "a law enacted under the clause must exercise a subsidiary rather than an independent power."[54] The mandate does not satisfy this requirement, because "the power to order someone to purchase a product is not a power subordinate or inferior to other powers."[55] An incident must be "a thing necessarily depending upon, appertaining to, or following another thing that is more worthy or principal."[56]

How are we to tell if one power is as "worthy" or "dignified" as another? To return to Marshall's example, how are we to know that the power to jail those who rob the mails is "less important or less valuable"[57] than the enumerated power to operate a post office?[58] These terms may have made sense in the eighteenth century. "By the founding era, the jurisprudence of principals and incidents had become a prominent and well-developed branch of the law. Numerous cases had specified which lesser interests were incident to which greater interests."[59] But how does one translate these terms from their then-familiar applications in property law or the law of corporations to the very different context of governmental powers? Marshall tried to do it in *McCulloch v. Maryland*.[60] So did others at the time who struggled with the question presented there: whether Congress had the power to charter a bank.[61]

Lawson and Kopel conceded in their article that "[m]ore recent cases no longer use the language of principals and incidents."[62] Their Supreme Court brief, evidently on the basis of later research, cited numerous cases that at least gestured toward the distinction.[63] However, every single one of those cases upheld the exercise of congressional power, so none of them provides any guidance as to where the line is to be drawn.

These terms take us into terra incognita. The debates at the time of *McCulloch* show that even then, there was deep uncertainty about how to apply the doctrine of principals and incidents to Article I of the Constitution. It is even harder to know how to apply them today. And what would be the consequence if we did?

All we are told is that the holdings of more recent cases—meaning, cases decided in the last century—"are broadly consistent with that framework,"[64] and that sustaining the constitutional objection to the individual mandate "does not require overruling any decision."[65] Lawson and Kopel add that "one could fairly argue that those decisions misapplied the original meaning of the Necessary and Proper Clause, but those arguments would involve issues not raised here."[66] It is, in short, an open question how much of existing law would have to be scrapped if this worth-and-dignity rule were adopted by the courts.

The federal government now exercises unenumerated powers that are not obviously lesser to the enumerated ones. Congress's plenary authority to regulate immigration and exclude aliens sure looks like a "great substantive and independent power," not merely derivative from the enumerated power "to establish a uniform Rule of Naturalization." The commerce power does not necessarily entail the power to regulate air and water pollution, or the sale of securities or adulterated food, neither of which typically is conducted across state lines. At the time of the framing and long after, it was taken for granted that eminent domain was a great power that the federal government could not exercise, yet it now routinely does so, and presumably Roberts did not mean to call this practice into question.[67]

Lawson and Kopel have defended themselves against the claim that the limits they would introduce into the doctrine would hamstring existing uses of congressional power:

> For example, federal water pollution regulation is straightforwardly derived from the federal power to regulate the waters of the United States, which in turn flows (no pun intended) from the fact that the channels of navigation can be regulated under the Commerce Clause. No strong inference from the Necessary and Proper Clause is necessary.[68]

If water is a means of interstate navigation, then apparently Congress can regulate entirely intrastate activity that pollutes it, even when that pollution does not in any way impair its usefulness as a means of transportation across state lines. This is a pretty generous way to read a supposedly subsidiary power. It appears that this reading is necessary in order to avoid ridiculous results.

Roberts also argued—here he is no longer relying on the "great substantive and independent power" idea—that an argument authorizing the mandate "vests Congress with the extraordinary ability to create the necessary predicate to the exercise of an enumerated power."[69] If this is permitted, "Congress could reach beyond the natural limit of its authority and draw within its regulatory scope those who otherwise would be outside of it."[70] His claim, essentially, is that Congress cannot arrogate to itself the power to solve problems that are of its own making.[71] But this problem is already present in *McCulloch*. Mail robbers are not ordinarily within the scope of the operation of a post office. If, however, Congress has no power to address negative consequences that follow from its own statutory scheme, then Marshall was wrong about mail robbery after all. Mail robbery is an adverse consequence of Congress's decision to establish a post office; had it not done that, all those valuable documents would not be gathered together in one place and susceptible to theft.[72]

In *Comstock*, Congress's ability to operate federal prisons—a power that, for the most part, is itself derived from the Necessary and Proper Clause—would not be impaired by the release of dangerous, mentally ill sex offenders into the general population. The *Comstock* Court noted that some of those offenders "would likely *not* be detained by the States if released from federal custody, in part because the Federal Government itself severed their claim to 'legal residence in any State' by incarcerating them in remote federal prisons."[73] But that is only to say that the statutory scheme generates negative consequences, and that Congress has the power to address those consequences.

*Comstock* also presses hard on the "great substantive and independent power" principle. Roberts tries to distinguish *Comstock*, because the law it upheld permitted "continued confinement of those *already in federal custody* when they could not be safely released."[74] It thus "involved exercise[] of authority derivative of, and in service to, a granted power."[75] But this is a pretty broad understanding of what constitutes a derivative power. If, in the course of exercising an enumerated power the federal marshals ever take you into custody, they apparently have a "derivative" power to keep you locked up, forever if necessary.

Roberts thought that a new expansion of the "proper" limitation to prohibit the mandate was necessary because permitting Congress to choose this means would permit it "to reach beyond the natural extent of its authority, 'everywhere extending the sphere of its activity and drawing all power into its impetuous vortex.'"[76] The "proper" limitation was exceeded if a law would "undermine the structure of government established by the Constitution."[77] The argument here is remarkably crude: (1) There must be some limit on federal power; (2) I can't think of another one; and therefore, (3) the limit must preclude the individual mandate.[78]

## 4. The Joint Dissent

The joint dissent of Justices Scalia, Kennedy, Thomas, and Alito is even murkier on the Necessary and Proper point. They argue that "one does not regulate commerce that does not exist by compelling its existence,"[79] but do not explain why the mandate is not a useful means to achieving the preexisting conditions regulation that is authorized. They purport to distinguish *Gonzales v. Raich* on the ground that prohibition of marijuana cultivation was "the only practicable way"[80] to stop interstate trafficking:

> With the present statute, by contrast, there are many ways other than this unprecedented Individual Mandate by which the regulatory scheme's goals of reducing insurance premiums and ensuring the profitability of insurers could be achieved. For instance, those who did not purchase insurance could be subjected to a surcharge when they do enter the health insurance system. Or they could be denied a full income tax credit given to those who do purchase the insurance.[81]

So *McCulloch* to the contrary notwithstanding, Congress does not have a choice of means in carrying out its enumerated powers. The joint dissenters seem to think that *McCulloch* adopted the rule that the decision specifically rejected: the trouble with the mandate is that it was not *absolutely* necessary. And their support even for this conclusion is weak. When the "regulatory scheme's goals" are enumerated, they omit its overriding one: reducing the number of Americans who have no health insurance. (Later on, they remember this and use it to show that Congress wickedly aimed to force all states to participate in the law's Medicaid expansion.) As we saw earlier, the only reason why the unpopular mandate got written into the law was that Congress and President Obama were both reluctantly convinced, on the basis of extensive analysis by the Congressional Budget Office and outside economists, that there was no other way that the statute could achieve its goals.[82]

What basis have the dissenters for rejecting that reasoning? It's impossible to know, because there are no citations to any empirical evidence whatsoever in the passage just quoted (which I have not edited). In other words, they are ready to destroy a carefully crafted congressional scheme on the basis of their own seat-of-the-pants intuitions about how the world works.

The joint dissenters claimed that without the limits they imposed, "then the Commerce Clause becomes a font of unlimited power, or in Hamilton's words, 'the hideous monster whose devouring jaws ... spare neither sex nor age, nor high nor low, nor sacred nor profane.'"[83] Roberts had the same concern: "The Commerce Clause is not a general license to regulate an individual from cradle to grave, simply because he will predictably engage in particular transactions."[84] But neither explains why the commerce power is not already sufficiently constrained by the limits the Court already placed upon it in *Lopez* and *Morrison*.

The joint dissenters went on to vindicate the liberties of those who "have no intention of purchasing most or even any [health care] goods or services and thus no need to buy insurance for those purchases."[85] Justice Ginsburg responded: "a healthy young person may be a day away from needing health care."[86] Those who go without health care are not entirely unrelated to that market, any more than drunk drivers are entirely unrelated to other people on the highway. Both are imposing substantial risks on others—in the health care context, the risk of having to pay large amounts for an uninsured person's medical bills. It remains mysterious why this should be thought to exceed the Necessary and Proper power.

## 5. Conclusion

Even if the distinction that Roberts drew makes no sense, perhaps we are stuck with it. Lawson and Kopel, steadfast originalists, argue that we are bound by the original meaning of "Necessary and Proper." In my earlier exchange with them, I worried that their principle, if adopted, would "randomly blow up large parts of the U.S. Code."[87] They denied that, but from the standpoint of their constitutional method, it doesn't matter. The limits they describe are, they acknowledge, unfamiliar rules of law, "perhaps strange-sounding to modern ears."[88] But if we are to believe in a written constitution, we have to live with its consequences, or else amend the Constitution.[89] If new research—as a nonhistorian I'm not competent to evaluate theirs, but it sure looks impressive[90]—shows that the original semantic meaning of the Necessary and Proper Clause is different than we thought, then we must upend our legal system in response. At least until the next bit of historical research comes along: if some later scholar shows us that the first one was wrong, then we lurch back to the law we had before. Large federal programs may disappear and reappear, depending on the state of the latest scholarship. This would be an insane way to run a civilization. It is, however, what you are committed to if you think that original meaning is the sole legitimate source of constitutional law. Roberts didn't give the credit that Lawson and Kopel deserved, but perhaps he just didn't want to be perceived as endorsing their methodological commitments.

The U.S. Constitution is hard to amend—as it happens, harder than any other constitution in the world.[91] That's why there have been so many judicial workarounds, which marginalized limitations that, in the modern context, made no sense. (The power to control immigration, omitted from the enumerated powers, is a prominent example.) This is appropriate in terms of the largest purposes of the Constitution. The Constitution was adopted specifically in order to give Congress power adequate to address the nation's problems. That is its fundamental and overriding purpose. A situation in which neither the states nor the federal government could solve the country's problems was what we had under the Articles of Confederation. It is precisely what the Constitution was intended to prevent. Yet if the Necessary and Proper Clause means that we are now constrained by obscure eighteenth-century norms, then that may be our situation.

If one stipulates that Natelson's history is correct, and that the great power limitation can be given determinate effect, then from the standpoint of original meaning the Constitution is fundamentally ambiguous. Its largest and most fundamental purpose (which obviously was part of its original public meaning) was, in Robert Stern's words, that the people of the United States should not "be entirely unable to help themselves through any existing social or governmental agency."[92] That is in tension with what Natelson claims is the specific original meaning of the Necessary and Proper Clause. Any resolution of this tension should be mindful of the enormous success of the American regime, and the flourishing of individual freedom therein, during the long period when this potentially explosive limitation of federal power was entirely ignored.

In the first paragraph of the Federalist Papers, Alexander Hamilton wrote: "It has been frequently remarked that it seems to have been reserved to the people of this country, by their conduct and example, to decide the important question, whether societies of men are really capable or not of establishing good government from reflection and choice, or whether they are forever destined to depend for their political constitutions on accident and force."[93] If the joint dissenters are correct, then accident is indeed what shapes the fate of contemporary Americans, and Hamilton's aspiration is a failure. The Constitution enumerates the powers that were thought necessary in the 1800s. If there are Americans who will die today unless the federal government exercises powers that were omitted from that list, then die they must. This is not because the framers thought this a just result. Whatever they thought they were creating, they in fact erected a cautionary monument to the limits of human foresight.

But perhaps the news is not so bad. Lawson and Kopel energetically denied that the limits they advocate would have the destructive results that I feared, and, as we have seen, Roberts even claims that the "great and independent" principle is consistent with *Comstock*. Perhaps the "great substantive and independent power" limitation is so malleable that it is no limitation at all. Certainly neither Roberts, nor Lawson and Kopel, could figure out how to show that the mandate either does or does not transgress it. The major premise is no constraint if you can do anything you like with the minor premise.

What actually ends up supplying the determination of what counts as a "great substantive and independent power" is the interpreter's pretheoretical intuitions about which government powers are particularly scary. The Lawson group, in its amicus brief, argued that the authority "to compel private citizens to purchase approved products from other, designated private persons" is "a power truly awesome in scope, and one that, if granted to Congress, the Constitution surely would have enumerated separately."[94] But how do they know?

Roberts's intuitions are most starkly revealed in his attempt to distinguish *Comstock*. The mandate, an obligation to pay money if you impose risks on other people, is an extraordinary power. Locking someone up indefinitely is a mere incident. Here we come to the dark heart of the case against the ACA: the notion that the law's trivial burden on individuals was intolerable, an outrageous invasion of liberty, "not the country the Framers of our Constitution envisioned,"[95] even when the alternative was a regime in which millions were needlessly denied decent medical care.

## Acknowledgments

Thanks to Marcia Lehr for research assistance, to David Kopel, Gary Lawson, Kurt Lash, Gillian Metzger, and Stephen Sachs for comments on an earlier draft, and to Josh Kleinfeld and Ilya Somin for helpful conversations.

## Notes

1. U.S. Const. art. I, § 8, cl. 18.
2. Pub. L. No. 111-148, 124 Stat. 119 (2010) (codified as amended in scattered sections of 26 and 42 U.S.C.).

3. NFIB v. Sebelius, 132 S. Ct. 2566, 2593 (2012) (Roberts, C.J.).

4. Other aspects of the challenge are addressed in ANDREW KOPPELMAN, THE TOUGH LUCK CONSTITUTION AND THE ASSAULT ON HEALTH CARE REFORM (2013).

5. 26 U.S.C. § 5000A (2010).

6. 42 U.S.C. § 300gg-3 (2010).

7. JOHN E. MCDONOUGH, INSIDE NATIONAL HEALTH REFORM 120 (2011).

8. LAWRENCE R. JACOBS & THEDA SKOCPOL, HEALTH CARE REFORM AND AMERICAN POLITICS: WHAT EVERYONE NEEDS TO KNOW 20 (2010).

9. STUART ALTMAN & DAVID SHACTMAN, POWER, POLITICS, AND UNIVERSAL HEALTH CARE: THE INSIDE STORY OF A CENTURY-LONG BATTLE 11–12 (2011); INSTITUTE OF MEDICINE, CARE WITHOUT COVERAGE: TOO LITTLE, TOO LATE 162 (2002), http://www.iom.edu/Reports/2002/Care-Without-Coverage-Too-Little-Too-Late.aspx.

10. John Z. Ayanian et al., *The Relation Between Health Insurance Coverage and Clinical Outcomes among Women with Breast Cancer*, 329 NEW ENG. J. MED. 326 (1993).

11. See STAN DORN, URBAN INST., UNINSURED AND DYING BECAUSE OF IT: UPDATING THE INSTITUTE OF MEDICINE ANALYSIS ON THE IMPACT OF UNINSURANCE ON MORTALITY 3 (2008), http://www.urban.org/publications/411588.html; Andrew P. Wilper et al., *Health Insurance and Mortality in US Adults*, 99 AM. J. PUB. HEALTH 2289, 2294 (2009).

12. INSTITUTE OF MEDICINE, *supra* note 9, at 18.

13. For a short and clear introduction to the ACA, see JONATHAN GRUBER, HEALTH CARE REFORM: WHAT IT IS, WHY IT'S NECESSARY, HOW IT WORKS (2011). For more detailed accounts, see STAFF OF THE WASHINGTON POST, LANDMARK: THE INSIDE STORY OF AMERICA'S NEW HEALTH-CARE LAW AND WHAT IT MEANS FOR US ALL (2010); see also JACOBS & SKOCPOL *supra* note 8, at 121–146; and MCDONOUGH, *supra* note 7.

14. U.S. GOV'T ACCOUNTABILITY OFFICE, GAO-12-439, PRIVATE HEALTH INSURANCE: ESTIMATES OF INDIVIDUALS WITH PRE-EXISTING CONDITIONS RANGE FROM 36 MILLION TO 122 MILLION (March 2012), *available at* http://www.gao.gov/assets/590/589618.pdf.

15. 42 U.S.C. §§ 300gg, 300gg-1(a), 300gg-3(a).

16. 26 U.S.C. § 5000A(c).

17. Paul Starr, *The Mandate Miscalculation*, NEW REPUBLIC ONLINE (Dec. 14, 2011), http://www.tnr.com/article/politics/magazine/98554/individual-mandate-affordable-care-act. The CBO has reaffirmed its earlier analysis. CONG. BUDGET OFFICE, REDUCING THE DEFICIT: SPENDING AND REVENUE OPTIONS 199–200 (March 2011), *available at* http://www.cbo.gov/sites/default/files/cbofiles/ftpdocs/120xx/doc12085/03-10-reducingthedeficit.pdf.

18. JONATHAN GRUBER, CTR. FOR AM. PROGRESS, HEALTH CARE REFORM WITHOUT THE INDIVIDUAL MANDATE: REPLACING THE INDIVIDUAL MANDATE WOULD SIGNIFICANTLY ERODE COVERAGE GAINS AND RAISE PREMIUMS FOR HEALTH CARE CUSTOMERS 3–5 (Feb. 2011), http://www.americanprogress.org/issues/2011/02/pdf/gruber_mandate.pdf. That analysis is reasonably contestable, since any analysis depends on educated guesses about how people will behave. For a strong argument in favor of the opt-out option, see Starr, *supra* note 17.

19. U.S. CONST. art. 1, § 8, cl. 18.

20. McCulloch v. Maryland, 17 U.S. 316 (1819).

21. *Opinion on the Constitutionality of a Bill for Establishing a National Bank, in* 19 PAPERS OF THOMAS JEFFERSON 275, 279 (Julian P. Boyd ed., 1974).

22. *McCulloch*, 17 U.S. at 418.

23. *Id.* at 408.

24. *Id.* at 417.

25. *Id.* at 428.

26. *Id.* at 411.

27. *Id.* at 421.

28. *Id.*

29. See Luxton v. N. River Bridge Co., 153 U.S. 525, 529 (1894); see also Union Pac. R.R. Co. v. Peniston, 85 U.S. 5, 28 (1873).

30. United States v. Comstock, 130 S. Ct. 1949 (2010).

31. *Id.* at 1955.

32. JACK M. BALKIN, LIVING ORIGINALISM 154–155 (2011). My argument here is elaborated in KOPPELMAN, *supra* note 4.

33. United States v. Darby, 312 U.S. 100, 118 (1941).

34. Barnett did not develop this claim in his first formulation of the objection to the ACA, which ignored the Necessary and Proper problem. RANDY BARNETT ET AL., HERITAGE FOUND., WHY THE PERSONAL MANDATE TO BUY HEALTH INSURANCE IS UNPRECEDENTED AND UNCONSTITUTIONAL (Dec. 9, 2009), http://www.heritage.org/research/reports/2009/12/why-the-personal-mandate-to-buy-health-insurance-is-unprecedented-and-unconstitutional. Despite this huge gap, the argument quickly gathered a large following: exactly two weeks after it was published, every Republican voted to support Senator John Ensign's point of order against the ACA on the ground that it exceeded Congress's commerce power. 153 CONG. RECORD. 13,830–13831 (2009). Later work noted the interdependence. Randy E. Barnett, *Commandeering the People: Why the Individual Health Insurance Mandate is Unconstitutional*, 5 N.Y.U. J.L. & LIBERTY 581 (2010). But this argument still doesn't work without specifying some additional reason why this particular choice of means is improper.

35. United States v. Lopez, 514 U.S. 549 (1995).

36. United States v. Morrison, 529 U.S. 598 (2000).

37. *Lopez*, 514 U.S. at 567–568.

38. NFIB v. Sebelius, 132 S. Ct. 2566, 2592 (2012) (Roberts, C.J.).

39. *Id.* at 2593.

40. Printz v. United States, 521 U.S. 898 (1997).

41. *Id.* at 923–924.

42. *Id.* at 923.

43. Alden v. Maine 527 U.S. 706 (1999).

44. *Id.* at 732.

45. *NFIB*, 132 S. Ct. at 2627 (Ginsburg, J., concurring in part, concurring in the judgment in part, and dissenting in part).

46. *Id.* at 2627–2628.

47. *Id.* at 2627 n.10.

48. Einer Elhauge, *If Health Insurance Mandates Are Unconstitutional, Why Did the Founding Fathers Back Them?* NEW REPUBLIC ONLINE (Apr. 13, 2012), http://www.tnr.com/article/politics/102620/individual-mandate-history-affordable-care-act.

49. *NFIB*, 132 S. Ct. at 2586 n.3.

50. Emergency Banking Relief Act of 1933, Pub. L. No. 73-1, 48 Stat. 1 (1933).

51. Gary Lawson & David B. Kopel, *Bad News for Professor Koppelman: The Incidental Unconstitutionality of the Individual Mandate*, 121 YALE L.J. ONLINE 267 (2011), http://yalelawjournal.org/2011/11/08/lawson&kopel.html. They repeated their arguments in an amicus brief, coauthored with Robert G. Natelson and Guy Seidman, in the Supreme Court. Brief of Authors of The Origins of the Necessary and Proper Clause as Amici Curiae Supporting Respondents, Dep't of Health & Human Servs. v. Florida, 132 S. Ct. 2763 (2012) (No. 11-398) [hereinafter Brief of Authors of The Origins]. I respond to their argument in Andrew Koppelman, *Bad News for Everybody: Lawson and Kopel on Health Care Reform and Originalism*, 121 YALE L.J. ONLINE 515 (2012), http://yalelawjournal.org/2012/03/06/koppelman.html. They respond to my response in Gary Lawson & David B, Kopel, *Bad News for John Marshall*, 121 YALE L.J. ONLINE 529 (2012), http://yalelawjournal.org/2012/03/06/lawson&kopel.html. The present chapter will be the first time that I have responded to that rejoinder. The exchange was provoked by Andrew Koppelman, *Bad News for Mail Robbers: The Obvious Constitutionality of Health Care Reform*, 121 YALE L.J. ONLINE 1 (2011), http://yalelawjournal.org/2011/04/26/koppelman.html.

52. David B. Kopel, *The Bar Review Version of* NFIB v. Sebelius, SCOTUSBLOG (July 6, 2012), http://www.scotusblog.com/2012/07/online-symposium-the-bar-review-version-of-

nfib-v-sebelius/. In this piece, Kopel did not mention his own earlier work, but he did attribute to Roberts ideas from that work that did not appear in the opinion.

53. That it is dictum is shown by Neil Siegel in his chapter in this volume.

54. Lawson & Kopel, *Bad News for Professor Koppelman, supra* note 51, at 270.

55. *Id.* at 271. They also argued, in both their article and their Supreme Court brief, that an exercise of power must treat citizens impartially, "with an eye towards the interests of *all* affected persons." *Id.* at 288; Brief of Authors of The Origins, *supra* note 51, at 33–36. This requirement is violated by a mandate that requires people to buy insurance "in order to subsidize other people." *Id.* at 37; Lawson & Kopel, *Bad News for Professor Koppelman, supra* note 51, at 288. This argument misconstrues the purpose of the mandate. See Koppelman, *Bad News for Everybody, supra* note 51, at 521. Roberts ignored it.

56. Lawson & Kopel, *Bad News for Professor Koppelman supra* note 51, at 273 (quoting Giles Jacob, A New Law-Dictionary (London, Strahan et al., 10th ed. 1782)).

57. Robert G. Natelson, *The Legal Origins of the Necessary and Proper Clause, in* Gary Lawson et al., The Origins of the Necessary and Proper Clause 52, 61 (2010) [hereinafter Origins].

58. Lawson and Kopel respond to this difficulty by arguing that, under a 1711 English statute, "the power to 'establish' a post office seems directly to have included the power to define and punish crimes against the post office." Lawson & Kopel, *Bad News for Professor Koppelman, supra* note 51, at 278 n.2. But the only evidence they offer for this proposition is the title of the English statute, "An Act for Establishing a General Post Office," the substance of which extends to defining crimes against the post office. It will take more than one statute's casual use of a label to establish that the shared semantic meaning of "post office," evident to any reasonable person in the eighteenth century, included the apparatus of criminal justice.

59. Natelson, *The Legal Origins of the Necessary and Proper Clause, supra* note 57, at 62.

60. *McCulloch,* 17 U.S. at 413–421.

61. See Robert G. Natelson, *The Framing and Adoption of the Necessary and Proper Clause, in* Origins, at 84, 114–119.

62. Lawson & Kopel, *Bad News for Professor Koppelman, supra* note 51, at 283.

63. Brief of Authors of The Origins, *supra* note 51, at 25–27.

64. Lawson & Kopel, *Bad News for Professor Koppelman supra* note 51, at 283. They do, however, express doubt that the federal government has any power to regulate the insurance industry. *Id.* at 271 n.14.

65. *Id.* at 284 n.66.

66. *Id.* at 283.

67. See William Baude, *Rethinking the Federal Eminent Domain Power,* 122 Yale L.J. (forthcoming 2013).

68. Lawson & Kopel, *Bad News for John Marshall, supra* note 51, at 535–556.

69. NFIB v. Sebelius, 132 S. Ct. 2566, 2592 (2012) (Roberts, C.J.).

70. *Id.* Here Roberts threatens to obliterate the Necessary and Proper Clause, which, if it does anything at all, adds to the regulatory scope of the enumerated powers.

71. District Court Judge Roger Vinson (N.D. Fla.), the district court judge who tried to invalidate the entire statute, was drawn to the same argument. See Koppelman, *Bad News for Mail Robbers, supra* note 51, at 9.

72. Stephen Sachs disputes my use (in earlier writings) of the analogy. The mandate, he observes, is designed to keep the Act from destroying insurance companies, which could religiously observe the pre-existing-conditions rule until the day they file for bankruptcy. In that sense, the mandate doesn't help carry the ban on preexisting-condition discrimination *into effect,* in the way that a ban on robbing the mail helps execute the power to move letters from Point *A* to Point *B.* What the mandate does is prevent entirely collateral consequences of the ACA's other provisions, which otherwise might make the ACA a really lousy idea. Stephen E. Sachs, *The Uneasy Case for the Affordable Care Act,* 75 L. & Contemp. Probs. 17, 24 (2012). But it's not clear that Sachs has entirely succeeded in rehabilitating the ban on mail robbery.

Post offices sell services and so are repositories of currency, like any other business. If the robber simply empties the till, without disturbing mail awaiting delivery, then it is not clear that he has brought himself within congressional power, on Sachs's account. It is possible to deliver mail while enduring the occasional robbery. More generally, the proposition that Congress has no power to deal with the collateral consequences of its own actions would hamstring it in multiple areas. The law upheld in *Comstock* prevents entirely collateral consequences of the federal criminal code's other provisions.Sachs adds: "Of course, Congress can accompany a valid law with other measures 'conducive to its beneficial exercise'—but only when those measures are in fact 'incidental to the power' actually granted." *Id.* at 24 (citing *McCulloch*, 17 U.S. at 418); see also Natelson, The Legal Origins of the Necessary and Proper Clause, *in* ORIGINS, *supra* note 57, at 60–68 (2010) (discussing the doctrine of incidental powers). Here he cites the Natelson-Lawson-Kopel thesis, which it is the burden of this chapter to rebut.

73. United States v. Comstock, 130 S. Ct. 1949, 1961 (2010) (internal citation omitted).
74. *NFIB*, 132 S. Ct. at 2592.
75. *Id.*
76. *Id.* at 2589.
77. *Id.* at 2592. A similar argument was offered to the Court in a brief by Prof. Ilya Somin, which may have influenced Roberts. It claimed that the mandate is "improper" because upholding it would give Congress virtually unlimited power. Brief of Washington Legal Foundation and Constitutional Law Scholars as Amici Curiae Supporting Respondents at 3, Dep't of Health & Human Servs. v. Florida, 132 S. Ct. 2763 (2012) (No. 11-398).
78. Thanks to Steve Lubet for this formulation.
79. *NFIB*, 132 S. Ct. at 2644 (2012) (Scalia, Kennedy, Thomas, and Alito, JJ., dissenting).
80. *Id.* at 2647.
81. *Id.*
82. Their last sentence is correct that the functional equivalent of the mandate would be a tax credit for purchasing insurance. But then they would need to explain, first, why the functional equivalence does not run both ways, thus sustaining the statute that Congress actually passed, and second, why they are sure that the tax credit would have the same behavioral effects.
83. *Id.* at 2646 (quoting ALEXANDER HAMILTON, THE FEDERALIST NO. 33, at 202 (Clinton Rossiter ed., 1961)). In context, Hamilton was caricaturing the views of those who opposed broad federal power under the Necessary and Proper Clause.
84. *Id.* at 2591.
85. *Id.* at 2647.
86. *Id.* at 2619 n.5.
87. Koppelman, *Bad News for Everybody, supra* note 51, at 522.
88. Lawson & Kopel, *Bad News for Professor Koppelman, supra* note 51, at 270.
89. Lawson & Kopel, *Bad News for John Marshall, supra* note 51, at 535–536.
90. Whatever one's views about constitutional methodology, knowledge of history is valuable for its own sake, and nothing I write here should be taken as impugning their contribution to that field.
91. See the comparative data in Donald S. Lutz, *Toward a Theory of Constitutional Amendment, in* RESPONDING TO IMPERFECTION: THE THEORY AND PRACTICE OF CONSTITUTIONAL AMENDMENT 261 (Sanford Levinson ed., 1995). The only constitution in Lutz's chart that is more difficult to amend is that of Yugoslavia, which has since ceased to exist.
92. Robert L. Stern, *The Commerce That Concerns More States Than One*, 47 HARV. L. REV. 1335, 1335 (1934).
93. *NFIB*, 132 S. Ct. at 2589.
94. Brief of Authors of The Origins, *supra* note 51, at 30. Randy Barnett makes essentially the same argument in his own brief, thus relying upon it to fill the gap in his earlier claims about the limits of the Necessary and Proper Clause: "The awesome power to compel commerce

is the type of 'great and substantive independent power' that the Framers never would have left to mere inference from the traditional power to regulate commerce." Brief for Private Respondents on the Individual Mandate at 57–58, Dep't of Health & Human Servs. v. Florida, 132 S. Ct. 2763 (2012) (No. 11-398). See also Caleb Nelson, Sovereign Immunity as a Doctrine of Personal Jurisdiction, 115 Harv. L. Rev. 1559, 1640 (2002) (suggesting that powers are "great substantive and independent powers" if they "seem like things that the Constitution would specifically grant if Congress was to have them")). Natelson and Kopel offer a somewhat different formulation in another article, writing, in an imaginary Marshall opinion invalidating the ACA, that "regulation of health within the several states" is "a subject at least as substantive and independent, and as 'worthy,' as the regulation of commerce among the states." Robert G. Natelson & David B. Kopel, *"Health Laws of Every Description": John Marshall's Ruling on a Federal Health Care Law*, 12 Engage 49, 52 (2011). This argument reaches beyond the mandate; it would dissolve the entire structure of federal regulation of medicine, and might invalidate Medicare and Medicaid as well.

95. *NFIB*, 132 S. Ct. at 2589.

# CHAPTER 8

# The Presumption of Constitutionality and the Individual Mandate

*Gillian E. Metzger and Trevor W. Morrison*

## 1. Introduction

Every American law student learns that there is a difference between a statute's meaning and its constitutionality. A given case might well present both issues, but law students are taught that the questions are distinct and that their resolution requires separate analyses. This is all for good reason: the distinction between statutory meaning and constitutional validity is both real and important. But it is not complete. Any approach to statutory interpretation depends on a view about the appropriate role of the judiciary (or other institutional interpreter) in our constitutional system; "[a]ny theory of statutory interpretation is at base a theory about constitutional law."[1] Moreover, some specific rules of statutory interpretation can themselves be understood as modes of constitutional implementation.

*NFIB v. Sebelius*[2]—and, in particular, the constitutionality of the Affordable Care Act (ACA)'s "individual mandate" under the tax power—is a prime example of constitutional and statutory intertwining. The crux of the tax question in the case was whether Congress permissibly exercised its tax power when it enacted the individual mandate. This was a question of both statutory meaning and constitutional validity: was the mandate permissibly understood to impose a tax, and did it represent a constitutional exercise of Congress's tax authority? According to some—including, critically, Chief Justice Roberts—the tax power cannot be used to impose commands. In the Chief Justice's view, Congress can tax an otherwise lawful action or failure to act, but it cannot use its tax power to enforce a command that individuals act or not act in a particular way. Under that standard, the mandate could be upheld under the tax power only if it could be interpreted as taxing the decision not to purchase insurance without rendering that decision unlawful. Hence, whether the mandate could be upheld as a tax turned on whether it could be construed, as a matter of statutory meaning, to fit this constitutional definition of a tax.

The correct answer was not obvious from the text of the mandate or the ACA as a whole. On the one hand, under the ACA the sole legal consequence of a covered individual's failure to purchase insurance is that it triggers an additional fee, payable on the individual's annual tax return. That fact—combined with the ACA's multiple references to the tax code and Congress's reliance on estimates that the mandate would raise $4 billion annually—weighed in favor of viewing the mandate as a tax but not a command. On the other hand, and in contrast to the ACA's express references to taxes elsewhere in the legislation, the ACA refers to the mandate and its fee in terms of a "requirement" and a "penalty," not a tax. For those and other reasons, it could be argued that the mandate was most naturally viewed as an exercise of the commerce power, not the tax power.

Although the parties and the justices did not acknowledge the point with any great clarity, resolving this statutory ambiguity required choosing between two constitutionally based rules of statutory construction: the principle that statutes should be construed, where possible, to avoid serious doubts about their unconstitutionality, and the requirement that Congress must clearly invoke its tax power before a court will review the challenged legislation as an exercise of that power. Chief Justice Roberts's controlling opinion embraced the first of these rules, commonly known as the canon of constitutional avoidance. By contrast, the joint dissent implicitly opted for the second, essentially imposing a clear statement rule on invocations of the tax power.

We think that the Chief Justice took the right approach, but the choice of which of these rules to apply requires fuller justification than the Chief Justice supplied. In particular, we argue that adequately answering this question necessitates a more forthright engagement with statutory interpretation as a mode of constitutional implementation. That engagement should be framed around one of the bedrock principles governing judicial review of most legislation— the presumption of constitutionality. Ultimately, we show that analyzing the tax question in *NFIB* against the presumption of constitutionality not only supports the Chief Justice's application of the canon of constitutional avoidance, but also indicates that the proper clear statement rule to apply with respect to Congress's use of its tax power is the opposite of that suggested by the joint dissent: The Court should not conclude that Congress refused to exercise its tax power, or any other head of legislative authority, unless Congress expressly stated that refusal in the statute at issue.

## 2. Constitution-Implementing Rules of Statutory Interpretation

We begin by describing two familiar interpretive approaches, the canon of constitutional avoidance and clear statement rules. As noted above, these principles were invoked, explicitly or implicitly, by the contending sides in *NFIB v. Sebelius*. Both approaches blend inquiries into statutory meaning with enforcement of constitutional norms. Yet in certain contexts they can have dramatically different consequences.

### A. THE CANON OF CONSTITUTIONAL AVOIDANCE

In its most common articulation, the canon of constitutional avoidance provides that "where an otherwise acceptable construction of a statute would raise serious constitutional problems, the Court will construe the statute to avoid such problems unless such construction is plainly contrary to the intent of Congress."[3] Most famously associated with Justice Brandeis's concurrence in *Ashwander v. Tennessee Valley Authority*,[4] the avoidance canon has long been embraced by the Court as a "'cardinal principle' of statutory interpretation."[5]

Although it is common to speak of a single avoidance canon, in fact there are two different versions of the rule. The first, which Adrian Vermeule helpfully terms "classical avoidance,"[6] provides that "as between two possible interpretations of a statute, by one of which it would be unconstitutional and by the other valid, [a court's] plain duty is to adopt that which will save the Act."[7] The second, which Vermeule calls "modern avoidance,"[8] is the one quoted in the above paragraph and most frequently invoked by courts today. The key difference between the two is that classical avoidance applies only when the otherwise preferred reading of a statute is in fact unconstitutional, while modern avoidance applies whenever there is serious doubt about the constitutionality of that reading.[9]

The Supreme Court's early practice employed classical avoidance, which it justified on dual grounds: first, that due respect for a coordinate branch of government entails assuming that its work product was intended to pass constitutional muster; and second, that unelected federal courts should minimize, to the extent consistent with their *Marbury* duty, the occasions on which they invalidate the work of the political branches.[10] But in a 1909 case, *United States ex rel. Attorney General v. Delaware & Hudson Co.*, the Court expressed concern that classical avoidance entails providing what amounts to an advisory opinion.[11] To address that concern, the Court reasoned that rather than finding a particular statutory reading unconstitutional only to reject it in favor of a saving construction, courts should instead construe statutes to avoid readings that raise serious constitutional concerns, without finally resolving those concerns. Courts, in other words, should employ modern avoidance.

Like classical avoidance, modern avoidance is typically justified as an instrument of judicial restraint.[12] And although the Court did not initially put it this way, contemporary accounts of modern avoidance also suggest that the canon respects congressional intent.[13] On this account, Congress is presumed to intend to legislate within constitutional limits and to avoid legislating in a way that pushes the constitutional envelope.

More than classical avoidance, modern avoidance has been subject to substantial academic criticism. Two lines of criticism are dominant. The first targets the notion that Congress truly intends to avoid constitutional doubts, not just outright unconstitutionality. As Judge Friendly explained, a rational legislator would likely prefer a court to resolve decisively any constitutional doubts it has about the otherwise best reading of a statute: "[T]here is always the chance...that the doubts will be settled favorably, and if they are not, the conceded rule of construing to avoid unconstitutionality will come into operation and save the day. People in such a heads-I-win, tails-you-lose position do not readily sacrifice it."[14] There is also the fact that Congress is a "they," not an "it."[15] Attributing a collective belief in the constitutionality of its work product may assign to the full body something not actually present in the mind of each member who voted for a given bill.

On the other hand, given that the initial move from classical to modern avoidance was not justified on congressional intent grounds but was instead aimed at avoiding the advisory opinion problem, this criticism of the canon as deviating from actual congressional intent may be something of a non sequitur. If classical avoidance tracks congressional intent, and if modern avoidance is the closest the courts can come to classical avoidance without creating advisory opinion concerns, modern avoidance's poor fit with congressional intent might be tolerable. Moreover, even if classical avoidance does not lead to truly impermissible advisory opinions,[16] it does generate fully elaborated constitutional analyses in a way that modern avoidance does not. Thus, following Justice Brandeis's desire to minimize the number of judicial pronouncements on the Constitution one way or the other, modern avoidance might again be justifiable despite not always closely tracking congressional intent.

The second main criticism of modern avoidance takes issue with the premise of the defense just offered: it asserts that modern avoidance does not, in fact, avoid the unnecessary making of constitutional law. In cases where the canon applies, the reviewing court engages the constitutional issue enough to discard its otherwise preferred reading of the statute. As Judge Posner puts it, even if such engagements do not yield definitive rulings on constitutional questions, they nevertheless create a "judge-made constitutional 'penumbra' that has much the same prohibitory effect as the...Constitution itself."[17] That might go a bit too far; there are important differences between modern avoidance's engagement with the Constitution and an analysis that reaches a definitive conclusion on a constitutional question. Still, Judge Posner and others leveling this criticism are clearly correct that modern avoidance does not avoid the Constitution altogether. In that sense, it arguably fails the task Justice Brandeis set for it in *Ashwander*.[18]

There is, however, an alternative account of the avoidance canon. As Ernest Young has described, modern avoidance can be viewed as "designed not to reflect what Congress might have wanted under particular conditions, but rather to give voice to [the] normative values" that are "embodied in the underlying constitutional provisions that create the constitutional 'doubt.'"[19] When implemented through the avoidance canon, those constitutional provisions operate as what Young calls "resistance norms"—constitutionally grounded "rules that raise obstacles to particular governmental actions without barring those actions entirely."[20] Put another way, the modern avoidance canon is a tool of both statutory construction and constitutional implementation. Indeed, it renders statutory construction a mode of constitutional implementation.

This resistance norm account of avoidance is decidedly not how Justice Brandeis or other early proponents of modern avoidance understood it.[21] It is, however, largely immune to the two criticisms of modern avoidance described above. If the purpose of avoidance is to protect constitutional values by "rais[ing] the cost of any congressional encroachment within a particular area of constitutional sensitivity,"[22] then its divergence from congressional intent is not deeply troubling. The constitutional resistance norm simply trumps congressional intent. Meanwhile, Judge Posner's complaint that avoidance creates a penumbral Constitution becomes not so much an indictment of avoidance as a description of its purpose.[23]

## B. CONSTITUTIONAL CLEAR STATEMENT RULES

Clear statement rules represent yet another method of statutory construction with a deep connection to constitutional norms. In a number of contexts the Court requires Congress to speak clearly before a statute will be read as trenching on important constitutional values. Prominent among these "constitutionally inspired 'clear statement rules'" are requirements aimed at protecting federalism.[24] Examples include the rule that Congress must expressly state its intention to abrogate state sovereign immunity, the presumption against preemption, and *Gregory v. Ashcroft*'s insistence that "if Congress intends to alter the usual constitutional balance between the States and the Federal Government, it must make its intention to do so unmistakably clear in the language of the statute."[25]

Some of these federalism clear statement rules apply more stringently than others. In particular, the Court often finds state law preempted on an implied basis, whereas it does not conclude Congress intended to abrogate state sovereign immunity absent fairly clear statutory language to that effect.[26] These variations notwithstanding, these rules are all techniques of using statutory construction, rather than direct constitutional adjudication, to protect a constitutionally based balance between federal and state authority. As John Manning has put it, these "clear statement rules share the defining feature of trying to safeguard constitutional values without the more obviously countermajoritarian step of invalidating acts of Congress."[27]

Clear statement rules bear a close resemblance to the canon of constitutional avoidance in that both implement constitutional norms through statutory interpretation.[28] Indeed, they often operate in the same fashion, with courts interpreting statutes to avoid trenching on the constitutional values at stake. One notable difference, however, is that constitutional clear statement rules often apply in contexts in which no constitutional bar prevents Congress from undertaking the action at issue. In such cases, Congress usually can respond to judicial decisions applying a clear statement requirement by expressly authorizing the action, and the Court will not hold Congress's action unconstitutional. By contrast, in constitutional avoidance contexts there is often a real risk that the alternative disfavored interpretation would be found unconstitutional, and thus Congress does not have the same room to respond with express authorization.[29] Yet the significant practical obstacles to reenacting a statutory provision with the requisite clarity minimize the import of this distinction in practice, and the constitutional avoidance canon is often characterized as one species of the wider genus of constitutional clear statement rules.[30]

Not surprisingly then, many of the complaints lodged against the avoidance canon are also raised against constitutional clear statement rules more generally. They are attacked for leading courts to deviate from likely congressional intent and for illegitimately increasing constitutional constraints on the legislature.[31] The latter criticism is even more applicable to constitutional clear statement rules than to the avoidance canon, since such rules typically apply in circumstances where Congress undoubtedly has the authority to take the underlying legislative step at issue. Defenders of constitutional clear statement rules often respond that the constitutional norms served by such rules tend to be underenforced in direct litigation, due to limits on judicial competence and a doctrinal tendency to treat the underlying norm as better suited to political enforcement. On this view, constitutional clear statement rules are a legitimate means of ensuring that constitutional norms are given their due weight by the legislature.[32] Thus, for example, some argue that requiring Congress to clearly state when it is burdening the states helps reinforce the political safeguards of federalism found in the Constitution—an approach often referred to as "process federalism."[33] Requiring such clear language from Congress engages these political safeguards by obliging Congress to confront the issue directly in order to achieve the federalism-implicating result.[34]

Whether justified or not, little debate exists over the effect of constitutional clear statement rules. They make it more difficult for Congress to legislate in certain ways and contexts or on certain issues. In addition, clear statement rules serve to make Congress's specific legislative language more constitutionally important than is usually the case. Although rooted in substantive normative concerns, clear statement rules put a premium on congressional choice of labels and other procedural legislative choices.[35] As a result, clear statement rules stand in some tension with the Court's general approach of not policing congressional procedures or requiring proof that Congress adequately considered the merits of enacted legislation unless the legislation implicates individual constitutional rights that trigger heightened scrutiny.[36] On the other hand, at least in the federalism context, constitutional clear statement rules find some support in recent decisions suggesting that Congress must identify the factual predicate for a statute in order for it to fall within certain heads of legislative authority.[37]

Despite their overlap and shared underpinnings, there is one area in which the avoidance canon and clear statement rules lead to diametrically opposed results. That area involves questions about the precise head of legislative authority pursuant to which Congress enacted the statute in question. If the courts were to require Congress to expressly invoke particular sources of legislative authority each time it acts (and if they were to judge the constitutionality of the enactment only against the invoked heads of authority), the result could be a large increase in the number of measures found unconstitutional. Potential bases for upholding a statute that Congress did not explicitly invoke would be off the table. The avoidance canon, in contrast, has the opposite effect. If a measure would be a constitutional exercise of a particular head of legislative power, and if it is plausible to read the measure as an exercise of that power, then under the avoidance canon courts should adopt that interpretation whether or not Congress expressly embraced the power in question. Far from requiring Congress to state clearly the authority under which it acts, the avoidance canon suggests that congressional failure to invoke a particular authority should not matter if the measure nonetheless can be read as enacted on that basis.

Interestingly, notwithstanding the Court's growing affection for clear statement rules in recent decades as well as its general affinity for process federalism, it has not adopted clear statement rules of the sort just described—that is, rules requiring Congress to state expressly the head of legislative authority pursuant to which it acts. Instead, the Court has continued to adhere to its long-standing view that "the constitutionality of action taken by Congress does not depend on recitals of the power which it undertakes to exercise."[38] Indeed, at times the Court has analyzed whether federal legislation falls within the scope of powers that Congress plainly did not invoke.[39] Thus, for example, although over the last fifteen years the Court has imposed greater limits on Congress's power under Section 5 of the Fourteenth Amendment, it has not demanded that Congress expressly invoke Section 5 before assessing whether the statute in question satisfies its substantive standards. In short, clear statement rules have been applied to determine a statute's substantive scope, but generally not to determine whether it falls within a particular head of legislative authority.[40]

## 3. THE ACA LITIGATION AND THE TAX POWER QUESTION

The canon of constitutional avoidance, clear statement rules, and the choice of which to apply when determining whether Congress acted under a particular head of authority all took center stage in *NFIB*. A number of lower courts refused to address the constitutionality of the individual mandate under the tax power on the ground that Congress had not signaled its intent to invoke that power with adequate clarity. In so holding, those courts emphasized several textual features of the ACA, in particular that Congress denominated the financial imposition for failing to purchase insurance a "penalty," despite describing it as a tax in earlier drafts of the legislation and despite calling other ACA impositions taxes. They also noted that Congress had included numerous findings to demonstrate that the mandate fell under the commerce power but none to support invocation of the tax power, such as findings on the amount of revenue the measure was expected to generate from those who paid the penalty rather than purchase insurance.[41]

The opinion that devoted the most attention to Congress's purported refusal to invoke the tax power may have been that of the district court in *Health and Human Services v. Florida*. There, Judge Vinson argued that "regardless of whether the exaction could otherwise qualify as a tax …, it cannot be regarded as one if it clearly appears that Congress did not intend it to be," and "it is inarguably clear that Congress did not intend for the exaction to be regarded as a tax."[42] He relied on the Supreme Court's early twentieth-century opinion in *Helwig v. United States* for the proposition that congressional intent controls, and that "in the absence of any declaration by Congress affecting the manner in which the provision shall be treated, courts must decide the matter in accordance with their views of the nature of the act."[43] Although acknowledging that current doctrine does not require Congress to identify a particular source of power in order for it to apply, Judge Vinson nonetheless stressed Congress's failure to invoke the tax power explicitly:

> Congress should not be permitted to secure and cast politically diffi-
> cult votes on controversial legislation by deliberately calling something

one thing, after which defenders of that legislation take an "Alice-in-Wonderland" tack and argue in court that Congress really meant something else entirely, thereby circumventing the safeguard that exists to keep their broad power in check. If Congress intended for the penalty to be a tax, it should go back and make that intent clear (for example, by calling it a tax, relying on Congress's Constitutional taxing power, allowing it to be collected and enforced as a tax, or identifying revenue to be raised).[44]

This was tantamount to imposing a clear statement rule. Judge Vinson's embrace of that approach does not appear to have been deterred by the fact that it would lead to finding a federal statute unconstitutional. That is, Judge Vinson neither acknowledged the novelty of imposing a clear statement rule for the purposes of identifying the source of legislative authority pursuant to which Congress legislates, nor justified the dramatically different consequence of applying such a rule in that context as compared to the contexts in which clear statement rules are typically imposed.

The joint dissent at the Supreme Court acknowledged that under the canon of constitutional avoidance, the Court "must, if fairly possible, construe the provision to be a tax rather than a mandate-with-penalty, since that would render it constitutional rather than unconstitutional."[45] Nonetheless, in practice the dissenters' approach was similar to Judge Vinson's, emphasizing statutory evidence that, they thought, precluded reading the mandate as a tax. According to the joint dissent, "to say that the Individual Mandate merely imposes a tax is not to interpret the statute but to rewrite it." Moreover, such rewriting in the tax context raised constitutional accountability concerns: "Imposing a tax through judicial legislation inverts the constitutional scheme, and places the power to tax in the branch of government least accountable to the citizenry."[46] Its acknowledgment of the avoidance canon notwithstanding, the joint dissent's analysis thus seems more in line with a clear statement approach, especially in its insistence that the Court had "never—never—treated as a tax an exaction which faces up to the critical difference between a tax and a penalty, and explicitly denominates the exaction a penalty."[47]

Chief Justice Roberts saw the statutory text and the governing constitutional considerations quite differently. He criticized the joint dissent for treating the labels Congress used as determinative of the constitutional inquiry, and emphasized instead the broad scope of Congress's taxing authority, together with the avoidance canon. In his view, it was sufficient under the Court's precedents that "Congress had the power to impose the exaction in [the mandate] under the taxing power, and that [the mandate] need not be read to do more than impose a tax."[48] On the latter point, the Chief Justice agreed that "[t]he most straightforward read-ing of the mandate is that it commands individuals to purchase insurance," which he deemed to be beyond Congress's authority under the Commerce and Necessary and Proper Clauses. But he maintained that determining "the most natural interpretation of the mandate" was not the proper inquiry. In light of the avoidance canon, the question instead was whether it was "fairly possible" or "reasonable" to read the mandate as imposing a tax on the deci-sion not to purchase insurance. Finding that the mandate could reasonably be so characterized, Roberts sustained it under the tax power.[49]

Some have criticized the Chief Justice for applying the canon of constitutional avoidance to the tax power question at all. According to Nicholas Rosenkranz, it was fundamentally misguided to apply avoidance in this case because avoidance applies only to questions of statutory interpretation, and not to matters of what Rozenkranz calls "constitutional characterization." In Rosenkranz's view, by con-struing the mandate to afford a choice between purchasing insurance and paying a tax, "The Chief is not *interpreting* the meaning of a statute to avoid a constitu-tional problem. Instead he is *characterizing* a statute—whose meaning is not in doubt—to be a tax for purposes of the Constitution."[50] And that, Rosenkranz maintains, was a kind of category mistake: it applied the avoidance canon where it does not belong.

The problem with this argument is its premise—that the "meaning" of the mandate and its accompanying exaction is "not in doubt." Rosenkranz sees no doubt on the matter because he sees no operative difference between a provision that makes it unlawful not to purchase insurance and then sanctions offenders by requiring them to pay a penalty, and a provision that allows individuals to choose between purchasing insurance and paying a tax equal in size to the penalty in the first scenario. In making this argument, Rosenkranz endorses a view (com-monly associated with Holmes's "bad man") that all that matters in determining legal meaning is the law's material consequences.[51] But that is not the only way to view the law, and clearly the Chief Justice did not adopt that view in *NFIB*. Instead, he saw a difference in legal meaning (as well as constitutional permissibil-ity, for purposes of the tax power) between (1) a command to purchase insurance that renders nonpurchases unlawful and (2) a choice between the equally lawful alternatives of purchasing insurance and paying a tax. In a sense, the difference is largely expressive: it has to do with whether the law expresses a view that the failure to purchase insurance is unlawful. But because the Chief Justice saw that difference as significant as a matter of statutory meaning, and because that same difference also tracked his view of the contours of Congress's legislative authority under the tax power, it was not a category mistake for him to invoke avoidance.

The Chief Justice's use of avoidance is vulnerable to other criticisms, however. First, he construed the mandate as a tax only after considering and definitively rejecting the constitutionality of a command-based reading of the mandate under the Commerce Clause. The Chief Justice claimed that he had to structure his analysis that way:

> [T]he statute reads more naturally as a command to buy insurance than as a tax, and I would uphold it as a command if the Constitution allowed it. It is only because the Commerce Clause does not authorize such a command that it is necessary to reach the taxing power question. And it is only because we have a duty to construe a statute to save it, if fairly possible, that [the mandate] can be interpreted as a tax. Without deciding the Commerce Clause question, I would find no basis to adopt such a saving construction.[52]

By claiming he needed to resolve the Commerce Clause question and not simply note the existence of a serious doubt as to the mandate's constitutionality under that head of authority, the Chief Justice embraced classical, not modern, avoidance. In that respect, his approach is at odds with the dominant way the Court has employed the avoidance canon for the last century. And for that reason, he was simply wrong, doctrinally and logically, to say that he would have no basis to adopt the saving construction of the mandate without first deciding the Commerce Clause question. Applying modern avoidance, he needed only to note a serious question as to the mandate's constitutionality under the Commerce Clause before proceeding directly to the tax question.

The Chief Justice's analysis is open to a second criticism as well. In contrast to having said too much about the commerce issue, he did too little to justify the sharp contrast he drew between statutory and constitutional questions. When determining the constitutionality of the mandate under the tax power, the Chief Justice treated the ACA's key statutory language very differently than when he addressed the threshold question whether the Anti-Injunction Act (AIA) barred the courts from hearing any constitutional challenges to the mandate until it went into effect. In addressing the latter issue, he placed great weight on the particular label Congress used in the ACA. Because Congress denominated the imposition a penalty instead of a tax, he reasoned, the AIA's prohibition of suits "for the purpose of restraining the assessment or collection of any tax" did not apply.[53] Yet the term penalty did not stop the Chief Justice from construing the mandate as a tax for constitutional purposes. He justified the divergence on the ground that one issue is purely statutory while the latter is constitutional:

> It is of course true that the Act describes the payment as a "penalty," not a "tax." But while that label is fatal to the application of the [AIA], it does not determine whether the payment may be viewed as an exercise

of Congress's taxing power. It is up to Congress whether to apply the [AIA] to any particular statute, so it makes sense to be guided by Congress's choice of label on that question. That choice does not, however, control whether an exaction is within Congress's constitutional power to tax.[54]

Simply invoking the difference between the statutory and constitutional domains is not enough, however. The avoidance canon and clear statement rules are both examples of techniques that blend statutory interpretation and constitutional implementation. Yet in insisting that "Congress cannot change whether an exaction is a tax or a penalty for *constitutional* purposes simply by describing it as one or the other,"[55] the Chief Justice failed to acknowledge that many clear statement rules accord great weight to the particular terms Congress uses, or fails to use, in a statute. At the same time, the Chief Justice himself allowed Congress's choice of language to affect his constitutional analysis, in that his deployment of the avoidance canon depended on his determination that the saving construction (i.e., that the mandate is a tax, not a command) is "fairly possible" as a matter of the statutory text.

The Chief Justice thus did not come fully to terms with the critical analytical questions at the heart both of this case and, more broadly, of a range of related issues linking statutory meaning and constitutional validity. When and how should Congress's choice of particular statutory language affect whether a statute is properly understood as an exercise of a particular head of legislative power? To what extent can Congress reject a particular head of power as the basis for sustaining an enactment against constitutional challenge? And why is the constitutional avoidance canon the appropriate device here, rather than a clear statement approach? To be sure, the joint dissent itself fares no better. It never squarely addresses the critical questions. To make matters worse, it obscures the key interpretive decisions by applying a clear statement requirement while invoking the avoidance canon.

# 4. Statutory Interpretation and Congressional Power: Implications from the Presumption of Constitutionality

These questions about the proper relationship between statutory interpretation and underlying congressional authority admit of no easy answers. A logical place to start, however, is with the basic posture courts adopt when reviewing most constitutional challenges, including to tax legislation: the presumption of constitutionality. In the areas where it applies, the presumption of constitutionality is a fundamental premise of judicial review. By attending to it, we can establish a fuller justification for the constitutional avoidance-based approach favored by the Chief Justice and also isolate the key shortcomings in the joint dissent's preference for a clear statement requirement.

## A. THE PRESUMPTION OF CONSTITUTIONALITY

The presumption of constitutionality states that, except where fundamental rights are implicated, courts should not hold legislation unconstitutional unless the unconstitutionality is clear.[56] In its most aggressive form, articulated famously by James Bradley Thayer, the presumption of constitutionality regards Congress as the institution with primary responsibility for interpreting the Constitution.[57] As Thayer put it, "the constitution often admits of different interpretations; ... there is often a range of choice and judgment; ... in such cases the constitution does not impose upon the legislature any one specific opinion, but leaves open this range of choice; and ... whatever choice is rational is constitutional."[58]

Although influential and "attractive to great judges,"[59] Thayer's particular approach sits uneasily with how the Supreme Court has come to understand its role. Invoking *Marbury v. Madison* for the proposition that it is the judiciary's special role to "say what the law is," the modern Court has insisted that the power of judicial review is the power to exercise independent judgment about a law's constitutionality.[60] Yet at the same time, the Court has retained a somewhat more modest version of the presumption, repeatedly stating that "[r]espect for a coordinate branch of Government forbids striking down an Act of Congress except upon a clear showing of unconstitutionality."[61] Put another way, although the Court's determination of constitutional invalidity always trumps the contrary judgment of a coordinate branch, the Court should not lightly arrive at such a determination.

In this form, the presumption of constitutionality represents the standard approach that courts take to questions of legislative constitutionality. To be sure, the Court has pulled a number of constitutional challenges outside of the presumption's ambit. In particular, laws implicating fundamental individual rights are typically viewed with judicial suspicion and will be upheld only after searching judicial scrutiny. But legislation merely "adjusting the burdens and benefits of economic life come[s] to the Court with a presumption of constitutionality,"[62] with courts presuming that facts exist to demonstrate the reasonableness of such legislative judgments.[63] Although not immune from scholarly criticism, the presumption of constitutionality is firmly rooted as a matter of judicial practice.

Admittedly, the presumption of constitutionality is by its terms a principle of constitutional adjudication, not statutory interpretation. But it would be a mistake to assume the presumption has no impact on how courts assign statutory meaning. If the presumption of constitutionality leads courts to uphold enactments in the absence of evidence of clear unconstitutionality, then ambiguity in statutory meaning can be one reason why a statute might not be clearly unconstitutional.

## B. THE PRESUMPTION, THE AIA, AND THE TAX POWER

Like the avoidance canon and clear statement requirements, the presumption of constitutionality also surfaced in *NFIB*. The Chief Justice included it in his introductory statement of background constitutional principles,[64] and he referred to it obliquely at the outset of his tax power analysis by emphasizing the importance of "[g]ranting the [ACA] the full measure of deference owed to federal statutes." But when it came to interpreting the ACA's terms, the Chief Justice turned more directly to the avoidance canon. This was not a huge leap, since both the avoidance canon and the presumption tilt in favor of upholding legislation against constitutional attack. Yet had he devoted greater attention to the basis and operation of the presumption, the Chief Justice might have been in a position to offer a more complete defense of his interpretive approach.

One place where Chief Justice Roberts could have put the presumption to good use was in explaining why Congress's choice of the "penalty" label was determinative of the AIA jurisdiction question, but not of whether the mandate could be upheld under the tax power. As noted above, the Chief Justice's insistence that the statutory and constitutional domains are simply separate is unsatisfying, given the obvious connections between the two in some contexts (including in his own opinion, when he turned to the avoidance canon). The presumption of constitutionality, however, offers a more convincing justification.

Whether or not a statutorily denominated "penalty" triggers the AIA jurisdictional bar does not implicate the presumption, because neither answer to that question places the challenged statute in constitutional jeopardy. In contrast, allowing Congress's choice of label to take the tax power completely off the table would have run headlong into the presumption of constitutionality. It would have resulted in the mandate being held unconstitutional even if the substantive operation of the provision fell entirely within Congress's legislative authority. As the Chief Justice explained, it would mean that "even if the Constitution permits Congress to do exactly what we interpret this statute to do, the law must be struck down because Congress used the wrong labels."[65] Such an unforgiving stance is very difficult to square with the idea at the heart of the presumption—that Congress should be presumed to intend to legislate within constitutional bounds. The presumption of constitutionality thus offers a more robust basis for treating the ACA's text quite differently when determining the AIA's application than when assessing the tax power's applicability.

## C. THE PRESUMPTION, AVOIDANCE, CLEAR STATEMENT
## RULES, AND CONGRESSIONAL POWER

It should be clear by now that the presumption of constitutionality and the avoidance canon are closely aligned. Both lead the Court to construe statutes to preserve their constitutionality, where possible. The Court has defended both on similar grounds—respect for Congress's own duty of constitutional fidelity and mindfulness of the countermajoritarian character of judicial review, in addition to Congress's superior institutional ability to make the factual determinations upon which an enactment's constitutionality might depend.[66] The Chief Justice's reliance on the avoidance canon in *NFIB* is thus defensible as consistent with those basic reasons.

What of a clear statement approach? It, too, provides an analytical method for determining whether, in a given case, a particular source of constitutional power is in play. And it at least arguably does so in service of some venerable underlying values. As Judge Vinson suggested in the Florida ACA litigation, process concerns provide the strongest argument for requiring Congress to invoke the tax power clearly before the mandate is upheld as a tax. In recognizing the constitutional breadth of the tax power, the Court has emphasized that "[t]he remedy for excessive taxation is in the hands of Congress, not the courts."[67] A clear statement rule for invoking the tax power could reinforce that political constraint by ensuring that members of Congress were aware that a measure constituted a tax and were on record supporting it as such. As noted above, other constitutional clear statement rules are frequently justified on similar process grounds.[68]

There are a number of problems, however, with adopting a clear statement approach to resolving questions like the tax power issue in *NFIB*. First, even on its own terms, a process-based defense of a tax power clear statement rule is open to question. To begin with, it simply assumes that additional clarity is needed in order to ensure political accountability for exercises of the tax power. But that assumption could be wrong. It seems especially questionable in the context of legislation like the ACA, which was passed after one of the most politically contentious and closely watched legislative battles in recent years, with the ACA's opponents frequently attacking the mandate as a tax.[69] At a minimum, if the assumption about the need for additional clarity is meant to reflect how clear statement rules actually operate on Congress, then further empirical investigation is warranted. In a legislative system like ours that is so replete with "vetogates," any requirement of specific text makes legislation harder to enact.[70] Clear statement rules might simply make certain types of legislative enactments more difficult to pass, without necessarily increasing political accountability in the form of greater congressional or public awareness.

In fact, a clear statement rule might actually undermine democratic values by transferring power from legislative majorities to legislative minorities.[71] True, the process constraints imposed by the constitutional requirements of bicameralism and presentment already inhibit the power of simple majorities in either the House or Senate. But those rules are expressly provided in the Constitution. The mere fact of their existence does not justify heightening minorities' control over legislation still further through the crafting of a new clear statement rule.[72] Indeed, a clear statement requirement for the invocation of the tax power would stand in substantial tension with the breadth of the constitutional grant of the tax power and the lenient standard by which tax legislation is generally reviewed.[73] This marks a stark contrast with other clear statement rules, which aim at protecting well-established constitutional norms such as sovereign immunity.

More fundamentally, subjecting the tax power to a clear statement requirement would not just break new doctrinal ground, it would also have a very different effect than the various federalism-enforcing and other clear statement rules contained in existing doctrine. The existing rules generally narrow the *substantive scope* of the laws to which they apply, not the *source of legislative authority* pursuant to which Congress may be deemed to have acted. The difference is significant. Whereas clear statement rules focusing on the former generally lead courts to confine statutes to constitutionally safe terrain and then uphold them on those grounds, a clear statement rule operating on the latter would lead courts to invalidate a statute when it is not sufficiently clear that Congress intended to exercise a head of legislative authority that would be sufficient to uphold the law.

In addition to departing dramatically from existing clear statement rules, a clear statement rule that narrows the available sources of legislative authority would conflict sharply with the presumption of constitutionality. By directing that legislation be upheld except where clearly unconstitutional, the presumption gives Congress the benefit of the constitutional doubt. But a rule requiring Congress to clearly invoke its tax authority before an enactment is upheld on that ground would have precisely the opposite effect, as the *NFIB* joint dissent and lower-court decisions like Judge Vinson's so vividly illustrate.

Respecting the presumption of constitutionality thus entails rejecting any requirement that Congress expressly identify the head of legislative authority under which it acts. To be sure, Congress may need to demonstrate that the substantive predicates for invoking a particular authority are met. Thus, for example, the Court has stated that Congress must establish an ongoing pattern of unconstitutional state action in order to pass legislation enforcing the relevant constitutional norm pursuant to Section 5 of the Fourteenth Amendment.[74] But imposing such evidentiary requirements is quite different from invalidating legislation because Congress did not invoke its Section 5 power with adequate clarity. These substantive constitutional requirements must be satisfied regardless of whether Congress expressly invokes the Section 5 power as the basis for legislation. If they are met, then a legislative measure can fall within the Section 5 power even though Congress was silent about its intent to exercise its Section 5 power.

## D. A MORE DIFFICULT QUESTION ABOUT A DIFFERENT KIND OF CLEAR STATEMENT

Although not raised in *NFIB* itself, a related question involves whether and to what extent Congress can prevent the courts from upholding the constitutionality of challenged legislation based on a particular head of legislative authority. That is, even if the courts should not impose a clear statement requirement on Congress's use of the tax (or any other) power, what should courts do if Congress clearly states an intent *not* to use a particular power when enacting a particular provision?

We regard this as a difficult question. On the one hand, respecting Congress might seem to entail crediting its decisions about which sources of legislative authority to invoke. A judicial refusal to honor such congressional choices could undermine the political checks against Congress's abuse of its powers. On the other, some political checks would still remain even if Congress were not able to preclude judicial consideration of a given head of authority. Legislation would still need to be actually enacted before courts could consider any challenges to its constitutionality, and so the constraints of bicameralism and presentment would continue to apply.

In addition, congressional efforts to preclude courts from sustaining legislation on a particular constitutional basis could risk unwarranted legislative intrusion into the core judicial function of constitutional adjudication. On this view, in rejecting certain heads of authority Congress is not simply exercising its own independent interpretive authority, but is also seeking to dictate the terms of constitutional adjudication by the courts. Requiring courts to defer to such manuevers could thus threaten basic separation-of-powers principles. Yet at the same time, judicial refusal to credit Congress's announcement about which powers it is exercising in a given context might also be thought to risk serious damage to other separation-of-powers principles that reserve the discretion inherent in legislating to Congress, not the courts.

The presumption of constitutionality cannot solve this puzzle, but it can limit the problem's scope. To honor the presumption of constitutionality, we think courts should at least require clear evidence before concluding that Congress has in fact rejected a particular power. And interestingly, this suggests that the appropriate clear statement rule in this context is actually the opposite of the one suggested by the *NFIB* joint dissent and Judge Vinson's opinion. Instead of requiring Congress to expressly invoke a given head of legislative power before examining the constitutionality of a given enactment under that power, courts should require Congress to expressly renounce a particular head of power before taking it off the table for purposes of assessing the enactment's constitutionality. Put another way, courts should err on the side of keeping any available source of legislative authority on the table unless Congress clearly and expressly disavows it.

## 5. Conclusion: Why the Presumption of Constitutionality?

In relying on the presumption of constitutionality to sort out the choice between the avoidance canon and a clear statement rule in a case like *NFIB*, our analysis has largely accepted the legitimacy of the presumption. Our project has been to explore the presumption's implications, as well as its relationship to the other interpretive principles discussed here. Some commentators—including, tellingly, one of the architects of the constitutional challenge to the ACA's individual mandate—have urged courts to abandon the presumption of constitutionality altogether, and instead to approach all or most legislation with much greater constitutional skepticism.[75] Similarly, in the *NFIB* oral argument, Justice Kennedy expressed skepticism about the presumption's applicability to assessing the constitutionality of the individual mandate: "I understand that we must presume laws are constitutional, but, even so, when you are changing the relation of the individual to the government in ... what we can stipulate is, I think, a unique way, do you not have a heavy burden of justification to show authorization under the Constitution?"[76]

For those attracted to limiting or abandoning the presumption of constitutionality in such ways, our argument is unlikely to persuade. But the presumption is a well-established, long-standing tenet of the American constitutional tradition.[77] Abandoning it would be a radical departure from established judicial practice. Both sides in *NFIB* purported to operate within the bounds of that established practice. Justice Kennedy's statement at oral argument notwithstanding, all members of the Court did likewise. Within those bounds, the presumption of constitutionality yields a robust justification of Chief Justice Roberts's reliance on the canon of constitutional avoidance to uphold the individual mandate under the tax power, and it counts powerfully against the sort of clear statement rule preferred by the joint dissent.

## Notes

1. Jerry Mashaw, *As If Republican Interpretation*, 97 YALE L.J. 1685, 1686 (1988).
2. 132 S. Ct. 2566 (2012).

3. Edward J. DeBartolo Corp. v. Fla. Gulf Coast Bldg. & Constr. Trades Council, 485 U.S. 568, 575 (1988).

4. 297 U.S. 288 (1936) (Brandeis, J., joined by Stone, Roberts, and Cardozo, JJ., concurring).

5. Zadvydas v. Davis, 533 U.S. 678, 689 (2001) (quoting Crowell v. Benson, 285 U.S. 22, 62 (1932)). For a list of recent invocations of the avoidance canon by the Court, see Trevor W. Morrison, *Constitutional Avoidance in the Executive Branch*, 106 COLUM. L. REV. 1189, 1193 n.10 (2006) (collecting cases).

6. Adrian Vermeule, *Saving Constructions*, 85 GEO. L.J. 1945, 1949 (1997).

7. Blodgett v. Holden, 275 U.S. 142, 148 (1927) (Holmes, J., concurring in the judgment of an equally divided Court).

8. Vermeule, *supra* note 6, at 1949.

9. See John Copeland Nagle, Delaware & Hudson Revisited, 72 NOTRE DAME L. REV. 1495, 1496–1497 (1997).

10. See Morrison, *supra* note 5, at 1203–1204.

11. 213 U.S. 366, 408 (1909).

12. See Morrison, *supra* note 5, at 1206–1207 (describing the elements of the standard defense of the modern avoidance canon and calling it the "judicial restraint" theory of avoidance).

13. See, e.g., Clark v. Martinez, 543 U.S. 371, 381 (2005) (describing modern avoidance as "a tool for choosing between competing plausible interpretations of a statutory text, resting on the reasonable presumption that Congress did not intend the alternative which raises serious constitutional doubts"); Immigration & Naturalization Serv. v. St. Cyr, 533 U.S. 289, 336 (2001) (Scalia, J., dissenting) (describing the avoidance canon as "conform[ing] with Congress's presumed intent not to enact measures of dubious validity").

14. Henry J. Friendly, *Mr. Justice Frankfurter and the Reading of Statutes*, in FELIX FRANKFURTER: THE JUDGE 30, 44 (Wallace Mendelson ed., 1964), reprinted in HENRY J. FRIENDLY, BENCHMARKS 196, 210 (1967).

15. *Cf.* Kenneth A. Shepsle, *Congress is a "They," Not an "It": Legislative Intent as Oxymoron*, 12 INT'L REV. L. & ECON. 239 (1992).

16. One of us is on record saying that the application of classical avoidance does not entail the issuing of a truly unconstitutional advisory opinion. See Morrison, *supra* note 5, at 1205.

17. Richard A. Posner, *Statutory Interpretation—In the Classroom and in the Courtroom*, 50 U. CHI. L. REV. 800, 816 (1983).

18. See Frederick Schauer, Ashwander Revisited, 1995 SUP. CT. REV. 71, 87.

19. Ernest A. Young, *Constitutional Avoidance, Resistance Norms, and the Preservation of Judicial Review*, 78 TEX. L. REV. 1549, 1585, 1551 (2000).

20. *Id.* at 1585.

21. See Henry P. Monaghan, *On Avoiding Avoidance, Agenda Control and Related Matters*, 112 COLUM. L. REV. 003, 070 (2012).

22. Young, *Constitutional Avoidance*, *supra* note 19, at 1606.

23. *Id.* at 1598.

24. John F. Manning, *Clear Statement Rules and the Constitution*, 110 COLUM. L. REV. 399, 406–407 (2010); see also William N. Eskridge Jr. & Philip P. Frickey, *Quasi-Constitutional Law: Clear Statement Rules as Constitutional Lawmaking*, 45 VAND. L. REV. 593 (1992).

25. 501 U.S. 452, 460 (1991) (internal quotations omitted); Manning, *supra* note 24, at 407–410 (discussing federalism clear statement rules).

26. *Compare* Altria v. Good, 555 U.S. 70, 76–77 (2009) (noting that preemption analysis begins with a presumption against preemption, but "Congress may indicate pre-emptive intent through a statute's express language or through its structure and purpose"), *with* Atascadero State Hosp. v. Scanlon, 473 U.S. 234, 242 (1985) ("Congress may abrogate the States' constitutionally secured immunity from suit in federal court only by making its intention unmistakably clear in the language of the statute").

27. Manning, *supra* note 24, at 402.

28. *Cf.* Gonzales v. Oregon, 126 S. Ct. 904, 935 (2006) (Scalia, J., dissenting) (categorizing cases employing the avoidance canon as a "line of clear-statement cases").

29. Manning, *supra* note 24, at 414.

30. See Eskridge & Frickey, *supra* note 24, at 599–600, 637–638; Manning, *supra* note 24, at 414; Cass R. Sunstein, *Nondelegation Canons*, 67 U. CHI. L. REV. 315, 331 (2000).

31. See, e.g., Eskridge & Frickey, *supra* note 24, at 632–638 (critiquing clear statement rules for prioritizing judicial value choices over legislative and as representing unwarranted judicial enforcement of constitutional norms left to the legislature); Schauer, *supra* note 18, at 74, 83, 89 (arguing that application of constitutional clear statement rules lead to statutory interpretations that Congress did not intend, has difficulty overcoming, and are insufficiently justified); see also Manning, *supra* note 24, at 418–419, 423–426 (detailing frequent criticisms and arguing that even if clear statement rules are not as intrusive as some argue, they produce interpretations at odds with the obvious reading of the text and represent unjustified judicial value balancing).

32. See Sunstein, *supra* note 30, at 316–317; Young, Constitutional Avoidance, *supra* note 19, at 1552 (arguing that some constitutional principles take the form of resistance norms rather than absolute limitations on Congress). For doubts about this defense, see Eskridge & Frickey, *supra* note 24, at 633–634 (noting that arguments against judicial enforcement of structural federalism norms through direct constitutional review also apply to statutory interpretation).

33. See Ernest A. Young, *Two Cheers for Process Federalism*, 46 VILL. L. REV. 1349 (2001). For the canonical statement of the view that constitutional federalism is primarily politically enforced, see Herbert Wechsler, *The Political Safeguards of Federalism: The Role of the States in the Composition and Selection of the National Government*, 54 COLUM. L. REV. 543 (1954).

34. See Young, Two Cheers, *supra* note 33.

35. See, e.g., Arlington Cent. Sch. Dist. Bd. v. Murphy, 548 U.S. 291, 296–298 (2008) (noting that conditions on federal grants to the states must be "unambiguously" stated and holding that statutory reference to "attorneys' fees" did not unambiguously include expert fees).

36. See, e.g., United States R.R. Retirement Bd. v. Fritz, 449 U.S. 166, 179 (1981).

37. See, e.g., Bd. of Trustees v. Garrett, 531 U.S. 356, 368 (2001); United States v. Lopez, 514 U.S. 549, 562–563 (1995).

38. Woods v. Cloyd W. Miller Co., 333 U.S. 138, 144 (1948); see Equal Employment Opportunity Comm'n v. Wyoming, 460 U.S. 226, 243 n.18 (1983); see also *Lopez*, 514 U.S. at 562–563 ("Congress normally is not required to make formal findings as to the substantial burdens that an activity has on interstate commerce").

39. See, e.g., Kimel v. Fla. Bd. of Regents, 528 U.S. 62, 78 (2000).

40. See Goshtasby v. Bd. of Trustees, 141 F.3d 761, 768 (7th Cir. 1998), *abrogated on other grounds by* Kimel v. Fla. Bd. of Regents, 528 U.S. 62 (2000); see also Mills v. State of Maine, 118 F.3d 37, 43–44 (1st Cir. 1997).

41. See Florida *ex rel.* Bondi v. U.S. Dep't of Health & Human Servs., 648 F.3d 1235, 1314–1320 (11th Cir. 2011), *aff'd in part, rev'd in part sub nom. NFIB*, 132 S. Ct. 2566 (2012); Thomas More Law Ctr. v. Obama, 651 F.3d 529, 550–554 (6th Cir. 2011) (Sutton, J., concurring), *cert. denied*, No. 11-117 (June 29, 2012).

42. Florida *ex rel.* McCollum v. U.S. Dep't of Health & Human Servs., 716 F. Supp. 2d 1120, 1133 (N.D. Fla. 2010) (internal quotations omitted).

43. *Id.* (quoting United States v. Helwig, 188 U.S. 605, 612–613 (1903)) (emphasis omitted).

44. *Id.* at 1136–1137 & n.7, 1143.

45. NFIB v. Sebelius, 132 S. Ct. 2566, 2651 (2012) (Scalia, Kennedy, Alito, Thomas, JJ., dissenting).

46. *Id.* at 2655.

47. *Id.* at 2653.

48. *Id.* at 2598.

49. *Id.* at 2594, 2600.
50. Nicholas Quinn Rozenkranz, *Roberts Was Wrong to Apply the Canon of Constitutional Avoidance to the Mandate*, SCOTUS REPORT (July 11, 2012, 8:36 AM), http://www.scotusreport.com/2012/07/11/roberts-was-wrong-to-apply-the-canon-of-constitutional-avoidance-to-the-mandate/.
51. See Oliver Wendell Holmes, *The Path of the Law*, 10 HARV. L. REV. 457, 459 (1897) ("If you want to know the law and nothing else, you must look at it as a bad man, who cares only for the material consequences which such knowledge enables him to predict").
52. *NFIB*, 132 S. Ct. at 2600–2601 (Roberts, C.J.).
53. *Id.* at 2583–2584.
54. *Id.* at 2594.
55. *Id.* at 2583.
56. See, e.g., Fletcher v. Peck, 10 U.S. (6 Cranch) 87, 128 (1810) (Marshall, C.J.) (stating that courts should not pronounce a law unconstitutional "on slight implication and vague conjecture," but instead that "[t]he opposition between the constitution and the law should be such that the judges feel a clear and strong conviction of their incompatibility with each other"); THE FEDERALIST NO. 78 (Alexander Hamilton) (stating that courts should hold unconstitutional only those laws that are "contrary to the manifest tenor of the Constitution" such that they create an "irreconcilable variance").
57. James B. Thayer, *The Origin and Scope of the American Doctrine of Constitutional Law*, 7 HARV. L. REV. 129, 136 (1893).
58. *Id.* at 144. Thayer did not shy away from the implications of this standard:[O]ne who is a member of a legislature may vote against a measure as being, in his judgment, unconstitutional; and, being subsequently placed on the bench, when this measure, having been passed by the legislature in spite of his opposition, comes before him judicially, may there find it his duty, although he has in no degree changed his opinion, to declare it constitutional.*Id.* (attributing this illustration to Judge Cooley, Const. Lim., 6th ed., 68).
59. Henry P. Monaghan, *Marbury and the Administrative State*, 83 COLUM. L. REV. 1, 7 n.35 (1983).
60. See Monaghan, *Avoiding Avoidance, supra* note 21, at 675 ("In *City of Boerne v. Flores*, to take a prominent example, the Court, invoking *Marbury*, admonished Congress for attempting to define the substantive content of the rights secured by the Fourteenth Amendment. That task was part of the judicial duty, not part of Congress's legislative responsibility").
61. Salazar v. Buono, 130 S. Ct. 1803, 1820 (2010); see Mistretta v. United States, 488 U.S. 361, 384 (1989) ("When this Court is asked to invalidate a statutory provision that has been approved by both Houses of Congress and signed by the President …, it should only do so for the most compelling constitutional reasons").
62. Pension Benefit Guar. Corp. v. R.A. Gray & Co., 467 U.S. 717, 729 (1984) (quoting Usery v. Turner Elkhorn Mining Co., 428 U.S. 1, 15 (1976)); see United States v. Carolene Prods. Co., 304 U.S. 144, 152 (1938) (courts should generally assume an adequate basis for legislating unless "facts made known or generally assumed … preclude the assumption that it rests upon some rational basis within the knowledge and experience of the legislature").
63. Andrew Hessick, *Rethinking the Presumption of Constitutionality*, 85 NOTRE DAME L. REV. 1447, 1452–1455 (2010) (describing well-entrenched deference to legislative factual judgments).
64. NFIB v. Sebelius, 132 S. Ct. 2566, 2679 (2012) ("'Proper respect for a coordinate branch of the government' requires that [the Court] strike down an Act of Congress only if 'the lack of constitutional authority … is clearly demonstrated'") (quoting United States v. Harris, 106 U.S. 629, 635 (1883)).
65. *Id.* at 2597.
66. Hessick, *supra* note 63, at 1449 ("Courts have based the presumption of constitutionality on three reasons: to show due respect to the judgments of legislators …; to promote democracy by preventing courts from interfering with decisions by an elected legislature; and to take

advantage of the legislature's superior institutional design" when it comes to making factual determinations).

67. United States v. Kahriger, 345 U.S. 22, 28 (1954).

68. See, e.g., Young, *Two Cheers, supra* note 33.

69. Dan Balz, *Introduction, in* STAFF OF THE WASH. POST, LANDMARK: THE INSIDE STORY OF AMERICA'S NEW HEALTH-CARE LAW AND WHAT IT MEANS FOR US ALL 1, 7 (2010); see also Robert Weiner, Much Ado: The Potential Impact of the Supreme Court Decision Upholding the Affordable Care Act, in this volume.

70. William N. Eskridge, Jr., *Vetogates, Chevron, Preemption*, 83 NOTRE DAME L. REV. 1441, 1444–1448 (2008).

71. See Eskridge & Frickey, *supra* note 24, at 637–640 (underscoring countermajoritarian concerns raised by clear statement rules).

72. See Manning, *supra* note 24, at 427–439 (challenging the legitimacy of clear statements rules that seek to enforce general constitutional values beyond the specific embodiment of such values in the Constitution).

73. See Regan v. Taxation with Representation, 461 U.S. 540, 547 (1983); Gillian E. Metzger, *To Tax, To Spend, To Regulate*, 126 HARV. L. REV. 86, 89–91 (2012).

74. See, e.g., Bd. of Trustees v. Garrett, 531 U.S. 356, 368 (2001) (holding Title I of the ADA exceeded Congress's Fourteenth Amendment enforcement power because "[t]he legislative record of the ADA... simply fails to show that Congress did in fact identify a pattern of irrational state discrimination in employment against the disabled"). The Court has sometimes sustained measures based on evidence of unconstitutional state actions not expressly invoked by Congress, raising questions about the extent to which Congress itself must give voice to this evidence for the enforcement power to apply. See Tennessee v. Lane, 541 U.S. 509, 524 (2003) (upholding Title II of the ADA based in part on evidence of discrimination against the disabled "documented in this Court's cases").

75. See RANDY BARNETT, RESTORING THE LOST CONSTITUTION: THE PRESUMPTION OF LIBERTY 259 (2004) (urging "shifting the background interpretive presumption of constitutionality whenever legislation restricts the liberties of the people" and adopting instead a "Presumption of Liberty").

76. Transcript of Oral Argument at 12, Dep't of Health & Human Servs. v. Florida, 132 S. Ct. 2566 (2012) (No. 11-398), *available at* http://www.supremecourt.gov/oral_arguments/argument_transcripts/11-398-Tuesday.pdf.

77. Hessick, *supra* note 63, at 1455.

CHAPTER 9

# The Individual Mandate and the Proper Meaning of "Proper"

*Ilya Somin*

## 1. Introduction

The Necessary and Proper Clause of the Constitution has often been at the center of debates over the limits of federal power. But in the first 220 years of its history, the Supreme Court never gave us anything approaching a comprehensive analysis of what it means for a law to be "proper." The Court's recent decision on the constitutionality of the Affordable Care Act (ACA) individual health insurance mandate in *NFIB v. Sebelius*[1] helps fill this gap. In doing so, it moves our jurisprudence closer to the proper meaning of proper.

The individual mandate at issue in *NFIB* requires most Americans to purchase government-approved health insurance by 2014 or pay a fine of $695 or up to 2.5 percent of an individual's annual income.[2] Defenders of the law argue that the mandate is needed to force people to purchase health insurance before they become sick, since another provision of the ACA forbids insurers from rejecting customers with preexisting conditions.

In this article, I explain why Chief Justice John Roberts's key swing-vote opinion was right to conclude that the individual health insurance mandate is outside the scope of Congress's power under the Necessary and Proper Clause. As Roberts put it, "Even if the individual mandate is 'necessary' to the Act's insurance reforms, such an expansion of federal power is not a 'proper' means for making those reforms effective."[3] Although Roberts ultimately cast the key vote for upholding the mandate as a tax authorized by the Constitution's Taxing Clause,[4] he also concluded that it was not authorized by either the Necessary and Proper Clause or Congress's power to regulate interstate commerce.

146

The text of the Necessary and Proper Clause gives Congress the power to "make all Laws which shall be necessary and proper for carrying into Execution the foregoing Powers, and all other Powers vested by this Constitution in the Government of the United States, or in any Department or Officer thereof."[5] In section 1, I explain why it makes sense to read this language as compelling laws authorized by the clause to meet two separate requirements: necessity and propriety. Both the original meaning of the clause and Supreme Court precedent support this interpretation.

Section 2 argues that the individual health insurance mandate is improper because upholding it under the clause would have given Congress virtually unlimited power to impose other mandates, and also rendered large parts of the rest of Article I redundant. This is consistent with a relatively minimalistic reading of the word "proper."

I also briefly discuss a broader interpretation of "proper" that leads to the same result: that the power to impose mandates on the general population is not a power "incidental" to Congress's other enumerated powers, but rather a major independent power of its own.[6] The minimalist interpretation of the clause is consistent with the broader version, but does not require it.

Finally, section 3 briefly discusses the possible future implications of Roberts's interpretation of propriety. Here, much depends on the future composition of the Supreme Court and other contingent factors. But it is possible that the ruling will have a noteworthy impact in curtailing future federal mandates. Future courts might also build on *NFIB*'s interpretation of "proper" as a tool for incrementally strengthening limits on federal power.

In this chapter, I do not consider two other important issues addressed by the Court in *NFIB*: whether the mandate is permissible under the Commerce Clause or the Taxing Clause.[7] But some of my analysis has implications for the former issue. If I am right that the argument in favor of the mandate fails the test of propriety because it would give Congress virtually unlimited power to enact other mandates, that conclusion also weakens the government's case under the Commerce Clause.[8]

## 2. Why a "Necessary" Law Isn't Necessarily Proper

The Necessary and Proper Clause imposes a requirement of propriety that is distinct from necessity. This conclusion follows from the text and original meaning of the Constitution, and is also consistent with the Court's precedents going all the way back to *McCulloch v. Maryland*.[9] There is no good reason to transform the Necessary and Proper Clause into a mere "Necessary Clause."

In his Supreme Court brief defending the individual mandate on behalf of the federal government, Solicitor General Donald Verrilli did not even consider the possibility that the mandate might be improper even if it is necessary.[10] Several leading academic defenses of the constitutionality of the mandate that rely on the Necessary and Proper Clause also neglect the distinction between necessity and propriety.[11] Conflating the two is a common but unfortunate error.

## A. THE TEXT

The text of the Necessary and Proper Clause authorizes only laws that are both "necessary *and* proper for carrying into Execution the foregoing Powers and all other Powers vested by this Constitution in the Government of the United States, or in any Department or Officer thereof."[12] If the clause was intended to simply authorize any laws that might be "necessary" for implementing the federal government's other powers, the framers could have omitted the word "proper." Instead of a Necessary and Proper Clause, we would have a "Necessary Clause." To reduce the language of the clause to a requirement of necessity would be to read the word "proper" out of the Constitution.[13]

That conflicts with both an ordinary language reading of the text and with the Supreme Court's long-standing insistence that "[i]n expounding the Constitution of the United States, every word must have its due force, and appropriate meaning" and that "[n]o word in the instrument...can be rejected as superfluous or unmeaning."[14] This idea has long been considered an "elementary canon of construction which requires that effect be given to each word of the Constitution."[15] It is also a standard rule of statutory interpretation.[16]

In this case, refusing to give "proper" any distinct meaning seems especially strange, given that there is no grammatical or linguistic necessity for including it in the clause otherwise. The word "proper" is not mere filler or a useful conjunction such as "and" or "the." The clause would be perfectly comprehensible without it: it would then give Congress the power to "make all Laws which shall be necessary for carrying into Execution the foregoing Powers."

## B. THE ORIGINAL MEANING

The textual case for giving "proper" a distinct meaning from "necessary" is reinforced by what we know about the word's original meaning. There seems to have been a fairly broad consensus on this point at the time of the Founding, even though there was great disagreement on other aspects of the Necessary and Proper Clause, such as the meaning of "necessary."

At the 1787 Constitutional Convention, the Committee of Detail deliberately inserted the word "proper" into a previous draft of the clause that included only the word "necessary."[17] This suggests a conscious effort on the part of the framers to insert the term "proper" in order to change the meaning the clause would otherwise have had. To be sure, this evidence from the secret proceedings of the Convention is only indirectly relevant for originalists who emphasize the "original public meaning" of the Constitution rather than the original intent of the framers.[18] But it is noteworthy that the drafters on the Committee of Detail apparently believed that the insertion of "proper" would make a difference to the interpretation of the clause by readers and courts. These knowledgeable insiders' expectations are at least relevant evidence of original meaning.

In Federalist 33, Alexander Hamilton, one of the strongest supporters of federal power among the framers, insisted that we must "judge of the *necessity* and *propriety* of the laws to be passed for executing the powers of the Union."[19] This clearly implies that "necessity" and "propriety" are two separate requirements. Hamilton goes on to state that "[t]he propriety of a law, in a constitutional light, must always be determined by the nature of the powers upon which it is founded," and then gives several examples of improper federal legislation, including an "attempt to vary the law of descent in any State" and a statute that "undertake[s] to abrogate a land tax imposed by the authority of a State."[20]

Obviously, federal laws that alter state inheritance laws or abrogate state land taxes may be necessary in the broad sense of "useful" or "convenient" for the execution of other enumerated powers. That, of course, is the broad definition of "necessary" long advocated by Hamilton and eventually adopted by the Supreme Court in *McCulloch v. Maryland*.[21] For example, both inheritance laws and state land taxes surely have an impact on interstate commerce. A federal law overriding or altering them therefore could be a "useful" or "convenient" means for changing patterns of interstate commerce, just as the federal government claimed that the individual mandate is a useful or convenient means for regulating the health insurance market. But such a law, Hamilton explained, would be *improper*.

Many other framers, political leaders, and legal commentators of the Founding era also recognized that propriety and necessity are separate and distinct requirements. For example, the first U.S. attorney general, Edmund Randolph, argued that "no power is to be assumed under the [Necessary and Proper] clause, but such as is not only necessary, but proper, or perhaps expedient also."[22] Others held similar views.[23]

## C. PRECEDENT

As Chief Justice Roberts notes in his *NFIB* opinion, the Court's "jurisprudence under the Necessary and Proper Clause has ... been very deferential to Congress's determination that a regulation is 'necessary.'"[24] By contrast, the Court has been far less clear on the meaning of "proper." But what it has said clearly shows that it imposes a limit on federal power distinct from that of necessity.

This is most clearly evident in two federalism cases decided in the 1990s: *Printz v. United States* and *Alden v. Maine*. In *Printz*, the Court held that "[w]hen a 'La[w] . . . for carrying into Execution' the Commerce Clause violates the principle of state sovereignty reflected in . . . various constitutional provisions . . . [,] it is not a 'La[w] . . . *proper* for carrying into Execution the Commerce Clause,' and is thus, in the words of *The Federalist*, 'merely [an] ac[t] of usurpation' which 'deserve[s] to be treated as such.'"[25]

The law invalidated in *Printz* required "state and local law enforcement officers to conduct background checks on prospective handgun purchasers."[26] It was clearly "useful" or "convenient" to carrying into execution Congress's authority to regulate commerce in handguns. Yet the Court concluded that it exceeded the bounds of congressional power because it was improper. *Printz's* holding relied in part on the concept of "state sovereignty" embedded in the Tenth Amendment.[27] But Justice Antonin Scalia's opinion for the Court emphasized that "[w]hat destroys the dissent's Necessary and Proper Clause argument . . . is not the Tenth Amendment but the Necessary and Proper Clause itself."[28] Nothing in the Court's analysis suggests that a law is only improper if it somehow threatens state sovereignty.

The Court relied on *Printz's* approach to propriety in *Alden v. Maine*.[29] In *Alden*, the Court concluded that states enjoy a constitutionally protected immunity from suit that is not limited by the express terms of the Eleventh Amendment, but applies in state court as well as federal court. *Alden* held that the Necessary and Proper Clause does not give Congress "the incidental authority to subject the States to private suits as a means of achieving objectives otherwise within the scope of the enumerated powers," because such authority is not "proper."[30]

*Printz* and *Alden* are relatively recent decisions that were part of the Rehnquist Court's controversial "federalism revolution." But their separation of necessity and propriety was prefigured in the Court's best-known early Necessary and Proper Clause decision: *McCulloch v. Maryland*.

In *McCulloch*, Chief Justice Marshall famously adopted a broad definition of "necessary," as anything that might be "useful" or "convenient" to the execution of an enumerated power.[31] But the Court also outlined several limitations on Congress's power under the Necessary and Proper Clause: "Let the end be legitimate, let it be within the scope of the constitution, and all means which are appropriate, which are plainly adapted to that end, which are not prohibited, but consist with the letter and spirit of the constitution, are constitutional."[32] This passage lists four constraints on the range of statutes authorized by the Necessary and Proper Clause: (1) the "end" pursued must be "legitimate" and "within the scope of the constitution"; (2) the means must be "appropriate" and "plainly adapted to that end"; (3) the means must "not [be] prohibited" elsewhere in the Constitution; and, finally (4) the means must be "consist[ent] with the letter and spirit of the Constitution."

While the first and second of these requirements might potentially be considered elements of necessity, the third and fourth clearly cannot. A statute "prohibited" elsewhere in the Constitution, or one that is inconsistent "with the letter and spirit of the Constitution," might still be a "useful" or "convenient" means of enforcing one of Congress's enumerated powers. If a statute exceeds the scope of the Necessary and Proper Clause for either of these reasons, it must be because it is not "proper," not because it fails the test of necessity.

Arguably, the same point applies to *McCulloch's* stricture that "should congress, under the pretext of executing its powers, pass laws for the accomplishment of objects not intrusted to the government; it would become the painful duty of this tribunal, should a case requiring such a decision come before it, to say, that such an act was not the law of the land."[33] A law adopted for the purpose of pursuing "objects not intrusted to the government" might still be useful or convenient for executing some enumerated power as well. For example, almost any regulation that affects commerce in some way would still fit the broad definition of "necessary."[34] If such a law is inherently beyond the scope of the clause, it must be because it is improper.

*United States v. Comstock*, the Court's most recent Necessary and Proper Clause case before *NFIB*,[35] is also consistent with the notion that propriety and necessity are separate standards, though it did not clearly distinguish between the two. *Comstock* reiterated the rule that Congress has broad discretion in determining necessity.[36] But the Court also based its decision on five other considerations, most of which are best understood as interpretations of "proper" rather than "necessary."[37] At least three of the five conditions—the broad "scope" of the statute, the history of federal involvement in the area, and the statute's lack of accommodation of state interests, count against the mandate, while a fourth is ambiguous.[38]

Finally, it is worth noting that the distinction between necessity and propriety is emphasized in Justice Antonin Scalia's 2005 concurring opinion in *Gonzales v. Raich*,[39] which some commentators cited as committing him to vote to uphold the individual mandate.[40] In that concurrence, Scalia defended a broad interpretation of "necessary."[41] But he also noted that "there are other restraints upon the Necessary and Proper Clause authority," besides merely the requirement of a necessary connection to an enumerated power. As an example of these additional "restraints," Scalia cited "cases such as *Printz v. United States* ... , [which] affirm that a law is not '*proper* for carrying into Execution the Commerce Clause' '[w]hen [it] violates [a constitutional] principle of state sovereignty.'"[42]

At the *NFIB* individual mandate oral argument, Scalia pointedly emphasized that "in addition to being necessary, [the mandate] has to be proper," explaining that a law backed by a rationale that implies unlimited federal power is not "proper."[43] As he recognized, the distinction between necessity and propriety provides a justification for invalidating the mandate while still endorsing a broad interpretation of "necessary."

## 3. Why the Mandate Is Not Proper: A Minimalistic Approach

Merely concluding that propriety is a distinct requirement from necessity does not tell us either what that requirement means or whether it renders the mandate unconstitutional. I contend that the mandate violates a relatively minimalistic definition of proper: one that excludes legislation that can only be justified by a line of reasoning that would give Congress unlimited power to impose other mandates, or render large parts of the rest of the Constitution redundant. This minimalistic interpretation does not necessarily foreclose the possibility that propriety also imposes other restrictions on the scope of congressional power under the clause. But it is enough to justify concluding that the individual mandate is improper without attempting a comprehensive definition of the term. As such, this approach might appeal to advocates of "judicial minimalism" who urge courts to decide cases on narrow grounds, where feasible.[44] But even defenders of a broader interpretation of "proper" are likely to agree that the requirement goes at least this far.

### A. WHY AN UNLIMITED POWER TO IMPOSE MANDATES IS IMPROPER

Text, original meaning, and precedent all support the notion that a "proper" law cannot be justified by a rationale that would give Congress unconstrained authority to impose other mandates. The textual argument is very simple: If unconstrained federal power is "proper," there would be no point to the careful enumeration of numerous other powers in Article I of the Constitution. As Chief Justice John Marshall put it in the famous 1824 case of *Gibbons v. Ogden*, "enumeration presupposes something not enumerated."[45]

Evidence of original meaning from the Founding era strongly supports the same conclusion.[46] As James Madison emphasized in a 1791 speech on the Necessary and Proper Clause, "Whatever meaning this clause may have, none can be admitted that would give an unlimited discretion to Congress."[47] Akhil Reed Amar, a leading legal historian who forcefully defended the constitutionality of the mandate,[48] notes that "Federalist" defenders of the Constitution "repeatedly explained that these words [of the clause] did not constitute some free-floating grant of near-plenary power."[49]

Founding-era jurists and other commentators in the nineteenth century concluded that the word "proper" prevented the federal government from using the Necessary and Proper Clause from intruding on the powers of the states. Chief Justice John Marshall, St. George Tucker, and Andrew Jackson were all among those who interpreted the term in that way.[50] As we have seen, Alexander Hamilton wrote that the propriety restriction would serve to protect such state prerogatives as the power to establish inheritance laws and taxes on land from federal interference—a clear indication that the term "proper" was intended to protect the states.[51]

While the Court has never expounded on the exact scope of the reserved state authority that is protected from federal interference by the requirement of propriety, it is safe to say that a virtually unlimited federal power to impose mandates goes beyond what is permissible.

Much modern precedent also supports the conclusion that there must be limits to congressional power under the clause. The Court has often emphasized that "[t]he Constitution requires a distinction between what is truly national and what is truly local."[52]

All of this precedent cuts against claims that "[a]bsent overt tension with independent constitutional norms, the Supreme Court has regarded 'necessary and proper' as a single construct," thereby requiring the Court to uphold the mandate.[53] Alternatively, the requirement that a law cannot be justified by a rationale that leads to unlimited power might itself be seen as an "independent constitutional norm" that qualifies as an element of propriety.

The same point applies to claims that propriety forbids only laws that violate some other part of the Constitution, such as the Bill of Rights or the Tenth Amendment.[54] No precedent limits propriety in this way. If it did, the term "proper" would become redundant, since a law that violates another part of the Constitution would be invalid even if "proper" were not included in the Necessary and Proper Clause.[55]

Some scholars have argued that the word "proper" merely requires an "appropriate relationship between congressional ends and means" under the Necessary and Proper Clause.[56] But this approach would interpret "proper" as serving much the same purpose as "necessary." If necessity means anything, it is some reasonable connection between ends and means. Such a definition of proper would also require the Supreme Court to overrule its interpretation of the meaning of the term in cases such as *Printz* and *Alden*.[57]

Chief Justice Roberts's interpretation of "proper" in *NFIB* is consistent with the view that it excludes interpretations that would give Congress unconstrained power. He emphasizes that "[e]ach of our prior cases upholding laws under th[e Necessary and Proper] Clause involved exercises of authority derivative of, and in service to, a granted power."[58] On the other hand, "The individual mandate, by contrast, vests Congress with the extraordinary ability to create the necessary predicate to the exercise of an enumerated power."[59] It does so by allowing Congress to go beyond regulation of people who fall within the scope of federal regulation because of "some preexisting activity" they have engaged in, and instead giving it the authority to regulate anyone it wants so long as doing so is in some way "useful" or "convenient" for regulating commerce, which in practice creates a power to "regulate an individual from cradle to grave."[60]

The four conservative dissenters who would have invalidated the mandate entirely also endorsed this interpretation of propriety, concluding that "the scope of the Necessary and Proper Clause is exceeded not only when the congressional action directly violates the sovereignty of the States but also when it violates the background principle of enumerated (and hence limited) federal power."[61]

If unlimited congressional power is improper, it is important to consider what it means for power to be unlimited. It may be impossible to prove that the rationale justifying any law is literally unlimited, in the sense that there is no conceivable law that wouldn't be authorized by it. Since the range of theoretically conceivable federal laws is infinite, it is impossible to consider all of them and show that each one would be authorized under the constitutional theory put forward to justify either the individual mandate or any other law.

Ironically, therefore, requiring those challenging a law to prove that its rationale is literally infinite would itself be a road to literally infinite federal power. Since no challenger could ever analyze the full range of conceivable laws, none could prove that the government's assertion of power was completely unlimited.

Moreover, the mere possibility that there is some conceivable law that the government's position would not authorize should not be enough to show that it is "proper." After all, there is no point to carefully enumerating a list of federal powers if the only power excluded from the list is that of enacting some hypothetical law that has no practical significance. Enumeration does not simply "presuppose" that "something [is] not enumerated," but that the something must be significant.[62]

In practice, therefore, it should be sufficient if the plaintiffs prove that the government's rationale for the law in question does not exclude anything with any practical significance, and refute the possible limiting principles put forward by the law's defenders. In the case of the individual health insurance mandate, these standards were met. Requiring plaintiffs to prove that the government's theory is literally unlimited would only ensure that federal power really *would* become literally unlimited. Such a burden of proof can never be met, and every challenged law would always be "proper."

## B. WHY THE CASE FOR THE MANDATE HAS
## NO STRUCTURAL LIMIT

In previous work, I have explained in detail why the constitutional rationales offered in defense of the individual mandate amount to rationales for unconstrained congressional power.[63] Here, I briefly cover some of the most commonly advanced rationales, especially those that claim that the health insurance mandate is a special case that would not require the Court to uphold other kinds of mandates.

Some defenses of the mandate assert that Congress has the power to regulate any "economic decision," including any decision *not* to engage in economic activity.[64] It is easy to see why this logic has no limit. Any decision to do or not do anything is inevitably an "economic decision" because the person in question could have chosen to spend the same time and effort doing something that affects the economy, such as working or purchasing a product.[65] The same point applies to arguments that Congress has the power to regulate any inactivity that has an economic effect.[66] *Any* kind of inactivity qualifies on that basis, since the inactive person could always have chosen to engage in some kind of economic activity instead. A person who spends an hour lying in bed could instead have used that time in productive labor or going to the supermarket to buy some broccoli.

The most widely asserted argument for the supposed uniqueness of the individual mandate is the claim that everyone eventually uses health care in some form. This point was made in virtually every lower-court decision upholding the mandate,[67] and also in Justice Ruth Bader Ginsburg's concurring opinion on behalf of the four liberal justices in the Supreme Court.[68]

Yet the fact that nearly everyone uses health care does nothing to differentiate health insurance from any other market. If we define the relevant "market" broadly enough, it is easy to characterize any decision not to purchase a good or service in exactly the same way. Tellingly, the mandate's defenders do not argue that everyone will inevitably use health *insurance*. Instead, they define the relevant market as "health *care.*" The same frame-shifting works for any other mandate.

Consider the much-discussed example of the broccoli purchase requirement raised by Judge Fred Vinson in the district court decision striking down the health insurance mandate.[69] Not everyone eats broccoli. But everyone inevitably participates in the market for food. Therefore, a mandate requiring everyone to purchase and eat broccoli would be permissible under the federal government's argument. The same holds true for a mandate requiring everyone to purchase General Motors cars in order to help the auto industry. There are many people who do not participate in the market for cars. But everyone does participate in the market for "transportation." As Chief Justice Roberts put it, "Everyone will likely participate in the markets for food, clothing, transportation, shelter, or energy; that does not authorize Congress to direct them to purchase particular products in those or other markets today."[70]

Justice Ginsburg misses the point when she responds to this argument by asserting that "[a]lthough an individual *might* buy a car or a crown of broccoli one day, there is no certainty she will ever do so," whereas everyone will eventually use health care at some point in their lives.[71] There is no "certainty" that the individual will ever use health insurance either, which is the product the mandate actually requires her to buy. But if health insurance can be viewed as just one of several ways of participating in the broader market for health care, then buying broccoli is just one of many ways of participating in the market for food, and buying a car is just one of many ways of participating in the market for transportation. And both food and transportation are practically unavoidable aspects of life.

This reasoning is broad enough to cover virtually any noneconomic mandate as well. For example, a mandate requiring people to exercise regularly might be justified on the grounds that everyone benefits from physical exertion at some point in their lives. A mandate requiring all American adults to read my posts at the Volokh Conspiracy legal blog could be justified on the grounds that virtually everyone seeks out information at one time or another.

Many also argue that the mandate case is special because medical providers are required to render emergency services to the uninsured, which is not true of most other markets.[72] But it is difficult to see why this distinction is constitutionally relevant. The answer advanced by the mandate's defenders seems to be that failure to purchase a given good or service thereby has an adverse economic effect on the producers, who end up having to provide free services.[73] In that respect, however, failure to purchase health insurance turns out to be no different from failure to purchase any other product. Every time someone fails to purchase a product, the producers of those goods and services are made economically worse off than they would have been if the potential buyer had made a different decision. This is true regardless whether the producers must provide goods and services to some consumers for free. At most, the latter condition exacerbates the negative impact on producers. Numerous other market conditions and government regulations can negatively affect producers as well. But it is not clear why a free service requirement has a special constitutional status denied to other conditions that also reduce producer profits.

Mandate defenders' other reasons for claiming that this is a special case have similar flaws. For example, the federal government's brief emphasized that health care is a large part of the American economy, that the need for health care is difficult to predict in advance, and that the use of health care by the uninsured imposes costs on others.[74] But almost any product can be described as part of a larger market that constitutes a major sector of the economy. For example, a broccoli-purchase mandate could be defended on the basis that broccoli is part of the food market and food is a major part of the economy.

Unpredictability of need is also ubiquitous. It applies, for example, to virtually every other type of insurance, including homeowners' insurance, life insurance, property insurance, and auto insurance. Even with respect to most ordinary consumer products, there are occasional needs that arise suddenly. For example, an individual's car might break down unexpectedly, necessitating an unforeseen purchase of a new car. The same goes for most noncommercial needs. People cannot always predict when they will want rest, companionship, or entertainment. Health care needs may be unpredictable more often than some of these other examples. But courts cannot base constitutional distinctions on such matters of degree, because there is no nonarbitrary way to determine how much unpredictability is enough to make any given market a special case.

Likewise, in an interdependent economy, failure to purchase almost any product has economic ripple effects that impact other sectors. Thus, failure to purchase nutritious foods such as broccoli might reduce the health of the workforce, thereby reducing overall economic productivity.[75]

Finally, some defenders of the mandate argue that it is a special case because it addresses a "national problem" that the states cannot solve due to collective action constraints.[76] Elsewhere, I have explained why this rationale for the law can only work if the concept of collective action problem is expanded broadly enough to justify almost any other mandate, including even one requiring people to purchase healthy food, such as broccoli.[77] If, on the other hand, Congress is required to prove that there really is a collective action problem that states are genuinely incapable of solving, the federal mandate would have to be invalidated because state governments are perfectly capable of enacting mandates of their own if such laws actually increase access to health care and decrease costs, as their defenders claim.[78]

If the requirement of propriety bars laws that can only be justified by a rationale that gives Congress unlimited power, then the case for the individual mandate fails.

## C. PROPRIETY AND REDUNDANCY

A decision upholding the individual mandate under the Necessary and Proper Clause would have also run afoul of propriety because it would make many of Congress's other enumerated powers completely redundant. This is improper because of the long-standing principle that a proper statute must "consist with the letter and spirit of the constitution."[79] The "letter and spirit of the Constitution" surely include respect for the Constitution's "careful enumeration of federal powers," which would be undermined by a decision rendering many of them superfluous.[80]

As discussed above,[81] the various rationales for upholding the mandate under the clause would give Congress the power to impose virtually any regulation that has an economic effect or might be useful or convenient for executing some enumerated power. The sweeping scope of this authority is accentuated by the Supreme Court's relatively broad interpretation of the Commerce Clause. The Court has held that the Commerce Clause gives Congress nearly unlimited power to regulate "economic activity," defined as any activity that involves "'the production, distribution, and consumption of commodities.'"[82] Virtually any mandate might be useful, convenient, or rationally related to a regulation of economic activity defined in this way. Any purchase mandate would obviously qualify, since it can be seen as a way of regulating the market for whatever commodity it requires people to buy. Almost any other regulation could potentially qualify as well. Forcing people to do anything ensures that at least some of them will forgo economic activity or other kinds of activity that have an effect on markets and so might be a useful or convenient way to regulate those markets. Obviously, some mandates might not be very effective regulatory mechanisms. But at least under current precedent, courts are not allowed to question Congress's judgment about the effectiveness of the regulatory measures it adopts under the Necessary and Proper Clause.[83]

The result of this kind of reasoning would render many of Congress's other powers completely superfluous. The very same clause that gives Congress the authority to regulate interstate commerce also gives it the power to regulate commerce with "Foreign nations" and "with the Indian Tribes."[84] But foreign and Indian commerce clearly have effects on interstate commerce and the overall economy more generally. Regulating these forms of commerce is surely a useful or convenient way to affect interstate commerce.

Similarly, Congress would no longer need its powers to organize and regulate the state militia, nor to "make rules for the Government and regulation of the land and naval Forces."[85] After all, the militia and the armed forces clearly affect economic activity in numerous ways, and virtually any regulations imposed on them would have at least some impact on the economy. The same reasoning applies even to the power to declare war, since a state of war inevitably has a substantial effect on economic activity.

Some overlap between powers is inevitable and even desirable.[86] But such an enormous degree of it makes a hash of Article I's scheme of enumerated powers, and seems clearly at odds with the "letter and spirit" of the Constitution. It is therefore improper.

## D. THE INDIVIDUAL MANDATE AS A
## NON-INCIDENTAL POWER

My analysis so far has relied on a minimalistic definition of propriety that only bars statutes whose rationale leads to unlimited congressional power or renders large parts of the rest of Article I redundant. But this approach does not preclude a more stringent definition of propriety that would bar any new claims of authority that are major independent powers as opposed to mere "incidents" of one of the other enumerated powers.[87] The more confining definition would inevitably bar any regulation that would be forbidden by the less restrictive one.

Interestingly, Chief Justice Roberts's reasoning appears to adopt the broader reading of propriety. He writes that the clause "vests Congress with authority to enact provisions 'incidental to the [enumerated] power, and conducive to its beneficial exercise,'" and concludes that the mandate is improper in part because it is not "'incidental' to the exercise of the commerce power," and "would work a substantial expansion of federal authority."[88] This language is, of course, borrowed from *McCulloch v. Maryland,* which distinguished between "incidental" powers that the clause gives to Congress, and "great substantive and independent power[s]," which it does not.[89]

The core argument here is that the power to impose mandates on general populations unconnected to any preexisting activity is a broad independent power that is not merely incidental. As discussed above, this power could potentially justify imposing an extraordinarily wide range of mandates and regulations— broad enough to compel almost anyone to do almost anything not specifically forbidden by a constitutional individual right.[90]

Due to space considerations, I do not attempt a full evaluation of the incidental powers argument here, especially since it has already been effectively defended by other scholars.[91] I will only note two relevant points.

First, if this interpretation of propriety is correct, it is difficult to save the mandate by arguing that it qualifies as merely "incidental." If the power to impose mandates is not a "great substantive and independent power," it is difficult to see what is. Second, the incidental powers analysis might invalidate the health insurance mandate even if its defenders could find some example of a mandate that would not be justified by its logic. So long as the argument for the health insurance mandate still justifies an extremely broad range of other possible mandates, it would still give Congress a "great substantive and independent power," even if there were a few types of mandates excluded from the scope of its authority.

# IV. Implications for the Future

The future effects of *NFIB's* Necessary and Proper holding are difficult to predict. It is possible that it will have a significant impact, but also possible that its effects will be extremely limited.

Some contend that Chief Justice Roberts's conclusion that the mandate exceeds Congress's powers under the Commerce Clause and Necessary and Proper Clause is mere dictum because it was not necessary to decide the case.[92] After all, he did ultimately uphold the mandate under the Taxing Clause.[93] If so, lower courts will not be bound by Roberts's necessary and proper analysis.

Such claims are undercut by Section IIIC of Roberts' opinion, which was joined by the four liberal justices who voted to uphold the mandate. It unequivocally states that "[t]he Court today holds that our Constitution protects us from federal regulation under the Commerce Clause so long as we abstain from the regulated activity."[94] Presumably, this applies to the Commerce Clause as augmented by the Necessary and Proper Clause as well.

Moreover, Chief Justice Roberts's key swing-vote opinion only concludes that the mandate is a tax because he adopts a "saving" construction that rejects the unconstitutional "more natural" reading of the provision, which would require it to be invalidated as a regulatory penalty.[95] He would not have rejected the "natural" reading if that reading were constitutionally permissible under the Commerce or Necessary and Proper Clauses.[96] Therefore, the necessary and proper analysis was essential to the result he ultimately reached. Finally, lower courts might well be influenced by the fact that a total of five justices concluded that the mandate is improper: Roberts and the four conservative dissenters who would have invalidated the mandate entirely.[97]

That said, there is enough uncertainty here that some lower courts could potentially refuse to apply NFIB's commerce and necessary and proper rulings on the grounds that they are dicta. And a future Supreme Court majority could even more easily choose to reject it for that reason.

A recent Ninth Circuit Court of Appeals opinion has treated NFIB's Necessary and Proper Clause reasoning as binding.[98] Whether other judges follow suit remains to be seen.

Assuming that future courts do follow Roberts's Necessary and Proper Clause reasoning, Congress would not have the power, under the clause, to "regulate individuals precisely *because* they are doing nothing."[99] That would prevent future mandates that are not predicated on some form of preexisting activity that brings individuals within the scope of federal authority.[100] Elsewhere, I have argued that mandates of this type are a genuine political danger, since industry interest groups have incentives to lobby for laws requiring people to buy their products, and Congress sometimes has incentives to cater to their demands.[101] But it is possible that future mandates could be structured as taxes in order to fall within the scope of Roberts's ruling upholding the mandate as a tax.[102] These mandates would, however, have to meet Roberts's requirements that the only penalty be a monetary fine that is not so high as to be coercive, that the fine be collected by the IRS, and that violation of the mandate should not be considered lawbreaking if the fine is paid.[103]

Roberts's endorsement of the "incidental powers" theory of propriety could have significant impact in the future, depending on the definition of what counts as an independent power that cannot be considered incidental. Unfortunately, Roberts offers little precise guidance on this question. As Justice Ginsburg asks in her concurring opinion, "How is a judge to decide, when ruling on the constitutionality of a federal statute, whether Congress employed an 'independent power...,' or merely a 'derivative' one...?"[104] Her question may well·need to be answered in a future decision.

Ultimately, much will depend on who gets appointed to the Supreme Court in the next few years. *NFIB* shows that the justices remain deeply divided over federalism issues. The five conservatives are willing to countenance judicial enforcement of at least some substantial constraints on federal power. With rare exceptions,[105] the four liberal justices remain dead set against it. Much could change if either side achieves a firm six-to-three or seven-to-two majority on the Court. If the liberals achieve such a majority, they are likely to overrule or confine to their facts recent precedents enforcing limits on federal power. By contrast, a firm conservative majority would no longer be at the mercy of any one swing voter such as Chief Justice Roberts in *NFIB*. Such a majority might therefore take a more aggressive posture in limiting congressional authority.

President Barack Obama's victory in the 2012 election ensures that he will get to fill any Supreme Court vacancies that arise in the next four years. Should one of the five conservative justices retire, the resulting liberal majority on the Court could easily eviscerate *NFIB*'s limits on federal power. But, in part for that very reason, the Court's conservatives might choose to wait Obama out and avoid stepping down unless forced to leave the Court by death or severe illness. If Obama is able to replace one of the older liberal justices, that would not change the immediate balance on the Court. But it would make it more difficult for any future Republican president to expand the size of the present tenuous conservative majority, since the new appointees would likely stay on the Court for decades.

If Obama's 2012 victory presages an era of liberal political dominance, the fate of *NFIB* will ultimately be sealed by a more liberal future Supreme Court. If, on the other hand, presidential politics remains highly competitive or the GOP makes major political gains as it did in the 2010 midterm elections, the composition of the Supreme Court will be much harder to predict. The future of the Necessary and Proper Clause—like that of constitutional federalism generally—remains very much in doubt.[106]

## 5. Conclusion

*NFIB* is the Court's most important decision expounding on the definition of "proper" in the Necessary and Proper Clause. Chief Justice Roberts's opinion has much to commend it, especially insofar as it bars interpretations of the clause that would give Congress unlimited power to impose other mandates. But the long-term impact of this case remains to be seen.

## Acknowledgments

The argument developed in this chapter is in part adapted from that which I presented in an amicus brief in *NFIB v. Sebelius* on behalf of the Washington Legal Foundation and a group of constitutional law scholars. See Brief of the Washington Legal Foundation and Constitutional Law Scholars as Amici Curiae in Support of Respondents (Individual Mandate Issue), NFIB v. Sebelius, 132 S. Ct. 2566 (2012) (No. 11–398), 2012 WL 1680857. However, the views expressed here do not necessarily represent those of the WLF and my other amicus clients. For helpful comments and criticisms, I would like to thank Randy Barnett, David Kopel, Gary Lawson, Andrew Koppelman, Trevor Morrison, and Nathaniel Persily.

## Notes

1. 132 S. Ct. 2566 (2012).
2. *Id.* at 2580.
3. *Id.* at 2592.
4. *Id.* at 2593–2600.
5. U.S. Const. art. I, § 8, cl. 13.
6. This argument was presented in an important amicus brief by constitutional law scholars Gary Lawson, Robert G. Natelson, and Guy Seidman. See Brief of Authors of the Origins of the Necessary and Proper Clause and the Independence Institute as Amici Curiae in Support of Respondents (Minimum Coverage Provision), 132 S. Ct. 2566 (No. 11–398). See also Gary Lawson & David Kopel, Bad News For Professor Koppelman: The Incidental Unconstitutionality of the Individual Mandate, 121 Yale L.J. Online 267 (2011).
7. I have briefly addressed these other issues in previous writings. See, e.g., Ilya Somin, *Why the Individual Health Care Mandate is Unconstitutional*, The Jurist (May 4, 2011), http://jurist.org/forum/2011/05/ilya-somin-mandate-is-unconstitutional.php.
8. Chief Justice Roberts reached this same conclusion in his opinion. *NFIB*, 132 S. Ct. at 2587–2591.
9. 17 U.S. (4 Wheat.) 316, 413–415 (1819).
10. See Brief for Petitioners (Minimum Coverage Provision), 132 S. Ct. 2566 (No. 11-398) [hereinafter Pet. Br.].
11. See, e.g., Erwin Chemerinsky, *Political Ideology and Constitutional Decision-making: The Coming Example of the Affordable Care Act*, 75 L. & Contemp. Probs. 1 (2012); Andrew Koppelman, *Bad News for Mail Robbers: The Obvious Constitutionality of Health Care Reform*, 121 Yale L.J. Online 1, 7–9 (2011); David B. Rivkin, Lee A. Kasey, & Jack Balkin, Debate, The Constitutionality of an Individual Mandate for Health Insurance, 158 U. Pa. L. Rev. PENNumbra 93, 105 (2009); Akhil Amar, *The Lawfulness of Health Care Reform* (Yale Law Sch. Pub. Law Working Paper No. 228, 2011), *available at* http://papers.ssrn.com/sol3/

papers.cfm?abstract_id=1856506. *But see* Mark A. Hall, *Commerce Clause Challenges to Health Reform*, 159 U. PA. L. REV. 1825, 1852–1858 (2011) (arguing that the mandate is "proper").

12. U.S. CONST. art. I, § 8, cl. 18 (emphasis added).

13. Two prominent academic defenders of a unitary approach to the clause conclude that their theory requires us to read "necessary and proper" as "an internally redundant phrase." Eric Posner & Adrian Vermeule, *Interring the Nondelegation Doctrine*, 69 U. CHI. L. REV. 1721, 1728 n.20 (2002).

14. Holmes v. Jennison, 39 U.S. 540, 570–571 (1840).

15. Knowlton v. Moore, 178 U.S. 41, 87 (1900). See also Dep't of Revenue v. Ass'n of Wash. Stevedoring Cos., 435 U.S. 734, 759 (1978) (rejecting the claim that "'Imposts or Duties' encompasses all taxes [because it] makes superfluous several of the terms of Art. I, § 8, cl. 1 of the Constitution, which grants Congress the 'Power To lay and collect Taxes, Duties, Imposts and Excises'"); Powell v. Alabama, 287 U.S. 45, 66 (1932) (holding that "no part of this important amendment [the Fifth Amendment] could be regarded as superfluous").

16. See, e.g., WILLIAM N. ESKRIDGE, JR., PHILLIP FRICKEY, & ELIZABETH GARRETT, CASES AND MATERIALS ON LEGISLATION: STATUTES AND THE CREATION OF PUBLIC POLICY 865–866 (4th ed. 2007) (citing numerous cases).

17. See Robert G. Natelson, *The Framing and Adoption of the Necessary and Proper Clause, in* GARY LAWSON ET AL., THE ORIGINS OF THE NECESSARY AND PROPER CLAUSE 84, 88–90 (2010); *cf.* Randy E. Barnett, *The Original Meaning of the Necessary and Proper Clause*, 6 U. PA. J. CONST. L. 183, 215 (2003) ("One thing that stands out from the records of the Constitutional Convention is how frequently the term 'necessary' was paired with 'proper' (or 'unnecessary' with 'improper') in contexts suggesting that each term has a distinct meaning").

18. Original public meaning originalism is now the dominant version of the theory. For leading defenses of the theory, see, e.g., RANDY E. BARNETT, RESTORING THE LOST CONSTITUTION: THE PRESUMPTION OF LIBERTY (2004); JACK M. BALKIN, LIVING ORIGINALISM (2011). For other citations to the relevant literature, see Ilya Somin, Originalism and Political Ignorance, 97 MINN. L. REV. 625, 625–627 (2012).

19. THE FEDERALIST NO. 33 (Alexander Hamilton).

20. *Id.*

21. See *McCulloch*, 17 U.S. (4 Wheat.) at 413–415. Alexander Hamilton was probably the originator of this broad interpretation of necessity. See Alexander Hamilton, Opinion on the Constitutionality of the Bank, Feb. 23, 1791, *in* 3 THE FOUNDERS' CONSTITUTION 247–249 (Philip B. Kurland & Ralph Lerner eds., 1987) (arguing that "necessary" should be interpreted to mean "no more *than needful, requisite, incidental, useful,* or *conducive to*").

22. Quoted in Gary Lawson & Patricia Granger, *The "Proper" Scope of Federal Power: A Jurisdictional Interpretation of the Sweeping Clause*, 43 DUKE L.J. 267, 290 (1993).

23. See *id.* at 290–308 (citing many examples).

24. NFIB v. Sebelius, 132 S. Ct. 2566, 2591–2592 (2012) (Roberts, C.J.).

25. 521 U.S. 898, 923–924 (1997) (quoting THE FEDERALIST NO. 33 (Alexander Hamilton)).

26. *Printz*, 521 U.S. at 902.

27. *Id.* at 923–924.

28. *Id.* at 923.

29. 527 U.S. 706, 733 (1999).

30. *Id.* At least one federal circuit court also concluded that "proper" and "necessary" are separate requirements prior to *NFIB*. See United States v. Sabri, 326 F.3d 937, 949 n.6 (2003), *aff'd* 541 U.S. 600 (2004) (holding that a statute is "proper" for reasons independent of its necessity).

31. *McCulloch*, 17 U.S. (4 Wheat.) at 413–415.

32. *Id.* at 421.

33. *Id.* at 423.

34. I expounded on this point in detail in Ilya Somin, *A Mandate for Mandates: Is the Individual Health Insurance Case a Slippery Slope?* 75 L. & CONTEMP. PROBS. 75, 84–93 (2012) [hereinafter Somin, *A Mandate for Mandates*].

35. 130 S. Ct. 1949 (2010).

36. See *id.* at 1956 (holding that necessity is satisfied if Congress adopts "a means that is rationally related to the implementation of a constitutionally enumerated power").

37. For my pre-*NFIB* assessment of *Comstock's* potential significance for the individual mandate case, see Ilya Somin, *Taking Stock of Comstock: The Necessary and Proper Clause and the Limits of Federal Power*, 2010 CATO SUP. CT. REV. 239, 260–267. In that article, I first explained why the *Comstock* five-part test was likely to cut against the government's position in the mandate case.

38. For a more detailed discussion of *Comstock's* applicability to the mandate, see *id.* and Brief of the Washington Legal Foundation and Constitutional Law Scholars as Amici Curiae in Support of Respondents (Individual Mandate Issue) at 32–35, NFIB v. Sebelius, 132 S. Ct. 2566 (2012) (No. 11-398).

39. 545 U.S. 1 (2005).

40. See, e.g., Lawrence Lessig, *Why Scalia Could Uphold Obamacare*, THE ATLANTIC, Apr. 13, 2012, *available at* http://www.theatlantic.com/national/archive/12/04/why-scalia-might-uphold-obamacare/255791/; Chemerinsky, *supra* note 11, at 11.

41. *Raich*, 545 U.S. at 34–38 (Scalia, J., concurring).

42. *Id.* at 39 (quoting *Printz*, 521 U.S. at 923–924) (emphasis in the original).

43. As Scalia put it, "The argument here is that this...may be necessary, but it's not proper, because it violates an equally evident principle in the Constitution, which is that the Federal Government is not supposed to be a government that has all powers; that it's supposed to be a government of limited powers." Quoted in Ilya Somin, *Thoughts on the Individual Mandate Oral Argument*, THE VOLOKH CONSPIRACY (Mar. 27, 2012, 7:15 PM), http://www.volokh.com/2012/03/27/thoughts-on-the-individual-mandate-oral-argument/.

44. See CASS R. SUNSTEIN, ONE CASE AT A TIME: JUDICIAL MINIMALISM ON THE SUPREME COURT (1999); *but see* Cass R. Sunstein, Beyond Judicial Minimalism (Harvard Pub. Law Working Paper No. 08–40, 2008), *available at* http://papers.ssrn.com/sol3/papers.cfm?abstract_id=1274200 (outlining some drawbacks of minimalism).

45. 22 U.S. (9 Wheat.) 1, 195 (1824).

46. See, e.g., Randy E. Barnett, *The Original Meaning of the Necessary and Proper Clause*, 6 U. PA. J. CONST. L. 183, 215–220 (2003) (discussing the relevant evidence); Kurt T. Lash, *A Textual-Historical Theory of the Ninth Amendment*, 60 STAN. L. REV. 895, 921 (2008) (citing evidence that the original meaning of the Constitution precludes any reading of the Necessary and Proper Clause that has "the effect of completely obliterating the people's retained right to local self-government"); Lawson & Granger, *supra* note 22, at 297 (explaining that the evidence shows that "proper" means that laws "must be consistent with principles of separation of powers, principles of federalism, and individual rights").

47. James Madison, *Speech on the Bank Bill, House of Representatives, Feb. 2, 1791, in* JAMES MADISON: WRITINGS 480, 484 (Jack N. Rakove ed., 1999).

48. See, e.g., Akhil Reed Amar, Op-Ed., *Constitutional Showdown: A Florida Judge Distorted the Law in Striking Down Healthcare Reform*, L.A. TIMES, Feb. 6, 2011, *available at* http://articles.latimes.com/2011/feb/06/opinion/la-oe-amar-health-care-legal-20110206 (comparing a district court ruling striking down the mandate to *Dred Scott v. Sanford*, arguably the most reviled decision in Supreme Court history).

49. AKHIL REED AMAR, AMERICA'S CONSTITUTION: A BIOGRAPHY 110 (2005).

50. Lawson & Granger, *supra* note 22, at 301–308.

51. THE FEDERALIST No. 33 (Alexander Hamilton); see also § 2.B, *infra* (discussing Hamilton's argument).

52. United States v. Morrison, 529 U.S. 598, 617–618 (2000). See also United States v. Lopez, 514 U.S. 549, 566 (1995) (emphasizing that Congress does not have "a plenary police power

that would authorize enactment of every type of legislation"); NLRB v. Jones & Laughlin Steel Co., 301 U.S. 1, 29 (1937) (noting "[t]hat the distinction between what is national and what is local in the activities of commerce is vital to the maintenance of our federal system").

53. Hall, *supra* note 11, at 1854. Justice Ginsburg's concurring opinion advances a similar argument. See *NFIB*, 132 S. Ct. at 2651 (Ginsburg, J., concurring in part, concurring in judgment in part, and dissenting in part) (claiming that previous cases asserting a separate requirement of propriety apply only to situations where the federal governments commandeers state officials in violation of the Tenth Amendment).

54. See, e.g., Charles Fried, *The June Surprises: Balls, Strikes, and the Fog of War*, in this volume (claiming that "since the New Deal...the conception has been that propriety is a matter of not contravening some distinct constitutional prohibition or principle" and that a law is only improper if it "bumps up against an explicit or implicit constitutional barrier").

55. See *infra* § 2.A (explaining why it is incorrect to interpret "proper" in a way that makes it redundant).

56. See, e.g., J. Randy Beck, *The New Jurisprudence of the Necessary and Proper Clause*, 2002 U. ILL. L. REV. 581, 581 (2002).

57. See *id.* (claiming that these cases interpreted the Necessary and Proper Clause incorrectly).

58. NFIB v. Sebelius, 132 S. Ct. 2566, 2592 (2012) (Roberts, C.J.).

59. *Id.*

60. *Id.* at 2590–2591, 2592.

61. *Id.* at 2646.

62. *Gibbons*, 22 U.S. (9 Wheat.) at 195.

63. See Somin, *A Mandate for Mandates, supra* note 34, at 84–93.

64. See *id.* at 82–83 (citing lower-court decisions adopting this rationale).

65. For a more detailed critique of the "economic decisions" rationale, see *id.* at 83–84.

66. See *id.* at 80–81 (citing examples).

67. See Seven-Sky v. Holder, 661 F.3d 1, 18 (D.C. Cir. 2011), *cert. denied*, No. 11–679 (June 29, 2012) (emphasizing that "the health insurance market is a rather unique one, both because virtually everyone will enter or affect it, and because the uninsured inflict a disproportionate harm on the rest of the market as a result of their later consumption of health care services"); Thomas More Law Ctr. v. Obama, 651 F.3d 529, 544 (6th Cir. 2011), *cert. denied*, No. 11-117 (June 29, 2012) (emphasizing that "[v]irtually everyone requires health care services at some point"); Mead v. Holder, 766 F. Supp. 2d 16, 37 (D.D.C. 2011), *aff'd sub nom. Seven-Sky*, 661 F.3d 1 (emphasizing "the inevitability of individuals' entrance into th[e] health care] market"); Liberty Univ. v. Geithner, 753 F. Supp. 2d 611, 633–634 (W.D. Va. 2010), *vacated*, 671 F.3d 391 (4th Cir. 2011), *cert. denied*, No. 11–438 (June 29, 2012) ("Nearly everyone will require health care services at some point in their lifetimes, and it is not always possible to predict when one will be afflicted by illness or injury and require care"); Thomas More Law Ctr. v. Obama, 720 F. Supp. 2d 882, 894 (E.D. Mich. 2010), *aff'd*, 651 F.3d 529 ("The health care market is unlike other markets. No one can guarantee his or her health, or ensure that he or she will never participate in the health care market.... The plaintiffs have not opted out of the health care services market because, as living, breathing beings...they cannot opt out of this market").

68. See *NFIB*, 132 S. Ct. at 2619–2620 (Ginsburg, J., concurring in part, concurring in judgment in part, and dissenting in part).

69. Florida *ex rel.* Bondi v. U.S. Dep't of Health & Human Servs., 780 F. Supp. 2d 1256, 1289 (N.D. Fla. 2011), *aff'd in part, rev'd in part*, 648 F.3d 1235 (11th Cir. 2011), *aff'd in part, rev'd in part sub nom. NFIB*, 132 S. Ct. 2566 ("Congress could require that people buy and consume broccoli at regular intervals, not only because the required purchases will positively impact interstate commerce, but also because people who eat healthier tend to be healthier, and...put less of a strain on the health care system.").

70. *NFIB*, 132 S. Ct. at 2590–2591. Other judges made similar points previously. See Virginia *ex rel.* Cuccinelli v. Sebelius, 728 F. Supp. 2d 768, 781 (E.D. Va. 2010), *vacated on other grounds*,

656 F.3d 253 (4th Cir. 2011), *cert. denied,* No. 11-420 (June 29, 2012) ("the same reasoning could apply to transportation, housing, or nutritional decisions"). See also Florida *ex rel.* Bondi, 780 F. Supp. 2d at 1289 (noting that "there are lots of markets—especially if defined broadly enough—that people cannot 'opt out' of. For example, everyone must participate in the food market"); *Seven-Sky,* 661 F.3d at 51–52 (Kavanaugh, J., dissenting) (noting that this theory "extend[s] as well to mandatory purchases of retirement accounts, housing accounts, college savings accounts, disaster insurance, disability insurance, and life insurance, for example").

71. *NFIB,* 132 S. Ct. at 2619–2620.

72. See, *eg., id.* at 2619–2620; Pet. Br., *supra* note 10, at 40. See also *Mead,* 766 F. Supp. 2d at 36–37 (emphasizing this point).

73. *Mead,* 766 F. Supp. 2d at 36–37; Pet. Br., *supra* note 10, at 40.

74. See Pet. Br., *supra* note 10, at 34–36. Unpredictability is also noted as a distinguishing factor by Justice Ginsburg. *NFIB,* 132 S. Ct. at 2619–2620.

75. Studies show that broccoli has significant health benefits. See Somin, *A Mandate for Mandates, supra* note 34, at 82 n.27 (citing several studies).

76. See, e.g., Neil Siegel, *Free Riding on Benevolence: Collective Action Federalism and the Minimum Coverage Provision,* 75 L. & CONTEMP. PROBS. 29 (2012).

77. See Somin, *A Mandate for Mandates, supra* note 34, at 90–94.

78. *Id.* at 93–94.

79. *McCulloch,* 17 U.S. at 421.

80. *Morrison,* 529 U.S. at 618 n.8. For a more detailed argument as to why a law whose rationale would make other parts of Article I redundant is "improper," see Gary Lawson, *Discretion As Delegation: The "Proper" Understanding of the Nondelegation Doctrine,* 73 GEO. WASH. L. REV. 235, 249–255 (2005).

81. See § 3.B, *infra.*

82. *Raich,* 545 U.S. at 25–26 (quoting WEBSTER'S THIRD NEW INTERNATIONAL DICTIONARY 720 (1966)).

83. See, e.g., United States v. Comstock, 130 S. Ct. 1949, 1956–1957 (2010) (holding that the requirement of necessity is satisfied so long as there is a "rational relationship" between Congress's ends and the means it chooses to adopt).

84. U.S. CONST. art. I, § 8, cl. 14, 16.

85. *Id.*

86. See, e.g., Akhil Reed Amar, *Constitutional Redundancies and Clarifying Clauses,* 33 VAL. U. L. REV. 1 (1998).

87. For arguments that this is the correct definition of "proper" and that the mandate fails it, see works cited *supra* in notes 6 and 17. For the originalist case that propriety bars non-incidental powers, see Robert G. Natelson, *The Legal Origins of the Necessary and Proper Clause, in* LAWSON ET AL., *supra* note 17, at 52–83.

88. NFIB v. Sebelius, 132 S. Ct. 2566, 2591–2592 (2012) (Roberts, C.J.) (quoting *McCulloch,* 17 U.S. (4 Wheat.) at 418).

89. *McCulloch,* 17 U.S. (4 Wheat.) at 411, 421.

90. For example, Congress could not force people to give up their First Amendment rights to freedom of speech or freedom of religion because legislation that violates constitutional rights is barred even if it falls within the scope of Congress's enumerated powers.

91. See works cited *supra* in notes 6 and 17.

92. See, e.g., David Post, *Dicta on the Commerce Clause,* THE VOLOKH CONSPIRACY (July 1, 2012, 6:40 PM), http://www.volokh.com/2012/07/01/dicta-on-the-commerce-clause/.

93. *NFIB,* 132 S. Ct. at 2593–2600.

94. *Id.* at 2599. I have elaborated on the importance of this part of the opinion in Ilya Somin, *A Simple Solution to the Holding vs. Dictum Mess,* THE VOLOKH CONSPIRACY (July 2, 2012, 3:47 PM), http://www.volokh.com/2012/07/02/a-simple-solution-to-the-holding-vs-dictum-mess/.

95. *NFIB*, 132 S. Ct. at 2601–2602.
96. *Id.*
97. *Id.* at 2644–2647.
98. See United States v. Elk Shoulder, 696 F.3d 922, 930–931 (9th Cir. 2012) (applying *NFIB*'s rulings that the Necessary and Proper authority extends "only [to] 'those who by some preexisting activity bring themselves within the sphere of federal regulation'" and that "the Necessary and Proper Clause provides no justification for laws effecting 'a substantial expansion of federal authority'" (quoting *NFIB*, 132 S. Ct at 2592)). Two district courts have also applied Roberts's position on the Commerce Clause as binding precedent. See United States v. Moore, No. CR-12-6023-RMP, 2012 WL 3780343, at *3 (E.D. Wash. Aug. 31, 2012) (treating it as a binding concurring opinion under Marks v. United States, 430 U.S. 188 (1977)); United States v. Williams, No. 12-60116-CR-RNS, 2012 WL 3242043, at *3 (S.D. Fla. Aug. 7, 2012) (stating that Chief Justice Roberts was "writing for the Court" when discussing Congress's commerce power). One has gone the other way. See United States v. Spann, No. 3:12-CR-126-L, 2012 WL 4341799, at *3 (N.D. Tex. Sept. 24, 2012).
99. *NFIB*, 132 S. Ct. at 2587.
100. *Id.* at 2590–2591.
101. Somin, *A Mandate for Mandates*, *supra* note 34, at 96–98.
102. I describe this possibility in greater detail in Ilya Somin, *A Taxing, But Potentially Hopeful Decision*, SCOTUSBLOG (June 28, 2012, 6:13 PM), http://www.scotusblog.com/2012/06/a-taxing-but-potentially-hopeful-decision.
103. *NFIB*, 132 S. Ct. at 2593–2599.
104. *Id.* at 2627.
105. One such is *NFIB*'s invalidation of part of the ACA's expansion of the Medicaid health care program as beyond Congress's powers under the Spending Clause. Two liberal justices, Stephen Breyer and Elena Kagan, joined this part of Chief Justice Roberts's opinion. See *NFIB*, 132 S. Ct. at 2601–2608.
106. *Cf.* Lawrence B. Solum, *The Effects of NFIB v. Sebelius and the Constitutional Gestalt* (Georgetown Pub. Law Research Paper No. 12-152, 2012), *available at* http://papers.ssrn.com/sol3/papers.cfm?abstract_id=2152653 (arguing that the Court's federalism jurisprudence is "unsettled" in the wake of *NFIB*).

# THE IMPORTANT ROLE
# OF THE CHIEF JUSTICE

# CHAPTER 10

# Judicial Minimalism, the Mandate, and Mr. Roberts

*Jonathan H. Adler*

Chief Justice John Roberts's opinion to uphold the individual mandate as a constitutional exercise of the taxing power caught most commentators by surprise. Few who hoped or expected the mandate to prevail foresaw that the Chief would control the outcome. Even fewer anticipated that Roberts would simultaneously reject the Commerce and Necessary and Proper Clause rationales for the mandate while salvaging the law's constitutionality as an exercise of the taxing power.

Postdecision reports that Roberts changed his vote at some point after the initial conference, and resulting discord at One First Street, fueled speculation that the Chief may have been swayed by political considerations, or perhaps even buckled to external pressure.[1] Critics on the right castigated the Chief for his alleged capitulation and challenged Roberts's conservative bona fides, while many on the left praised his judicial statesmanship.[2] Some even compared John Roberts to Chief Justice John Marshall, going so far to characterize his *NFIB v. Sebelius* (*NFIB*) opinion as a *Marbury v. Madison* for our time; an exercise of judicial jujitsu that embraced the Right's constitutional arguments even as it avoided issuing a judgment that could provoke a political backlash.[3] That few commentators found Roberts's opinion wholly persuasive only fueled suspicion that politics drove Roberts's decision.

Much commentary assumes it is necessary to ascribe political motivations to the Chief Justice. On such accounts, Roberts must have feared the consequences for the Court and its legitimacy, if not for his own legacy as Chief Justice. What such commentary overlooks is the extent to which Chief Justice Roberts's *NFIB* opinion is consistent with his own stated judicial philosophy and his record on the bench. The key elements of his opinion are of a piece with his prior opinions as a justice and circuit court judge and his accounts of the proper judicial role. Whether or not one agrees with Roberts's conclusions, there is no need to ascribe him political motives, or worse.

A majority of the Court in *NFIB* held that the individual mandate did not constitute a valid exercise of the Commerce Clause power, even if supplemented by the Necessary and Proper Clause.[4] For Justices Scalia, Kennedy, Thomas, and Alito, this was enough to seal the individual mandate's fate.[5] As they read the Affordable Care Act (ACA), Congress sought to mandate the purchase of health insurance, not impose a tax on a failure to purchase it.[6] Chief Justice Roberts agreed this was the "most straightforward reading" of the relevant statutory language. But this did not end the matter for him. Rather, Roberts concluded, it was "necessary" to consider whether the mandate's constitutionality could be sustained by an alternative reading of the text.[7]

Section 5000A(a) directs that all nonexempt individuals "shall" obtain qualifying health insurance.[8] This language "commands individuals to purchase insurance."[9] Yet Roberts insisted the Court should also consider whether an alternative interpretation—an interpretation that would treat the mandate and enforcement penalty as a tax—was sufficiently "reasonable" for the Court to sustain it. "The question is not whether that is the most natural interpretation of the mandate, but only whether it is a fairly possible one." As Roberts explained, the Court had an obligation to consider "every reasonable construction" of a duly enacted federal law before striking it down.[10]

Intent on finding a way to salvage the constitutionality of the individual mandate, Roberts turned away from the text to consider how the mandate and associated penalty would function in practice. Setting aside Congress's decision to label the exaction a "penalty," Roberts noted it would function as a tax, much like other provisions of the Internal Revenue Code. Whereas a universal mandate to purchase insurance was "novel" and unprecedented, using taxes to encourage purchases was old hat. Thus, Roberts concluded, the "requirement that certain individuals pay a financial penalty for not obtaining health insurance may reasonably be characterized as a tax," and such a tax would be well within Congress's constitutional authority.[11]

*NFIB* was not the first case in which Chief Justice Roberts embraced a strained "saving construction" of a statute in order to preserve its constitutionality. Most notably, Roberts did the same thing in *Northwest Austin Municipal Utility District No. 1 v. Holder* (*NAMUDNO*) to preserve Section 5 of the Voting Rights Act (VRA) against a constitutional challenge.[12] His opinion for the Court in *NAMUDNO* adopted a strained and scarcely plausible interpretation of Section 5, and yet was joined by all but one of the justices.[13]

Congress enacted the VRA to enforce the Fifteenth Amendment guarantee that the "right of citizens of the United States to vote shall not be denied or abridged...on account of race, color, or previous condition of servitude." The law bars discriminatory election procedures and practices nationwide and imposes additional restrictions on those portions of the country with a history of voting discrimination. Specifically, Section 5 requires designated jurisdictions (so-called "covered jurisdictions") to obtain the federal government's permission before making any changes to existing voting procedures or practices, including voter eligibility requirements and polling locations.

"Covered jurisdictions" are those jurisdictions that had employed discriminatory or otherwise prohibited voting practices and in which fewer than 50 percent of eligible voters were registered or voted in the 1964 presidential election. Such jurisdictions may only alter voting practices or procedures by obtaining "preclearance" from the attorney general or a three-judge federal district court on the basis that the change neither "has the purpose nor will have the effect of denying or abridging the right to vote on account of race or color."[14] "Covered jurisdictions" that wish to be free of Section 5's limitations may file a declaratory judgment seeking to "bail out" from the preclearance requirements.[15] In this suit the jurisdiction must show that it has not engaged in any proscribed voting rights violations within the previous ten years and that it has taken steps to prevent voter intimidation and harassment.[16]

The Northwest Austin Municipal Utility District No. 1 filed suit challenging the preclearance provisions on the basis that these requirements could no longer be considered "congruent and proportional" to the rights violations they were designed to address. This claim received some force from the fact that Congress had twice renewed the VRA without updating the formula upon which the "covered jurisdiction" determinations are made. Whatever the scope of voting rights violations today, NAMUDNO argued, they bear little relationship to those in 1964. In the alternative, NAMUDNO also argued that it was a "political subdivision" that should be permitted to bail out from the preclearance requirements. The problem with this argument was that the plain text of Section 5 seemed to limit bailout suits to states and those political subdivisions separately designated for coverage under the Act, and a local utility district in Texas would not seem to qualify.[17]

Despite the text of the VRA, eight justices concluded that NAMUDNO could bail out of Section 5's preclearance requirements. Chief Justice Roberts's opinion for the Court noted the potential constitutional difficulties posed by Section 5, but shrunk from confronting them. Quoting Justice Oliver Wendell Holmes's admonition that overturning a duly enacted act of Congress is "the gravest and most delicate duty that this Court is called on to perform," Roberts noted that the Court should avoid reaching constitutional questions "if there is some other ground upon which to dispose of the case."[18] NAMUDNO's alternative statutory argument provided this alternative basis, even if the text of the VRA did not.

Roberts's opinion acknowledged that the text of the VRA did not appear to support NAMUDNO's bailout claim, as the district court had concluded. Yet the "underlying constitutional concerns" with such an interpretation "compel[led] a broader reading of the statute," even if there was little basis in the VRA's text or history to support it.[19] By comparison Roberts's interpretation of the ACA is thoroughly persuasive.

NAMUDNO showed Chief Justice Roberts willing to lead the Court toward adopting a strained and scarcely plausible reading of a statute in order to avoid declaring a law unconstitutional and unnecessarily splintering the Court. NAMUDNO is not an isolated case, however.[20] Roberts has joined a few decisions overturning federal statutes on First Amendment grounds, but such decisions have been the exception.[21] Chief Justice Roberts has repeatedly joined, if not always himself written, opinions that adopted statutory interpretations enabling the Court to avoid difficult constitutional questions, particularly where such interpretations could produce greater unanimity on the Court. As Roberts explained in a 2006 commencement address, his aim is to produce narrower opinions that more justices can join. "Division should not be artificially suppressed, but the rule of law benefits from a broader agreement," he told Georgetown University Law Center's graduating class. "The broader the agreement among the justices, the more likely it is a decision on the narrowest possible grounds."[22]

Roberts has also shown a preference for as-applied challenges, a preference that avoids broader-than-necessary constitutional rulings (if it also makes constitutional challenges to federal statutes more difficult).[23] Just as Roberts seeks saving constructions of federal statutes to preserve their constitutionality, he embraces as-applied challenges as a means to excise potentially unconstitutional applications of an otherwise constitutional statutory scheme. In each case, Roberts has shown a willingness to elevate this conception of judicial restraint above plain readings of statutory text. Thus in *Federal Election Commission v. Wisconsin Right to Life* (*WRTL*), Roberts concluded that the Bipartisan Campaign Reform Act's limitations on corporate funding of "electioneering communications" were unconstitutional as-applied to the appellants' issue advertisements, effectively rewriting the relevant statutory provisions in the process.[24] In *WRTL* Roberts both rejected Justice Scalia's entreaty to invalidate the challenged provision on its face and eschewed reliance on the statute's "backup" definition of electioneering communications that would have been triggered as a result.

*Citizens United v. Federal Election Commission* would appear to provide a prominent counterexample to NAMUDNO. *Citizens United* overturned two of the Court's precedents and declared key portions of the Bipartisan Campaign Reform Act (BCRA) unconstitutional under the First Amendment.[25] Although he did not write the opinion for the Court, Roberts joined Justice Kennedy's opinion in full, embracing a broad constitutional holding when narrower statutory holdings were available. Does this undermine the claim that Roberts prefers to avoid constitutional questions and is particularly averse to unnecessarily invalidating an act of Congress? Not necessarily.

At issue in *Citizens United* was Section 203 of the BCRA, which barred corporations and unions from spending general treasury funds on an "electioneering communication," defined as a "broadcast, cable or satellite communication that refers to a candidate for federal office" aired within thirty days of a primary or sixty days of a general election. The petitioners in this case, Citizens United, had sought to air an anti–Hillary Clinton video on cable networks as a video-on-demand feature. As this would constitute a "cable...communication," distributing the video in this way would have been covered by the Act. Holding otherwise, and defining cable video-on-demand as something other than a "cable...communication," would have required adopting a fairly implausible reading of the statutory text—a reading not a single justice on the Court was willing to endorse.

Although Chief Justice Roberts ultimately joined Justice Kennedy's opinion rejecting a potential saving construction of the BCRA, reporting by Jeffrey Toobin for the *New Yorker* suggests Roberts—and Roberts alone—had been willing to adopt a saving construction of the statute.[26] As Toobin tells the tale, after *Citizens United* was first argued Roberts drafted a narrow opinion holding for Citizens United on statutory grounds. This opinion interpreted the BCRA so as to avoid the constitutional question lurking within the case. Unlike in *NAMUDNO*, however, this approach did not foster near unanimity. Four justices saw no constitutional problems with limiting electioneering communications that could justify stretching the statute's text.[27]

After Roberts circulated this opinion, Justice Kennedy circulated a concurrence reiterating his view that the BCRA was unconstitutional under the First Amendment. The other conservative justices apparently found Kennedy's opinion convincing, as they all reportedly signed on. This left Roberts as the only justice willing to adopt a saving construction of the statute. Faced with the alternative of authoring a solo opinion embracing a statutory interpretation rejected by every other justice on the Court, Roberts reportedly acquiesced to Kennedy's approach. As Toobin recounts, some of the dissenters complained that the broader First Amendment questions were not properly before the Court, prompting the Court to schedule a re-argument with supplemental briefing that would place the First Amendment question front and center.

In his *New Yorker* article, Toobin dwells on Justice Stevens's complaint that the Court's broad holding in *Citizens United* was unnecessary, as the Court could have held for the petitioners on narrower, statutory grounds. Yet as Toobin's own reporting recounts, Roberts was the only justice on the Court willing to resolve the case on such a basis. Four justices were ready to declare BCRA unconstitutional, and four saw no constitutional problem at all.

Assuming Toobin's account of *Citizens United* is correct, this is further evidence of Chief Justice Roberts's reluctance to invalidate federal statutes. Where possible, the Chief prefers to adopt saving constructions and avoid constitutional rulings. Yet this preference has limits, particularly when it conflicts with other jurisprudential commitments, such as Roberts's distaste for fractured rulings and solo opinions that announce the holding of the Court. Roberts has been critical of the Court's tendency to produce splintered majorities that make it more difficult for litigants and lower courts to understand and apply the Court's holdings. So when the Court split four-one-four in *Rapanos v. United States*, Roberts lamented that no opinion could command a majority of the Court, depriving lower courts and regulated entities of a clear rule for future cases.[28]

Given the conservative dissenters' approach to severability, a splintered opinion was unavoidable if Roberts sought to avoid invalidating the ACA in its entirety. As he testified at his confirmation hearing, Roberts believes courts should decide no more than necessary in a given case and should strive to avoid unnecessary conflict with the political branches. This approach recommends a narrow approach to severability just as it encourages the adoption of saving statutory constructions. In each instance the aim is to leave as much of Congress's handiwork undisturbed as the case allows.

After concluding that conditioning receipt of existing Medicaid funds on a state's willingness to accept the ACA's Medicaid expansion was unduly "coercive," Roberts sought to invalidate as little of the ACA as possible. Thus he concluded that the Medicaid expansion itself was constitutional, even if one associated provision was not. Just as *NFIB* was not Roberts's first embrace of a saving construction, it was not the first time Roberts adopted a narrow approach to severability. Roberts wrote for the Court in *Free Enterprise Fund v. Public Company Accounting Board* (*PCAOB*), voiding a limitation on the president's ability to influence the PCAOB while leaving all other aspects of the agency (and its authorizing statute) undisturbed.[29]

Roberts's reluctance to invalidate federal statutes is evidence of his minimalist orientation—an orientation that often puts him at odds with other conservative justices on the Court. *NFIB* was not the first case in which his reluctance to embrace a broader holding prompted discord. In one case Roberts's reticence to act more boldly prompted Justice Scalia to accuse him of "faux judicial restraint."[30] Whatever its merits, Roberts's approach has been relatively consistent. Just as he has been reluctant to strike down federal statutes and embrace broad holdings, he has eschewed clear opportunities to overturn long-standing, if poorly regarded, precedents. So while he voted to deny standing in *Hein v. Freedom from Religion Foundation*,[31] he refused to overrule *Flast v. Cohen*,[32] preserving an anomaly in the law of standing.

A common thread in Roberts's minimalism is a preference for maintaining the status quo and, where possible, not upsetting established legal rules and creating new law. This is reinforced by a demonstrated preference to narrow the role of the Court in public affairs. Not only does Roberts seek to avoid contradicting the political branches, he has also voted fairly consistently to narrow the scope of Article III standing, heighten pleading requirements, and deny new opportunities for private plaintiffs to file suit against public and private plaintiffs alike.

Throughout, Chief Justice Roberts's minimalism aims to lessen the role of the Court in the nation's politics. In this regard, the important part of the infamous umpire analogy Roberts shared at his confirmation hearing was not his reference to the umpire's role calling balls and strikes, but his comment that "Nobody ever went to a ball game to see the umpire."[33] His judicial approach narrows the range of cases the Court will hear and lessens the likely impact of any individual case, either by seeking narrow holdings that can attract broad agreement or by refusing to overturn federal laws or the Court's own precedents unless absolutely necessary. This tendency has also been observed in the Court's behavior as a whole since Roberts was confirmed as Chief Justice. The Supreme Court, under Roberts's leadership, has invalidated federal statutes and overturned precedents at a slower rate than under Chief Justices Rehnquist, Burger, and Warren[34] and, in most areas, has only moved legal doctrine slightly, if at all.[35] This commitment to judicial minimalism (albeit a judicial minimalism with a rightward tilt), helps explain his reach for a saving construction of the individual mandate's penalty provision.

Chief Justice Roberts's decision to salvage the individual mandate's constitutionality and preserve as much of the ACA as was possible is of a piece with a demonstrated commitment to judicial minimalism. But what of Roberts's conclusion that the mandate could not be justified under the Commerce or Necessary and Proper Clauses? Before reaching for a saving construction that would enable the Court to uphold the mandate's penalty as a tax, Roberts concluded the mandate itself exceeded the scope of Congress's power to regulate commerce among the several states, even as supplemented. Here Roberts embraced a formalist analysis of the Commerce Clause power that focused on first characterizing the nature of the activity subject to federal regulation under the mandate, and then determining whether the mandate could be properly characterized as a regulation of "commerce." This was not a novel approach for the Court or for Roberts. From the New Deal to the present, the Court had never "sustained federal regulation of intrastate activity based upon the activity's substantial effects on interstate commerce" without also concluding "the activity in question had been some sort of economic endeavor."[36] Thus if the activity subject to regulation by the mandate were not itself "economic" in a meaningful sense, its constitutionality was not assured under existing precedent, no matter how much the mandate itself could affect health insurance markets or the economy at large. This is the same approach Roberts used in his very first opinion as a federal judge, where Roberts noted that whether a given regulation constitutes a valid exercise of the commerce power turns on "whether the *activity* being regulated" is sufficiently economic that it "can be said to be interstate commerce," and not whether a regulatory scheme itself has substantial economic effects.[37]

Whether the individual mandate could be said to be a regulation of economic activity was always central to the Commerce Clause question in *NFIB*. For this reason, mandate supporters generally characterized the mandate as a regulation of identifiable economic activities. Congress, for instance, declared the mandate regulated "economic and financial decisions about how and when health care is paid for, and when health insurance is purchased."[38] Judge Boyce Martin of the U.S. Court of Appeals for the Sixth Circuit characterized the relevant class as "the practice of self-insuring for the cost of health care delivery."[39] Mandate opponents, on the other hand, claimed it was not a regulation of economic activity at all, but rather a regulation of "inactivity," or a requirement that all Americans engage in activity that would then subject them to regulation.[40] They noted that even those who would never purchase health insurance, or perhaps even never purchase health care, were still subject to the mandate.

The resolution of this debate over how to characterize that which the mandate regulated would go a long way toward determining whether the mandate was, in fact, a permissible regulation of commerce. Setting aside (for a moment) the supplemental authority of the Necessary and Proper Clause, the Commerce Clause only grants Congress the power to regulate commerce. Although the power to regulate commerce has been considered broad enough to reach all economic activity, the Rehnquist Court repeatedly stressed that this power is still subject to a meaningful outer limit.

Whether a given exercise of the commerce power is constitutional is determined by how the power is exercised, not whether a given statute reaches otherwise regulable conduct. Consider *United States v. Lopez*.[41] Alfonso Lopez was arrested while he was participating in a commercial transaction. He possessed a gun within a school zone because he was to deliver a gun to a local gang member. This activity was unquestionably subject to the federal commerce power as it had been understood. Why, then, did the federal government lose its case? Because the Gun-Free School Zones Act (GFSZA) did not regulate gun sales or commercially related gun possession, nor did the statute contain a jurisdictional element that could serve to confine its application to those instances of gun possession with a sufficiently commercial nexus to fit within the commerce power.[42] Had the statute been written in this way, Alfonso Lopez would have gone to jail.

Although the GFSZA could be applied to economic conduct within the scope of federal power, that was not what it regulated on its own terms. The class of activities subject to regulation under the GFSZA—gun possession in or near schools—was not economic, and this was so whether or not a given defendant had possessed a gun in school for economic purposes, brought the gun across state lines, or even whether the majority of those who would violate the GFSZA's prohibition would be otherwise engaged in regulable conduct. What matters is what Congress actually did.

Chief Justice Roberts made this very point in his *Rancho Viejo* opinion, in which he challenged the Commerce Clause analyses embraced by his colleagues on the U.S. Court of Appeals for the D.C. Circuit.[43] As he noted, *Lopez* and *Morrison* were both facial challenges to federal statutes. Under *United States v. Salerno*, a facial challenge "can succeed only if there are no circumstances in which the Act at issue can be applied without violating the Commerce Clause."[44] As each law arguably reached some conduct that could be subject to regulation under the Commerce Clause, this means that the relevant question is not whether the laws themselves could substantially affect commerce, nor whether the specific activities taken by a party in a specific case could substantially affect commerce, even when aggregated with all other instances of like conduct. Rather, the question is whether the class of activity subject to regulation by the statute—gun possession near a school, gender-motivated violence, or the failure to be insured—substantially affects commerce, which is another way of asking whether the activity identified and made subject to federal regulation by the statute is itself economic.

Viewed in this way, the constitutionality of the individual mandate was anything but a slam dunk. It may well be that the vast majority of Americans engage in health care transactions of one sort or another that are readily subject to federal control. Engaging in such transactions is not what made an individual subject to the mandate, however. To the contrary, an individual who has never purchased health care (let alone health insurance)—and never plans to—was still obligated to purchase insurance. Although the legislative purpose may have been to regulate health-related financial decisions, and reduce the adverse selection that threatens health insurance markets, the class of activities subject to regulation under the mandate was not limited to those who are or would be engaged in such economic decisions. Under Roberts's understanding of *Lopez*, as outlined in his *Rancho Viejo* decision, this was a problem.

The mandate, by its terms, applied to everyone within the country, save those expressly exempted. (The penalty, on the other hand, was only imposed on those meeting certain criteria.) The activity subject to regulation was not the purchase or pursuit of health care, as it applied whether or not someone had sought health care, and whether or not an individual would become a free rider, imposing health care costs on others. A hermit living off the grid in Montana, growing his own food, making his own herb-based medicines, and not engaged in economic exchange with anyone would be subject to the requirement to obtain health insurance just the same as everyone else. Application of the mandate was not tied to any preexisting economic or commercial activity. As Roberts noted, the mandate "does not regulate existing commercial activity. It instead compels individuals to become active in commerce by purchasing a product."[45] This was a problem, in Roberts's eyes, because the Court's Commerce Clause precedents "recognize[d] Congress's power to regulate 'class[es] of activities' not classes of individuals, *apart from any activity in which they are engaged*," or due to some hypothesized activity they are likely to undertake in the future.[46]

It was not enough to say that the ACA as a whole, or even the mandate in particular, had an economic purpose or that most of those subject to the mandate's requirements were or would be engaged in economic activity. Legislative purpose, as such, has long been irrelevant to Commerce Clause decisions. The Civil Rights Act of 1964 was no more enacted to facilitate commerce than the ban on interstate shipment of lottery tickets.[47] The motivations for such laws were moral ideals, not economics. The constitutionality of such statutes did not rely upon legislative intent, but on what the laws actually did.[48] That the ACA was focused on restructuring and regulating health insurance markets was likewise not determinative, as what matters for this analysis is what a specific provision actually did in service of this economically related end. The regulation of noneconomic, intrastate activity—in the case of *NFIB*, "inactivity" or the failure to engage in a desired economic activity—would not suffice.

Whether or not Chief Justice Roberts's treatment of the Commerce Clause claim was compelled by precedent, it represented a plausible interpretation of the Court's Commerce Clause jurisprudence as modified by the Rehnquist Court. Well before the ACA was proposed (let alone enacted), commentators had noted the importance of identifying the precise class of activities subject to regulation when considering whether a given legislative measure could be justified as a valid regulation of commerce.[49] Roberts adopted this approach as a judge on the D.C. Circuit without much controversy. Thus it should not surprise that he persisted with this analytical approach once on the Supreme Court, or that he ultimately found a naked mandate to purchase health insurance could not be justified as a regulation of commerce.

The individual mandate did not merely pose a question under the Commerce Clause. The strongest argument for the mandate's constitutionality was never that it was a regulation of commerce, as such, but that it was necessary to carry into execution other regulation of commerce enacted by the ACA, and was thus a valid exercise of the Necessary and Proper Clause. This argument had an analytical clarity most efforts to characterize the mandate as commerce regulation lacked, and had the additional benefit of replicating the arguments that convinced six justices to uphold the federal prohibition on the possession of marijuana, even when possessed for medical purposes, in *Gonzales v. Raich*.[50]

In *Raich* the Court held Congress could have reasonably concluded that it was necessary and proper to prohibit marijuana possession in order to make the federal prohibition on the sale of marijuana more effective. By the same token, mandate supporters could argue that requiring the purchase of health insurance would make the ACA's other health insurance regulations more effective. In particular, a universal coverage requirement could help prevent adverse selection in health insurance markets after the imposition of community rating and rules against denying coverage due to preexisting conditions. If these regulations were permissible exercises of the commerce power—and under existing precedent they clearly were—there would seem to be a strong argument for the mandate as a means of helping to carry such regulations into execution.

Whereas Chief Justice Roberts's rejection of the pure Commerce Clause argument was foreshadowed by his analytical approach in *Rancho Viejo*, no prior opinion suggested his approach to the Necessary and Proper Clause, nor his approach to the Spending Clause, when the question turned to the constitutionality of the Medicaid expansion. What, then, explains these portions of his opinion?

Roberts's narrow reading of the Necessary and Proper Clause and limitation of the spending power are probably best understood as an application and continuation of the Rehnquist Court's insistence that all enumerated powers be subject to meaningful, judicially enforced limits. As the late Chief Justice Rehnquist announced in *United States v. Lopez*, the need for such limits was a matter of "first principles," and the Court was obligated to reject any assertion of federal power that was without meaningful limit. From this standpoint, the unprecedented nature of the individual mandate and Medicaid expansion weighed against their constitutionality.

Roberts's fealty to the Rehnquist Court's federalism jurisprudence may be an outgrowth of his time clerking for then–Associate Justice Rehnquist on the Supreme Court. The term Roberts worked for Rehnquist, the future architect of the "New Federalism" previewed his commitment to meaningful, judicially enforced limits on federal power with a separate concurrence in *Hodel v. Virginia Surface Mining & Reclamation Association*.[51] While most of the Court had little difficulty concluding Congress could enact a comprehensive regulatory scheme governing the mining industry, Rehnquist had his doubts. Though he joined the judgment, he penned a separate opinion concurring in the judgment lamenting the Court's failure to take its role as enforcer of limits on federal power more seriously. He even edited his opinion after publication to stress the commerce power's constitutional limits.[52] Foreshadowing Roberts's opinion in *Rancho Viejo*, he made it clear the activity subject to regulation had to have a substantial effect on interstate commerce for the exercise of federal power to be constitutional. That a regulatory scheme could have such an effect would not be sufficient.

The *Hodel* concurrence set the stage for the federalism jurisprudence that would later be a hallmark of the Rehnquist Court. In *Lopez* and *Morrison*, Rehnquist effectively turned his *Hodel* concurrence into a majority holding of the Court. In *Lopez* specifically, Rehnquist stressed that "first principles" required judicially enforceable limits on federal power.[53] Yet the Rehnquist Court did not trim back federal power so much as it refused to let Congress extend its reach further. In effect these decisions said "go forth and sin no more."

The laws invalidated in *Lopez* and *Morrison* were characterized by Rehnquist as the most expansive assertions of federal power to date. To uphold these laws, Rehnquist explained, would be to countenance a federal power without limit. In much the same way, Roberts characterized both the mandate and the Medicaid expansion as the most expansive exercises of the commerce and conditional spending power to date. To uphold the federal government's necessary and proper rationale for the mandate would, Roberts suggested, have allowed the federal government a power without limit—a potential outcome the Rehnquist Court had time and again rejected. To uphold the Medicaid expansion would have made it too easy for Congress to coerce states with threats to withhold large, preexisting grants of federal funds, potentially undermining the limits on conditional spending Rehnquist had articulated in *South Dakota v. Dole*.[54] Either outcome would have compromised the Rehnquist Court's insistence on meaningful limits to federal power. Perhaps this is why Roberts thought each went too far.

*NFIB* confirms that John Roberts, as Chief Justice, is precisely what one would have expected: a conservative judicial minimalist.[55] Justice Roberts is conservative, to be sure. One would expect no less from a Bush nominee and Reagan Justice Department alum. Yet unlike others, Roberts is not clearly a movement conservative and does not appear wedded to originalism or any other particular conservative judicial ideology.[56] Whereas some of his colleagues on the right flank are ready to embrace broad rulings, sweeping away whatever precedents and statutes their interpretations would require, Roberts is a minimalist. His tendency is to take each case at a time, leaving the status quo as undisturbed as possible. Whereas others are quick to pen solo concurrences and dissents distinguishing their views from the Court's, Roberts seeks greater unanimity. For him a narrow but unanimous ruling that obscures divisions within the Court is a virtue, not a vice. And though unanimity was not possible in *NFIB*, he sought to be a part of majority rationales while voiding as little of the statute as possible.

When John Roberts was nominated to the Supreme Court, many predicted he would be a conservative judicial minimalist. That is, he would have a generally conservative outlook, but would try to decide cases narrowly, avoid disturbing precedents, and defer to the other political branches. This is what he has tended to do since becoming Chief Justice. From this perspective, his opinion in *NFIB* makes sense. This is not a defense of Roberts's opinion on the merits, for there is much in his *NFIB* opinion with which to disagree. It is merely to claim the opinion is understandable given Roberts's record to date. If, for Chief Justice Roberts, his opinion in *NFIB v. Sebelius* is defining, it is because it defines and encapsulates the tendencies he has exhibited since joining the Court.

# Notes

1. See, e.g., Jan Crawford, *Roberts Switched Views to Uphold Health Care Law*, CBS News (July 1, 2012, 1:29 PM), http://www.cbsnews.com/8301-3460_162-57464549/roberts-switched-views-to-upholdhealth-care-law/; see also Jeffrey Toobin, The Oath (2012).
2. See, e.g., John Yoo, *Chief Justice Roberts and His Apologists*, Wall St. J., June 29, 2012, *available at* http://online.wsj.com/article/SB1000142405270230356150457749652001139252 92.html; Jeffrey Rosen, *Welcome to the Roberts Court: How the Chief Justice Used Obamacare to Reveal His True Identity*, The New Republic, June 29, 2012, *available at* http://www.tnr.com/blog/plank/104493/welcome-the-roberts-court-who-the-chief-justice-was-all-along.
3. See, e.g., Bradley Joondeph, *A Marbury for Our Time*, SCOTUSblog (June 29, 2012, 2:36 PM), http://www.scotusblog.com/2012/06/a-marbury-for-our-time/; David Kopel, *Major Limits on the Congress's Powers, in an Opinion Worthy of John Marshall*, SCOTUSblog (June 28, 2012, 6:33 PM), http://www.scotusblog.com/2012/06/major-limits-on-the-congresss-powers-in-an-opinion-worthy-of-john-marshall/.
4. See NFIB v. Sebelius, 132 S. Ct. 2566, 2599 (2012) ("The Court today holds that our Constitution protects us from federal regulation under the Commerce Clause so long as we abstain from the regulated activity").
5. *Id.* at 2650 ("As far as § 5000A is concerned, we would stop there. Congress has attempted to regulate beyond the scope of its Commerce Clause authority, and § 5000A is therefore invalid").
6. *Id.* at 2651 ("The issue is not whether Congress had the power to frame the minimum-coverage provision as a tax, but whether it did so").
7. *Id.* at 2593–2594.
8. 26 U.S.C. § 5000A(a).
9. *NFIB*, 132 S. Ct. at 2593.
10. *Id.* at 2594 (citations and internal quotations omitted).
11. *Id.* at 2599–2600. But see Erik M. Jensen. *The Individual Mandate and the Taxing Power*, 134 Tax Notes 97 (2012); Steven J. Willis & Nakku Chung, *Of Constitutional Decapitation and Healthcare*, 128 Tax Notes 169 (2010).
12. 557 U.S. 193 (2009).
13. See Richard L. Hasen, *Constitutional Avoidance and Anti-Avoidance by the Roberts Court*, 2009 Sup. Ct. Rev. 181, 182 (2009) (the *NAMUDNO* opinion "embraced a manifestly implausible statutory interpretation" of the VRA "to avoid the constitutional question").
14. 42 U.S.C. § 1973c(a).
15. 42 U.S.C. §§ 1973b (a)(1), 1973c(a).
16. 42 U.S.C. §§1973b(a)(1)(A)–(F).
17. See Nw. Austin Mun. Util. Dist. No. 1 v. Mukasey, 573 F. Supp. 2d 221, 230–231 (D.D.C. 2008).
18. *NAMUDNO*, 557 U.S. at 205 (citations omitted).

19. *Id.* at 207.
20. See Hasen, *supra* note 13, at 192–195 (surveying references to constitutional avoidance during the Roberts Court).
21. See, e.g., United States v. Alvarez, 127 U.S. 2537 (2012) (invalidating the Stolen Valor Act); United States v. Stevens, 130 S. Ct. 1577 (2010) (invalidating a federal statute barring depictions of animal cruelty); Citizens United v. Fed. Election Comm'n, 558 U.S. 310 (2010) (invalidating the Bipartisan Campaign Reform Act of 2002).
22. The Associated Press, *Chief Justice Says His Goal Is More Consensus on Court*, N.Y. TIMES, May 22, 2006, *available at* http://www.nytimes.com/2006/05/22/washington/22justice.html?_r=1&oref=slogin.
23. See Nathaniel Persily & Jennifer S. Rosenberg, *Defacing Democracy? The Changing Nature and Importance of As-Applied Challenges in the Supreme Court's Recent Election Law Decisions*, 93 MINN. L. REV. 1644 (2009).
24. 551 U.S. 449 (2007). See also Persily & Rosenberg, *supra* note 23, at 1662 ("In doing so, the Court rewrites a law that does not need to be rewritten and does so in a way that Congress specifically avoided").
25. 558 U.S. 310 (2010) (overturning McConnell v. Fed. Election Comm'n, 540 U.S. 93 (2003) and Austin v. MI Chamber of Commerce, 494 U.S. 652 (1990)).
26. See Jeffrey Toobin, *Money Unlimited*, THE NEW YORKER, May 21, 2012, *available at* http://www.newyorker.com/reporting/2012/05/21/120521fa_fact_toobin.
27. See Tom Goldstein, *Jeff Toobin on Citizens United (slightly expanded)*, SCOTUSBLOG (May 14, 2012, 9:30 PM), http://www.scotusblog.com/2012/05/jeff-toobin-on-citizens-united/.
28. See Rapanos v. United States, 547 U.S. 715, 757 (2006) (Roberts, C.J., concurring).
29. See Free Enterprise Fund v. Pub. Co. Accounting Oversight Bd., 130 S. Ct. 3138 (2010).
30. See Fed. Election Comm'n v. WI Right-to-Life, 551 U.S. 449, 499 n. 7 (2007) (Scalia, J., concurring in part and concurring in the judgment) ("This faux judicial restraint is judicial obfuscation").
31. 551 U.S. 587 (2007).
32. 392 U.S. 83 (1968). See generally, Jonathan H. Adler, *God, Gaia, The Taxpayer and the Lorax: Standing, Justiciability, and Separation of Powers after Massachusetts and Hein*, 20 REG. U.L. REV. 175 (2008).
33. *Confirmation Hearing on the Nomination of John G. Roberts, Jr., to be Chief Justice of the United States: Hearing Before the S. Comm. on the Judiciary*, 109th Cong. 55 (2005) (statement of John G. Roberts, Jr., Nominee to be Chief Justice of the United States), *available at* http://www.gpo.gov/fdsys/search/pagedetails.action?granuleId=&packageId=GPO-CHRG-ROBERTS.
34. See Adam Liptak, *Court Under Roberts Is Most Conservative in Decades*, N.Y. TIMES, July 24, 2010, *available at* http://www.nytimes.com/2010/07/25/us/25roberts.html?pagewanted=all. Despite the article's title, the data presented in the article showed that the Roberts Court invalidates fewer federal statutes and overturns fewer Supreme Court precedents per year than did the Rehnquist, Burger, or Warren Court.
35. See Jonathan H. Adler, *Getting the Roberts Court Right: A Response to Chemerisnky*, 54 WAYNE L. REV. 983 (2008).
36. United States v. Morrison, 529 U.S. 598, 613 (2000).
37. Rancho Viejo, LLC v. Norton, 334 F.3d 1158, 1160 (D.C. Cir. 2003) (Roberts, Circuit Judge, dissenting from denial of reh'g en banc) (emphasis in original).
38. 42 U.S.C. § 18091(a)(2)(A).
39. Thomas More Law Ctr v. Obama, 651 F.3d 529, 544 (6th Cir. 2011), *cert. denied*, No. 11-117 (June 29, 2012).
40. See, e.g., Randy Barnett, Nathaniel Stewart, & Todd F. Gaziano, *Why the Personal Mandate to Buy Health Insurance Is Unprecedented and Unconstitutional* (Heritage Found. Legal Memorandum No. 49, Dec. 9, 2009), http://www.heritage.org/research/

reports/2009/12/why-the-personal-mandate-to-buy-health-insurance-is-unprecedented-and-unconstitutional.

41. 514 U.S. 549 (1995).

42. *Cf.* Jones v. United States, 529 U.S. 848 (2000).

43. *Rancho Viejo*, 334 F.3d at 1160.

44. *Id.* (citing United States v. Salerno, 481 U.S. 739 (1987)).

45. NFIB v. Sebelius, 132 S. Ct. 2566, 2587 (2012) (Roberts, C.J.).

46. *Id.* at 2590 (emphasis added, internal citations omitted).

47. See Katzenbach v. McClung, 379 U.S. 294 (1964) (rejecting a Commerce Clause challenge to the Civil Rights Act); Heart of Atlanta Motel v. United States, 379 U.S. 241 (1964) (same); Champion v. Ames, 188 U.S. 321 (1903) (rejecting a Commerce Clause challenge to a ban on interstate shipment of lottery tickets).

48. *Cf.* Hammer v. Dagenhart, 247 U.S. 251, 277 (1918) (Holmes, J., dissenting) ("if an act is within the powers specifically conferred upon Congress, it seems to me that it is not made any less constitutional because of the indirect effects that it may have, however obvious it may be that it will have those effects").

49. See, e.g., Nathaniel S. Stewart, Note, *Turning the Commerce Clause "On Its Face": Why Federal Commerce Clause Statutes Demand Facial Challenges*, 55 CASE WES. L. REV. 161 (2004); Jonathan H. Adler, *Is Morrison Dead? Assessing a Supreme Drug (Law) Overdose*, 9 LEWIS & CLARK L. REV. 751 (2005); see also Nicholas Rosenkranz, *The Subjects of the Constitution*, 62 STAN. L. REV. 1210, 1273–1281 (2010).

50. 545 U.S. 1 (2005).

51. 452 U.S. 264, 307 (1981) (Rehnquist, J., concurring).

52. See Robert V. Percival, *Environmental Law in the Supreme Court: Highlights from the Blackmun Papers*, 35 ENVTL. L. REP. 10637, 10647 (2005).

53. *Lopez*, 514 U.S. at 552 ("We start with first principles. The Constitution creates a Federal Government of enumerated powers").

54. 483 U.S. 203 (1987).

55. See also Timothy P. O'Neill, *Harlan on My Mind: Chief Justice Roberts and the Affordable Care Act*, 3 CAL. L. REV. CIRCUIT 170 (2012).

56. See David G. Savage & Maura Reynolds, *High Court Nominee Sides with Restraint*, L.A. TIMES, Aug. 3, 2005, *available at* http://articles.latimes.com/2005/aug/03/nation/na-roberts3.

# CHAPTER 11

# Is It the Roberts Court?

*Linda Greenhouse*

The lonely path Chief Justice Roberts traveled in *NFIB v. Sebelius*[1] was the Supreme Court's most consequential solo performance since Justice Lewis Powell's opinion in the *Bakke* case[2] thirty-five years ago. Just as Powell's singular view of the constitutional boundary between impermissible racial quotas and acceptable consideration of race defined for a generation the contours of affirmative action in university admissions, so does John Roberts's response to the challenge to the Affordable Care Act (ACA) define the current constitutional boundaries of congressional authority over the economy and federal bargaining power with the states.

*Bakke*, coming midway through a fifteen-year tenure, also defined Justice Powell's place in Supreme Court history. Even assuming that Chief Justice Roberts, in his eighth term, is years away from the midpoint of his own tenure, it isn't too soon to ask how his dispositive vote in *NFIB* might shape history's assessment of his chief justiceship. And even without peering far into the future, it certainly isn't premature to wonder how the experience of separating himself from his usual ideological allies to uphold a Democratic president's signature policy initiative might influence his role on the Court in the near term.

Of course, I don't mean to suggest that Justice Powell and Chief Justice Roberts were identically situated, or to ignore the differences, starting with the obvious fact that the spotlight necessarily shines more brightly on a chief justice than on his colleagues (an important and perhaps even crucial fact, as I will elaborate). Justice Powell spoke only for himself in *Bakke*, without any justice joining any part of his opinion. While that was a notable feature of the decision, Lewis Powell was known as the Burger Court's "swing justice," so it wasn't particularly surprising to find him in the middle of a spectrum that ran from William Brennan and Thurgood Marshall on one end to William Rehnquist and Warren Burger on the other.

No one had ever called John Roberts a swing justice. Anyone so tempted might have been dissuaded by rereading what until *NFIB* had been his most important opinion, *Parents Involved*.[3] More to the point, in contrast to Justice Powell in *Bakke*, Chief Justice Roberts actually wrote for a five-member majority in upholding as a tax the individual mandate's penalty for not obtaining health insurance. (While six justices agreed with him that the Spending Clause condition that Congress placed on the Medicaid expansion was unconstitutionally coercive, only two of the six—Justices Breyer and Kagan—signed that part of his opinion.) To that extent, of course, he was not alone, and *NFIB* was not a replay of *Bakke*. Nonetheless, no other member of the Court saw the case as he did in all its aspects: Commerce Clause, taxing power, Spending Clause, severability.

And no member of his tax-authority majority bought the logic in which he clothed his deus ex machina, namely that it was necessary to reach the tax issue only because the ACA exceeded congressional authority under the Commerce Clause. In fact, Justice Ginsburg, speaking for herself and the other three members of the tax majority (Justices Breyer, Sotomayor, and Kagan) not only disagreed with the Chief Justice's Commerce Clause analysis, but dismissed that entire portion of his opinion as gratuitous.[4] In filling fifty-nine pages of the slip opinion, Chief Justice Roberts spoke for the Court for only twenty-one pages, nine of which recited the facts of the case and established the Court's jurisdiction to decide it. Remarkably, the remaining thirty-eight pages are simply "Opinion of Roberts, C.J."[5]

"It's now the Roberts Court" proclaims the title of Erwin Chemerinsky's summary of the 2011 Term in the summer 2012 issue of *The Green Bag*.[6] Not exactly. Not yet, anyway.

Or is it?

Others in this book analyze the health care decision from the perspectives of constitutional law and social policy. My focus is on the Chief Justice: what his performance in *NFIB* tells us about him and what it might portend.

To start with the first obvious point: this was not just any case. Aside from *Bush v. Gore*,[7] it is hard to think of any modern case that came before the Court with such a clear political valence. And *Bush v. Gore* was over in a flash. By contrast, the national Republican Party spent the two years after passage of the ACA staking its identity on opposition to the law and to the promise to see it eradicated either in court or in the next Congress. The twenty-seven states that went to court to have the law declared unconstitutional all had either Republican governors, Republican attorneys general, or both. (Surely one of the most disingenuous questions ever posed in a Supreme Court opinion is this one, from the Scalia-Kennedy-Thomas-Alito dissent: "[W]hy have more than half the states brought this lawsuit … ?"[8] The answer the dissenters gave to their own question was asserted coercion under the Spending Clause, but the real answer, as they had to know, was partisan politics.)

The Court's own politically identifiable cleavage, already well established in the public mind by a series of five-to-four decisions with five Republican-appointed justices on one side and four Democratic-appointed justices on the other, served to heighten the impression that the Supreme Court was not only being invited to render a political decision, but that it would happily accept the invitation. A Kaiser Family Foundation poll in January 2012, soon after the Court's grant of certiorari, showed 59 percent of the respondents believing that "the justices will let their own ideological views influence their decision." Only 28 percent said they thought the justices "will base their decision on legal analysis without regard to ideology or politics."[9] A Gallup poll at the start of the term had shown a surprisingly steep decline in public approval of the Court, down to 46 percent from 51 percent the previous year and a more typical 61 percent two years earlier.[10] These two troubling measures of public confidence in the institution and in the intellectual integrity of its members could not have escaped the Chief Justice's notice.

And that leads to a second obvious point: just as this was not just any case, John Roberts was not just any justice. Confronting the most important decision of his judicial life, he was Chief Justice, and if he couldn't function as Chief Justice of the Supreme Court—a general with no troops—he must have decided, as spring turned to summer and the country held its breath, that he had to be all that his official title implied: Chief Justice of the United States. With his usual allies seemingly on a partisan wrecking mission, determined to invalidate the entire statute by declaring none of it severable,[11] Chief Justice Roberts was unable to save the Court from his friends, so he decided to save the Court he revered by saving a statute that he clearly disliked intensely.

The distaste jumps out from the pages of his separate Commerce Clause opinion. His writing is muscular, embracing the Commerce Clause attack on the ACA in all its colorful imagery and reductios ad absurdum. "Under the Government's theory, Congress could address the diet problem by ordering everyone to buy vegetables."[12] "That is not the country the Framers of our Constitution envisioned."[13] By contrast to his thirty pages on the Commerce Clause, the prose in the fourteen pages of the tax holding is flat, mechanical, almost apologetic: "And it is only because we have a duty to construe a statute to save it, if fairly possible, that Sec. 5000A can be interpreted as a tax."[14] "Sec. 5000A is therefore constitutional, because it can reasonably be read as a tax."[15] Having imputed to Chief Justice Roberts a thought process for which I have no direct proof, I will take one more leap and suggest that had he been a mere associate justice, and a rather junior one at that, he might well have given his vote to the anti–Commerce Clause four and let the ACA fall.

Assuming that the narrative I offer here bears some relationship to what actually happened inside the Court,[16] what are we to make of Chief Justice John Roberts? A brave, even tragic hero who took a bullet for the Court? A "strategic genius," in Jeffrey Toobin's newly published account?[17] A sincere advocate of judicial moderation and pragmatism, learned, as John Fabian Witt suggests, at the feet of his early mentor, Judge Henry Friendly?[18] A Reagan-era as opposed to a new-style conservative, in the view of the political scientist Steven Teles, that is to say, someone with a genuine dislike of "judicial activism" rather than someone who condemns "activism" while being happy enough to call upon the right kind of activist judges when they come in handy?[19]

Or is he a traitor, a turncoat, a type whom no respectable Republican president should think about nominating in the future, as John Yoo fulminated in the *Wall Street Journal*?[20] A coward who abandoned principle and let himself be browbeaten by the liberal establishment, as anxious conservative commentators began hinting weeks before the decision was issued, when rumors began to circulate?[21]

The vituperation unleashed on Chief Justice Roberts from the Right was startling, bespeaking a sense of entitlement, of ownership betrayed. The howling tone was one of "how dare he, he is supposed to be one of ours." The attacks, with their deeply personal nature, raise the question of how the Chief Justice might respond, consciously or otherwise. Judge Richard Posner posed this question in characteristic pithy fashion in an interview with Nina Totenberg of NPR:

> What's he supposed to think? That he finds his allies to be a bunch of crackpots? Does that help the conservative movement? I mean, what would you do if you were Roberts? All the sudden [*sic*] you find out that the people you thought were your friends have turned against you, they despise you, they mistreat you, they leak to the press. What do you do? Do you become more conservative? Or do you say, "What am I doing with the crowd of lunatics?" Right? Maybe you have to re-examine your position.[22]

So where does John Roberts go from here? Supreme Court justices do "evolve," history shows us,[23] although John Roberts, with his inside-the-Beltway credentials and executive branch ticket-punching, does not fit the mold of Republican-appointed Supreme Court justices since the middle of the last century who have trended leftward.[24] I find it hard to imagine him becoming less conservative on the questions that seem to matter to him most: affirmative action, church and state, standing. But as the health care experience shows, the question is what "conservative" means, not as a set of abstract preferences, but as a prescription for judicial behavior—or, more precisely, for behavior in a specific context.

In listing the various ways one might understand Chief Justice Roberts in *NFIB*, I failed to signal my own choice. As I suggested at the beginning of this essay, I choose none of the above. I see John Roberts as having been carried by events, or perhaps as scrambling to get out of the way of an oncoming train while standing on a bridge over a fast-moving river. He jumped, and he came up still breathing. Good for him, and for us. But does that make him a leader of the "Roberts Court?"

Jeffrey Toobin's new book on the Roberts Court, *The Oath*, offers a fascinating backstory account of how *Citizens United* came to be reargued.[25] In this account, which I have verified to my own satisfaction, after the first argument in March 2009, Chief Justice Roberts assigned the opinion to himself. He circulated an opinion addressing the narrow question that the petitioner had presented: whether the McCain-Feingold law's bar against corporate-sponsored political broadcasts during the weeks immediately preceding a federal election could apply to a ninety-minute anti–Hillary Clinton film. As limited to such a broadcast, the Roberts opinion draft answered no. Jeffrey Toobin reports that Justice Kennedy then circulated a concurring opinion that expanded the Court's inquiry to include the constitutionality of the broadcast bar as applied to any corporate (or union) political speech. As the Court's other conservatives "began rallying" to the Kennedy opinion, Roberts proposed to withdraw his own and to permit the sweeping Kennedy opinion to become the opinion for the Court. When the liberal justices objected vociferously that the Court was addressing an issue on which it had not granted certiorari (and Justice Souter, on the eve of his retirement announcement, proposed to publish a dissenting opinion revealing the internal struggle), the Chief Justice led the Court in setting the case over for re-argument in the following term with explicitly expanded "questions presented."

Jeffrey Toobin proclaims this scenario "a stroke of strategic genius" by the Chief Justice. Assuming the facts, I think a different assessment is called for, one that foreshadows what was to come three years later in *NFIB*. John Roberts was not in charge of the *Citizens United* narrative. He was carried along by it, riding a wave he could not control. "There is a difference between judicial restraint and judicial abdication," he offered by way of explanation in his concurring opinion.[26] Was there a hint of apology, even embarrassment, in his tone? Or perhaps he was looking ahead to a future in which, he now had some reason to believe, his professed adherence to restraint would be put to an even greater test, to the test of his judicial life, to the making of the Roberts Court.

## Notes

1. 132 S. Ct. 2566 (2012).
2. Regents of Univ. Cal. v. Bakke, 438 U.S. 265 (1978).
3. Parents Involved in Cmty. Sch. v. Seattle Sch. Dist. No. 1, 551 U.S. 701 (2007). The Chief Justice's refusal to accommodate Justice Kennedy's concerns left him writing for a hard-edged plurality in rejecting racially conscious K-12 student assignments, while Justice Kennedy wrote a separate, more moderate concurrence in the judgment.

4. NFIB v. Sebelius, 132 S. Ct. 2566, 2629 n.12 (2012) (Ginsburg, J., concurring in part, concurring in the judgment in part, and dissenting in part). Of course, while the Chief Justice's invocation of the avoidance canon speaks the language of judicial modesty, see *id.* at 2593–2594, many scholars have pointed out that any judge who uses the avoidance canon is making the inherently normative judgment that there is a constitutional problem to be avoided. See, e.g., Lisa A. Kloppenberg, *Avoiding Constitutional Questions,* 35 B.C. L. Rev. 1003 (1994). By rehearsing at length his Commerce Clause objections to the ACA, Chief Justice Roberts gave his support, a fifth vote, for a Commerce Clause interpretation that he could easily have—dare I say—avoided had he gone immediately to his tax-power analysis as a straightforward exercise of statutory interpretation.

5. *NFIB,* 132 S. Ct. at 2585–2594, 2600–2601.

6. Erwin Chemerinksy, *It's Now the Roberts Court,* 15 Green Bag 2d 389 (2012).

7. Bush v. Gore, 531 U.S. 98 (2000).

8. *NFIB,* 132 S. Ct. at 2666.

9. The Henry J. Kaiser Family Found., Kaiser Health Tracking Poll: Public Opinion on Health Care Issues (Jan. 2012), www.kff.org/kaiserpolls/upload/8274-F.pdf.

10. Jeffrey M. Jones, *Supreme Court Approval Rating Dips to 46%,* Gallup Politics (Oct. 3, 2011), http://www.gallup.com/poll/149906/supreme-court-approval-rating-dips.aspx.

11. *NFIB,* 132 S. Ct. at 2676–2677.

12. *Id.* at 2588.

13. *Id.* at 2589.

14. *Id.* at 2600–2601.

15. *Id.* at 2601.

16. I should note that in a column published on the afternoon of the decision, Linda Greenhouse, *A Justice in Chief,* N.Y. Times, June 28, 2012, *available at* http://opinionator.blogs.nytimes.com/2012/06/28/a-justice-in-chief/, before the "leak" about the Roberts vote switch, Jan Crawford, *Roberts Switched Views to Uphold Health Care Law,* CBS News (July 1, 2012, 1:29 PM), http://www.cbsnews.com/8301-3460_162-57464549/roberts-switched-views-to-uphold-health-care-law/, I suggested the likelihood that the Chief Justice had changed his position during the decisional process.

17. Jeffrey Toobin, The Oath: The Obama White House and the Supreme Court 295 (2012).

18. John Fabian Witt, *The Secret History of the Chief Justice's Obamacare Decision,* Balkinization (June 29, 2012), http://balkin.blogspot.com/2012/06/secret-history-of-chief-justices.html.

19. Steven M. Teles, *On the Affordable Care Act Decision,* Wash. Monthly Blog (June 28, 2012, 9:49 AM), http://www.washingtonmonthly.com/ten-miles-square/2012/06/on_the_affordable_care_act_dec038239.php.

20. John Yoo, *Chief Justice Roberts and His Apologists,* Wall St. J., June 29, 2012, *available at* http://online.wsj.com/article/SB10001424052702303561504577496520011395292.html.

21. See Greenhouse, *supra* note 16.

22. Nina Totenberg, *Federal Judge Richard Posner: The GOP Has Made Me Less Conservative,* NPR Blog (July 5, 2012, 5:15 PM), http://www.npr.org/blogs/itsallpolitics/2012/07/05/156319272/federal-judge-richard-posner-the-gop-has-made-me-less-conservative.

23. See, e.g., Lee Epstein et al., *Ideological Drift Among Supreme Court Justices: Who, When, and How Important?* 101 Nw. U. L. Rev. 1483 (2007).

24. Michael C. Dorf, *Does Federal Executive Branch Experience Explain Why Some Republican Supreme Court Justices "Evolve" and Others Don't?* 1 Harv. L. & Pol'y Rev. 457 (2007).

25. Toobin, *supra* note 17, at 167–169. See also Jeffrey Toobin, *Money Unlimited,* New Yorker, May 21, 2012, at 36–47.

26. Citizens United v. Fed. Election Comm'n, 130 S. Ct. 876, 918 (2010) (Roberts, C.J., concurring).

CHAPTER 12

# More Law Than Politics

## THE CHIEF, THE "MANDATE," LEGALITY, AND STATESMANSHIP

*Neil S. Siegel*

In *National Federation of Independent Business v. Sebelius* (*NFIB*),[1] Chief Justice Roberts concluded for himself that the Affordable Care Act's (ACA)'s minimum coverage provision—the so-called individual mandate—was beyond the scope of Congress's power to regulate interstate commerce. He further concluded that the provision was unjustified by Congress's power to pass laws that are necessary and proper to carrying into execution other concededly valid regulations of interstate commerce, such as the ACA's requirement that insurers cover individuals with pre-existing conditions.[2] Pivoting dramatically, however, the Chief Justice then held for the Court that the minimum coverage provision was a permissible exercise of Congress's tax power.[3] As Roberts pivoted, so changed the fate of the most consequential piece of American social welfare legislation in nearly half a century.[4]

Some defenders of the ACA's constitutionality responded by praising the Chief Justice's judicial statesmanship, political savvy, and personal courage. For example, Jeffrey Rosen reported in the *New Republic* that "liberals found themselves in the unexpected position of applauding Roberts for his act of judicial statesmanship," as "he set aside his ideological preference to protect the Court from a decision along party lines that would have imperiled its legitimacy."[5] Jeffrey Toobin, writing in the *New Yorker*, celebrated "a singular act of courage" of "a professional Republican" who "was disappointing those closest to him."[6] David Von Drehle of *Time* magazine, invoking King Solomon's offer to split the baby, wrote that Roberts had "vindicated the virtue of compromise in an era of Occupiers, Tea Partyers and litmus-testing special interests."[7]

Constitutional critics of the ACA were less congratulatory. Some responded by condemning Roberts's legal infidelity, political motivation, and personal cowardice. For instance, Randy Barnett wrote in the *Washington Examiner* that Roberts's "maneuvers made constitutional law worse, even if they did save this law in hope of avoiding political attacks on the court." James Taranto, writing in the *Wall Street Journal*, acidly wondered whether Roberts had acted "as a finger-to-the-wind politician" basking in the "strange new respect" of liberals.[8] Taranto counseled Roberts "to reflect on ... just how respectful it is to think of the chief justice of the Supreme Court [*sic*] as an easily bullied politician."[9] Mark Thiessen declared in the *Washington Post* that Roberts had "effectively redrafted the statute, making the mandate a tax in order to declare it constitutional."[10] He accused Roberts of "the kind of sophistry we expect from liberals" and opined that conservatives "need jurists who have not only a philosophy of judicial restraint but the intestinal fortitude not to be swayed by pressure from the *New York Times*, the Georgetown cocktail circuit and the legal academy."[11]

The assessments of such constitutional defenders and critics differed significantly in obvious ways. Yet there was subtle and substantial agreement lurking beneath the normative dissensus: Roberts's defenders and critics appeared to share the belief that his decisive vote to uphold the ACA's minimum coverage provision is best understood on nonlegal grounds. Conservative critics eagerly claimed the mantle of legality for themselves, and some liberal defenders were quick to concede it. Thus Toobin, while lavishing praise upon Roberts and four of his colleagues for doing "the right thing in one of the most important cases they will ever decide," dismissed the Court's tax-power rationale as "[f]rankly ... not a persuasive one," but "good enough for Roberts" because "[a]ny port will do in a constitutional storm."[12] Similarly, Rosen wrote that "[i]t would be easy, of course, to question the coherence of the combination of legal arguments that Roberts embraced, but it would also be beside the point," because "Roberts's decision was above all an act of judicial statesmanship."[13]

Claims that Roberts acted politically (in either a bad or a good sense) in upholding the minimum coverage provision appear to go to his motives—to his reasons for deciding the case the way that he did. So conceived, the question of whether Roberts's opinion is law or politics is impossible to answer. None of us knows why Roberts wrote the opinion that he wrote, and thus none of us can demonstrate that he was (or was not) politically motivated in whatever sense of "political" one has in mind. If, however, acting politically means acting without adequate legal justification, then it is possible to assess Roberts's performance.

In this chapter, I will inquire whether the various parts of Roberts's opinion on the minimum coverage provision are legally justifiable. I will focus on what Roberts decided, not why he decided it that way. I will therefore not opine on whether or why Roberts switched his vote, which is open to different interpretations and may turn substantially on which part(s) of his opinion one finds persuasive. Nor will I focus on the Medicaid portion of Roberts's opinion. The question of when, if ever, a federal financial incentive to the states tips from permissible inducement to unconstitutional coercion is sufficiently difficult that I will reserve my answer for future work.

In my view, law is fully adequate to explain the Chief Justice's vote to uphold the minimum coverage provision as within the scope of Congress's power "[t]o lay and collect Taxes."[14] Roberts embraced the soundest constitutional understanding of the Taxing Clause. He also showed fidelity to the law by applying—and not just giving lip service to—the deeply entrenched presumption of constitutionality that judges are supposed to apply when federal laws are challenged on federalism grounds.

Roberts's opinion was unpersuasive in concluding that the minimum coverage provision was beyond the scope of the Commerce and Necessary and Proper Clauses. Roberts failed to apply the modern doctrine of "constitutional avoidance," thereby needlessly deciding these questions. What is more, he decided them wrongly. Fortunately, the doctrinal consequences of this portion of his opinion will likely (although by no means certainly) prove insignificant.

In the final part of this chapter, I move from the internal perspective of the faithful legal practitioner to the external perspective of the analyst of the constitutional system. I ask what Roberts may have accomplished in responding to *NFIB* as he did. By prohibiting Congress from requiring Americans to purchase products against their will, Roberts partially expressed new popular and professional constitutional arguments—arguments developed by those who had mobilized against the prevailing view among legal experts that the minimum coverage provision is constitutional. By upholding the minimum coverage provision under the Taxing Clause, he validated the values of the ACA's supporters and respected the post–New Deal convention that the Court should uphold momentous social welfare legislation. By partially validating the sincerely held moral beliefs of both sides, Roberts may have succeeded in sustaining a modest measure of social solidarity amid intense disagreement over health care reform, thereby enhancing the public legitimacy of constitutional law.

Roberts may or may not have intended to practice judicial statesmanship, and his statesmanship may not be enough to justify his contradictions of sound legal reasoning.[15] But statesmanship probably would provide the most persuasive way to try to justify his analyses of the Commerce and Necessary and Proper Clauses. Such a defense, however, would require the application of criteria that are difficult to justify as legal from the internal point of view.

## 1. Good Law

I will first consider the portion of the Chief Justice's opinion that upheld the ACA's minimum coverage provision as within the scope of Congress's power to tax. He wrote this part for the Court.

## A. THE "MANDATE" IS A CONDITION ATTACHED TO A TAX

Exhibit A for commentators who interpret Roberts's opinion in political terms is his allegedly implausible conclusion that the minimum coverage provision and shared responsibility payment were within the scope of Congress's tax power. Such commentators wonder how that could be. Congress not only referenced a "Requirement" to maintain minimum coverage and provided that every applicable individual "shall" obtain it,[16] but also used the "penalty" label many times to describe the required payment for going without insurance.[17]

This objection emphasizes the seemingly mandatory language that Congress used in drafting the minimum coverage provision. One possible response is that the provision nonetheless expresses a tax, not a penalty. For example, Congress placed the required payment provision in the Internal Revenue Code, called individuals who must make the payment "taxpayers," and calculated the amount of the payment in part based on the taxpayer's household income for the taxable year. Moreover, the statute requires taxpayers to indicate whether they have health insurance on their tax returns and instructs the Internal Revenue Service to include the amount owed in the taxpayer's tax return liability.[18] Thus, Congress also used the language of taxation in drafting the minimum coverage provision.

While the ACA's defenders are right to stress this point, the ACA's opponents still have the stronger argument regarding the expressive form of the provision. The statutory language is closer to that of a penalty than a tax for two main reasons. First, Congress used the words "Requirement" and "shall." Second, Congress repeatedly called the exaction for noninsurance a "penalty" after labeling it a "tax" in earlier versions of the bill.[19]

However one resolves this debate about expressive form, the ACA's required payment for going without insurance is a tax for purposes of the Taxing Clause, not a penalty. To see why, it is most important to focus on the anticipated effects of the exaction.[20] Ordinarily, the effects of an exaction are determined more by its material characteristics than by its expressive form.[21] The material characteristics of the ACA's required payment provision are plainly those of a tax, not a penalty. First, the payment is less than the cost of insurance for many people—indeed, for almost everyone. By 2016, the annual exaction for noninsurance will be the greater of $695 or 2.5 percent of income, but not more than the average yearly premium for the minimum level of health insurance specified in the ACA.[22] Second, there is no scienter requirement; and third, the amount of the penalty does not go up each month or year that an individual goes without insurance. Thus, an individual does not have to pay at an increasing rate for intentional or repeated failures to obtain health insurance.[23]

Because of these material characteristics—Roberts called them "practical characteristics"[24]—the required payment will reduce the number of people who go without insurance without preventing such conduct, thereby raising several billion dollars in revenue each year. The nonpartisan Congressional Budget Office (CBO) estimates that four million people each year will choose to make the shared responsibility payment instead of obtaining coverage.[25] The CBO further predicts that the statute's payment provision will produce $54 billion in federal revenue from 2015 to 2022.[26]

If the ACA had required a yearly payment of, say, $15,000 per uninsured person, then the payment would be a penalty, not a tax. A $15,000 exaction would prevent almost everyone from going without insurance, and thus would raise little or no revenue. Such an exaction would raise even less revenue if its amount went up by $5,000 each year that an individual remained uninsured. Likewise, an initial "tax" of $25,000 on carrying a firearm in a school zone (with enhancements for intentionality and recidivism) would prevent such behavior and raise minimal revenue.[27] In distinguishing a tax from a penalty, the effect of a payment to the federal government on individual behavior matters most. The so-called individual mandate is a modest financial incentive, not a coercive regulation. It is not a pure tax in light of its expressive form, but it is a tax equivalent in light of its material characteristics and anticipated consequences.[28] Thus, it lies within Congress's tax power.

Constitutional text, structure, history, and precedent indicate that it is constitutionally irrelevant whether Congress primarily intended to raise revenue or to regulate behavior in enacting the minimum coverage provision.[29] The Constitution gives Congress the power to tax in order to "provide for the common Defence and general Welfare."[30] Providing for the general welfare through taxation sometimes involves regulatory objectives. Indeed, many federal exactions have long been intended both to raise revenue and to regulate behavior, from the federal tax on imports at the time of the Founding to cigarette taxes today.[31] Thus the modern Court has referenced approvingly "mixed-motive taxes that governments impose both to deter a disfavored activity and to raise money."[32]

Moreover, it is not decisive for purposes of the tax power whether Congress calls a required payment a tax.[33] The Court has long de-emphasized the constitutional significance of the label that Congress uses to describe such payments.[34] Just as Congress does not gain a power that it lacks by calling it a power that it has, so too does Congress not lose a power that it has by calling it a power that it lacks. The expressive form of a required payment matters only to the extent that it affects individual behavior.[35] To reiterate, the expressive form of the ACA's shared responsibility payment as more a penalty than a tax will not tip the practical operation of the exaction from a tax to a penalty. The amount imposed is sufficiently modest that many Americans are expected to pay it.

For some observers, however, the tax power rationale for the minimum coverage provision may still seem like a cheat. Hadn't opponents of the ACA framed the public debate in terms of the Commerce Clause? Indeed, the label created by opponents—"individual mandate"—presupposes a regulation backed by a penalty, not a tax. At oral argument, Justice Scalia deemed it "extraordinary" that the Solicitor General would invoke the tax power as an independently sufficient basis for the minimum coverage provision, with the implication that "all the discussion we had earlier about how this is one big uniform scheme and the Commerce Clause … really doesn't matter."[36]

It is bedrock constitutional law, however, that the tax power is an independent source of constitutional authority. The tax power may thus be available to Congress regardless of whether other sources of legislative authority are available, and regardless of how a debate is framed in the political arena. Congress needed only one source of constitutional authority to justify the minimum coverage provision, and three were potentially available: the tax power, the power to "regulate Commerce … among the several States,"[37] and the power to "make all Laws which shall be necessary and proper for carrying into Execution" other, concededly constitutional provisions of the ACA.[38] The challengers, by contrast, had to win all three of their constitutional arguments. The federal government's reliance on the tax power was ordinary, not extraordinary.

What about political accountability? Some argue that the federal government will avoid accountability if it may call an exaction a penalty in the political arena and a tax in court.[39] But political accountability in this context usually depends on who must pay and how much they must pay, not on what Congress calls what they must pay—which most people may not know anyway. Neither President Obama nor the Democrats in the ACA Congress escaped political accountability for supporting the minimum coverage provision, which remains controversial. The expressive form of the ACA's required payment provision does not appear to compromise political accountability.

More fundamentally, it is far from clear that political accountability is a judicially enforceable constitutional value in this setting. I know of no constitutional authority for the assertion that Congress's tax power is circumscribed by a requirement of accurate labeling, so that an exaction with the material characteristics and effects of a tax must be deemed a penalty in order to hold Congress accountable. Federal commandeering of states, which the Court has held to violate the Tenth Amendment, is readily distinguishable.[40] With commandeering, the federal government is requiring states to regulate individuals on its behalf. With a purchase mandate or incentive, the federal government is itself regulating individuals.

Perhaps the Court has declined to impose such a "clear statement" requirement because the consequences would prove severe and destabilizing. For example, many federal statutes have titles and preambles that misstate their contents, whether by labeling civilian spending "military" or by announcing public-regarding purposes for self-serving logrolls. For decades, Congress has hidden tax breaks in the tax code instead of exposing them in the budget.[41] The Court has never hinted that these practices raise constitutional concerns. If the Court were to hold that the tax power justifies an exaction only if Congress calls it a "tax," other kinds of mislabeling logically should also fall under such a requirement. Policing these practices would require a massive judicial undertaking, which presumably no member of the Roberts Court wishes to pursue.

## B. THE PRESUMPTION OF CONSTITUTIONALITY, NOT UNCONSTITUTIONALITY

For the foregoing reasons, the Taxing Clause justifies the minimum coverage provision even without putting a judicial thumb on the scales in favor of acts of Congress. Roberts, however, did not see it this way, which is why he stressed the legal principle of judicial deference to Congress in federalism cases.[42] This principle requires judges to presume that federal laws are constitutional when they are challenged as beyond the scope of Congress's enumerated powers, and to practice constitutional avoidance by reading them in ways that render them constitutional if they can reasonably be so read.[43] "[I]t is well established," Roberts wrote, "that if a statute has two possible meanings, one of which violates the Constitution, courts should adopt the meaning that does not do so."[44]

Roberts did not just pay lip service to the presumption of constitutionality; he actually applied it in his tax power analysis, construing the minimum coverage provision as a tax because it "may reasonably be characterized as a tax."[45] "[B]ecause the Constitution permits such a tax," he recognized, "it is not our role to forbid it, or to pass upon its wisdom or fairness."[46] Roberts appropriately deferred to Congress even though he apparently did not share the political vision that produced the ACA. "It is not our job," he pointedly wrote, "to protect the people from the consequences of their political choices."[47]

## 2. Bad Law

While Roberts's analysis of the tax power was legally sound, the same cannot be said of his analyses of the Commerce and Necessary and Proper Clauses. He offered unpersuasive legal reasoning to justify why and how he was deciding that the minimum coverage provision was beyond the scope of these clauses.

## A. CONSTITUTIONAL AVOIDANCE, NOT PURSUIT

Roberts did not need to decide whether the minimum coverage provision was within the scope of Congress's power to regulate interstate commerce. Nor did he need to decide whether the provision was a constitutionally "necessary and proper" measure to execute other congressional regulations of interstate commerce in the ACA. To reiterate, Congress required only one source of constitutional authority to support the minimum coverage provision, and Roberts concluded that the provision was within the scope of the tax power.

Roberts explained that he was first deciding whether the minimum coverage provision was justified by the Commerce and Necessary and Proper Clauses because the provision "reads more naturally as a command to buy insurance than as a tax."[48] He reasoned that he could not resort to the "saving construction" entailed in viewing the provision as a tax until he concluded that no other clause supported the provision.[49]

During the nineteenth century, Roberts's legal reasoning would have been persuasive. Back then, the canon of "constitutional avoidance" in statutory interpretation was narrow: a judge was justified in construing a statute so as to save it from constitutional invalidation only after concluding that the statute would indeed be unconstitutional if read free of any such substantive canon.[50] The problem for Roberts is that the modern avoidance canon is much broader than the classical canon he applied.[51] The modern canon kicks in when a jurist has significant constitutional doubts about the constitutionality of a statutory provision. The judge is supposed to engage in the saving construction if such a construction is reasonably available without initially deciding the constitutionality of the first-best reading of the statute.[52] "'If there is one doctrine more deeply rooted than any other in the process of constitutional adjudication,'" the Court stated as recently as 1999, "'it is that we ought not to pass on questions of constitutionality … unless such adjudication is unavoidable.'"[53]

I cannot know why Roberts proceeded in this fashion. Perhaps he simply confused classical avoidance with modern avoidance. Perhaps he instead meant to reject modern avoidance. Perhaps he made a factual mistake when he wrote that "[t]he Government asks us to interpret the mandate as imposing a tax, if it would otherwise violate the Constitution."[54] (The government argued that the tax power provides an *additional* basis for upholding the minimum coverage provision, not an *alternative* basis.)[55]

Whatever the explanation, Roberts's legal reasoning on the avoidance question is unsatisfactory. If he was embracing the classical avoidance canon going forward— perhaps in light of criticism of the modern canon[56]—then he owed the legal system an explanation to this effect in light of the rule-of-law values of guidance, predictability, reliance, and transparency. If he was instead embracing old avoidance for this case only, then such a limited embrace seems difficult to square with the rule-of-law requirement that judges discipline themselves to the virtue of consistency.[57]

One might defend Roberts as having used dicta to reduce uncertainty. The legal system now knows that he (and thus a majority of justices) accept a distinction between regulating and requiring commerce, and future Congresses can plan accordingly. But this defense is just an argument for abandoning the modern canon of constitutional avoidance in favor of the classical canon, which Roberts did not do. It is not a strong argument for applying the classical canon in this case only. As I discuss below, it is unlikely that Congress would have imposed purchase mandates in the future even if the Court had upheld the minimum coverage provision under the Commerce Clause. Accordingly, the legal system did not appear to require guidance concerning the validity of such mandates under the commerce power.

## B. INTERSTATE AND COMMERCE, NECESSARY AND PROPER

Roberts not only decided constitutional questions that he did not need to decide. He also decided them wrongly. Under at least two decades of case law,[58] the Commerce Clause justifies the minimum coverage provision because it regulates economic conduct that substantially affects interstate commerce. Specifically, the provision regulates (through a financial incentive) how people pay for—or do not pay for—the health care that almost all of us inevitably consume and may not lawfully be denied, at a time we cannot predict, at a cost we may not be able to afford.[59] Americans who lack health insurance, as a general class, undeniably impact the costs borne by other participants in health care and insurance markets. In passing the ACA, Congress found that, in 2008 alone, the uninsured shifted $43 billion in health care costs to health care providers, which "pass on the cost to private insurers, which pass on the cost to families."[60] Cost shifting is an economic problem, and its aggregate effects on interstate commerce are substantial.

The minimum coverage provision also finds support in recent normative scholarship on constitutional federalism, which stresses that Congress may invoke the Commerce Clause if it reasonably believes it is ameliorating a significant problem of collective action that exists "among the several States." This account offers a multigenerational synthesis and justification of post–New Deal and pre–NFIB case law.[61] If Congress has no reasonable basis to believe that it is solving a significant collective action problem involving multiple states—whether races to the bottom or interstate spillovers—then Congress may not invoke its commerce power.[62]

Roberts stressed that Congress may not use the Commerce Clause to force people into commerce.[63] Even assuming (notwithstanding the cost shifting noted above) that the uninsured as a general class are presently inactive in commerce, a proper Commerce Clause inquiry does not ask whether Congress is mandating private action. Congress may mandate private action using its commerce power, just as it may otherwise regulate private action using its commerce power, in order to address a commercial problem of collective action facing the states—when the states are separately incompetent to solve the problem on their own because the scope of the problem disrespects state borders. The states are separately incompetent when they impose significant costs on one another without paying for them.

The idea of separate state incompetence comes from the Constitutional Convention of 1787. The Convention instructed the midsummer Committee of Detail that Congress would be empowered to legislate in, among other things, "those Cases to which the States are separately incompetent."[64] This language originated in Resolution VI of the Virginia Plan. The Committee of Detail changed the indefinite language of Resolution VI into an enumeration closely resembling Article I, Section 8 as adopted.[65]

As Justice Ginsburg emphasized in one of the most important opinions of her career,[66] Congress reasonably concluded that the minimum coverage provision would address significant collective action problems involving multiple states. These problems arise when financially able individuals decline to purchase health insurance. These individuals can free ride on the benevolence of others in two ways. First, because of federal and state laws and the charitable practices of most hospitals in the United States, other institutions and individuals will pay a significant share of the cost of stabilizing medical care rather than let uninsured people go untreated.[67] Second, even when the uninsured do not receive medical care for the time being, they benefit from the existence of the health care infrastructure and can rely on its availability in case of emergency. Indeed, insurers must account for such reliance in pricing policies. A requirement to obtain health insurance coverage or pay for going without insurance is designed in part to overcome risk-taking in reliance on benevolence. This rationale does not apply to uninsured individuals who are able to pay the full cost of their health care, but a severe injury or illness can bankrupt even wealthy individuals who lack insurance.

Theoretical reasoning and empirical evidence suggest that this free-rider problem is interstate in scope—that this collective action problem involving individuals causes a collective action problem for the states. For example, many insurance companies operate in multiple states, and the costs that insurers must bear in one state may affect their ability to operate in more marginal markets in other states. Moreover, millions of Americans have access to health care in states in which they do not reside, and many patients cross state lines to seek medical care.[68] Congress could reasonably conclude that these interstate effects and movements partially reflect costs that some states impose on other states. Internalizing these interstate externalities requires collective action by the affected states, which they are unlikely to accomplish on their own.

Turning to the Necessary and Proper Clause, it gives Congress the power to pass laws that are necessary and proper to carrying into execution Congress's other enumerated powers. It was common ground in the ACA litigation that the Commerce Clause gives Congress the authority to prohibit insurance companies from denying coverage based on preexisting conditions, canceling coverage absent fraud, charging higher premiums based on medical history, and imposing lifetime limits on benefits.[69] These ACA provisions solve collective action problems for the states by facilitating labor mobility, discouraging the flight of insurers from states that guarantee insurance access to states that do not, and disincentivizing states from free riding on the more generous health care systems of sister states.

Under established law, the minimum coverage provision is necessary and proper for carrying into execution these undeniably valid regulations of insurers. "[T]he relevant inquiry is simply 'whether the means chosen are 'reasonably adapted' to the attainment of a legitimate end under the commerce power.'"[70] Guaranteeing access to health insurance is a legitimate end, and the minimum coverage provision is reasonably adapted to the attainment of this end. Without the minimum coverage provision, there would be a perverse incentive for uninsured, financially able individuals to buy insurance only when they require expensive care, thereby free riding on people who pay for insurance when they are healthy. This "adverse selection" problem would substantially undermine insurance markets.

Notwithstanding this straightforward application of preexisting law, Roberts created new limits on the Commerce and Necessary and Proper Clauses. Regarding the commerce power, his opinion echoed Republican and Tea Party scare tactics about mandatory purchases of broccoli;[71] about losing "the country the Framers of our Constitution envisioned";[72] about "fundamentally changing the relation between the citizen and the Federal Government";[73] and about congressional use of the Commerce Clause as "a general license to regulate an individual from cradle to grave, simply because he will predictably engage in particular transaction."[74] Roberts thereby asserted that upholding the minimum coverage provision under the Commerce Clause would annihilate judicially enforceable limits on the commerce power.

Rhetoric aside, Roberts's opinion voiced the strongest argument of opponents of the minimum coverage provision: the perceived need for a judicially enforceable limiting principle on the commerce power. A good response is that other judicially enforceable limits on the Commerce Clause would remain in place even if Roberts had rejected the novel distinction between regulating and requiring commerce. These limits are evident in the above discussions of pre-NFIB doctrine and collective action federalism. They include the Court's distinction between regulating economic conduct and regulating noneconomic conduct, and the structural distinction between problems that require collective action by states and problems that states can solve on their own.[75]

These limits would not prohibit Congress from ever imposing a purchase mandate, nor is there any good reason that they should. But these limits would rule out some of the scarier hypotheticals crafted by opponents of the ACA, such as forced purchases of broccoli or gym memberships on the ground that healthier citizens impose fewer health care costs on others. The causal relationship between such purchases and good health is highly speculative and attenuated when the regulated individuals do not want to buy the good or service in question. That is not the case concerning the relationship between possession of health insurance and cost shifting in health care markets. Health insurance is how most of us routinely pay for health care.

Roberts also ignored political constraints on Congress, which often count in the Court's jurisprudence. Political constraints, not judicially enforceable limits, prevent Congress from raising the minimum wage to $1,000 per hour. Political realism ensures that Congress will not prohibit people from purchasing unhealthy foods—or vegetables for that matter—even though the Court's Commerce Clause doctrine allows Congress to enact such fundamental changes in the relationship between the citizen and the federal government. Registering appropriate concerns about constitutional limits requires the human faculty of judgment—an ability to distinguish real threats to constitutional values from mere shadows.

As for the Necessary and Proper Clause, Roberts seemed to concede that the minimum coverage provision was necessary (that is, convenient or useful) to effectuate the admittedly constitutional ACA provisions that require insurers to cover people with preexisting conditions. He nonetheless concluded that the provision was improper.[76] It was improper, as best I can discern, because it violated a new structural limit on federal power that disables Congress from compelling people to buy a product. He deemed such compulsion the exercise of a "'great substantive and independent power'" beyond those specifically enumerated, not an exercise of authority "derivative of, and in service to, a granted power."[77]

I do not understand why this is so. The minimum coverage provision is a means to the end of guaranteeing people access to health insurance without unraveling insurance markets. This rationale for the provision is narrower than the Commerce Clause theory because it requires a comprehensive regulatory scheme, and because many markets do not even arguably suffer from adverse selection problems. So the adverse selection rationale is another limiting principle that Roberts could have elected to embrace.

With respect to both the Commerce and Necessary and Proper Clauses, Roberts's new constitutional prohibition on purchase mandates appears to lack a sound basis in constitutional text, history, structure, or precedent.[78] Nor does it seem grounded in a sensible functional understanding of the vertical division of powers in a federal system. If states may impose purchase mandates when commercial problems are intrastate in scope, why may not Congress impose them when such problems are interstate in scope? "The authority of the federal government over interstate commerce," the Court instructed in the landmark case of *United States v. Darby*, "does not differ in extent or character from that retained by the states over intrastate commerce."[79]

## C. DOCTRINAL IMPLICATIONS

Fortunately for the integrity of constitutional law, Roberts's interpretation of the Commerce Clause (which Justices Scalia, Kennedy, Thomas, and Alito share) seems unlikely to prove significant. Congress never used the Commerce Clause to impose purchase mandates prior to the ACA—it actually imposed only a purchase incentive in the ACA—and it is unlikely to impose a purchase mandate in the future. Purchase mandates are politically unpopular, and Congress has a variety of other means to achieve its objectives. The parade of horribles invoked by opponents of the ACA—from forcing Americans to purchase broccoli to compelling them to buy American cars—seemed to have more to do with persuading the Court to invalidate the minimum coverage provision (and the entire ACA) than with future congressional legislation.

Roberts's interpretation of the Necessary and Proper Clause may prove more consequential. Indeed, the four dissenters went even further than Roberts in restricting the scope of this power. It is hard to know what will happen, however, because Roberts's language is vague and difficult to apply. Going forward, how should Congress and the courts distinguish between a "great substantive and independent power" beyond those enumerated in the Constitution, and a power merely "derivative of, and in service to, a granted power?"[80]

I suspect, although I cannot prove, that Roberts wrote this part of his opinion more for this case than for the future. Having just denied Congress the power to impose purchase mandates under the Commerce Clause, he may have been determined not to allow such mandates under the Necessary and Proper Clause. Quoting selectively from *McCulloch v. Maryland*,[81] while ignoring most of its language and structural logic, Roberts may have been insisting that Congress may not impose a purchase mandate under the Necessary and Proper Clause if Congress may not impose one under the Commerce Clause. Such a rationale risks denying the undeniable—that the Necessary and Proper Clause is an independent source of constitutional authority—but the damage may prove modest partly for this reason.

Moreover, following through on what Roberts wrote to justify his conclusion might have radical implications. If a requirement to buy a product is always a great substantive and independent power, then perhaps Congress has long used the Necessary and Proper Clause to exercise other great substantive and independent powers, such as creating a national bank. Federal power to charter corporations was so controversial at the time of the Founding that the framers declined to vote on whether to grant Congress such authority.[82] Roberts likely did not contemplate that his analysis might call into question the constitutionality of a national bank—or, for that matter, criminal laws whose violation can result in long prison terms or execution. Unlike the joint dissenters in *NFIB*, he had recently joined all of Justice Breyer's broad interpretation of the Necessary and Proper Clause in *United States v. Comstock*.[83]

My best guess is that the commerce and necessary and proper portions of Roberts's opinion will come to be regarded as exercises in symbolic federalism. I read Roberts as prohibiting Congress from imposing purchase mandates, not as prohibiting Congress from ever regulating "inactivity" under the Commerce Clause or Necessary and Proper Clause. Federal power to quarantine or mandate vaccination might be critical in a public health emergency, such as a flu pandemic that disrespects state borders.

Of course, I cannot be certain that the Roberts opinion will be limited to purchase mandates. If I am wrong, then the consequences could be quite significant. For example, given the conceptual instability of the distinction between regulating "activity" and regulating "inactivity," it is possible that a differently composed Court will use the Roberts opinion (and the joint dissent) to aggressively scale back the scope of federal power. But given how extreme it would be to conclude, say, that a restaurant owner who refuses to serve African Americans is "inactive" in commerce for constitutional purposes, I doubt we will end up in such a place. Parties that practiced racial discrimination infamously made such claims in *Heart of Atlanta Motel, Inc. v. United States*[84] and *Katzenbach v. McClung*,[85] in which the Court held that the Commerce Clause justified provisions of the Civil Rights Act of 1964 that prohibited racial discrimination in hotels and restaurants. My sense of the Chief Justice, who presumably will be on the Court for decades, is that he has no desire to go there. He is too much of a believer in judicial deference to acts of Congress.

## 3. Outside Law

For the most part, I have so far occupied the perspective of the faithful legal practitioner, who has views about sound and unsound constitutional arguments. In this final section, I will occupy the external perspective of the analyst of the constitutional system. I will ask what Chief Justice Roberts potentially accomplished in responding to *NFIB* as he did. I will focus on the possible effects of his intervention, not on whether he intended these effects. As I noted at the outset, no one knows why he did what he did.

What may Roberts have accomplished by prohibiting Congress from using the Commerce and Necessary and Proper Clauses to require Americans to purchase products against their will? Any answer to this question is necessarily speculative at this point. The effects of a Supreme Court decision are a matter of empirical causation, which may be difficult to measure and may depend on whether one focuses on the short term or the long term.[86] There may also be a difference between the effects of judicial speech on elite opinion and the effects on public opinion, even if the latter is partially a function of the former. I cannot do more here than note these difficulties and proceed anyway.

In validating a legal position that was widely dismissed as near-frivolous just two years earlier,[87] Roberts expressed new popular and professional constitutional arguments. These arguments were developed by those who had mobilized against the predominant view among legal experts that the minimum coverage provision is constitutional. These experts including some of the most prominent legal conservatives in the nation, such as Charles Fried, Henry Monaghan, Richard Posner, Laurence Silberman, Jeffrey Sutton, and J. Harvie Wilkinson III.

Many millions of Americans balked at being forced by Congress to buy a product.[88] Perhaps they were misinformed about the rationales for the minimum coverage provision, given that the ACA provisions requiring insurers to cover individuals with preexisting conditions remain very popular.[89] And perhaps much of the public was misinformed because so much more money was spent attacking the law than defending it.[90] But it can be perilous to dismiss the opposition of a majority of Americans over a sustained period of time on grounds of public ignorance. Perhaps the Obama administration would have defended the ACA more vigorously in the court of public opinion if doing so had entailed less political risk.[91]

Republican and libertarian lawyers acted in harmony, and in concert, with the popular constitutional commitments of groups that had mobilized against the minimum coverage provision. These lawyers conceptualized Congress's enumerated powers in libertarian terms. The best instance may have been Randy Barnett's ingenious argument that the minimum coverage provision "commandeered the people," thereby turning citizens into "subjects."[92] From the standpoint of orthodox legal reasoning, it would have made more sense to present this liberty-based, freedom-from-contract objection to the minimum coverage provision as an economic substantive due process claim.[93] From the standpoint of conventional legal reasoning, it makes little sense from either a federalism or a liberty perspective to invalidate the minimum coverage provision while conceding that a more centralizing and coercive single-payer system of Medicare for all is clearly constitutional.[94] But from the standpoint of emerging and contrarian constitutional arguments, such observations may be beside the point. In rejecting the Commerce and Necessary and Proper Clauses as justifications for the minimum coverage provision, Roberts's opinion was congruent with mobilization claims on the Republican right.

But Roberts's opinion also differed from these mobilization claims. By upholding the minimum coverage provision under the Taxing Clause, Roberts validated the commitments of the ACA's supporters, including the President and the political party that he leads. In addition, Roberts honored what Adrian Vermeule has identified as a fundamental post–New Deal constitutional convention: "the Court should not invalidate major social welfare statutes enacted by the federal government."[95] The ACA is deadly serious business. Almost all Americans will be personally affected by the legislation, just as they would have been personally affected by the Court's invalidation of it. The ACA is much closer to Social Security, Medicare, and Medicaid than it is to any federal law invalidated by the Rehnquist Court on federalism grounds. A principal effect of Roberts's intervention was that the Court avoided striking down—by a vote of five Republicans to four Democrats—much or all of the most important piece of domestic legislation in nearly half a century.

Roberts did not give the ACA's opponents and proponents half a loaf: opponents lost this part of the case and won a limit on federal commerce power that seems unlikely to come into play much in the future. But Roberts did accept their key constitutional, moral, and symbolic claim: Congress may not coerce people into commerce the better to regulate them. Whether intentionally or unwittingly, Roberts partially validated the sincerely held moral beliefs of both sides. This is precisely what Professor Paul Mishkin understood Justice Powell to have done when the Court initially established constitutional standards for affirmative action in higher education.[96] Like Powell in the *Bakke* case,[97] Roberts thereby may have helped to sustain some measure of social solidarity amid intense disagreement over the meaning of the Constitution—and of the nation's commitments to the general welfare and individual liberty.

Justices sometimes respond to momentous cases by practicing judicial statesmanship. They "seek not only the 'right answer' to legal questions as a matter of professional reason, but also an answer that sustains the social legitimacy of law."[98] Such judges take some account of the conditions of the public legitimacy of the constitutional law that they craft. They may succeed in sustaining the public legitimacy of constitutional law by fashioning judicial opinions that express social values as social circumstances change, and by sustaining social solidarity amid reasonable, irreconcilable disagreement. Statesmanship is political in the sense of attempting to secure the political foundations of the rule of law,[99] which requires attention to the subtle relationships of "trust" that make the rule of law possible.[100] Statesmanship is not political in the "low politics" sense of seeking partisan advantage.[101]

As I observed at the beginning of this chapter, liberal supporters of the ACA praised Roberts's judicial statesmanship in upholding the minimum coverage provision under the Taxing Clause. If the foregoing account of Roberts's conduct is persuasive, then these commentators were right to stress his statesmanship, but wrong to locate it exclusively in his reliance on the tax power. His statesmanship also lay in his conclusions that the minimum coverage provision was beyond the scope of the Commerce and Necessary and Proper Clauses.

Several clarifications of this account are appropriate. First, an act of judicial statesmanship may succeed or fail, and it is unclear whether Roberts's opinion is a success or a failure in this regard. Because the general public does not read Supreme Court opinions, the meaning of these opinions is communicated to the public in complex, highly mediated ways—especially through various news media. When *NFIB* came down, some conservative and libertarian elites registered their partial victory and declared it publicly.[102] At the same time, media headlines mostly emphasized that the Court had upheld almost all of the ACA. Accordingly, many low-information citizens on the political right may not have received a message of partial vindication from Roberts's opinion. Low-information citizens—that is, the vast majority of the population—may not have internalized much more from media accounts than the Court's bottom line.[103]

Second, I have underscored some possible consequences of Roberts's conduct from the external perspective, and I have noted its similarity to the practice of judicial statesmanship. I have not approved his commerce and necessary and proper analyses from the internal perspective. I am loath to endorse these parts of Roberts's opinion on grounds of statesmanship because I believe that they contradict sound legal reasoning. If one were going to defend these portions of his opinion, however, statesmanship likely would provide the most persuasive means of doing so. But such a defense would entail the application of criteria that sound in social solidarity and judicial legitimacy, which are difficult to justify as legal from the internal point of view.[104]

Third, a focus on judicial statesmanship does not suggest that Roberts disbelieved his own interpretations of the Commerce and Necessary and Proper Clauses. To reiterate, I am examining the potential effects of his intervention, not whether he intended these effects. Moreover, Roberts easily could have believed his interpretations of these clauses even if he intended to practice statesmanship. Statesmanship might then explain why he needlessly decided these questions, not whether he believed in the soundness of the resolutions that he reached.

Finally, this account of Roberts's statesmanship in *NFIB* may seem most persuasive to those who agree with me on the merits—that is, those who think the tax part of his opinion is legally persuasive and the commerce and necessary and proper parts are unpersuasive. I am not so sure. Although views about judicial statesmanship are not entirely independent of views about the merits,[105] nor are the two coextensive. For example, one might agree with certain liberal defenders of the ACA's constitutionality that Roberts's opinion is statesman-like for the reasons I have offered while still concluding that all three parts of his opinion on the minimum coverage provision are legally unpersuasive. One could also appreciate the potentially positive systemic effects of his intervention even after concluding that legality required him to invalidate the minimum coverage provision.

## 4. Conclusion

There is adequate legal justification for Chief Justice Roberts's conclusion that the minimum coverage provision was within the scope of Congress's tax power. There is inadequate legal justification for why and how Roberts concluded that the minimum coverage provision was beyond the scope of the Commerce and Necessary and Proper Clauses. But in partially responding to conservative mobilization against the ACA, Roberts may have practiced judicial statesmanship—not just by upholding the minimum coverage provision under the Taxing Clause, but also by rejecting it under the Commerce and Necessary and Proper Clauses. The ACA's opponents thereby won something, even if mostly symbolic, in their quest to defeat health care reform.

It is difficult to approve this facet of Roberts's opinion if one believes, as I do, that the minimum coverage provision is a valid regulation of interstate commerce, as well as a constitutionally appropriate means of effectuating other valid regulations of interstate commerce. But to the extent that Roberts succeeded in enhancing the social legitimacy of constitutional law, this consequence of his opinion should, perhaps, give some pause to those inclined to judge him in exclusively legal terms—and to judge him harshly. American constitutional discourse requires resources to distinguish the different senses in which judges may act "politically." Statesmanship and partisanship are not the same.

## Acknowledgments

For illuminating discussions or suggestions, I am grateful to Jack Balkin, Randy Barnett, Katharine Bartlett, Joseph Blocher, Robert Cooter, Heather Gerken, R. Craig Green, Linda Greenhouse, Andy Koppelman, Gillian Metzger, Trevor Morrison, Nathaniel Persily, Robert Post, Theodore Ruger, Reva Siegel, Lawrence Solum, Robert Weiner, participants in Columbia Law School's conference on *NFIB*, and workshop participants at the University of Miami Law School.

# Notes

1. 132 S. Ct. 2566 (2012).
2. *Id.* at 2584–2593 (Roberts, C.J.).
3. *Id.* at 2593–2600. Justices Ginsburg, Breyer, Sotomayor, and Kagan joined this part of Chief Justice Roberts's opinion for the Court.
4. See THE STAFF OF THE WASH. POST, LANDMARK: THE INSIDE STORY OF AMERICA'S NEW HEALTH-CARE LAW AND WHAT IT MEANS FOR US ALL 66–68 (2010).
5. Jeffrey Rosen, *Big Chief: How to Understand John Roberts*, THE NEW REPUBLIC, July 13, 2012, *available at* http://www.tnr.com/article/politics/magazine/104898/john-roberts-supreme-court-aca.
6. Jeffrey Toobin, *To Your Health*, THE NEW YORKER, July 9, 2012, *available at* http://www.newyorker.com/talk/comment/2012/07/09/120709taco_talk_toobin.
7. David Von Drehle, *Roberts Rules: What the Health Care Decision Means for the Country*, TIME, June 29, 2012, *available at* http://swampland.time.com/2012/06/29/roberts-rules-what-the-health-care-decision-means-for-the-country/.
8. James Taranto, *We Blame George W. Bush*, WALL ST. J., June 28, 2012, *available at* http://online.wsj.com/article/SB10001424052702304058404577494622616505142.html.
9. *Id.*
10. Mark A Thiessen, *Why Are Republicans So Awful at Picking Supreme Court Justices?* WASH. POST, July 2, 2012, *available at* http://www.washingtonpost.com/opinions/marc-a-thiessen-why-Are-republicans-so-awful-at-picking-supreme-court-justices/2012/07/02/gJQAHFJAIW_story.html.
11. *Id.*
12. Toobin, *supra* note 6, at 30.
13. Jeffrey Rosen, *Welcome to the Roberts Court: How the Chief Justice Used Obamacare to Reveal His True Identity*, THE NEW REPUBLIC, June 29, 2012, *available at* http://www.tnr.com/blog/plank/104493/welcome-the-roberts-court-who-the-chief-justice-was-all-along.
14. U.S. CONST. art. I, § 8, cl. 1. For a theory of the tax power that Roberts's opinion tracks closely, see generally Robert D. Cooter & Neil S. Siegel, *Not the Power to Destroy: An Effects Theory of the Tax Power*, 98 VA. L. REV. 1195 (2012).
15. For an account of judicial statesmanship, see generally Neil S. Siegel, *The Virtue of Judicial Statesmanship*, 86 TEX. L. REV. 959 (2008).
16. 26 U.S.C. § 5000A(b)(1).
17. 26 U.S.C. § 5000A(b), (c).
18. For documentation of these facts, see Cooter & Siegel, *supra* note 14, at 1241.
19. See, e.g., Liberty Univ., Inc. v. Geithner, 671 F.3d 391, 424 (4th Cir. 2011) (Davis, J., dissenting) ("Congress deliberately deleted [previous] references to a 'tax' in the final version of the Act and instead designated the exaction a 'penalty.'" (citations omitted)).
20. See generally Cooter & Siegel, *supra* note 14.
21. See *id.* at 1226–1228.
22. 26 U.S.C. § 5000A(c).
23. See Cooter & Siegel, *supra* note 14, at 1222–1224.
24. NFIB v. Sebelius, 132 S. Ct. 2566, 2595, 2600 (2012).
25. CONGRESSIONAL BUDGET OFFICE, PAYMENTS OF PENALTIES FOR BEING UNINSURED UNDER THE PATIENT PROTECTION AND AFFORDABLE CARE ACT (April 2010), at 1, http://www.cbo.gov/publication/21351.
26. CONGRESSIONAL BUDGET OFFICE, UPDATED ESTIMATES FOR THE INSURANCE COVERAGE PROVISIONS OF THE AFFORDABLE CARE ACT (March 2012), at 11, http://www.cbo.gov/sites/default/files/cbofiles/attachments/03–13-Coverage%20Estimates.pdf.
27. *Cf.* United States v. Lopez, 514 U.S. 549 (1995) (holding a ban on firearm possession in school zones beyond the scope of the commerce power).

28. For a distinction between pure taxes and tax equivalents, see generally Cooter & Siegel, *supra* note 14.

29. These claims are defended in Cooter & Siegel, *supra* note 14, at 1200–1222.

30. U.S. CONST. art. I, § 8, cl. 1.

31. See Cooter & Siegel, *supra* note 14, at 1205–1206 (discussing Alexander Hamilton's program for industrialization and quoting Joseph Story's *Commentaries*).

32. Dep't of Revenue of MT v. Kurth Ranch, 511 U.S. 767, 782 (1994).

33. I do not address here the applicability of the federal tax Anti-Injunction Act. For my views, see generally Michael C. Dorf & Neil S. Siegel, *"Early-Bird Special" Indeed! Why the Tax Anti-Injunction Act Permits the Present Challenges to the Minimum Coverage Provision*, 121 YALE L.J. ONLINE 389 (2012), http://yalelawjournal.org/2012/01/19/dorf&siegel.html.

34. See, e.g., New York v. United States, 505 U.S. 144, 169–174 (1992); Bailey v. Drexel Furniture Co., 259 U.S. 20, 35 (1922); License Tax Cases, 72 U.S. (5 Wall.) 462 (1866).

35. See Cooter & Siegel, *supra* note 14, at 1226–1227.

36. Transcript of Oral Argument at 52–53, NFIB v. Sebelius, 132 S. Ct. 2566 (2012).

37. U.S. CONST. art. I, § 8, cl. 3.

38. U.S. CONST. art. I, § 8, cl. 18.

39. See, e.g., Randy E. Barnett, *Commandeering the People: Why the Individual Health Insurance Mandate is Unconstitutional*, 5 N.Y.U. J.L. & LIBERTY 581, 632 (2010).

40. See Printz v. United States, 521 U.S. 898 (1997); New York v. United States, 505 U.S. 144 (1992).

41. For discussions, see Cooter & Siegel, *supra* note 14, at 1244–1245.

42. See NFIB, 132 S. Ct. at 2579 ("Our permissive reading of [Congress's enumerated] powers is explained in part by a general reticence to invalidate the acts of the Nation's elected leaders."); *id.* at 2594 (stressing "the full measure of deference owed to federal statutes.").

43. See, e.g., Nw. Austin Mun. Util. Dist. No. One v. Holder, 557 U.S. 193, 197 (2009). For use of the presumption of constitutionality to privilege constitutional avoidance over clear statement rules in tax power cases, see generally Gillian E. Metzger & Trevor W. Morrison, The Presumption of Constitutionality and the Individual Mandate, in this volume.

44. *NFIB*, 132 S. Ct. at 2593.

45. *Id.* at 2600.

46. *Id.*

47. *Id.* at 2579.

48. *Id.* at 2600.

49. *Id.* at 2601 ("Without deciding the Commerce Clause question, I would find no basis to adopt such a saving construction.").

50. For a discussion of the change from an "unconstitutionality" understanding of the avoidance canon to a "doubts" understanding, see RICHARD H. FALLON JR. ET AL., HART AND WECHSLER'S THE FEDERAL COURTS AND THE FEDERAL SYSTEM 78–80 (6th ed. 2009); see *id.* at 78–79 ("Under the unconstitutionality approach, which was commonly practiced during the nineteenth century, the courts adopted an alternative interpretation only after first deciding that the preferred interpretation would render the statute unconstitutional.").

51. On the distinction between "classical avoidance" and "modern avoidance," see generally Adrian Vermeule, *Saving Constructions*, 85 GEO. L.J. 1945, 1949 (1997).

52. See FALLON ET AL., *supra* note 50, at 79 ("Modern avoidance … rejects the unconstitutionality approach on the ground that the former practice still requires an unnecessary constitutional ruling."). The canonical citation is *Ashwander v. TN Valley Auth.*, 297 U.S. 288, 348 (1936) (Brandeis, J., concurring).

53. Dep't of Commerce v. U.S. House of Representatives, 525 U.S. 316, 343 (1999) (quoting Spector Motor Serv. v. McLaughlin, 323 U.S. 101, 105 (1944)).

54. *NFIB*, 132 S. Ct. at 2594.

55. See Brief for Petitioners at 52, *NFIB*, 132 S. Ct. 2566 (No. 11-398) (Minimum Coverage Provision) ("The minimum coverage provision is independently authorized by Congress's tax power").

56. For a cogent discussion and citations to the literature, see FALLON ET AL., *supra* note 50, at 79–80.

57. For a discussion of rule-of-law values, see Robert C. Post & Neil S. Siegel, *Theorizing the Law/Politics Distinction: Neutral Principles, Affirmative Action, and the Enduring Legacy of Paul Mishkin*, 95 CALIF. L. REV. 1473, 1474–1477 (2007).

58. See, e.g., Gonzales v. Raich, 545 U.S. 1 (2005); United States v. Morrison, 529 U.S. 598 (2000); United States v. Lopez, 514 U.S. 549 (1995).

59. See generally Neil S. Siegel, *Free Riding on Benevolence: Collective Action Federalism and the Minimum Coverage Provision*, 75 L. & CONTEMP. PROBS., no. 3, at 29 (2012).

60. 42 U.S.C. § 18091(a)(2)(F) (2010).

61. See generally Robert D. Cooter & Neil S. Siegel, *Collective Action Federalism: A General Theory of Article I, Section 8*, 63 STAN. L. REV. 115 (2010). For related accounts, see generally Jack M. Balkin, *Commerce*, 109 MICH. L. REV. 1 (2010); Donald H. Regan, *How to Think About the Federal Commerce Power and Incidentally Rewrite* United States v. Lopez, 94 MICH. L. REV. 554 (1995); Robert L. Stern, *That Commerce Which Concerns More States Than One*, 47 HARV. L. REV. 1335 (1934).

62. Reasonableness is the appropriate test. See, e.g., Thomas More Law Ctr. v. Obama, 651 F.3d 529, 564 (6th Cir. 2011) (Sutton, J., concurring in part and delivering the opinion of the court in part) ("The courts do not apply strict scrutiny to commerce clause legislation and require only an 'appropriate' or 'reasonable' 'fit' between means and ends.") (quoting United States v. Comstock, 130 S. Ct. 1949, 1956–1957 (2010)).

63. NFIB v. Sebelius, 132 S. Ct. 2566, 2585–2591 (2012) (Roberts, C.J.).

64. 2 THE RECORDS OF THE FEDERAL CONVENTION OF 1787 131–132 (Max Farrand ed., rev. ed. 1966).

65. See Stern, *supra* note 61, at 1340.

66. See, e.g., *NFIB*, 132 S. Ct. at 2612 (Ginsburg, J., concurring in part, concurring in judgment in part, and dissenting in part) ("States cannot resolve the problem of the uninsured on their own."); id. ("Congress' intervention was needed to overcome this collective-action impasse.").

67. For documentation of these laws and charitable hospital practices, see Siegel, *supra* note 59, at 57.

68. For a discussion, see id. at 56–61.

69. 42 U.S.C. § 300gg, 1(a), 3(a), 11, 12 (2010).

70. *Comstock*, 130 S. Ct. at 1957 (quoting *Raich*, 545 U.S. at 37 (Scalia, J., concurring in judgment) (quoting United States v. Darby, 312 U.S. 100, 121 (1941))).

71. See *NFIB*, 132 S. Ct. at 2588 ("Under the Government's theory, Congress could address the [unhealthy] diet problem by ordering everyone to buy vegetables.").

72. *Id.* at 2589.

73. *Id.*

74. *Id.* at 2591.

75. For a discussion of these limits, see generally Neil S. Siegel, *Four Constitutional Limits that the Minimum Coverage Provision Respects*, 27 CONST. COMMENT. 591 (2011).

76. *NFIB*, 132 S. Ct. at 2592 ("Even if the individual mandate is 'necessary' to the Act's insurance reforms, such an expansion of federal power is not a 'proper' means for making those reforms effective.").

77. *Id.* at 2591–2593 (quoting McCulloch v. Maryland, 17 U.S. (4 Wheat.) 316, 411 (1819)).

78. For substantiation of these claims, see generally Siegel, *Free Riding on Benevolence, supra* note 59.

79. 312 U.S. 100 (1941).

80. 132 S. Ct. at 2591–2593 (quoting *McCulloch*, 17 U.S. at 411).

81. *McCulloch*, 17 U.S. at 316.

82. See, e.g., PAUL BREST, SANFORD LEVINSON, JACK M. BALKIN, AKHIL REED AMAR, & REVA B. SIEGEL, PROCESSES OF CONSTITUTIONAL DECISIONMAKING: CASES AND MATERIALS 27–28 (5th ed. 2006).

83. 130 S. Ct. 1949 (2010).

84. 379 U.S. 241 (1964).

85. 379 U.S. 294 (1964).

86. For an empirical examination of certain short-term effects of *NFIB*, see generally Andrea Louise Campbell & Nathaniel Persily, The *Health Care Case* in the Public Mind: Opinion on the Supreme Court and Health Reform in a Polarized Era, in this volume.

87. See, e.g., Kevin Sack, *Judge Voids Key Element of Obama Health Care Law*, N.Y. TIMES, Dec. 13, 2010, *available at* http://www.nytimes.com/2010/12/14/health/policy/14health. html?pagewanted=1&%2359 (observing that a district court's invalidation of the minimum coverage provision was "striking given that only nine months ago, prominent law professors were dismissing the constitutional claims as just north of frivolous").

88. A variety of illuminating polls are available at PollingReport.com, http://pollingreport. com/health.htm.

89. See Peter Baker, *For Obama, A Signature Issue That the Public Never Embraced Looms Large*, N.Y. TIMES, June 29, 2012, *available at* http://www.nytimes.com/2012/06/30/us/politics/ health-care-overhaul-is-still-no-hit-with-public.html?_r=2&pagewanted=all (referencing "polls showing that elements of the law, like protections for those with pre-existing conditions, rate high with the public.").

90. See Abby Goodnough, *Distaste for Health Care Law Reflects Spending on Ads*, N.Y. TIMES, June 20, 2012, *available at* http://www.nytimes.com/2012/06/21/health/policy/health- care-law-loses-ad-war.html?hp&pagewanted=all ("In all, about $235 million has been spent on ads attacking the law since its passage in March 2010.... Only $69 million has been spent on advertising supporting it.").

91. See, e.g., Baker, *supra* note 89.

92. See generally Barnett, *supra* note 39.

93. For analysis of the liberty claim, see generally Jedediah Purdy & Neil S. Siegel, *The Liberty of Free Riders: The Minimum Coverage Provision, Mill's "Harm Principle," and American Social Morality*, 38 AM. J.L. & MED. 374 (2012).

94. For explication of these points, see Siegel, *Free Riding on Benevolence*, *supra* note 59, at 73–74.

95. Adrian Vermuele, *Constitutional Conventions*, NEW REPUBLIC, Aug. 2, 2012 (reviewing MICHAEL J. GERHARDT, THE POWER OF PRECEDENT (2012)), *available at* http://www.tnr. com/ book/review/power-precedent-michael-gerhardt?utm_source=The+New+Republic &utm _campaign=ce2825869c-TNR_B%26A_080212&utm_medium=email#.

96. Mishkin wrote and taught about judicial opinions that "both symbolically and actually rec- ognize[] the legitimacy of deeply held moral claims on both sides." Paul J. Mishkin, *The Uses of Ambivalence: Reflections on the Supreme Court and the Constitutionality of Affirmative Action*, 131 U. PA. L. REV. 907, 922 (1983).

97. Regents of the Univ. of Cal. v. Bakke, 438 U.S. 265 (1978).

98. Siegel, *supra* note 15, at 979.

99. See *id.* at 965–969.

100. See Carla A. Hesse & Robert Post, *Introduction, in* HUMAN RIGHTS IN POLITICAL TRANSITIONS: GETTYSBURG TO BOSNIA 13, 20 (Carla A. Hesse & Robert Post eds., 1999) ("[T]he relationship between the governed and the governors necessary to sus- tain the rule of law ... consists of specific practices that reflect trust and tacit social understandings.").

101. For a distinction between "high politics," in which judges pursue a political vision, and "low politics," in which judges seek partisan advantage, see generally Jack M. Balkin & Sanford Levinson, *Understanding the Constitutional Revolution*, 87 VA. L. REV. 1045 (2001).

102. See, e.g., George F. Will, *Conservatives' Consolation Prize*, WASH. POST, June 28, 2012 ("Conservatives distraught about the survival of the individual mandate are missing the considerable consolation prize they won when the Supreme Court rejected a constitutional rationale for the mandate — Congress's rationale — that was pregnant with rampant statism.").

103. I have elsewhere criticized the Court's anticommandeering doctrine as not advancing political accountability for low-information voters. See Neil S. Siegel, *Commandeering and Its Alternatives: A Federalism Perspective*, 59 VAND. L. REV. 1629, 1632 (2006) ("Even after factoring in search costs and rational ignorance, it seems likely that citizens who pay attention to public affairs and who care to inquire will be able to discern which level of government is responsible for a government regulation, and citizens who do not care to inquire may be largely beyond judicial or political help on the accountability front.").

104. See generally Robert C. Post, *Theorizing Disagreement: Reconceiving the Relationship Between Law and Politics*, 98 CALIF. L. REV. 1319 (2010).

105. See Siegel, *supra* note 15, at 999–1000 (discussing the relationship between views about judicial statesmanship and views about the constitutional values that courts enforce).

# CHAPTER 13

# The Secret History of the Chief Justice's Obamacare Decision

*John Fabian Witt*

A Democratic Party president's signature legislative victory is imperiled by an aging Supreme Court stocked by Republican appointees. Tricky constitutional law obstacles, including limits on the Congress's power under the Commerce Clause, threaten to undo a vast federal insurance program designed to solve a pressing social crisis. But then one of the justices identifies an alternative way to rescue the constitutional basis for the legislation: Congress's tax power,[1] he concludes, offers the basis for upholding the program.

The scenario sounds like Chief Justice John Roberts and the Affordable Care Act[2] (ACA), known as Obamacare, which the Supreme Court upheld in June 2012 on the basis of the Congress's tax power in *National Federation of Independent Business v. Sebelius* (*NFIB*).[3] But it also matches perfectly the story of Justice Louis Brandeis, President Franklin Roosevelt, and the Social Security Act of 1935.[4] And amid all the coverage of the Obamacare decision, the crucial connection between Roberts and Brandeis has gone missing. Right out of law school, the Chief Justice clerked for Judge Henry Friendly, long thought of as one of the great judges of the twentieth century, perhaps the greatest federal judge (alongside Learned Hand) never to serve on the Supreme Court. Friendly, in turn, clerked for none other than Justice Louis Brandeis. Brandeis's broad view of Congress's taxing authority is readily apparent in Friendly's widely respected taxation decisions. And now Brandeis's influence is apparent in the most important opinion of Chief Justice Roberts's tenure.

Tracing the influence of Brandeis and Friendly reveals a feature of the Roberts *NFIB* opinion that has been left out of most of the commentary on the case so far. For the Roberts opinion is not only the product of conservative movement politics, on the one hand, and prudent institutional judgment, on the other. The opinion is both of those things. But it was also shaped by a powerful set of professional traditions. The tax power strand in Roberts's Obamacare opinion was made available by a professional culture of lawyers stretching back into the beginnings of the modern state.

The story begins in 1933, when Depression-fueled unemployment rates hit an all-time high of 25 percent.[5] Progressive reformers, including Wisconsin's influential husband-and-wife crusaders Elizabeth and Paul Raushenbush, were desperately casting about for a constitutional basis for national unemployment insurance.[6] Action at the state level was paralyzed because no one state seemed able to adopt an expensive insurance plan without driving employers into neighboring states. But action at the federal level seemed impossible, too, because the conservative Supreme Court seemed unlikely to allow the Congress to enact a comprehensive unemployment system as a regulation of interstate commerce.[7]

That's where Brandeis comes in. The Justice had been involved in unemployment insurance debates going back to at least 1914, when he sat on a Massachusetts commission that studied the problem.[8] Elizabeth Raushenbush was his daughter, and when she and her husband visited with him in his summer cottage in Massachusetts, Brandeis suggested a novel solution to the constitutional dilemma: the tax power, he told them, would offer a constitutionally sound footing for the vast social insurance system they were contemplating.[9]

Justice Brandeis spent a great deal of time contemplating how the United States might escape the Depression. In many ways, his plan for economic recovery mirrored President Roosevelt's. Both men strongly supported minimum wage laws, protections for labor unions, and investments in public works projects. But Brandeis, who considered himself a conservative, was not entirely supportive of the New Deal.[10]

Brandeis harbored a deep distrust of centralized federal programs. He often spoke of "the curse of bigness" and dreamed of returning power from large corporations back to farmers and entrepreneurs. Thus, Brandeis's clerks remember that "[i]n the adjustment of interstate relations," the Justice "sought resourcefully for a via media between centralization and Balkanization."[11] He found in the Constitution one provision that enabled exactly this type of balance: Congress's tax power.[12]

Brandeis saw in the tax power a mechanism not only for raising revenue, but also for regulating. As he saw it, federal taxes should be used for two purposes: curbing the size of large corporations and drastically limiting the size of inheritances. Brandeis also wanted to use federal taxes to limit the activities of banks, to penalize out-of-state corporations, and to limit the power of public utility holding companies. In short, Brandeis "wanted the central government to use its power, and particularly its taxing power, to break up concentrations of power elsewhere and to ensure that society's underdogs would be treated fairly."[13]

Brandeis was hardly the only one to emphasize the tax power. Chief Justice Harlan Fiske Stone told Secretary of Labor Frances Perkins that he believed the tax power of the federal government would solve the constitutional difficulties facing social insurance legislation. But as President Roosevelt began developing his plan for an unemployment insurance system, Brandeis's theory of the tax power solved a special problem that Brandeis had identified with the emerging legislation. Roosevelt favored a nationalized program that would be administered from Washington. Brandeis shared Roosevelt's basic commitment to unemployment insurance but worried that unemployment relief might produce an oversized federal government. Brandeis instead proposed a state-run insurance program. To avoid a race-to-the-bottom among the states, Brandeis suggested that Congress could use its tax power to penalize states that did not create their own unemployment insurance programs.[14]

Roosevelt, however, was not convinced. By the spring of 1934, he was prepared to move forward with the nationalized program favored by his advisors. But before Roosevelt made his commitment public, Brandeis was able to use back channels to arrange a one-on-one meeting with the President. On June 7, 1934, the Justice personally lobbied President Roosevelt in a forty-five-minute Oval Office meeting. Roosevelt, keenly "concern[ed] with what the fate of the [unemployment insurance] law would be in the courts," left the meeting convinced that Brandeis's state-based system was the superior option. He reasoned that "[i]f Brandeis favored the plan, there was at least one vote for it, and perhaps it would be more palatable to the other justices as well."[15]

Four years later, the Supreme Court heard *Steward Machine Co. v. Davis*,[16] a challenge to the unemployment insurance provisions of the Social Security Act. During the oral argument, Brandeis appeared frustrated with the petitioner's argument that the unemployment insurance provision somehow exceeded the scope of the federal government's taxing authority. Brandeis interrupted the oral argument to note that a national unemployment insurance scheme "was needed and [had been] deemed necessary by [the federal government's] representatives."[17] As one of his clerks later recalled, it was "unthinkable" to Brandeis "that the federal government was powerless to act more constructively by inducing the states, through a credit against a federal tax, to establish unemployment compensation plans of their own."[18]

When the opinion came down the next month, Brandeis proved to be a decisive vote in the sharply divided five-to-four decision upholding the unemployment provisions.[19] The Court held that "[t]he subject-matter of taxation open to the power of the Congress is as comprehensive as that open to the power of the states," and suggested that Congress's broad taxing authority extended to "every form of tax appropriate to sovereignty."[20] Although the four conservatives dissented vigorously,[21] Justice Cardozo's opinion for the majority emphasized the dire economic situation and lauded the Social Security Act for "attempt[ing] to find a method by which ... public agencies may work together to a common end."[22] The tax theory had become a foundation stone in the new American social insurance state.

Brandeis's clerks generally found their boss aloof and distant. But when Henry Friendly went from Harvard Law School to clerk for Brandeis on the Supreme Court, the younger man quickly developed a case of what he frankly acknowledged as "hero worship." The feelings were mutual. "Don't you ever send me another such man as Friendly," Brandeis wrote in jest to Harvard Professor Felix Frankfurter: "If I had another man like [him], I would not have to do a lick of work myself."[23]

The two men had a good deal in common. Both were academic superstars—to this day, there remains some controversy over whether Brandeis or Friendly had the best grades in the history of Harvard Law School. Both were extraordinarily hard workers. Both were meticulous, disciplined, and thoughtful. On a personal level, Friendly admired Brandeis's ability to remain kind while also keeping an appropriate professional distance.[24]

Friendly, however, was no Brandeis clone. Friendly spent the bulk of his professional career in large corporate law firms, first at Root, Clark, and then as a founding partner at what is now Cleary Gottlieb Steen & Hamilton, LLP. Perhaps because of that experience, Friendly had virtually no distrust of "bigness" and typically favored efforts to reform institutions rather than reduce them. And, although his mentors Brandeis and Frankfurter were both prounion and proworker, Friendly's politics and jurisprudence were decidedly promanagement.[25]

Despite his business-friendly politics, Henry Friendly had a certain prudentialist quality that made it difficult for the media to label him as either as a liberal or a conservative. He hired clerks of all political stripes, believing that the most intelligent applicants would be most useful to him. He favored incrementalism over radical change, respected history and precedent, and drew inspiration directly from the text of the Constitution. Throughout his twenty-seven years on the federal bench, Friendly stood by the most important lesson he learned from Justice Brandeis: to humbly defer to the elected branches whenever possible.[26] And according to one close student of Friendly, he particularly "admired Brandeis's dissents that refused to invalidate state and federal taxation and regulation on equal protection or due process grounds."[27]

After his appointment to the U.S. Court of Appeals for the Second Circuit in 1959, Friendly quickly took up the project of carrying on his former boss's vision of Congress's taxation authority. Within just a few months of coming onto the bench, Friendly heard argument in *Sidney v. Commissioner*, which involved a challenge to the retroactive application of a new tax.[28] The petitioners in that case relied heavily on *Untermyer v. Anderson*,[29] in which the Supreme Court had held that retroactive application of new taxes violated due process. But Justice Brandeis had disagreed with that opinion, and, as his clerk, the young Henry Friendly had helped him write a dissent.[30] Thirty-two years later, Friendly dug up that dissent and used it as the basis for his opinion in *Sidney*. Friendly noted that the majority's opinion in *Untermyer* was now regarded as questionable; indeed, by the time *Sidney* was decided, "the Supreme Court ha[d] distinguished [*Untermyer*] on six occasions and ha[d] expressly followed it only once."[31] Accordingly, Friendly dismissed *Untermyer* wholesale and instead decided the case in front of him on the basis of Brandeis's dissent. Despite clear Supreme Court precedent to the contrary, Friendly ultimately held that the tax at issue in *Sidney* could apply retroactively.[32]

*Sidney* proved to be an accurate predictor of Friendly's later tax jurisprudence. Although the judge was no pushover for the government in tax cases, he adopted an approach that was distinctively aimed at avoiding formalities and allowing the government broad leeway to operate a well-functioning system of tax collection. That approach led not to only to the result in *Sidney*, but also to decisions affirming other IRS determinations—such as the IRS's rulings that investors cannot claim income tax deductions on interest payments resulting from simulated bond transactions,[33] and that a corporate president cannot claim deductions on bad business debt incurred through activities not proximately related to the president's trade or business.[34] As David Dorsen's recent biography of Friendly emphasizes, Friendly eschewed formal and textualist approaches to deciding tax cases when advancing the purposes and functions of the tax in question required him to do so. More than once, he invoked the statutory interpretation canon against absurdity to preserve the government's position in a tax dispute. And in one especially prominent tax case, he insisted on advancing the "policy of the legislation" and the "purpose of the act" as against the "literal words" and the "strict letter" of the text.[35]

Friendly's antiformalist approach to tax cases was on clear display during the 1979–1980 term, during which John Roberts clerked for him. In that year alone, the judge wrote opinions enforcing a congressional estate tax amendment against wealthy families' efforts to circumvent it[36] and upholding the government's collection of tax penalties against a company that had entered and then emerged from bankruptcy reorganization.[37] And, in *Laino v. United States*,[38] Friendly wrote a pointed opinion rejecting a taxpayer's effort to evade the Anti-Injunction Act (the same statute Chief Justice Roberts would later take up in *NFIB*).[39] In *Laino*, Friendly again sought to ease the burden of administering the tax code and appeared particularly indignant that the appellants chose not to petition the tax court for a redetermination in their case. Given their choice not to take advantage of this "generous avenue of relief," Friendly refused to hear their argument that they lacked an adequate opportunity to litigate their posi-tion.[40] Only once during Roberts's clerkship did his boss write an opinion ruling against the government in a tax case.[41]

Friendly's typical pattern continued after Roberts left Friendly's chambers. Only two years after Roberts's clerkship ended, Friendly wrote one of his most important and memorable tax decisions. In *Drucker v. Commissioner*, the judge ruled against a challenge to the tax code's controversial marriage penalty penal-izing married couples over singles.[42]

Judge Friendly hired John Roberts in part because the two men were so simi-lar. Both were raised by wealthy families in small towns. They both excelled at Harvard College, where each won the Bowdoin Essay Prize and graduated summa cum laude. Beyond mere biographical similarities, the two also shared "research and writing ability, love for history, and devotion to the law." Roberts was certainly more conservative than Friendly, but he was no partisan ideologue. Seeing a bit of himself in the young man from Indiana, Friendly decided to take a chance on Roberts.[43]

His gamble quickly paid off. Judge Friendly, like Justice Brandeis before him, tended to keep his distance from his clerks. But Roberts was able to endear him-self to the judge by showing up early for his clerkship and immediately produc-ing high-quality work. Friendly became so smitten with Roberts that he wrote then-Justice William Rehnquist a glowing recommendation of Roberts before he had completed even two months on the job. Later in life, Friendly openly rated Roberts among his favorite clerks.[44]

The affection was mutual. During his confirmation hearings to be Chief Justice, Roberts held Friendly up as a personal and professional role model. During his three years on the D.C. Circuit, Roberts quoted Friendly in six of the forty-nine opinions he wrote. (He never mentioned Rehnquist by name.) He quoted Friendly in his first opinion as Chief Justice of the United States. And as Chief Justice, he runs his chambers in the style of the judge for whom he clerked. Like Friendly (and like Brandeis), Roberts writes numerous longhand drafts of his opinions.[45]

A lot changed about American conservatism and the Republican Party between Eisenhower's nomination of Friendly in 1959 and George W. Bush's nomination of John Roberts in 2005. But one thing that stuck with Roberts from his clerkship was the same kind of deep admiration for Friendly that the older man had felt for Brandeis. One part of that, it has turned out, was Friendly's old-fashioned Republican view of the federal government's taxing authority. In 2006, in *Gonzales v. O Centro Espirita Beneficente Uniao do Vegetal*, the Chief Justice defended Social Security tax obligations on the theory that "mandatory participation is indispensable to the fiscal vitality of the social security system," noting that the "tax system could not function if denominations were allowed to challenge the tax system because tax payments were spent in a manner that violates their religious belief[s]."[46] The next year, in *Hinck v. United States*, Roberts ruled in the IRS's favor when taxpayers sought to avoid interest charges for late payment. ("Bad things happen if you fail to pay federal income taxes when due," the Chief Justice quipped.[47]) A year later, Roberts wrote an opinion upholding the government's efforts to collect taxes from three coal-mining companies[48] and upheld the IRS's view of the deductibility of certain investment costs.[49] And in 2011, he wrote an opinion deferring to a Treasury Department interpretation imposing Federal Insurance Contributions Act (FICA)[50] taxes on hospital residency programs employing recent medical school graduates.[51]

When it finally came to Obamacare, then, it should be no surprise that the Chief Justice had an intuitive feel for what, in his opinion, he called the "functional approach"[52] of the ACA's individual mandate as the equivalent of a tax. Roberts's practical evaluation of the ACA drew on a long professional history, going back eighty years to the beginnings of a remarkable line of American jurists yoked together by relations of mentorship and professional connections.

I do not mean for a minute to overclaim for the significance of the tax power story I have told here. Of course the deep roots of the tax power argument did not determine the result that Roberts reached. I am not committed to some notion of the perfect autonomy of the law, either as a description of what it is possible for judges to do, or even as a prescription for what they ought to do. How could one hold such a view after reading the opinions in *NFIB*? For they make clear better than any other decision just how much political transformations matter in constitutional law. The three-decade-old conservative movement to ratchet back the Commerce Clause to its pre–New Deal position comes to fruition in the opinions of five justices of the Court, Roberts included.[53] Nor do I mean to suggest that institutional considerations about the political stature of the Court played no role in Roberts's formulation of the decision. Quite the opposite. Roberts's reluctance to put the Supreme Court between the elected branches and the people on the President's signature policy achievement seems to have been crucial in the decision to uphold the statute.[54]

Even after allowing for the significance of political and institutional judgments, however, another basic question remains. What is it that made the tax power plausible as a pathway for solving the Chief's institutional dilemma? The transformation of the culture of the Commerce Clause and the rise of originalism in constitutional method demonstrate for all to see that the availability of moves in the game of constitutional law is culturally conditioned. That is not a bad thing. It is inevitable, and not something to be mourned. But if political movements can vie for pride of place in the shaping of constitutional law, so too does professional identity set conditions of plausibility and availability for judges maneuvering their way through the thickets of legal and political controversy. If Roberts's decision highlights a gap between the Supreme Court and crude partisan politics—and I think it does—it does so by bringing the significance of professional identity formation to the fore.[55]

And yet as the four Republican-appointed dissenters in *NFIB* make clear, the difference between constitutional law and partisanship is a razor's edge. The story of Brandeis, Friendly, and Roberts helps us see where this difference comes from and what sustains it. Law is not a mysterious science. It does not come to us from the heavens. It is located, in part, in the professional identities of the men and women who make it.

## Acknowledgment

Many thanks to James Dawson for excellent research assistance.

## Notes

1. "The Congress shall have Power to lay and collect Taxes, Duties, Imposts and Excises, to pay the Debts and provide for the common Defence and general Welfare of the United States; but all Duties, Imposts, and Excises shall be uniform throughout the United States." U.S. CONST. art. I, § 8, cl. 1.
2. Pub L. No. 111-148, 124 Stat. 119 (2010) (codified as amended in scattered sections of 26 and 42 U.S.C.).
3. See *NFIB*, 132 S. Ct. 2566 (2012).
4. Pub L. No. 74-271, 49 Stat. 620 (1935) (codified as amended in scattered sections of 42 U.S.C.).
5. Claudia Goldin, *Labor Markets in the Twentieth Century, in* THE CAMBRIDGE ECONOMIC HISTORY OF THE UNITED STATES 549, 590 (Stanley L. Engerman & Robert E. Gallman eds., 2000).
6. DAVID MOSS, SOCIALIZING SECURITY: PROGRESSIVE ERA ECONOMISTS AND THE ORIGINS OF AMERICAN SOCIAL POLICY 165–170 (1996); DANIEL NELSON, UNEMPLOYMENT INSURANCE: THE AMERICAN EXPERIENCE, 1915–1935, at 198–199 (1969); JOHN FABIAN WITT, THE ACCIDENTAL REPUBLIC: CRIPPLED WORKINGMEN, DESTITUTE WIDOWS, AND THE REMAKING OF AMERICAN LAW 198–199 (2004).
7. ALEXANDER KEYSSAR, OUT OF WORK: THE FIRST CENTURY OF UNEMPLOYMENT IN MASSACHUSETTS 292 (1986); NELSON, *supra* note 6, at 165.
8. KEYSSAR, *supra* note 7, at 265; MELVIN I. UROFSKY, LOUIS D. BRANDEIS: A LIFE 711 (2009) [hereinafter UROFSKY, LOUIS D. BRANDEIS].
9. See BRUCE ALLEN MURPHY, THE BRANDEIS/FRANKFURTER CONNECTION: THE SECRET POLITICAL ACTIVITIES OF TWO SUPREME COURT JUSTICES 165–167 (1982); LEWIS J. PAPER, BRANDEIS: AN INTIMATE BIOGRAPHY OF ONE OF AMERICA'S TRULY GREAT SUPREME COURT JUSTICES 354–355 (1983).
10. PHILIPPA STRUM, LOUIS D. BRANDEIS: JUSTICE FOR THE PEOPLE 193, 411 (1984); UROFSKY, LOUIS D. BRANDEIS, *supra* note 8, at 710; Paul A. Freund, *Mr. Justice Brandeis,*

*in* Mr. Justice 177, 185 (Allison Dunham & Phillip B. Kurland eds., 1964). According to Brandeis, New Deal liberals generally gave "[t]oo little thought ... to complex problems [when] drafting major economic and social legislation." Paper, *supra* note 9, at 362–363.

11. Freund, *supra* note 10, at 190.

12. Nelson L. Dawson, *Brandeis and the New Deal, in* Brandeis and America 38, 41 (Nelson L. Dawson ed., 1931); Melvin I. Urofsky, A Mind of One Piece: Brandeis and American Reform 41–55 (1971); Freund, *supra* note 10, at 190. Brandeis's plan, somewhat unlike Roosevelt's, "relied heavily on the use of the federal taxing power." Strum, *supra* note 10, at 390.

13. Strum, *supra* note 10, at 390, 413.

14. Michelle Landis Dauber, *The Sympathetic State*, 23 L. & Hist. Rev. 387, 387–388 (2005); *id.* at 382; Urofsky, Louis D. Brandeis, *supra* note 8, at 712–713.

15. Paper, *supra* note 9, at 357; Urofsky, Louis D. Brandeis, *supra* note 8, at 712–713.

16. 301 U.S. 548 (1937).

17. S. Doc. No. 75-53, at 71 (1937).

18. Freund, *supra* note 10, at 190.

19. *Steward*, 301 U.S. at 581–582, 590.

20. *Id.* at 581. In seeking to define the outer boundaries of Congress's taxing power, the Court noted that "[w]e do not say that a tax is valid, when imposed by act of Congress, if it is laid upon the condition that a state may escape its operation through the adoption of a statute unrelated in subject-matter to activities fairly within the scope of national policy and power. No such question is before us. In the tender of this credit Congress does not intrude upon fields foreign to its function." *Id.* at 590.

21. Justices McReynolds and Butler dissented in whole, see *id.* at 598, 616, and Justices Sutherland and Van Devanter dissented in part, see *id.* at 609.

22. *Id.* at 588.

23. David M. Dorsen, Henry Friendly: Greatest Judge of His Era 27–30 (2012).

24. *Id.* at 28–30; Bruce A. Ackerman, *In Memoriam: Henry J. Friendly*, 99 Harv. L. Rev. 1709, 1709 (1986).

25. Dorsen, *supra* note 23, at 279; Daniel Breen, *Avoiding "Wild Blue Yonders": The Prudentialism of Henry J. Friendly and John Roberts*, 52 S.D. L. Rev. 73, 81–82 (2007); Daniel Breen, Henry J. Friendly and the Pragmatic Tradition in American Law 7 (December 2002) (unpublished Ph.D. dissertation, Boston University).

26. Michael Boudin, *Memoirs in A Classical Style*, 133 U. Pa. L. Rev. 1, 3 (1984); Brad Snyder, *The Judicial Genealogy (and Mythology) of John Roberts: Clerkships from Gray to Brandeis to Friendly to Roberts*, 71 Ohio St. L.J. 1149, 1151 (2010) [hereinafter Snyder, *Judicial Genealogy*].

27. Snyder, *Judicial Genealogy*, *supra* note 26, at 1182.

28. 273 F.2d 928 (2d Cir. 1960).

29. 276 U.S. 440 (1928).

30. *Id.* at 446 (Brandeis, J., dissenting); Snyder, *Judicial Genealogy*, *supra* note 26, at 1177–1178.

31. *Sidney*, 273 F.2d at 932.

32. *Id.*

33. Lynch v. Comm'r, 273 F.2d 867, 871–873 (2d Cir. 1959).

34. Weddle v. Comm'r, 325 F.2d 849, 851–852 (2d Cir. 1963).

35. Dorsen, *supra* note 23, at 260–261 (referring to Friendly's opinion in J.C. Penny Co. v. Comm'r, 312 F.2d 65, 68 (2d Cir. 1962)).

36. Alperstein v. Comm'r, 613 F.2d 1213, 1221–1222 (2d Cir. 1979).

37. Jaylaw Drug, Inc. v. Internal Revenue Serv., 621 F.2d 524, 527–529 (2d Cir. 1980).

38. 633 F.2d 626, 633 (2d Cir. 1980).

39. 26 U.S.C. § 7421 (2000).

40. *Laino,* 633 F.2d at 629–630.
41. Estate of Schelberg v. Comm'r, 612 F.2d 25, 33–34 (2d Cir. 1979) (Friendly reversing the IRS commissioner's determination that survivor's income benefits ought to be counted as part of the decedent's gross estate for purposes of federal estate tax collection).
42. 697 F.2d 46, 54–56 (2d Cir. 1982).
43. DORSEN, *supra* note 23, at 109; JEFFREY TOOBIN, THE OATH: THE OBAMA WHITE HOUSE AND THE SUPREME COURT 15 (2012); Snyder, *Judicial Genealogy, supra* note 26, at 1218.
44. DORSEN, *supra* note 23, at 110–111; Snyder, *Judicial Genealogy, supra* note 26, at 1219.
45. DORSEN, *supra* note 23, at 357, 486 n.80; Snyder, *Judicial Genealogy, supra* note 26, at 1230–1234. Roberts's first opinion as Chief Justice was Martin v. Franklin Capital Corp., 546 U.S. 132, 139 (2005) (quoting Henry Friendly, *Indiscretion About Discretion,* 31 EMORY L.J. 747, 758 (1982)).
46. 546 U.S. 418, 435 (2006) (citing and quoting United States v. Lee, 455 U.S. 252, 258, 260 (1982)).
47. 550 U.S. 501, 502 (2007).
48. United States v. Clintwood Elkhorn Mining Co., 553 U.S. 1 (2008).
49. Knight v. Comm'r, 552 U.S. 181, 195 (2008).
50. 42 U.S.C. § 21 (2006).
51. Mayo Found. v. United States, 131 S. Ct. 704, 715–716 (2011); see Gillian E. Metzger, *Embracing Administrative Common Law,* 80 GW. L. REV. 1293, 1308–1309 (2012).
52. NFIB v. Sebelius, 132 S. Ct. 2566, 2595 (2012).
53. Neal Katyal, *A Pyrrhic Victory,* N.Y. TIMES, June 29, 2012, at A25; Randy Barnett, *The Unprecedented Uniqueness of Chief Justice Roberts' Opinion,* BALKINIZATION (July 5, 2012 5:14 PM), http://www.volokh.com/2012/07/05/the-unprecedented-uniqueness-of-chief-justice-roberts-opinion/.
54. See, e.g., TOOBIN, *supra* note 43, at 285–290; Jan Crawford, *Roberts Switched Views to Uphold Health Care Law,* CBS NEWS (July 1, 2012, 1:29 PM), http://www.cbsnews.com/8301-3460_162-57464549/roberts-switched-views-to-uphold-health-care-law/; John Fund, *The Flip that Will Flop?* NAT'L REV. ONLINE (July 2, 2012, 4:00 AM), http://www.nationalreview.com/articles/304533/flip-will-flop-john-fund?pg=1.
55. See David Hollinger, *T. S. Kuhn's Theory of Science and Its Implications for History, in* In the American Province: Studies in the History and Historiography of Ideas 106, 113–115, 121–122, 126–127 (1985).

# THE DECISION'S
# IMPLICATIONS

# CHAPTER 14

# FEDERALISM BY WAIVER AFTER THE *HEALTH CARE CASE*

*Samuel R. Bagenstos*

The Supreme Court's Spending Clause holding in *National Federation of Independent Businesses v. Sebelius* (*NFIB*) is likely to be consequential for many reasons. It will have a direct effect on the implementation of the Affordable Care Act (ACA), which relied on the expansion of Medicaid—now made voluntary by the Court—to obtain health care coverage for more than fifteen million previously uninsured people. At this writing, it remains unclear how many states will participate in the expansion. The Congressional Budget Office recently estimated that, as a result of the Court's decision, three million fewer people will obtain new Medicaid coverage under the law than it had originally predicted.[1]

But the Court's Spending Clause ruling will have potentially an even more far-reaching effect on the constitutionality of other federal statutes enacted pursuant to Congress's spending power, as states will be prompted to challenge other conditional spending laws in the education, social welfare, environmental, and civil rights areas as unconstitutionally coercive. The ultimate legal effect of *NFIB*'s Spending Clause holding on these laws is unlikely to be determined without years of litigation.

In this chapter, I focus on another likely effect of *NFIB*'s Spending Clause holding—the case's effect on the day-to-day bargaining between states and the federal agencies that administer cooperative spending programs.[2] I argue that *NFIB* gives states important new leverage in these negotiations. This new leverage is likely to accelerate the trend toward "federalism by waiver," in which important questions about the federal-state relationship are resolved by the federal executive branch granting tailored, conditional exemptions from the broad, general spending conditions adopted by Congress. And I will argue that this is not necessarily a bad thing.[3]

## 1. The Rise of Federalism by Waiver

As far as I can tell, Professor Hugh Heclo was the first academic to use the term "federalism by waiver."[4] The term refers to a pattern in the administration of cooperative state-federal spending statutes in which the federal executive branch has taken an increasingly large role. Federal conditional spending statutes typically impose detailed and prescriptive obligations on states. These obligations come directly from the statutory language adopted by Congress. But Congress has recognized that the detailed statutes it adopts cannot take account of all local conditions, and it has also recognized a value in giving states space to experiment with new means of achieving the goals of those statutes. Accordingly, at least since the 1960s, Congress has included provisions in its major conditional spending statutes that empower the federal agency that administers a given spending program to grant waivers of the statutes' requirements in various circumstances.[5]

Waivers like this might play a distinctly marginal and interstitial role. They might simply address particular circumstances that Congress did not anticipate. Or they might provide for narrowly drawn and carefully evaluated demonstration projects designed to build policy knowledge that Congress could take into account in subsequent reauthorizations of the statute. And, indeed, those seem to have been the occasions in which Congress anticipated that states would seek, and the federal executive branch would grant, waivers from the basic obligations imposed by conditional spending programs.[6]

But beginning in the 1980s, states and the federal executive branch cooperated to transform the use of waivers in cooperative spending programs. The transformation began during the Reagan administration, as the executive branch encouraged widespread use of waivers in the Medicaid program to promote home- and community-based services, and in the Aid to Families with Dependent Children (AFDC) program to jump-start a process of welfare reform.[7] These efforts carried out one of the original purposes of the waiver authority—to promote policy experimentation—but they occurred on such a wide scale that waivers were no longer a marginal or interstitial tool.

The George H. W. Bush administration was, in general, less interested in using waivers of conditional spending legislation as a policy tool. Indeed, the administration denied the most prominent request for such a waiver during its time in office—the waiver encompassing Oregon's ambitious effort to reform its Medicaid system.[8] As his reelection campaign picked up in 1992, however, President Bush did grant some notable waivers in the welfare area.[9]

Broad use of the waiver tool really took off during the Clinton administration.[10] President Clinton had been an innovative governor himself, and he came to the presidency determined to use waiver authorities aggressively to enable other governors to innovate as well. While his own welfare reform legislation stalled in Congress during the first few years of his administration, President Clinton sought to burnish his record as a welfare reformer by approving a number of states' requests for significant and far-reaching waivers of various requirements imposed by the AFDC program. And especially after the defeat of his health care plan in 1994, President Clinton used Medicaid waivers to promote health reform—and particularly to encourage states to move to more comprehensive coverage and cost controls imposed by managed care—on a state-by-state basis. By the end of the Clinton administration, federalism by waiver had become a key means for both the federal executive branch and the states to escape the detailed strictures of conditional spending statutes.

Notably, the Clinton administration was relatively ecumenical in the waivers it would approve. Prior to the enactment of comprehensive welfare reform legislation in 1996, the Clinton administration approved AFDC waivers that embraced a variety of different—and even conflicting—visions of the appropriate way to reform welfare.[11] A similar pattern was evident in the Medicaid area after the collapse of Clintoncare in 1994.[12]

The George W. Bush administration consolidated the rise of federalism by waiver. In 2002, it even sought from Congress the authority to issue "super waivers"—waivers that could dispense with the requirements of a range of different federal spending programs, often administered by different cabinet departments, in a single administrative act. The general "super waiver" legislation passed the House but died in the Senate.[13] (Congress did, however, grant the Secretary of Homeland Security a form of "super waiver" authority in connection with the construction of a border fence.)[14]

But the Bush administration also sought, much more aggressively than had the Clinton administration, to use waivers as a tool to achieve the President's substantive policy goals. Where the Clinton administration had seen flexibility and devolution as important ends in themselves, the Bush administration saw the waiver process largely in terms of the substantive results it could achieve. In the Medicaid area, the administration's Health Insurance Flexibility and Accountability (HIFA) initiative "encourage[d] states to finance expansions of coverage of the uninsured population through cuts in the optional services they currently provide[d]."[15] To many critics, HIFA appeared to reflect a backdoor effort by the Bush administration to implement its preferred block grant model for the program, in which Medicaid would no longer be an entitlement.[16] And in the education area, the administration's Department of Education took a hard line against waiver requests that would have provided relief from the strictures of President Bush's signature No Child Left Behind legislation.[17]

The Obama administration has also aggressively used waivers of conditional spending statutes as a policy tool. In doing so, it has adopted elements of both the Clinton administration's and the George W. Bush administration's approaches.

The Obama administration has used its Medicaid waiver authority to grant broad flexibility to the states in providing health care to indigent and disabled persons. Unlike in the second Bush administration, these waivers have not followed a particular substantive pattern. As in the Clinton administration, flexibility itself seems to have been the Obama administration's immediate goal. Part of the explanation for this may lie in the background of President Obama's Secretary of Health and Human Services, Kathleen Sebelius. As a former governor and state insurance commissioner, Sebelius had an appreciation for the importance of local conditions and state innovation in health care provision. But a more significant part of the explanation, I think, was the overriding importance President Obama placed on obtaining support for—and blunting the constitutional challenges to—the ACA, his signature measure. The ACA required state cooperation in its Medicaid expansion and in its system of health insurance exchanges. With the statute already a target of vigorous political attack, Obama administration officials felt an acute need not to unnecessarily alienate the state officials on whom they would rely for its implementation. And with the Medicaid expansion specifically under attack in the courts for being burdensome on and coercive of the states, administration officials were keen to limit the burdens imposed by Medicaid to the extent that they could do so. The administration (in a process implemented by the Department of Health and Human Services [HHS], but encouraged, if not driven, by the White House) thus adopted a relatively general policy of flexibility toward states' efforts to carry out their obligations under the ACA.[18]

In the education area, the Obama administration has been much more open to granting waivers than had the George W. Bush administration. But like the Bush administration, it has used its waiver authority to push its own substantive vision of education policy. Amid widespread discontent with the strictures imposed by the No Child Left Behind Act (NCLB), and a deadlock in Congress regarding how to change the statute, the Obama administration has offered to waive many of the statute's requirements for states that adopt the core elements of the administration's own preferred NCLB revision.[19] Some commentators have decried this offer as working an end run around Congress. But even some critics see the Obama administration's approach as a responsible, if not ideal, response to the legislative gridlock that has prevented Congress from updating an unpopular and perhaps impractical statute.[20]

Throughout his administration, President Obama's openness to waivers of the requirements of cooperative spending (and other) statutes has drawn criticism from right-wing critics.[21] These criticisms tended to lie at the margins of mainstream discourse until President Obama's HHS issued a letter, responding to requests made by a number of Republican governors, that expressed a willingness to entertain requests for waivers of certain of the work requirements of the 1996 welfare reform legislation.[22] HHS made clear that any request for waiver of those requirements would have to show how it would promote work by public assistance recipients, and it has not yet granted any such waiver. Nonetheless, Governor Romney's presidential campaign seized on the Obama administration's mere statement that it would *entertain* requests for waivers of 1996 legislation's work provisions and exploited that statement to argue (with some effect) that President Obama is gutting welfare reform.[23]

## 2. WHY THE *HEALTH CARE CASE* SHOULD ACCELERATE THE TREND

Because the statutes that authorize waivers of federal funding conditions are phrased in highly discretionary terms, one might hypothesize that, all else equal, a presidential administration will use the waiver authority to achieve its more general policy goals. When an administration's policy preferences are well reflected in the rules adopted by Congress (as was the case for the Bush administration in education policy after the passage of NCLB), we can expect the administration to grant relatively few waivers. When, by contrast, an administration has been unable to get Congress to adopt its preferred policy (as has been the case for the Obama administration in education policy, as efforts to reauthorize and reform NCLB have stalled), we can expect the administration to grant more waivers, but to grant only those waivers that serve its substantive policy preferences. And when an administration has a general policy preference toward devolution (as was the case for the Clinton administration in the AFDC and Medicaid programs), we can expect the administration to grant more waivers across the board.

But the incumbent presidential administration's policy preferences are not the only crucial variable here. Each waiver of a federal spending condition results from an iterative, negotiated process, in which the states hold a number of important cards. The process may be initiated by the federal agency that administers a given cooperative spending program, which can (formally or informally) let states know that it will entertain requests for particular sorts of waivers. Or the process may be initiated by individual states, or groups of states, themselves. These states may simply submit applications for individual waivers, or (as they did when they triggered the recent controversy over Temporary Assistance to Needy Families [TANF] waivers) they may ask the administration for more general guidance about what sorts of waiver requests it will entertain.

Once this process begins, a state has a number of bargaining advantages. States can sometimes threaten to opt out of a federal spending program entirely if the administration refuses to waive rules they find particularly noxious. Where this threat is credible, as it will occasionally be (especially for programs in which

the amount of federal money at stake for any given state is low), the federal officials who administer the program will be strongly inclined to grant the waiver in
order to salvage as much of the program as they can. For similar reasons, federal
agencies virtually never cut off all funds to states that fail to comply with the
terms of a given program, even though the relevant statute will often authorize
such a sanction. Federal officials simply do not want to harm a program's beneficiaries by cutting off funds to a noncompliant state.[24]

Even where the state lacks a credible opt-out option, the dynamics of the
waiver negotiation process push toward approval of waiver requests. For one
thing, the career officials who staff the federal agencies that administer cooperative spending programs have extensive day-to-day contacts with the state
officials to whom they provide money—far more extensive contacts than they
have with anyone else. They receive most of their information from those state
officials. All of these interactions engender a felt affinity and association between
the interests of state and federal officials working on cooperative programs.[25]

This affinity and association is enhanced by the career paths of the officials
who work in federal spending agencies. Those officials often move back and
forth between state and federal government jobs. The typical federal office
administering a cooperative program will contain a large number of staff who
formerly worked—and/or expect to work in the future—for the state agencies
receiving the office's money. They thus will readily be sympathetic to the state's
perspective and its analysis of the possibilities and constraints available to those
implementing federal policy on the ground.[26]

The argument in the preceding two paragraphs is in some ways the flip side of
the oft-expressed argument against "picket fence federalism."[27] As generally presented, that argument asserts the existence of an alliance between federal- and
state-level subject-matter expert bureaucrats, who join together to overcome
resistance to a federal program's goals from politicians and generalist agency officials at the state level. But the alliance can cut in both directions. Subject-matter
experts in the federal bureaucracy, supporting their allies in state government,
can work to overcome the resistance of generalist federal officials to state-level
innovations. As Frank J. Thompson and Courtney Burke argue, the rise of federalism by waiver helps to deepen and problematize the standard argument against
picket fence federalism.[28]

And the congressional connection is especially important. Federal agencies are responsive to members of the House and Senate—particularly, but not
exclusively, those on the agencies' authorizing committees or appropriations
subcommittees. And those legislators are often extremely responsive to the
desires of the governing administration in their home states. Agency officials'
desire to please important constituencies in Congress thus will lead them to seek
to please the governments of the states with whom they deal.[29] Steven Teles's

important study of welfare policy prior to the 1996 welfare reform legislation accordingly emphasized the role of states' congressional delegations in "act[ing] in concert to put pressure on the executive branch to expedite the processing of ... waiver proposal[s]."[30]

To the extent that members of Congress see particular sorts of waiver requests through a policy rather than a casework lens, they may be more skeptical of those requests and work to undermine them or bar them by appropriations riders or statutory amendments. The recently proposed requests for waivers of TANF's work requirements may fall into this category.[31] For the ordinary run of waiver requests, however, congressional delegations are likely to push in the same direction as their states' governors.

These dynamics do not ensure that the states will always get their way. To the contrary, the policy preferences of the incumbent presidential administration will also play a substantial role in determining which waiver requests will be granted. But, notwithstanding the broad discretion that the statutes authorizing waivers grant to the administration as a formal matter, the administration faces substantial constraints in exercising that discretion.

The Supreme Court's ruling in *NFIB* is likely to shift the waiver-bargaining dynamic—at least for a time—in an even more state-friendly direction.[32] By holding, for what Justice Ginsburg emphasized was *"the first time ever,"*[33] that a federal spending condition had coerced the states, the Court in *NFIB* gave states a new tool to use in their negotiations with federal agencies. Despite the suggestions of scholars such as Gillian Metzger that "greater scrutiny appears warranted when waiver authority is sought by a state and the waiver denial significantly restricts state regulatory autonomy," the courts have generally reviewed waiver denials "quite deferentially."[34] On some occasions in the past, states that unsuccessfully sought administrative exemptions from certain conditions imposed on federal funding recipients turned to the courts to argue that the conditions were unconstitutionally coercive. But that litigation typically proved unavailing.[35] Now, a state that does not receive the waiver it requested can threaten—more credibly than before *NFIB*—to challenge the constitutionality of the underlying spending program if the administering agency refuses its requested waiver.

But it is not just the *fact* that the Court found a spending condition unconstitutionally coercive that enhances states' bargaining positions. The *language* and *reasoning* in the Chief Justice's pivotal Spending Clause opinion may prove especially helpful to states in threatening to sue if waivers are denied. In concluding that the ACA's Medicaid expansion provisions unconstitutionally coerced the states, Chief Justice Roberts found it crucial that the expansion did not, in his view, simply make changes to the existing Medicaid program. Rather, it required states that wished to continue participating in that program *also* to participate in what he regarded as a "new health care program"—one that had different federal reimbursement rules and mandated a different benefits package that would apply to individuals who were eligible for preexpansion Medicaid.[36] That Congress sought to tie together what he thought were really separate and independent grants was key to the Chief Justice's conclusion. He argued that when federal funding conditions "take the form of threats to terminate other significant independent grants, the conditions are properly viewed as a means of pressuring the States to accept policy changes."[37] And he agreed with the plaintiff-states that the threat to bar future access to *all* Medicaid funds to states that failed to participate in the (in his view separate) Medicaid expansion "serves no purpose other than to force unwilling States to sign up for the dramatic expansion in health care coverage effected by the Act."[38]

This language might be understood as holding that Congress may not tie together conceptually or budgetarily separate programs in a single offer of federal funds. If a state wishes to accept federal funds to participate in one program, what reason could Congress have for denying it those funds for refusal to participate in some *other* program—aside from "forc[ing] unwilling States to sign up for" that other program? This reasoning has obvious implications for waiver requests. Imagine that a state is willing to participate in the Elementary and Secondary Education Act (ESEA) Title I program but is not willing to provide Title I funds to students enrolled in private schools, as required by NCLB.[39] Although the statute by its terms requires participating states to provide Title I funds to eligible private school students, the state agrees to forgo the federal money that would go to those students if it can obtain a waiver of that requirement. After *NFIB*, the state can credibly threaten that, if the waiver is denied, it will challenge the tying together of private and public school populations as unconstitutionally coercive—the only reason to tie them together, the state might say, is to force unwilling states to provide public funds to private school students.

I argue elsewhere that this is too broad a reading of the Chief Justice's opinion.[40] In my view, that opinion is best read not simply as prohibiting the tying together of two analytically or budgetarily separable funding streams, but instead as prohibiting a particular kind of leveraging. The Chief Justice's opinion bars Congress from telling states that they can continue to participate in an entrenched and lucrative cooperative spending federal program only if they *also* agree to participate in a new and independent program. It thus should not prohibit Congress from bundling together various separable funding streams from the start. The Chief Justice's opinion does not treat *every* analytically or budgetarily separable funding stream as reflecting an independent program in any event. Rather, the Chief Justice accepted that the many changes Congress had made to Medicaid itself through the years, including adding new mandatorily covered populations and new required services, merely "altered" the existing Medicaid program; it was only the very large expansion demanded by the ACA that sought to tie that existing program to an independent program. Finally, the Chief Justice limited his coercion analysis to those instances in which the amount of money a state stood to lose was so great as to deny states a real choice "not merely in theory but in fact."[41]

A federal agency that is sued for unconstitutional coercion after denying a waiver *ought* therefore to have three possible defenses against such a suit: first (if this is true), that the condition the agency refused to waive was not a new condition but existed from the time Congress created the program; second, that the condition the agency refused to waive was not independent from the conditions that the state had agreed to accept; and third, that the amount of money at stake is not so great as to deny the state a realistic choice. But it will take some time for the courts to settle on a reading of *NFIB*'s Spending Clause holding—particularly if agencies seek to avoid litigation of these issues.

In the interim, agencies faced with waiver requests must engage in risk management. They must decide how willing they are to risk a holding that the statutes they administer are unconstitutionally coercive. Given the great harm to those agencies if that risk eventuates—harm in unsettling expectations and in keeping the agencies from providing the services that they are set up to provide—they can be expected in many circumstances to be unwilling to take the risk. This is particularly likely to be true because what constitutes an "independent" program remains quite uncertain after the *NFIB* decision—and Chief Justice Roberts expressly overrode Congress's determination that the ACA's Medicaid expansion merely added to the existing Medicaid program without creating a separate program. By contrast, if the agency grants a questionable waiver request, it is unlikely even to be held to account by the courts. The erosion of private rights of action to enforce spending statutes, the difficulty in finding a plaintiff with standing, and the generally deferential posture of courts toward waiver grants will make granting the request the path of least resistance for the agency.[42]

The uncertainty created by *NFIB*'s Spending Clause holding is thus likely to embolden states to seek more and more extensive waivers of federal spending conditions. And it is likely, at least at the margins, to encourage federal agencies to grant those waivers more frequently. The *NFIB* case is therefore likely to accelerate the trend toward federalism by waiver.

## 3. An Initial Normative Assessment

Is the trend toward federalism by waiver, which the *NFIB* decision is likely to accelerate, something to be welcomed? Or to be greeted warily? Federalism by waiver—and the connected though broader phenomenon that has been labeled "government by waiver"[43]—has drawn substantial criticism from both liberals

and conservatives. These critics charge that increasing use of the waiver authority undermines both the goals set by Congress for particular statutes and, ultimately, the rule of law itself.

Although there is an essential similarity between the liberal and conservative criticisms of federalism by waiver, the criticisms sound in different regis-
ters. Liberal critics express a concern for statutory erosion. They contend that
waivers have been used to undermine hard-won statutory requirements that
would otherwise bind states to provide important services to less privileged and
less empowered individuals and communities. States may also use waivers as a
vehicle to cut costs during recessions—the worst possible time, from a programmatic perspective, to cut aid to poor people.[44] At their worst, waivers may enable
states to reprogram redirect money that had been designated for poor people
and people with disabilities and divert it to less needy groups.[45]

For conservatives, the criticisms of federalism by waiver form part of a larger
rule-of-law argument against the exercise of executive discretion in the administration of complex federal programs. The argument runs that constraints on
discretion are necessary to avoid arbitrary, favoritistic, and rent-seeking uses of
executive power, and to ensure that parties that operate in a space with extensive federal involvement can plan and order their affairs. Although quite common in early conservative challenges to the rise of the New Deal administrative
state, these rule-of-law arguments had migrated to a narrow fringe view until the
Obama administration's domestic policy efforts engendered Tea Party opposition and brought them back into the mainstream of conservative legal thought.[46]

I have a more optimistic view of federalism by waiver. The concerns regarding
statutory erosion are real, but they must be considered in the light of the realistic
alternatives to waivers. These alternatives, in turn, are likely to depend on the
nature of the spending condition that a state is asking the federal government to
waive. Where the spending condition forms a relatively minor part of a complex
scheme, a state that could not obtain a waiver might simply refuse to comply
and expect to get away with it. Federal agencies are unlikely to terminate funding for relatively minor violations of the rules governing a spending program.[47]
And the avenues for third-party private enforcement of those rules have been
increasingly closed off by the Supreme Court's restrictive private-right-of-action
jurisprudence.[48]

The alternative to a waiver regime in these cases is thus likely to be a regime
of de facto waivers determined by ability of the incumbent administration to
detect violations and its willingness to threaten fund cutoffs over them—a willingness that will necessarily depend on the administration's enforcement priorities, but that will often occur out of public view and accountability. An overt
waiver regime provides a mechanism for federal agencies to engage states before
they depart from the strict requirements of funding statutes; to negotiate for

provisions that preserve the key goals, according to the administration, of the statutes at issue; and to do so in a context that preserves a measure of public accountability. And where states pass up an opportunity to obtain waivers and instead simply violate the law in the hope that they will not get caught, the disregard of the waiver process will justify enforcement actions that might not be triggered by the state's violation in and of itself.

Federal agencies have often undertaken to give states and interested parties advance public notice of the criteria they will apply to waiver requests. Programs in which the Obama administration has undertaken to provide such advance notice include Medicaid (in which the Centers for Medicare and Medicaid Services have published detailed criteria for assessing home- and community-based services waiver requests)[49] and NCLB.[50] Indeed, the attacks on the Obama administration for "gutting" TANF's work requirement arose, not after HHS *granted* a waiver of that requirement (as of this writing, it still has not granted any such waiver), but after the Department published a notice informing states of the criteria it would apply in *considering* such a request.[51] Whatever one thinks of the merits of the very public political and legal dispute that ensued, the prominence of that dispute highlights a way in which executive branch waivers of statutory spending conditions can enhance public accountability.

Where the spending condition at issue is a more central requirement of the statute at issue—as is the case in many of the large Medicaid waivers and waivers of NCLB—the calculus is different. If waivers are not available in these cases, states that find themselves unable or unwilling to comply with the conditions may choose simply to opt out of the spending program entirely[52]—or to lobby in Congress for fundamental changes to the program that can have nationwide effects. Allowing waivers of such central requirements does take away some of the leverage that Congress presumably sought to employ to impel states to agree to those requirements. But if the alternative is a state opting out of the statute entirely—or a state prompting statutory changes that undermine these requirements in all states—the availability of a waiver provides a second-best option. In this way, as Professors Thompson and Burke have shown, a waiver regime can provide a safety valve that preserves conditional spending programs at the same time that it relieves states of some of the obligations these programs impose.[53] As Theodore Ruger argues in his contribution to this volume, waivers can be used to accommodate state concerns with particular implementation rules while firmly entrenching the cooperative spending programs that authorize them.[54] The executive branch, in exercising its waiver authority, can say yes only in those cases in which executive officials believe that the state will opt out of the program entirely if the waiver is denied, and it can otherwise exercise its leverage in the waiver process to negotiate waiver terms that promote its understanding of the statutory goals to the extent possible.

For the conservative rule-of-law critics, this degree of executive discretion is itself the problem. But their argument ultimately rests on a rejection of delegation—a rejection that would call into question huge swaths of the modern administrative state.[55] To be sure, one might accept the delegation inherent in the modern administrative state—if only as an accommodation to the reality that it will not be rolled back any time soon—but still argue that extensive reliance on executive waivers goes too far.[56] But this would be perverse. As David Barron and Todd Rakoff argue, the delegation inherent in waiver authority seems on balance to be *less* problematic from the perspective of accountability and congressional control than are more traditional delegations.[57] The most plausible justification for drawing a line of permissible delegation that forbids extensive use of waivers would be to raise the costs to Congress of imposing extensive and detailed conditions on federal spending.[58] An antiwaiver (or anti-too-extensive-reliance-on-waiver) principle could thus be understood as what Ernest Young has called a "resistance norm": a norm that "makes it harder—but still not impossible—for Congress to write statutes that intrude into areas of constitutional sensitivity."[59] For those who are grudging at best about the New Deal Settlement and its instantiation in the federalism arrangements of Great Society programs, limitations on federalism by waiver will no doubt be attractive. But for those of us who are comfortable with those basic federalism arrangements, limiting the use of waivers will lead to suboptimal policy outcomes without sufficient countervailing benefits.

The critics, in my view, fail to account for the positive contributions of a robust waiver regime to good policy and governance. A robust waiver regime can serve as a tool to negotiate the proper boundary between national standards and local variation, but with lower stakes, and at a lower temperature, than a regime that imposes strict statutory standards on states and provokes them to challenge those standards on constitutional grounds. Reliance on the waiver mechanism helps to realize many of the benefits of decentralization—notably the benefits of experimentation and accounting for local variation—within the context of a national program. In the Medicaid program, for example, the executive branch employed waiver-based demonstration projects to develop models for providing community-based services to older people and people with disabilities. These included the Long-Term Care Channeling Demonstration in twelve states in the early 1980s,[60] which laid the groundwork for the Home- and Community-Based Waiver program, and the Cash-and-Counseling Demonstration in three states in the 2000s.[61] Policymakers in both federal and state governments have learned substantial lessons from demonstrations like these; those lessons have helped them provide more effective—and more cost-effective—community-based services.[62]

A robust waiver regime can also provide a means of updating or revising statutory regimes that prove impractical or ill-conceived in the face of experience, but that, because of veto points in Congress, cannot be comprehensively revised.[63] The Obama administration's extensive use of waivers in the education area provides the best example here. Vanishingly few state or federal officials are happy with NCLB as it stands, but it has proven impossible to date to assemble a legislative coalition to reauthorize and amend that law. The Obama administration has offered states a way out of NCLB's unpopular strictures, but only on the condition that those states adopt policies that fit the administration's own preferred policy in the area. This waiver regime helps to bring the statute up to date, but it also focuses attention—and accountability—on the executive branch's own clearly expressed policy preferences.[64] There may be substantial reasons to object to the Obama administration's approach on its *policy* merits.[65] But the administration's use of the waiver tool has ensured that its policy decisions are made in full view of the public and that the states and Congress can push back if they are so disposed.[66]

A regime that relies heavily on executive branch waivers certainly has its dangers. The critics are right that waivers can be used by an administration that is hostile to a conditional spending statute as a tool to undermine that law. So, too, can waivers be used to facilitate rent-seeking or other arbitrary or venal conduct. As a practical matter, however, a hostile or venal administration has ample opportunity to undermine the requirements of a conditional spending statute simply by failing to enforce its terms against noncompliant states. Given the erosion of private rights of action and the extremely limited (at best) judicial review of an agency's failure to take enforcement action, there is likely to be no effective *legal* check on an agency that is bound and determined to resist the requirements Congress has imposed on states that receive federal funds. The most effective checks are likely to be political. And a waiver regime, honestly engaged, can provide the opportunity for political debate, contestation, and accountability.

I have argued that the Spending Clause ruling in *NFIB v. Sebelius* is likely to have a significant impact that goes beyond the Medicaid expansion provisions of the ACA. That ruling will affect the entire range of day-to-day bargaining between states and the federal executive branch in the administration of cooperative spending programs. Because *NFIB* marked the first time the Supreme Court invalidated a spending condition as coercing the states—and because of the structure and ambiguities of Chief Justice Roberts's pivotal opinion on the question—the case is likely, at least in the short term, to accelerate the trend toward federalism by waiver.

And, I have argued, that may not be such a bad thing. A robust waiver regime can achieve many of the goals of decentralization—experimentation and accounting for differences among the states—within the context of a program that serves objectives set by Congress and policed by the federal executive branch. A robust waiver regime provides a means of updating and harmonizing outdated or conflicting statutes—or statutes with provisions that have proven impractical in the light of experience—in the face of congressional gridlock. And a robust waiver regime can channel departures from the rules set by Congress through a process that promotes political accountability and deliberation. *NFIB*'s Spending Clause ruling might be criticized along many dimensions,[67] but the ruling's effects in promoting federalism by waiver are likely to be salutary.

# Notes

1. See CONGRESSIONAL BUDGET OFFICE, ESTIMATES FOR THE INSURANCE COVERAGE PROVISIONS OF THE AFFORDABLE CARE ACT UPDATED FOR THE RECENT SUPREME COURT DECISION 11 (2012).
2. This chapter thus has substantial affinities to Professor Ruger's contribution to this volume, which emphasizes the way in which *NFIB* "invites complex and ongoing strategic interaction between the states and the federal executive on multiple dimensions of health policy going forward." Theodore W. Ruger, Health Policy Devolution and the Institutional Hydraulics of the Affordable Care Act, in this volume. For an outstanding catalog of the various ways in which states and federal agencies bargain over federalism on a day-to-day basis, only a subset of which I treat in this chapter, see Erin Ryan, *Negotiating Federalism*, 52 B.C. L. REV. 1 (2011). Another notable recent discussion of the phenomenon is Jessica Bulman-Pozen & Heather K. Gerken, *Uncooperative Federalism*, 118 YALE L.J. 1256 (2009).
3. For another defense of administrative waiver, which shares broad similarities with my account, see David J. Barron & Todd D. Rakoff, In Defense of Big Waiver (unpublished manuscript, on file with author).
4. Hugh Heclo, *Poverty Politics, in* CONFRONTING POVERTY: PRESCRIPTIONS FOR CHANGE 396, 415 (Sheldon H. Danziger, Gary D. Sandefur & Daniel H. Weinberg eds., 1994).
5. See, e.g., 20 U.S.C. § 7861 (2011) (granting the Secretary of Education authority to waive various requirements of the Elementary and Secondary Education Act (ESEA)); 42 U.S.C. § 1315 (2010) (granting the Secretary of Health and Human Services general authority to issue waivers for "any experimental, pilot, or demonstration project which, in the judgment of the Secretary, is likely to assist in promoting the objectives of" various provisions of the Social Security Act, in which the Medicaid and Temporary Assistance to Needy Families (TANF) programs are embedded).
6. See Ryan, *supra* note 2, at 63 ("The Medicaid demonstration waiver programs were to function as the hallowed federalism laboratory of ideas would intend: the goal was to allow a limited degree of flexibility so that each state could experiment in a way that would yield learning benefits to the overall program").
7. Medicaid waivers to support home- and community-based services were initially issued under the Secretary's general demonstration waiver authority, see Bruce C. Vladeck, *Medicaid 1115 Demonstrations: Progress Through Partnership*, 14 HEALTH AFFAIRS 217, 218 (1995), but Congress in 1981 adopted a special provision authorizing home- and community-based services waivers, 42 U.S.C. § 1396n(c). On the Reagan administration's use of waivers to jump-start welfare reform, see STEVEN M. TELES, WHOSE WELFARE? AFDC AND ELITE POLITICS 124–130 (1996).
8. See *ADA Analyses of the Oregon Health Care Plan*, 9 ISSUES L. & MED. 397, 410 (1994).
9. See Thomas Gais & James Fossett, *Federalism and the Executive Branch, in* THE EXECUTIVE BRANCH 486, 508 (Joel D. Aberbach & Mark A. Peterson eds., 2005).

10. For a good summary of the use of waivers by the Clinton administration in welfare, Medicaid, and education programs, see Gais & Fossett, *supra* note 9, at 508–510. Professor Ruger provides an outstanding discussion of the Clinton administration's approach to Medicaid waivers in Ruger, *supra* note 2.

11. See TELES, *supra* note 7, at 136–141.

12. See Frank J. Thompson & Courtney Burke, *Executive Federalism and Medicaid Demonstration Waivers: Implications for Policy and Democratic Process*, 32 J. HEALTH POL. POL'Y & L. 971, 975–976 (2007).

13. See H.R. 4, 108th Cong., tit. VI (2d Sess. 2002).

14. See Office of the Secretary, Determination Pursuant to Section 102 of the Illegal Immigration Reform and Immigrant Responsibility Act of 1996 as Amended, 73 Fed. Reg. 19,077 (Apr. 8, 2008) (exercising this authority).

15. Samuel R. Bagenstos, *The Future of Disability Law*, 114 YALE L.J. 1, 60 (2004).

16. See, e.g., Jonathan R. Bolton, *The Case of the Disappearing Statute: A Legal and Policy Critique of the Use of Section 1115 Waivers to Restructure the Medicaid Program*, 37 COLUM. J.L. & SOC. PROBS. 91 (2003).

17. See Martha Derthick & Andy Rotherham, *Obama's NCLB Waivers: Are They Necessary or Illegal?* EDUC. NEXT, Spring 2012, at 56, 58 (discussing "the deeply intrusive, get-tough, and grant-no-waivers initial approach adopted by Congress and the Bush administration in 2001–02").

18. For a treatment of some of the dynamics discussed in this paragraph, see Timothy J. Conlan & Paul L. Posner, *Inflection Point? Federalism and the Obama Administration*, 41 PUBLIUS 421, 438–439, 442 (2011).

19. See, e.g., Gillian E. Metzger, *The Supreme Court, 2011 Term—Comment: To Tax, To Spend, To Regulate*, 126 HARV. L. REV. 83 (2012) (discussing the Obama Administration's NCLB waivers).

20. For a good treatment of this controversy, see Derthick & Rotherham, *supra* note 17.

21. See, e.g., Richard A. Epstein, *Government By Waiver*, NAT'L AFFAIRS, Spring 2011, at 39.

22. See OFFICE OF FAMILY ASSISTANCE, ADMIN. FOR CHILDREN & FAMILIES, U.S. DEPT. OF HEALTH & HUMAN SERVS., TO STATES ADMINISTERING THE TANF PROGRAM AND OTHER INTERESTED PARTIES: GUIDANCE CONCERNING WAIVER AND EXPENDITURE AUTHORITY UNDER SECTION 1115 (July 12, 2012), *available at* http://www.acf.hhs.gov/programs/ofa/resource/policy/im-ofa/2012/im201203/im201203.

23. See, e.g., Josh Barro, *Romney's Thin Welfare-Reform Attack*, BLOOMBERG VIEW (Aug. 8, 2012), http://www.bloomberg.com/news/2012-08-08/romney-s-thin-welfare-reform-attack.html.

24. Professors Tomlinson and Mashaw noted this phenomenon four decades ago, and nothing essential has changed since then. See Edward A. Tomlinson & Jerry L. Mashaw, *The Enforcement of Federal Standards in Grant-in-Aid Programs: Suggestions for Beneficiary Involvement*, 58 VA. L. REV. 600, 620 (1972); see also STEPHEN C. HALPERN, ON THE LIMITS OF THE LAW: THE IRONIC LEGACY OF TITLE VI OF THE 1964 CIVIL RIGHTS ACT 294–295 (1995) (noting reluctance of administrations of both political parties to cut off funds); Roderick M. Hills Jr., *Dissecting the State: The Use of Federal Law to Free State and Local Officials from State Legislatures' Control*, 97 MICH. L. REV. 1201, 1227–1228 (1999) ("[T]he the sanction of withdrawing federal funds from noncomplying state or local officials is usually too drastic for the federal government to use with any frequency: withdrawal of funds will injure the very clients that the federal government wishes to serve").

25. See, e.g., Abbe R. Gluck, *Interstatutory Federalism and Statutory Interpretation: State Implementation of Federal Law in Health Reform and Beyond*, 121 YALE L.J. 534, 570 (2011) ("[M]any federalism scholars have argued that state and federal specialist agencies share more connections with and loyalties to one another than they do with their particular level of government").

26. For the classic description of this "professional bureaucratic complex," see Samuel H. Beer, *Federalism, Nationalism, and Democracy in America*, 72 AM. POL. SCI. REV. 9, 17–18 (1978).

27. For a good statement of the argument against picket fence federalism, see Roderick M. Hills Jr., *The Eleventh Amendment as a Curb on Bureaucratic Power*, 53 STAN. L. REV. 1225, 1236–1246 (2001).

28. See Frank J. Thompson & Courtney Burke, *Federalism by Waiver: Medicaid and the Transformation of Long-Term Care*, 39 PUBLIUS 22, 38–40 (2009). For a similar point, see Bulman-Pozen & Gerken, *supra* note 2, at 1301 n.148.

29. See Frank J. Thompson & Courtney Burke, *Executive Federalism and Medicaid Demonstration Waivers: Implications for Policy and Democratic Process*, 32 J. HEALTH POL. POL'Y & L. 971, 995–998 (2007).

30. TELES, *supra* note 7, at 142.

31. See Rebecca Berg, *Shift in Welfare Policy Draws GOP Protests*, N.Y. TIMES, July 18, 2012, at A17.

32. Much of the analysis that follows draws on a far more extensive discussion in Samuel R. Bagenstos, *The Anti-Leveraging Principle and the Spending Clause After NFIB*, 101 GEO. L.J. (forthcoming 2013).Please update the reference.

33. NFIB v. Sebelius, 132 S. Ct. 2566, 2630 (2012) (Ginsburg, J., concurring in part, concurring in the judgment in part, and dissenting in part).

34. Gillian E. Metzger, *Administrative Law as the New Federalism*, 57 DUKE L.J. 2023, 2107 (2008).

35. See, e.g., California v. United States, 104 F.3d 1086, 1092 (9th Cir.), *cert. denied*, 522 U.S. 806 (1997) (rejecting claim that the Medicaid Act was coercive to the extent that it required them to provide coverage to unauthorized aliens as a condition of receiving Medicaid funds); Padavan v. United States, 82 F.3d 23, 29 (2d Cir. 1996) (same); *but cf.* Virginia Dept. of Educ. v. Riley, 106 F.3d 559 (4th Cir. 1997) (*en banc*) (upholding challenge, on notice grounds, to federal threat "to withhold Virginia's entire $60 million annual [Individuals with Disabilities Education Act] grant for fiscal years 1994 and 1995 unless Virginia amended its policies to provide private educational services to each of the State's 126 disabled students who had been expelled for reasons wholly unrelated to their disabilities").

36. *NFIB*, 132 S. Ct. at 2606.

37. *Id.* at 2603–2604.

38. *Id.* at 2603.

39. See 20 U.S.C. § 6320 (2011).

40. See Bagenstos, *supra* note 32.

41. *NFIB*, 132 S. Ct. at 2605 (internal quotation marks omitted).

42. On the tightening of private rights of action to enforce conditional spending statutes, see, e.g., Samuel R. Bagenstos, *Spending Clause Litigation in the Roberts Court*, 58 Duke L.J. 345, 393–410 (2008). See also Stephen I. Vladeck, *Douglas and the Fate of Ex Parte Young*, 122 YALE L.J. ONLINE 13, 14 (2012) (arguing that "there may already be five votes to" hold "that injunctive relief would seldom be available to private plaintiffs under the Supremacy Clause to enjoin governmental officers from violating federal statutes that do not themselves provide a cause of action"). On courts' deferential review of waiver grants, see Metzger, *supra* note 34, at 2107.

43. See Epstein, *supra* note 21.

44. Professor Huberfeld argues, with some justification, that Medicaid waivers have followed this precise pattern. See Nicole Huberfeld, *Federalizing Medicaid*, 14 U. PA. J. CONST. L. 431, 483 (2011). I have argued elsewhere that the budget-cutting imperative imposes its most direct risk on those services, such as home- and community-based services, that the Medicaid Act does not require but merely permits to be provided pursuant to waivers. See Samuel R. Bagenstos, *The Past and Future of Deinstitutionalization Litigation*, 34 CARDOZO L. REV. 1 (2012). The difference is largely one of emphasis, however. States may first look to cut those services that the Medicaid Act does not require, but in times of serious budget retrenchment they will no doubt seek out the savings that can be realized by aggressive use of waivers.

45. See, e.g., Bolton, *supra* note 16 (discussing use of waivers in Medicaid); David A. Super, *Laboratories of Destitution: Democratic Experimentalism and the Failure of Antipoverty Law,* 157 U. Pa. L. Rev. 541, 588–590 (2008) (discussing use of waivers in welfare programs).

46. For expressions of this conservative critique during the Obama administration, see Epstein, *supra* note 21; Todd Zywicki, *Economic Uncertainty, the Courts, and the Rule of Law,* 35 Harv. J.L. & Pub. Pol'y 195 (2012).

47. See sources cited *supra* note 24.

48. See sources cited *supra* note 42.

49. See Medicaid Program, State Plan Home- and Community-Based Services, 77 Fed. Reg. 26,362 (May 3, 2012) (to be codified at 42 C.F.R. pts. 430–447).

50. Extensive discussion of the criteria for NCLB waivers—including numerous guidance documents—can be found on the Education Department's "ESEA Flexibility" web page, http://www.ed.gov/esea/flexibility.

51. See Guidance Concerning Waiver and Expenditure Authority, *supra* note 22.

52. Although the justices who believed the ACA's Medicaid expansion provisions were unconstitutional in *NFIB* apparently found it unthinkable that any state would leave Medicaid, at least one state's governor had recently raised the possibility that his state would exit the program. See Corrie MacLaggan, *Is Texas Really Thinking of Opting Out of Medicaid?* Austin American-Statesman, Nov. 14, 2010, *available at* http://www.statesman.com/news/news/state-regional-govt-politics/is-texas-really-thinking-of-opting-out-of-medicaid/nRS5F/. And Medicaid is, by an order of magnitude, the largest federal grant-in-aid program to states. Even if it is unlikely that states will leave Medicaid, it is far more thinkable that they will leave other, smaller conditional-spending programs.

53. See Thompson & Burke, *supra* note 29.

54. See Ruger, *supra* note 2.

55. See Adrian Vermeule, *Same Old, Same Old,* New Republic, Feb. 22, 2012, *available at* http://www.tnr.com/article/books/magazine/100987/richard-epstein-design-liberty-private-property-law#.

56. *Cf.* Lawrence B. Solum, *The Legal Effects of NFIB v. Sebelius and the Constitutional Gestalt* (Georgetown Law Sch. Pub. Law Working Paper No. 12-152), *available at* http://papers.ssrn.com/sol3/papers.cfm?abstract_id=2152653 (discussing the "Frozen New Deal Settlement").

57. See Barron & Rakoff, *supra* note 3.

58. The notion that the law should give governments an all-or-nothing choice in order to raise the cost of regulation is a long-standing theme of Professor Epstein's work. See, e.g., Richard A. Epstein, *The Supreme Court, 1987 Term—Foreword: Unconstitutional Conditions, State Power, and the Limits of Consent,* 102 Harv. L. Rev. 4 (1988). It is also a theme of the joint dissent in *NFIB,* which suggested that the Court must preserve the "practical obstacle[s] that prevent[] Congress from using the tax-and-spend power to assume all the general-welfare responsibilities traditionally exercised by the States." NFIB v. Sebelius, 132 S. Ct. 2566, 2643 (2012) (Scalia, Kennedy, Alito, Thomas, JJ., dissenting).

59. Ernest A. Young, *Constitutional Avoidance, Resistance Norms, and the Preservation of Judicial Review,* 78 Tex. L. Rev. 1549, 1552 (2000).

60. See William G. Weissert, *The National Channeling Demonstration: What We Knew, Know Now, and Still Need to Know,* 23 Health Servs. Res. 175 (1988).

61. See Bagenstos, *supra* note 15, at 78.

62. For a recent discussion, see Holly C. Felix, Glen P. Mays, M. Kathryn Stewart, Naomi Cottoms, & Mary Olson, *Medicaid Savings Resulted When Community Health Workers Matched Those With Needs to Home and Community Care,* 30 Health Affairs 1366, 1366–1367 (2011).

63. For a similar defense of this updating function, see Barron & Rakoff, *supra* note 3.

64. See Derthick & Rotherham, *supra* note 17.

65. For a powerful critique, see Diane Ravitch, *How, and How Not, to Improve the Schools*, N.Y. Rev. of Books, Mar. 22, 2012, *available at* http://www.nybooks.com/articles/archives/2012/mar/22/how-and-how-not-improve-schools/.

66. Waivers enable policy updating to arise from the states as well as the federal government. Professors Bulman-Pozen and Gerken argue that various waivers granted in the AFDC program in the 1980s and 1990s enabled states to make the case for "for building a new kind of welfare system, one with a markedly different vision of welfare's purposes." Bulman-Pozen & Gerken, *supra* note 2, at 1275.

67. For a highly critical response to that ruling, see Nicole Huberfeld, Elizabeth Weeks Leonard, & Kevin Outterson, *Plunging into Endless Difficulties: Medicaid and Coercion in the Healthcare Cases*, B.U. L. Rev. (forthcoming 2013).

# CHAPTER 15

# The *Health Care Case* in the Public Mind

## OPINION ON THE SUPREME COURT AND HEALTH REFORM IN A POLARIZED ERA

*Andrea Louise Campbell and Nathaniel Persily*

The Supreme Court's decision in *NFIB v. Sebelius* (*NFIB*) achieved a level of media coverage and public salience reached by very few Supreme Court decisions. It represented a political moment, if not a constitutional one. Although legal scholars might focus on the doctrinal importance of the decision for shaping the contours of congressional power, this unusually high-profile case is also fascinating to study as an event that structured public opinion about the Affordable Care Act (ACA) and the Court itself. As such, it presented a unique test for larger theories about the role of the Supreme Court as an agenda-setter for public opinion.

Perhaps more than any case in the post–New Deal period, the *Health Care Case* evolved into a judicial referendum on a president and his signature legislative achievement. Leading up to the decision, media coverage resembled that of a sporting event or a campaign. It became clear that the case would end with a reported "win" or "loss" for the President. Coming, as it did, five months before the President would stand for reelection, the decision also threatened to frame the presidential race in unprecedented ways.

This chapter examines the effect of the Court's decision on public approval of the Court and the ACA. Section 1 briefly reviews previous research on Court decisions and opinion formation. Section 2 describes the predecision polling on both the ACA and the Roberts Court. Section 3 compares public opinion before and after the decision to evaluate the decision's short-term impact. Section 4 presents our conclusions.

The data suggest that the Court's decision had a small but noticeable impact on attitudes toward the Court and the ACA. Although the Court found itself with historically low approval ratings before the decision, approval dropped further soon after the opinion's release. Moreover, the structure of opinion toward the Court became more polarized along partisan lines following the decision. Given the partisan split in opinion over the ACA, perhaps this should come as little surprise. The Court gave a win to the President, so Court approval and presidential approval became more aligned following the decision. Less obvious, however, might be the effect of the decision on attitudes toward the ACA. The Court's perceived stamp of approval for the ACA led some Americans to switch their minds about it, leading to a small, short-term increase in approval of the law following the decision. Some of this opinion transformation might simply have come from the favorable media attention heaped on the law as a "winner" at the Court. In other words, the Court's upholding of the ACA sent a signal that the law represented good policy. For still others, the decision provided an occasion for elite discussion and persuasion, instituted in particular by the President, who either convinced them on the law's merits or triggered their latent approval for him, which they expressed in newfound support for the law. Precisely because the decision clearly defined the political stakes, and because discussion surrounding it became more politically polarized, support for the Act (which had lagged presidential approval) now became more closely correlated with it. We emphasize, however, that this shift in ACA approval due to the Court's decision was quite temporary: less than a year after the decision, other factors quickly took over as the principal determinants of public attitudes toward the ACA.

## 1. Previous Research on Public Opinion toward the Court and Its Decisions

### A. THE STRONG "RESERVOIR OF GOOD WILL" FOR THE SUPREME COURT

For most of the history for which we have polling, the public has held the Supreme Court in higher regard than either the President or Congress. Indeed, as compared to all public and private institutions, the Supreme Court has ranked quite high in the public mind. Although public support for the Court will wax and wane depending on both national trends and specific cases the Court decides, the range of approval is much narrower than for other institutions.

The sources for such support are varied. They include lack of knowledge of the Court's business (and personnel) and consequent deferral to the institution, the symbolism surrounding the institution (think marble columns, black robes, and life tenure), and the obvious fact that members of the political branches (but not the Court) are repeatedly subject to electoral fights where voters hear negative messages about their performance. The Court's relatively high favorability, then, comes both from its status as a black box and from the association many Americans continue to make between the Court and lessons learned in grade-school civics classes.

Political scientists, such as James Gibson and Gregory Caldeira, often remark on the Court's strong "reservoir of good will," which allows it to weather individual cases.[1] They distinguish between "diffuse support," which translates into beliefs as to the legitimacy of the institution, and "specific support," which relates to short-term evaluations of Supreme Court performance. Individual Court decisions may affect measures of specific support, such as approval ratings and confidence measures, but even the most controversial cases, such as *Bush v. Gore*, do not affect attitudes about the Court's legitimacy.[2]

Even with respect to specific support, though, very few cases are sufficiently salient to have much of an impact on public attitudes toward the Court. For a case to affect approval of the Court, not only must a certain segment of the public be paying attention to it (and receiving signals from the media and elites about it), but they must also care enough about the issue to let it determine their attitudes toward the Court. More still, for opinion to shift, the Court decision cannot have been factored into Court approval before the Court issues its decision. In other words, the greatest effect on Court approval should be seen when a large segment of the public is aware of the decision, thinks it involves an important issue that could affect their overall evaluation of the Court, and is somewhat surprised by the decision such that it disrupts settled expectations as to how the Supreme Court is performing its job.[3]

Although the Court has issued many controversial and popular decisions, it is quite difficult to identify individual salient decisions that have affected approval of the Court. Popular lore would have it that the decisions of the Warren Court in the 1960s regarding First Amendment and criminal rights, for example, led Americans to lower their support for the Court. This seems like a safe assumption, but unfortunately, we do not have good, consistent polling data on specific support for the Court before and after the relevant decisions of the time.

The best examples of short-term shifts in specific support for the Court following its decisions may come from the most controversial decisions over the past decade or so. Most notably, approval of the Court became more polarized along partisan lines in the immediate wake of *Bush v. Gore* (2000),[4] as Republicans became more supportive and Democrats less so. Approval appeared to decline in a more uniform fashion in the wake of the Supreme Court's decisions in *Kelo v. New London* (2005),[5] which upheld a local government's taking of private property, in *Citizens United v. FEC* (2010),[6] which struck down a federal ban on corporate campaign expenditures, and perhaps in the wake of the Supreme Court's 2003 decisions in *Lawrence v. Texas*[7] and *Grutter v. Bollinger*.[8] Over that same period it is difficult to attribute increases in public approval of the Court to decisions that were popular with the public. Instead, it appears that approval for the Court rose following presidential elections and the nominations of John Roberts, Samuel Alito, and Sonia Sotomayor (although, interestingly, not Elena Kagan).

Of course, drawing causal inferences from any of these events or decisions to shifts in approval is a tricky business. Polls gauging Supreme Court approval are not taken at regular intervals so many other potentially relevant events occur in the intervening period between Supreme Court approval polls. As with any political event, such as a presidential debate or party convention, the closer in time the polls are taken before and after the event, the more plausible the inference that the event led to the public opinion shift. As we discuss later, we are fortunate to have such data concerning the *Health Care Case*. Perhaps if comparable data were available for other decisions we might see similar effects.

## B. THE EFFECT OF COURT DECISIONS ON PUBLIC OPINION CONCERNING CONSTITUTIONAL QUESTIONS

The effect of Court decisions on public opinion toward the issues the Court considers presents a related, if somewhat different, dynamic to effect on approval of the Court itself. Once again, a Court decision will have the greatest effect concerning issues that are sufficiently salient to attract media coverage, but about which a significant share of the public does not yet hold firm beliefs. Given that most Court decisions occur below the public radar, very few will affect public attitudes on issues. For those few instances when a Court decision will affect issue attitudes, it does so only indirectly. The Court elevates an issue onto the national agenda with its decision, elites in politics and the media then send signals to the mass public about the issue, and depending on the character of the signals and the movability of the public, some share of the public may shift in its opinion.

The public can shift in one of three possible directions, which the literature describes as legitimation, backlash, and polarization.[9] First, legitimation occurs when the public moves in the same direction as the Court following its decision. For the *Health Care Case*, for example, legitimation would occur if the public became more favorable toward the ACA following the Court's decision upholding most of the law. For many years, political scientists thought the Court frequently had such a legitimating effect when it issued a decision.[10] However, closer analysis has found very few, if any, instances.[11] Although public attitudes toward issues of racial equality, such as school segregation or bans on intermarriage, became more liberal in the wake of liberal Court decisions on those subjects, it is unclear, given the scarcity of early polls, if the postdecision trajectory of opinion was steeper than it was before the relevant decision. Legitimation is a rare phenomenon. This is one reason, as we argue later, that the short-term rise in ACA favorability post-*NFIB* is so noteworthy.

Backlash refers to the opposite dynamic: that is, when the public moves in the direction opposite the Court's decision on the issue. *Lawrence v. Texas*, the 2003 Supreme Court decision striking down Texas' ban on sodomy, produced a short-term backlash on gay rights, albeit one that quickly evaporated within two years and was followed by steady approval on most issues concerning gay rights. *Kelo v. New London* and *Citizens United v. FEC* are often seen as backlash cases, given the high disapproval of government takings and unregulated corporate campaign expenditures expressed in polls taken after the decision. But existing data suggest most Americans were quite opposed to takings and unregulated corporate campaign spending even before those decisions. In contrast, some point to backlash from the Court's decision in *Furman v. Georgia*,[12] which suspended the use of the death penalty and was followed by rising approval of the death penalty. But public approval of the death penalty was rising even before the decision, and the trajectory of opinion afterward was identical. Indeed, even after the Court overturned *Furman* in *Gregg v. Georgia*,[13] reinstating the death penalty, the upward trajectory of pro-death penalty opinion continued unabated. Neither case had any independent effect—backlash or legitimation—on public opinion, because the predecision and postdecision paths of death penalty opinion were equally steep.

Finally, sometimes aggregate opinion may appear the same before and after a decision, but changes in the intensity or structure of opinion suggest polarization. Usually this occurs when attitudes on the issue become more closely correlated with particular demographic or political characteristics. *Roe v. Wade*[14] is often described in these terms.[15] Although aggregate support for abortion rights appeared unaffected by the decision, racial minorities and Catholics became significantly more opposed to abortion rights, while whites and non-Catholics expressed greater favorability. The "structure" of opinion changed, in that certain group characteristics became better predictors of opinion on abortion rights. In other contexts, the relevant groups might be partisan or ideological, as Republicans and Democrats, for instance, grow farther apart on an issue as a result of a decision.

Of course, legitimation, backlash, and polarization are not mutually exclusive, especially if one expands the time frame for analysis. As in *Lawrence*, a decision might produce short-term backlash on an issue, which quickly subsides and is replaced by long-term legitimation. Some suggest *Brown v. Board of Education*[16] and *Miranda v. Arizona*[17] are such examples, although public opinion data before those decisions on the relevant issues of desegregation and the right against self-incrimination are quite scant. Furthermore, the longer it takes to see an effect from a decision, the more difficult it is to conclude that the decision and contemporaneous discussion of it "caused" the public opinion change. The constitutional ban on school prayer erected by the Court in the 1960s, for example, remains highly unpopular today, but not as unpopular as it was in the immediate aftermath of the decision. So much has happened in the country's religious and political life since the Court issued those decisions that it would be difficult to draw anything but a very faint connection between those decisions and attitudinal change on questions of church and state.

The rich amount of available data concerning the ACA, both before and after the *Health Care Case*, provides a unique opportunity to analyze that decision in ways few other such decisions could be assessed. We should emphasize, though, that we are still viewing a public opinion snapshot in time. The independent effect of the decision (to the degree one exists) has now been overcome by other events, such as other Supreme Court cases, presidential elections, or legislative controversies. Indeed, just as many describe a decay in the bounce that presidential candidates typically receive after their party's national convention, we see public opinion toward the Court and the ACA returning to "normal" patterns over the year following the *NFIB v. Sebelius* decision. Moreover, as the ACA is implemented over its lifespan and perhaps becomes an accepted part of the administrative state, the independent effect of the Court's decision will become impossible to identify, except insofar as the law itself might not exist had the Court struck it down. Even with those caveats, the short-term effect of the decision is interesting to analyze in its own right. Very few decisions are followed by comparable, identifiable shifts in public attitudes toward the Court or the issues it considers.

## II. Predecision Public Opinion toward the Court and the ACA

### A. OPINION TOWARD THE SUPREME COURT

Much had been made in the months prior to the *Health Care Case* decision of the record lows in approval that the Supreme Court had posted. According to the Pew polls, favorability ratings of the Court in 2012 were at their lowest in twenty-five years of polling, with only 52 percent describing their opinion of the Court as "very" or "mostly" favorable. The June 2012 Gallup Poll found only 37 percent expressed "a great deal" or "quite a lot" of confidence in the Supreme Court and the New York Times / CBS News poll at the same time found just 44 percent approval.

For the most part, the Court has suffered the same fate as other powerful institutions. General distrust of those in power, fueled in part by the soured

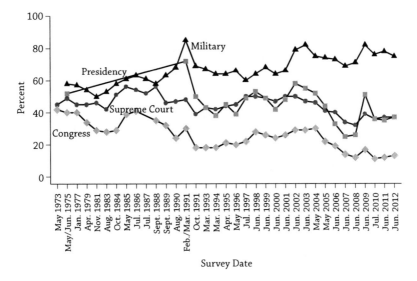

*Figure 1.* Confidence in American institutions, 1973–2012.

Source: Gallup Polls from the Roper Center. Question wording: "Now I am going to read you a list of institutions in American society. Please tell me how much confidence you, yourself, have in each one—a great deal, quite a lot, some or very little?" Figure refers to combined response of "great deal" / "quite a lot."

economy, has been a tide that has sunk all boats. Opinion toward Congress has been injured the most, with the proportion expressing confidence falling from 42 percent to 13 percent between 1973 and 2012 (see Figure 1). However, other institutions, such as banks, the church, and public schools all engendered historically low levels of confidence in recent years.

Even as it has posted historic lows, however, the Court still outranks many, but by no means all, other institutions in terms of confidence (Figure 2). With 37 percent expressing "a great deal" or "a lot of confidence," the Court ranked below the military, small business, the police, organized religion, and the medical system. Although the Court has often enjoyed greater confidence than the presidency, as of 2012 the two institutions were tied, with the presidency garnering a slightly higher percentage of Americans expressing a "great deal" of confidence, 17 percent compared to 15 percent for the Court.

With respect to these measures of specific support, the Court falls victim to political forces beyond its control in two respects. First, as mentioned, larger shifts in general attitudes toward government afflict opinion toward the Court. Second, the partisan structure of support for the Court will vary depending on which party holds the presidency. Because respondents' attitudes toward the federal government are often shaped by their approval of the President, and because such general governmental attitudes feed into attitudes toward the

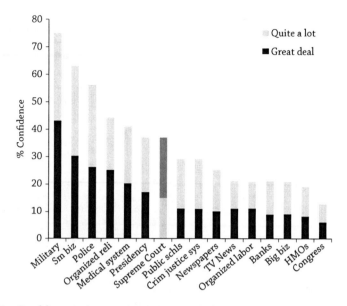

*Figure 2.* Confidence in American institutions, 2012.

Source: Gallup Poll, June 7–10, 2012. Question wording: "Now I am going to read you a list of institutions in American society. Please tell me how much confidence you, yourself, have in each one—a great deal, quite a lot, some or very little?" Figure refers to combined response of "great deal" / "quite a lot."

Court, copartisans of the President tend to express greater support for the Court than partisan opponents of the President. As Figure 3 demonstrates with respect to Gallup's approval ratings of the Court, Democrats displayed greater approval than Republicans of the Court during the last year of the Clinton presidency and throughout the Obama presidency, while Republicans generally had higher approval of the Court during George W. Bush's presidency. The correlation is not perfect, because approval will also vary somewhat based on highly salient decisions, such as the *Citizens United* case in 2010, but the dynamic is quite easy to see from the data.

In addition to measuring approval, favorability, and confidence, surveys tapping public attitudes toward the Supreme Court often attempt to gauge cynicism concerning the bases for the Court's decisions. Of course, experienced legal analysts might decry these polls for constructing an unrealistic and artificial law-versus-politics dichotomy. However, the interesting findings (or lack thereof) concern whether individual decisions shake respondents' confidence in the legal basis for judicial decision-making. For example, in a New York Times / CBS News poll administered in May 2012, shortly before the Court's ACA ruling, 13 percent of respondents said that generally Supreme Court justices decide the cases before them based on legal analysis, while a large majority—76 percent—said that the justices' own personal or political views mattered (Table 1). However, when the

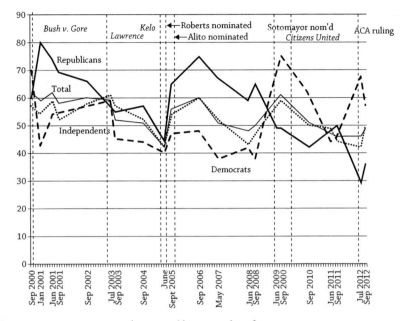

*Figure 3.* Supreme Court job approval by party identification.

Source: Gallup polls from the Roper Center. Question wording: "Do you approve or disapprove of the way the Supreme court is handling its job?"

same respondents were asked later in the survey about the bases for ruling on the ACA specifically, the proportion saying that the decision would be based on legal analysis rose to 32 percent, while the proportion citing personal or political views fell to 55 percent. There are no clear patterns of partisanship or ACA opinion in the "off-diagonals," that is, respondents whose views on the bases of court decision-making differed between general cases and the health care ruling. In other words, the group of respondents in this preruling poll who said that, in general, the Court makes its decisions based on legal analysis but that in the case of the ACA the decision would be made on the basis of the justices' own personal or political views was not dominated by one political party's adherents or by respondents who disapproved of the health care law.

Interestingly, there was no aggregate shift in the perceived basis of decision-making after the Court issued its ACA ruling. In a New York Times / CBS News poll administered in July 2012, after the ruling, the proportions of respondents saying that the Court's ruling on health care was based on legal analysis (31 percent) or the justices' own personal and political views (54 percent) was virtually the same as in the May predecision poll (Table 1).

However, this stasis in overall opinion hides partisan polarization following the decision. Prior to the ACA ruling, partisans did not have different views on how justices generally decide cases or how they thought the justices

*Table 1.* **Perceived Bases of Justices' Rulings**

| | May 2012 | | | | May 2012 | | | | July 2012 | | | |
| | How justices generally decide cases | | | | How justices will decide ACA | | | | How justices did decide ACA | | | |
| | Dem | Ind | Rep | Total | Dem | Ind | Rep | Total | Dem | Ind | Rep | Total |
|---|---|---|---|---|---|---|---|---|---|---|---|---|
| Legal analysis | 14 | 13 | 12 | 13 | 35 | 33 | 33 | 32 | 43 | 30 | 21 | 31 |
| Own personal or political views | 76 | 73 | 75 | 76 | 56 | 54 | 48 | 55 | 42 | 55 | 65 | 54 |
| Both (vol.) | 3 | 4 | 5 | 4 | 3 | 5 | 7 | 4 | 2 | 3 | 1 | 2 |
| Don't Know | 7 | 9 | 8 | 8 | 6 | 8 | 13 | 9 | 13 | 12 | 14 | 13 |

*Source:* New York Times / CBS News polls, May 31–June 3, 2012, and July 11–16, 2012.

would decide the ACA case (Table 1). The same proportion of Democrats and Republicans (14 and 12 percent) thought justices generally base their decisions on legal analysis, while larger, but similar proportions (35 percent of Democrats, 33 percent of Republicans) thought the ACA decision would be based on legal analysis. (Note that this May 2012 poll was taken subsequent to the oral argument in the *Health Care Case* but before the decision, suggesting that the argument itself did not generate polarized responses). However, after the ruling was announced, partisans polarized, with the proportion of Democrats saying that the ruling was based on legal analysis increasing to 43 percent, while the proportion of Republicans holding that view falling to 21 percent (with independents in between—and unchanged—at 30 percent). In the postdecision poll, almost two-thirds of Republicans thought the ACA decision had been based on the justices' own personal or political views, compared to just 42 percent of Democrats who thought so.

In sum, prior to the *Health Care Case* decision, the Supreme Court had suffered from the loss of confidence that afflicted many other powerful institutions. However, the reservoir of support that the Court uniquely enjoys kept approval ratings of the Court higher than those of many other institutions and branches of government. Although partisan differences in approval had narrowed, Democrats displayed marginally higher support for the Court as they had for most of President Obama's term in office. When the Court issued its decision, it remained to be seen whether and how attitudes toward the decision might affect support for the Court given the larger forces that had shaped opinion to that point.

## B. ACA OPINION BEFORE THE RULING

Public opinion toward the Affordable Care Act was divided throughout the legislation's development and passage. As time series from the New York Times / CBS News, Washington Post / ABC News, and Kaiser polls all demonstrate, prior to the Court's ruling, approval of the ACA overall never consistently hit 50 percent, and opposition exceeded support throughout (Figure 4). The Obama proposal never suffered the catastrophic drop in public support that plagued the 1993–1994 Clinton health care reform effort, but neither did it enjoy increased public support over time. As many observers have noted, this is somewhat curious, given that large majorities of the public supported individual provisions in the legislation, such as allowing children to stay on their parents' insurance until age twenty-six, prohibiting the denial of insurance for preexisting conditions, and providing tax breaks to small businesses that offer health insurance.[18] A hope among the legislation's proponents was that as individuals learned more about the legislation, they would come to support the overall package at greater rates. However, that effect never came to fruition during the preruling period.

Predecision ACA opinion was also characterized by substantial intergroup differences in support for the legislation. Figure 5 shows the proportion of various demographic and political groups approving of the ACA in a May 2012 New York Times / CBS News poll. There are statistically and substantively significant differences by level of education, marital status, and race/ethnicity. The largest differences, however, are found across political groups, with Republicans, conservatives, and Tea Party supporters much less supportive of the legislation than their Democratic, liberal, or non–Tea Party counterparts. The partisan and ideological polarization that characterizes contemporary public opinion is very much evident in ACA opinion.[19]

Even given these expected demographic and ideological differences, we should note that opponents of the ACA were not homogeneous in their reasons for opposition. CNN polls have asked respondents if they "generally favor or generally oppose" the "bill that makes major changes to the country's health care system." In May 2012, 42 percent favored and 51 percent opposed. But about a fourth of the opponents, when pressed, said they opposed the legislation because "it is not liberal enough." Thus, 43 percent favored the ACA, 34 percent opposed it because it was "too liberal," and 13 percent opposed it because it

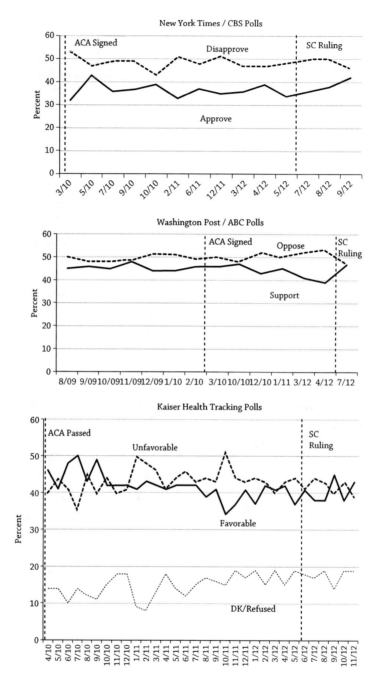

**Figure 4.** ACA opinion over time.

Source: New York Times / CBS News polls. Question wording: "From what you've heard or read, do you approve or disapprove of the health care law that was enacted in 2010?." *Source*: Washington Post / ABC News polls. Question wording: "Overall, do you support or oppose the federal law making changes to the health care system?." *Source*: Kaiser Health Tracking Polls. Question wording: "As you may know, a health reform bill was signed into law in 2010. Given what you know about the health reform law, do you have a generally favorable or generally unfavorable opinion of it?"

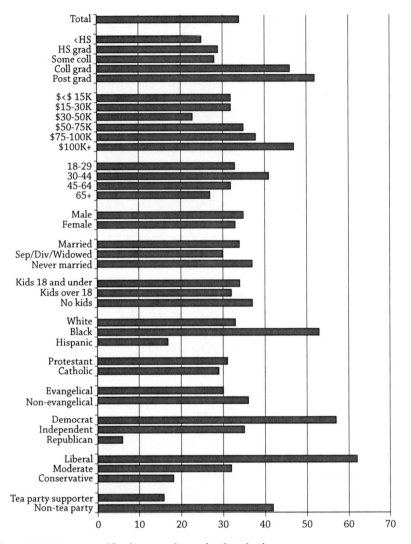

*Figure 5.* ACA approval by demographic and political subgroup.

Source: NYTimes / CBS News Poll, May 31–June 3, 2012. Question wording: "From what you've heard or read, do you approve or disapprove of the health care law that was enacted in 2010?"

was "not liberal enough." These data are consistent with Kaiser polls that asked, "What would you like to see Congress do when it comes to the health care law?" In the predecision period, a majority (or plurality) always supported the options "expand the law" or keep it "as is," whereas roughly 40 percent supported repealing the law and not replacing it, or repealing the law and replacing it with the Republican alternative.

## 3. Public Opinion after the Supreme Court Ruling

Given the close divide among the public on the ACA, would the Court's upholding of much of the law increase support for the ACA? Would it cause opinion on
the ACA—or on the Court itself—to become even more polarized?

### A. PUBLIC OPINION ON THE RULING ITSELF

In the immediate aftermath of the decision, opinion on the ruling was closely
divided. Some polls showed a small majority supporting the decision, while others showed small majorities opposing it. Most people had an opinion on the decision. However, in the first few days after the decision was issued ( June 28 to July 1
2012), a significant share of the public did not know how the Court had ruled on
the law. The Pew survey at the time asked, "From what you've read and heard, did
the Supreme Court [uphold or reject] most of the provisions in the health care
law?" Fifty-five percent correctly answered "uphold," 15 percent answered "reject,"
and 30 percent did not know or refused to answer. Of those who answered correctly, 50 percent approved of the decision and 42 percent disapproved.[20]

This initial lack of understanding, along with the differences in wording of survey questions, may explain some of the divergences in the poll items asking respondents to assess the ruling itself (table 2). In polling questions that did not mention
which way the Court ruled, disapproval of the decision exceeded approval, 44 to
42 percent (the Washington Post / ABC News item), or 40 to 36 percent (Pew
Poll of all respondents). However, in three polls that mentioned that the Court's
decision upheld the law, approval exceeded disapproval. In a June 2012 Kaiser
poll fielded immediately after the ruling was announced, 47 percent of respondents approved of the Court's decision "to uphold the health care law," compared
to 43 percent who disapproved. A Quinnipiac poll with nearly identical wording
revealed a comparable breakdown—48 percent approved, while 45 percent disapproved. Similarly, in a July 2012 New York Times / CBS News poll, 46 percent of
respondents said that it was a "good thing" that the Supreme Court kept the health
care law "mostly in place," versus 41 percent who said it was a "bad thing."

The impact of question wording and many Americans' uncertainty about
what the Court had ruled is apparent in Figures 6a and 6b, which contrast survey respondents' own feelings toward the ACA and their opinion of the Court
ruling. Figure 6a shows the results for the Washington Post / ABC News July
2012 poll, in which the horizontal axis represents each demographic and political group's level of support for "the federal law changing the health care system,"
while the vertical axis represents each groups' support for the Court's ruling. This
item did not specify which way the Court ruled, and more groups appear below
the 45-degree line than above, indicating that their support for the Court's ruling

Table 2. **Public Opinion about the Court Ruling**

| Direction of Court's ruling mentioned? | Date | Poll | Question | Approve/ agree | Disapprove/ disagree |
|---|---|---|---|---|---|
| No | July 2012 | Wash. Post/ABC | Regardless of your feeling about the law itself, do you approve or disapprove of the U.S. Supreme Court ruling on the health care law last week? | 42 | 44 |
| | June 28–July 1, 2012 | Pew | From what you have read and heard about the Supreme Court's ruling on the 2010 health care law, would you say you strongly approve, approve, disapprove, or strongly disapprove of their decision? | 36 | 40 |
| Yes | July 1–8, 2012 | Quinnipiac | The Supreme Court has heard a challenge to the health care law and voted to uphold it. Do you agree or disagree with the Supreme Court's decision to uphold the health care law? | 48 | 45 |
| | June 2012 | Kaiser | The Supreme Court recently decided to uphold the health care law. Do you approve or disapprove of the Court's decision in this case? | 47 | 43 |
| | July 2012 | NYT/CBS | As you may know, the Supreme Court upheld most of the 2010 health care law. Do you think the Supreme Court's decision to keep the health care law mostly in place was a good thing or a bad thing? | 46 (good thing) | 41 (bad thing) |

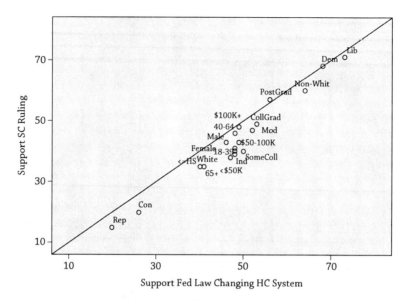

*Figure 6a.*  Court ruling support versus ACA support: Direction of ruling not given

Source: Washington Post / ABC Poll.

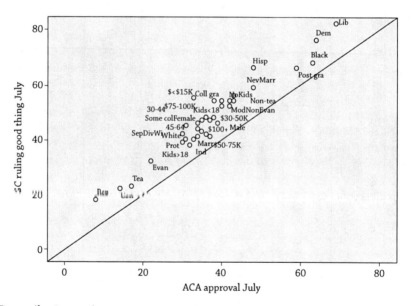

*Figure 6b.*  Court ruling support versus ACA support: Direction of ruling given

Source: New York Times / CBS Poll.

was lower than their own support for the ACA. In contrast, a similar graph of the New York Times / CBS News item (Figure 6b), in which respondents were asked whether the Court's decision to uphold "most" of the law was a good or bad thing, shows that the proportion of each subgroup saying the decision was a good thing was higher than their own approval of the ACA (all of the groups appear above the 45-degree line). This suggests that when survey respondents know that the Court ruled in favor of the ACA, a greater share support the decision.

Given that opposition to the health care law exceeded support for most of the predecision period, the narrow majority of the public supporting the Court's decision suggests some opinion leadership by the Court. To be more specific, some share of the population that opposed the law probably supported the decision because of their respect for the Court. Of course, for survey respondents as with judges, one can disapprove of a law while approving of a court decision upholding it under the Constitution. However, even beyond the possibility that respondents correctly disentangle favorability from constitutionality, some small share of the population is predisposed to agree with a Supreme Court decision, even if the result—upholding a law they dislike—is not the one they were hoping for from the Court. A recent panel study by Professors Katerina Linos and Kim Twist that interviewed the same people before and after the ruling confirms this finding, as well as the later finding that the Court decision increased support for the ACA.[21] They found that those who trusted the Court before the decision were more likely to change their position and become more favorable to the individual mandate provision of the ACA following the decision.

## B.  POSTDECISION OPINION ON THE ACA

For a decision to have a truly legitimating effect, opinion on the underlying law would need to move in the direction of the Court's decision. In this case, the public would need to become more supportive of the ACA itself. Time series of public opinion polls suggest, in fact, that the ruling had a small positive effect on ACA support in the very short term. In all three time series in Figure 4 and in most of the polls presented in Table 3, support of or favorability toward the law increased slightly in the first poll taken after the Court's decision. For the New York Times / CBS News poll, we have two additional postruling readings, for August and September 2012, and ACA approval continued to trend upward, to 42 percent in September, the highest level of approval since the 43 percent reached in May 2010, two months after the reform bill's passage. At least in the very short term, the Court's ruling seemed to have bolstered ACA support.

The Kaiser tracking polls paint a somewhat more complicated picture. Consistent with the other polls, they indicate that, as compared to a poll one month earlier, a greater share of the public held favorable views toward the ACA after the Court's decision, a jump of four percentage points, from 37 percent to 41 percent. That gain was immediately erased for the next two months, until in September following the Democratic National Convention, favorable views shot up to 45 percent, a level not seen in the previous two years and one where those holding favorable views outnumbered those holding unfavorable views. They dropped back down in October, but shot up to comparable levels in the November poll, which was

*Table 3.*  **Change in ACA Approval after the Supreme Court's Decision**

| Polling Organization | Question | Predecision ACA Approval/ Favorable (date) | Post-decision ACA Approval/ Favorable(date) |
|---|---|---|---|
| Wash. Post/ ABC | Overall do you support or oppose the federal law making changes to the health care system? | 39 (4/5–8/12) | 47 (7/5–8/12) |
| Pew | Do you approve or disapprove of the health care legislation passed by Barack Obama and Congress in 2010? | 43 (6/7–17/12) | 47 (6/28 – 7/9/12) |
| Quinnipiac | Do you think Congress should try to repeal the health care law, or should they let it stand? | 38 (4/11–17/12) | 43 (7/1–8/12) |
| NBC News/ Wall Street Journal | From what you have heard about barack Obama's health care plan that was passed by Congress and signed into law by the President in 2010, do you think his plan is a good idea or bad idea? | 35 (6/20–24/12) | 40 (7/18–22/12) |
| CNN/ORC | As you may know, a bill that makes major changes to the country's health care system became law in 2010. Based on what you have read or heard about that legislation, do you generally favor or generally oppose it? | 43 (5/29–31/12) | 42 (11/16–18/12) |

(*continued*)

Table 3. (Continued)

| Polling Organization | Question | Predecision ACA Approval/ Favorable (date) | Post-decision ACA Approval/ Favorable(date) |
|---|---|---|---|
| Kaiser | As you may know a health reform bill was signed into law in 2010. Given what you know about the health reform law, do you have a generally favorable or generally unfavorable opinion of it? | 37 (5/8–14/12) | 41 (6/28–30/12) |
| NYT/CBS | From what you've heard or read, do you approve or disapprove of the health care law that was enacted in 2010? | 34 (5/31–6/3/12) | 36 (7/11–16/12) |

*Source:* www.pollingreport.com.

conducted in the days following the presidential election. However, in the latest, February 2013 Kaiser poll (taken as this book went to press so not depicted here), favorable ratings of the ACA plummeted seven points, such that 42 percent held unfavorable views of the ACA, and 36 percent held favorable views.

In short, like the others, the Kaiser polls suggest that a Supreme Court decision, like other political events that present elites an opportunity for mass persuasion, can lead to short-term shifts in public attitudes on particular issues. However, these effects can become dwarfed by other political events, such as the public's general souring toward government, which occurred during the budget fights of early 2013. Also, we should expect that opinion toward the ACA might wax and wane with approval of President Obama. Shifts in attitudes toward the President might have spillover effects with respect to his signature legislative achievement.

To some extent, even the observed, short-term increase in ACA-approval after the decision can be explained by regression to the mean. In the period between the oral argument in the case and the release of the decision, opinion on the ACA appeared to drop somewhat. Perhaps this is due to the unfavorable media coverage the government received in the wake of the argument and the concomitant lowering of expectations as to whether the Court would uphold the law. Some of the post-decision increase in ACA favorability may be due to a return to a normal equilibrium interrupted by the oral argument. Nevertheless, as Table 3 indicates, the upward trend appeared to be almost uniform among the polls and to continue slightly upward in the six months following the decision.

Because the greatest change in postdecision attitudes occurred among Democrats, the ruling also appears to have exacerbated the other underlying characteristic of ACA opinion, its pronounced partisan divide. In the Kaiser time series, for which we have opinion by party identification, favorability toward the ACA increased by 9 points among Democrats immediately after the Court's ruling, from 62 to 71 percent, and increased by four points among independents, from 34 to 38 percent. In contrast, favorability among Republicans continued to slide after the ACA ruling, dropping a point to tie its historic low of 7 percent (Figure 7). Because the Kaiser data "bounce around" quite a bit from March through November 2012, we should be cautious in our assessments of polarization. It is clear that opinion was more polarized along partisan lines when comparing the postdecision poll to its immediate predecessor, but the extent of polarization in November was comparable to what it was in April 2012. Moreover, while aggregate favorability dropped over the summer of 2012, so did the polarization in opinions. Even when favorability rebounded following the Democratic Convention, the rise was evident among all partisan groups, so that the sixty-four-percentage-point gap between Democrats and Republicans in the

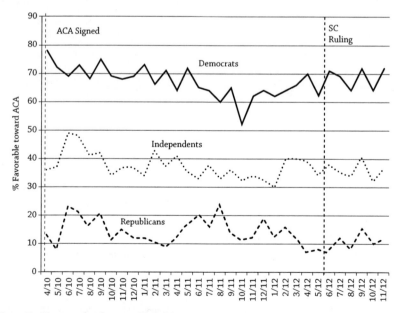

*Figure 7.* Partisan divide over the ACA.

Source: Kaiser Family Foundation Health Tracking Polls, kff.org. Question wording: "As you may know, a health reform bill was signed into law in 2010. Given what you know about the health reform law, do you have a generally favorable or generally unfavorable opinion of it?"

June poll had narrowed to fifty-six points. By the time of the November election, however, the gap was sixty points: 72 percent of Democrats had a favorable opinion of the law, as compared to 37 percent of Independents and 12 percent of Republicans. Of course, polarization declined between November 2012 and February 2013 as favorability toward the ACA unexpectedly plummeted. Most of this reduction can be attributed to drops in the share of Democrats expressing favorable views: that figure dropped from 72 percent in November 2012 to 57 percent in February 2013. Among Independents the figure dropped from 37 percent to 32 percent, while Republicans remained unchanged, as only 12 percent expressed a favorable view of the law. Thus, the gap between Democrats and Republicans toward the ACA shrank to 45 percentage points.

A look across demographic and political groups in the New York Times / CBS News polls for which we have individual-level data shows that approval of the ACA increased among most groups immediately after the Court's ruling (Figure 8a). Groups appearing above the 45-degree line exhibited an increase in ACA approval after the Court ruling, while groups whose ACA approval fell appear below the line. Note, however, that approval of the ACA remained below 50 percent for most groups, with majorities of only a few groups supporting the reform, notably liberals, Democrats, blacks, and those with postgraduate educations. Figure 8b shows the comparable data from April and July 2012 polls by the Washington Post / ABC News: there, the proportion of supportive responses to the question "Do you support or oppose the federal law making changes to the health care system" increased for all demographic and political groups.

Thus, the Court's ruling upholding most of the ACA had a positive effect on public opinion in the very short term, with most demographic and political groups more positive about the health reform than they had been. Shifts were most pronounced among groups that had been most supportive of the ACA prior to the decision. However, the aggregate opinion changes were small, and approval and support of the ACA remained below 50 percent for most groups. Even these small shifts suggest some short-term legitimating effect from the Court decision, and more likely, from favorable media coverage and elite discussion of the decision in its immediate aftermath.

## C. POSTDECISION ATTITUDES TOWARD THE COURT

The sports-like media coverage of the *Health Care Case*, which pitted Republicans against Democrats and the Court against the President, suggested that the decision might have fundamental consequences for the Court's reputation and political capital. As with the warnings surrounding *Bush v. Gore*, the case was described as a test of the Court's legitimacy, not a mere run-of-the-mill adjudication of a law's constitutionality. According to Jeffrey Toobin, Chief Justice Roberts perceived the case in this way, and his reported change of heart in moving to uphold

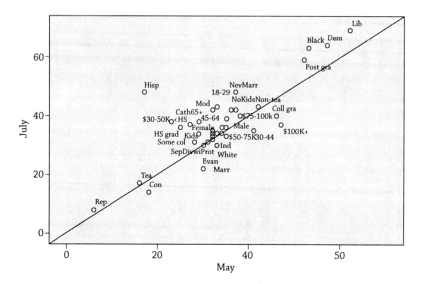

*Figure 8a.* Before and after ACA approval: New York Times / CBS News polls

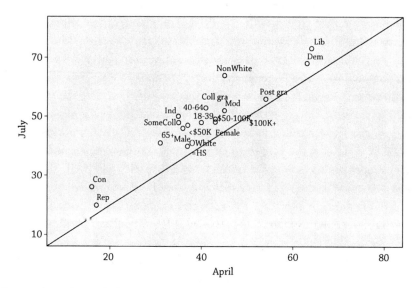

*Figure 8b.* Before and after ACA support: Washington Post / ABC News polls

the individual mandate and most of the other provisions may have derived from his perception that the Court's public reputation would suffer if five Republican appointees struck down President Obama's signature legislative achievement.[22] Given the threat the case (allegedly) posed to the Court as an institution, what would the ruling on this highly contentious and polarizing law mean for regard for the Court and its standing among the public?

The ruling may have had a slightly positive effect on ACA opinion, but it had an immediately negative effect on opinion toward the Court. Overall, the job approval rating of the Court in the New York Times / CBS News poll declined from 44 percent in May and early June, before the ruling, to 41 percent after the ruling in July. Approval also became more polarized, with Republican approval falling eleven points, from 42 to 31 percent, while Democratic approval fell just three points, from 51 to 48 percent, and Independents stayed the same (43 and 42 percent; Figure 9). (A September 2012 Gallup Poll suggests some rebound in Court approval, which reached 49 percent. The partisan divide declined but was still pronounced: 57 percent of Democrats approved of the Court compared to only 36 percent of Republicans.)

Figure 10 shows the same pre- and postdecision Court job approval ratings for a variety of demographic and political subgroups. Groups appearing above the 45-degree line exhibited an increase in Supreme Court job approval after the ACA ruling, while groups whose approval rating fell appear below the line. In contrast to favorability toward the ACA itself, which increased among most groups after the ruling (Figure 8), the Court's job approval fell among the majority of groups after the ACA decision, most notably among Tea Party supporters, those with household incomes between $15,000 and $30,000, conservatives, Republicans, and separated/divorced/widowed respondents. Job approval increased the most among college graduates, Catholics, those aged thirty to forty-four, and those with incomes between $30,000 and $50,000. Thus, Court job approval fell the most among groups most likely to be embittered by the ruling, namely political groups such as conservatives, Republicans, and Tea Party supporters (the changes in attitudes among the income and marital status groups are more mixed and difficult to interpret).

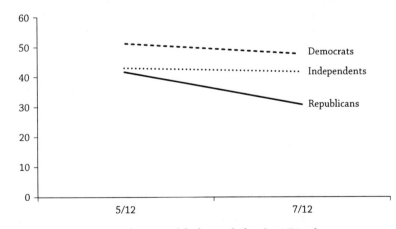

*Figure 9.* Supreme Court job approval, before and after the ACA ruling.

Source: New York Times / CBS News polls, May 31–June 3, 2012 and July 11–16, 2012

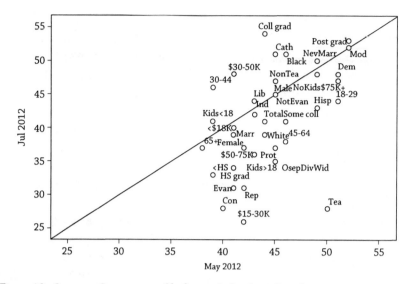

*Figure 10.* Supreme Court approval before and after the ACA ruling.

Source: New York Times / CBS News polls, May 31–June 3, 2012 and July 11–16, 2012

Multivariate analysis of the postruling July 2012 New York Times / CBS News poll for which we have the individual-level data allows us to examine similarities and differences in the structure of attitudes toward the Court, Obama, the ACA, and the Court's ACA ruling (Table 4); that is, whether the underlying correlates of opinion are the same or different. The analysis shows that Supreme Court approval after the decision was structured chiefly by education, race, and religion, and modestly by political variables (column 1), with Republicans and to some extent Tea Party iden-tifiers less approving of the Court. However, whether respondents thought the ruling a "good thing" (column 4) has a structure almost identical to that of underlying ACA approval (column 3) and Obama job approval (column 2), with political variables dominating. In other words, respondents' attitudes about Obama and the ACA are deeply partisan, as one would expect, and in turn the Court's ACA ruling was as well. Interestingly, whether respondents thought the Court's ruling was made on a legal basis versus a personal or political basis had a structure that seems some combina-tion of the factors behind the Supreme Court's job approval and ACA approval (with opinion varying by demographics like education and race just as Supreme Court job approval does, and opinion varying as well with political variables like conservative and Tea Party identification, as ACA approval does). What respondents thought of the basis of the Court's decision was thus shaped both by the underlying demograph-ics that shape general Court opinion, such as education and race, and by the partisan variables associated with attitudes toward this particular President and issue area.

Finally, did the ruling change the structure of Supreme Court job approval or ACA approval? That is, did the Court's stamp of approval change the underlying correlates of opinion on the Court itself or on the health care law? Table 5 shows

*Table 4.* **Post-ruling Supreme Court, Presidential, and ACA Attitudes: Multivariate Analysis**

| | Supreme Ct. job approval (1) | Obama job approval (2) | ACA approval (3) | SC ruling good thing (4) | SC ruling legal BASIS (5) |
|---|---|---|---|---|---|
| Education | .255*** | .137 | .175ᵃ | .348*** | .262** |
| Income | .135* | −.032 | .060 | .017 | .118ᵃ |
| Age | −.002 | .002 | .011 | .001 | .014ᵃ |
| Female | −.301ᵃ | −.522** | −.406* | −.521** | .057 |
| Black | 1.053*** | 2.182*** | 1.035*** | .394 | .774* |
| Hispanic | .054 | 1.424*** | 1.463*** | 1.192*** | .612* |
| Asian | .247 | .590 | −.695 | 1.009 | −.066 |
| Kids 18 and under | −.068 | .270 | −.776*** | −.399 | −.771** |
| Kids over 18 | −.221 | −.067 | −.771*** | −.604* | −.742** |
| Sep./div./widowed | −.050 | .169 | .025 | .354 | −.257 |
| Never married | .521ᵃ | 1.549*** | −.065 | .293 | −.664* |
| Catholic | .764*** | .056 | −.094 | .304 | −.107 |
| Evangelical | −.019 | −.392ᵃ | −.587* | −.170 | −.130 |
| Independent | −.347ᵃ | −1.940*** | −1.228*** | −1.490*** | −.234 |
| Republican | −.584** | −2.096*** | −2.732*** | −2.113*** | −.463ᵃ |
| Moderate | .427* | −1.047*** | −.917*** | −1.040*** | −.126 |
| Conservative | −.221 | −1.779*** | −2.212*** | −2.213*** | −.889*** |
| Tea Party | −.336ᵃ | −1.069*** | −.333 | −.761*** | −1.279*** |
| Constant | −1.350 | 1.609 | .975 | 1.596 | −.930 |
| Cox & Snell $R^2$ | .15 | .42 | .36 | .37 | .20 |
| % correctly predicted | 67.5 | 82.5 | 80.7 | 79.5 | 73.4 |
| N | 838 | 838 | 838 | 838 | 718 |

*Note:* Entries are logit coefficients. References categories are: White; no kids; married; Democrats; liberals. Dependent variables are proportion of respondents approving of the Supreme Court's job (compared to disapprove or don't know); approving of President Obama's job performance; approving of the Affordable Care Act (vs. disapproving or DK); thinking that the Supreme Court's ACA ruling was a "good thing" (vs. a bad thing, both good and bad, and DK); and thinking that the Court's ACA ruling was based on legal analysis (vs. personal or political views).

ᵃ $p < .10$; * $p < .05$; ** $p < .01$; *** $p < .001$.

*Source:* New York Times/CBS News Poll, July 11–16, 2012.

*Table 5.* **Pre- and Post-ruling Supreme Court and ACA Attitudes: Multivariate Analysis**

| | Supreme Ct. job approval | | ACA approval | |
|---|---|---|---|---|
| | *May* (1) | *July* (2) | *May* (3) | *July* (4) |
| Education | .105 | .255*** | .419*** | .175# |
| Income | −.041 | .135* | .027 | .060 |
| Age | −.016* | −.002 | .000 | .011 |
| Female | −.182 | −.301# | −.237 | −.406* |
| Black | −.096 | 1.053*** | .201 | 1.035*** |
| Hispanic | .452 | .054 | −1.245** | 1.463*** |
| Asian | −.480 | .247 | .889 | −.695 |
| Kids 18 and under | −.278 | −.068 | −.129 | −.776*** |
| Kids over 18 | .264 | −.221 | .011 | −.771*** |
| Sep/div/widowed | .281 | −.050 | .325 | .025 |
| Never married | .004 | .521# | .551# | −.065 |
| Catholic | −.199 | .764*** | −.009 | −.094 |
| Evangelical | −.211 | −.019 | .066 | −.587* |
| Independent | −.339 | −.347# | −1.257*** | −1.228*** |
| Republican | −.327 | −.584** | −3.315*** | −2.732*** |
| Moderate | .680** | .427* | −1.209*** | −.917*** |
| Conservative | .359 | −.221 | −1.122*** | −2.212*** |
| Tea Party | .279 | − .336# | −.779** | −.333 |
| Constant | .786 | −1.350 | .467 | .975 |
| Cox & Snell R2 | .05 | .15 | .34 | .36 |
| % correctly predicted | 60.5 | 67.5 | 74.3 | 80.7 |
| N | 619 | 838 | 664 | 838 |

*Note:* Entries are logit coefficients. References categories are white; no kids; married; Democrats; liberals. Dependent variables are proportion of respondents approving of the Supreme Court's job (compared to disapprove or don't know) and approving of the Affordable Care Act (vs. disapproving or DK).

# $p < .10$; * $p < .05$; ** $p < .01$; *** $p < .001$.

*Source:* New York Times / CBS News Polls, May 31–June 3, 2012 and July 11–16, 2012.

that after the ACA ruling was issued, education became a stronger predictor of Supreme Court job approval, which might make sense given that educated people were probably more likely to receive the positive signals from elites and the mass media regarding the news of the decision. Similarly, blacks and Catholics were more approving of the Court's job performance after the law, whereas there were no statistically significant differences among racial or religious groups in the predecision poll. Most notably perhaps, while there were no partisan differences in Supreme Court job approval before the ACA ruling, after it was issued Republicans were less approving of the Court than were Democrats.

The Court's ruling also had some modest effects on the structure of ACA approval. The ruling did little to change the basic effect of the political variables: Republicans and independents were much less supportive of the law than Democrats both before and after the ruling; similarly conservatives and moderates were much less supportive than liberals. A number of demographic correlates became statistically significant after the ruling, although in some cases the changes are difficult to interpret.

## 4. Conclusions

Available public opinion data suggest that the Court's ruling upholding much of the Affordable Care Act had a small, positive, short-term effect on public support for the law, but a mildly negative effect on public approval of the Court itself. Support for the ACA increased by ten or eleven points among a number of groups, including blacks, moderates, the never married, those under thirty or over sixty-five, the less educated, and those with incomes between $30,000 and $50,000, while approval of the Court fell the most among Republicans, conservatives, and Tea Party supporters.

In the immediate aftermath of the ACA ruling, opinion continued to polarize. Already divided by opinion gaps of fifty to sixty points on the health care reform, Democrats became even more supportive of the ACA, while already low Republican support may even have declined slightly. By November 2012, after the presidential election, favorability of the ACA appeared to rise among all partisan groupings, but in February 2013, the substantial gap between Democrats and Republicans narrowed as favorable attitudes toward the ACA appeared to fall significantly among Democrats.

Partisans also viewed the basis for the Court's decision differently, with Republicans much more likely than Democrats to say that the justices had made their decision on personal or political grounds rather than on a legal basis. The ruling seemed to sour Republicans on the Court, as their job approval rating of the Court was statistically the same as Democrats' before the ACA ruling, but more negative afterwards. Thus, the Court's upholding of much of the ACA may have increased popular support for the law, although the significant fluctuations in opinion since the decision suggest other political factors and events may have "taken over" soon after the Court released its decision. The decision's short-term effect for public attitudes toward the Court, however, was to project the partisan polarization in public attitudes that characterizes contemporary American politics. As the decision recedes further into the past, we should continue to see other forces, events, and decisions subsume the *Health Care Case* in importance in determining attitudes toward the Court. Indeed, as the presidential campaign entered its final month, it appeared that the Court had rebounded slightly in aggregate approval, even if the partisan divide in support begun by the *Health Care Case* still remained.

These results suggest that *NFIB v. Sebelius* may be in a public opinion class by itself among Supreme Court decisions. Never before, to our knowledge, has the Court's upholding of a federal law led to increased favorability of the law, yet polarization and lower approval toward the Court even in the short term. Indeed, even with the small effects noted, this case of judicial restraint may exist as a rare case of short-term judicial legitimation, but one that was accompanied by polarization in attitudes toward the Court. Such a result may have been inevitable, given the salience of the case and polarization in attitudes regarding the underlying issue before the Court. However the Court ruled on the constitutional challenge to the ACA, the winners and their supporters in the mass public would have rejoiced and the losers would have felt aggrieved. For the most part, concerns about backlash and polarization due to a constitutional decision arise when the Court shuts off democratic debate, for instance when it strikes down restrictions on abortions, same-sex marriage, or even campaign spending. The *Health Care Case* suggests that when all politics is perceived as a zero-sum game, even judicial affirmation of a result reached by the political branches can further split the public both on its attitudes toward the Court and the issues the Court decides.

# Notes

1. See James L. Gibson, Gregory A. Caldeira, & Lester Kenyatta Spence, *The Supreme Court and the U.S. Presidential Election of 2000: Wounds, Self-inflicted or Otherwise?* 33 BRIT. J. POL. SCI. 535 (2003).
2. *Id.*
3. This public opinion dynamic is similar to that observed by John Zaller, among others. See JOHN ZALLER, THE NATURE AND ORIGIN OF MASS OPINION (1992).
4. 531 U.S. 98 (2000).
5. 545 U.S. 469 (2005).
6. 558 U.S. 310 (2010).
7. 539 U.S. 558 (2003).
8. 539 U.S. 306 (2003).
9. See Nathaniel Persily, *Introduction, in* PUBLIC OPINION AND CONSTITUTIONAL CONTROVERSY (Nathaniel Persily, Jack Citrin, & Patrick Egan eds., 2008). The book

describes public opinion trends concerning most of the cases discussed herein, such as those concerning desegregation, abortion, gay rights, government takings of private property, school prayer, criminal rights, and the 2000 election controversy.

10. See Robert Dahl, *Decision Making in a Democracy: The Supreme Court as a National Policy Maker*, 6 J. Pub. L. 279 (1957); David Adamany, *Legitimacy, Realigning Elections, and the Supreme Court*, 3 Wisc. L. Rev. 790 (1973).

11. See Thomas Marshall, *The Supreme Court as an Opinion Leader*, 15 Am. Pol. Q. 147 (1987).

12. 408 U.S. 238 (1972).

13. 428 U.S. 153 (1976).

14. 410 U.S. 113 (1973).

15. See Charles H. Franklin & Liane C. Kosacki, *Republican Schoolmaster: The U.S. Supreme Court, Public Opinion and Abortion*, 83 Am. Pol. Sci. Rev. 751 (1989).

16. 347 U.S. 483 (1954).

17. 384 U.S. 436 (1966).

18. Robert J. Blendon & John M. Benson, *Public Opinion at the Time of the Vote on Health Care Reform*, 362 New Eng. J. Med. e55 (2010); Mollyann Brodie, Drew Altman, Claudia Deane, Sasha Busche, & Elizabeth Hamel, *Liking the Pieces, Not the Package: Contradictions in Public Opinion During Health Reform*, 29 Health Affairs 1125–1130 (2010).

19. Note that several authors have also found racial attitudes to be important in the structure of Obama health care reform attitudes. See Michael Henderson & D. Sunshine Hillygus, *The Dynamics of Health Care Opinion, 2008–2010: Partisanship, Self-Interest, and Racial Resentment*, 36 J. Health Pol. Pol'y & L. 945 (2011); Michael Tesler, *The Spillover of Racialization in Health Care: How President Obama Polarized Public Opinion by Racial Attitudes and Race*, 56 Am. J. Pol. Sci. 690 (2012). We lack measures of racial attitudes in the polls analyzed here.

20. Pew Research Center, Division, Uncertainty over Court's Health Care Ruling: Top One-Word Reactions—"Disappointed," "Surprised" (July 2012), http://www.people-press.org/2012/07/02/division-uncertainty-over-courts-health-care-ruling/.

21. Katerina Linos & Kim Twist, Citizen Responses to the Supreme Court's Health Care and Immigration Rulings: Comparing Experimental and Observational Methods (2012) (unpublished).

22. See Jeffrey Toobin, The Oath: The Obama White House and the Supreme Court (2012).

# CHAPTER 16

# Federalism from Federal Statutes

HEALTH REFORM, MEDICAID, AND
THE OLD-FASHIONED FEDERALISTS' GAMBLE

*Abbe R. Gluck*

How can the states retain relevance in an era of federal statutory law? The persistence of the states and our enduring attachment to "federalism" in an increasingly national and global regulatory environment have occupied the minds of many scholars. For the most part, however, the U.S. Supreme Court, because of its role as the final expositor of constitutional meaning, has been viewed as the primary arbiter of what federalism is and what is required to protect it. Less often explored has been *Congress's* role in giving meaning to federalism in the modern administrative state. Specifically, the possibility to which this chapter wishes to draw attention is that federal *statutes* may now be the primary way in which state power is created and protected. To be clear, the claim is not about federal statutes that are modest in ambition and leave most areas exclusively to state regulation. Rather, the claim is about major federal statutes that, even as they extend federal power, entrust to the states much of their implementation and elaboration.

The 2010 health reform legislation—The Patient Protection and Affordable Care Act (ACA)—is the most prominent recent example of such a statute. And the Supreme Court's 2012 decision about the constitutionality of that statute revealed that the Court emphatically disagrees with this chapter's claim. But federalism proponents may be doing their own cause a disservice with their reluctance to see federalism in federal statutes.

Congress seems to have taken a different view. Since the New Deal, Congress repeatedly has invited the states to be the frontline implementers of its new federal laws—federal-statutory design decisions that are often described by legislators as respectful of "federalism," even as the new national legislation displaces traditional state dominance over a particular area of policy. Health reform, for example, invited the states to serve as central policymakers and implementers in key areas of the statute, including its expansion of Medicaid and its lishment of insurance exchanges (the law's new "one-stop shopping" portal insurance purchase).

The Court, however, as well as some other self-identified state-power proponents, appears to believe that state power is undermined, not advanced, when Congress invites states into federal statutes in this manner. But from a federalism-protective perspective, the Court's position may well have the reverse of its intended effect. Insisting on separation is unlikely to stop Congress from legislating altogether. At most, it will encourage Congress to legislate without state partners—a course of action that is likely to increase, not decrease, national power.

The issue that brought these matters to the fore in health reform was the ACA's proposed Medicaid expansion. Medicaid is a half-century-old federal program that is jointly administered by states and the federal government, and has been incrementally expanded since its inception. Medicaid's paradigmatic "cooperative federalism" and its slow course of development are the direct result of policymakers' continued efforts to bring the federal government into an area dominated by the states while still respecting "federalism." But, in the health reform litigation, the Court held that Congress's most recent expansion of Medicaid went too far, and implied that Congress loses some power over how it may expand federal programs once it invites states to participate. In the name of federalism, seven justices held that states were free effectively to reject the amendments to the Medicaid statute that Congress had passed and the President had signed.

The Court's decision, however, relied on a vision of federalism that has been on the decline at least since the New Deal. The Court insisted that federalism and its benefits—including local control and the ability of states to check federal power—are best effectuated by state separation from federal law, rather than state participation in it. That vision depends on what no longer exists: significant areas of regulation that are reserved to the states and into which federal lawmaking may not tread. Today, the states' relevance on the national policymaking level comes mostly from *Congress's discretion*, not from the states' exclusive control over policy as a matter of (judicially monopolized) boundary-emphasizing constitutional law. Congress may design federal statutes that retain central roles for states, or Congress may design federal statutes that displace the state function entirely.

Health reform exemplifies this modern state of affairs. In designing the statute, Congress followed its typical legislative path—one of incremental federal lawmaking over a historical backdrop of state control—a path that, as in the case of numerous social programs enacted over the past century, produced a new federal statute that took some power from the states with one hand and gave the states new (federal-law-granted) power with the other. The Court interpreted these moves as fundamentally antifederalist. But would federalism really have been better served had Congress pushed the states to the periphery?

Since the decision, moreover, some state-power proponents have taken similar positions to the Court's with respect to other aspects of the statute. Specifically, the majority of Republican-controlled states have rejected Congress's offer to let the states, rather than the federal government, run the Act's new health insurance exchanges. Their effort, like the Court's, is to fight a battle already lost; that is, to try to derail the progress of this federal lawmaking altogether. But the Court *upheld* the constitutionality of the rest of the health reform statute, including the exchange provisions. The states' decision not to participate thus opens the door to a wholesale federal takeover of health-insurance regulation in those same states that opposed the federal law in the first place. What's more, that opening may pave the way for additional federal encroachment that might not otherwise occur if states implemented the Act themselves.

The gamble is a big one. Unlike the health-reform question that received far more public attention but is unlikely to arise again—Congress's authority to enact an insurance-purchase mandate using its commerce power[1]—the question at issue in the Medicaid expansion is certain to recur and to affect how Congress legislates. Nearly every major federal program in this country relies at least in part on the kind of state-led implementation that the Court's decision attempted to deter. The Court's opinion injected significant uncertainty into those cooperative federalism schemes and, ironically, may have given Congress an incentive to legislate in a more nationalist fashion going forward.

This is not to say that Congress's efforts to include the states always effectuate federalist, as opposed to nationalist, goals, or that it is easy to tell which federal-statutory moves are state protective. Different states might take divergent views of different statutes, and, of course, not everyone will agree that state-protective policy solutions are normatively ideal for every policy problem. Nor is it to say that Congress must not do a better job in making clear how much power it intends to delegate to the states relative to federal agencies or other implementers when it offers them roles in federal administration. The point, rather, is that these federal-statutory-implementation relationships are the critical federalism relationships of the statutory era. The real work to be done is not in eliminating these partnerships altogether, but in recognizing Congress's centrality in creating them and the need for legal rules to govern their successful operation.

## 1. The Stakes

Health reform offered both Congress and the Supreme Court the opportunity to address the modern conundrum of the states' place in a legal world dominated by federal statutes. Congress did so as a matter of health policy, the Court did so as a matter of constitutional law. Neither did so with particular clarity.

## A. HEALTH POLICY

Federalism has been the subject of robust debate in the health policy context for decades. The question in the policy context typically has been framed as a functional one; that is, which level of government, state or federal, is best situated to oversee health care regulation and finance? Proponents of state regulation have emphasized the benefits of local variation and the expertise of local health administrators in arguing for state control. On the other side, nationalists emphasize that local regulation does not work given the countercyclical nature of programs like Medicaid: expenses for assistance programs increase during difficult economic times when governments (especially states with balanced-budget requirements) have less revenue to cover them. Nationalists also argue that state-level health reform is impossible given the national market for health care: providers and insurers will simply leave aggressive states if other states have fewer restrictions.[2]

Congress essentially punted the answer to this health-policy question when it enacted the ACA. The statute is a paradigm of the kind of structural schizophrenia that results from incremental federal lawmaking—over terrain historically controlled by the states—by a Congress sensitive to undercutting federalism. The ACA offers few answers to the functional question of where health administration should be located. Instead, as detailed below, the statute doles out authority among, alternatively, the federal government alone, the states alone, the state and federal governments together, and private actors.

Of course, depending on the policy question at hand, such a varied structural approach is not always undesirable. In the context of health reform, however, the pre-ACA landscape of regulatory structural fragmentation had been much lamented,[3] and Congress disappointed the many health policy experts who had hoped that the ACA would address the field's structural issues head-on. Congress did not, for example, address why, as a matter of good policy, the nation's health insurance program for the elderly (Medicare) is run by the federal government, while the nation's health insurance program for the poor (Medicaid) is run jointly with the states. Instead, the structure of the ACA (which extended both programs) was the product of what might be called authority-allocating, federalism-inspired, path dependence: Congress gave the states a lead role in the new federal statute in those same areas in which states had previously exerted primary authority, namely, Medicaid and insurance regulation.

## B. LAW

On the legal side, this question of the modern state-federal relationship has been framed differently, as one of constitutional structure; namely, whether the

Constitution's protections of state sovereignty limit the way in which the federal government uses (or does not use) the states in administering federal legislation. But here is a more provocative way to ask the same question and one that makes clearer the stakes of the answer: what is the continuing relevance of "federalism" *at all* in an era in which our most important laws come from federal legislation that Congress has the power to enact without any role for the states in the first place?

"Constitutional" federalism is typically a federalism defined by the allocation of powers in our founding document and one that has been understood by many to prescribe separate spheres of state and federal responsibility. But, as many scholars have noted, that brand of federalism is increasingly irrelevant. The New Deal brought the federal government squarely into most areas of traditional state regulation, including the world of social policy, and today, if statutes are crafted properly, there are few areas into which the federal government may not go. As such, the apposite question is not how federalism should protect what are now mostly nonexistent areas of exclusive state authority. Rather, the apposite question is whether there might be a new type of federalism—which might be called *intrastatutory* federalism—that functions *within* the world of federal statute making. Is there a federalism in which state power comes from federal statutes—from Congress's decision to design federal laws that rely on state administration—rather than a federalism in which state power derives from its separation from federal law?

In the health reform case, seven justices refused to acknowledge the possibility of this modern expression of our foundational state-federal relationship. The joint dissent (for Justices Scalia, Kennedy, Thomas, and Alito) expressly disputed the proposition that Congress's decision to allow "state employees to implement a federal program is more respectful of federalism than using federal workers alone," and asserted that "[t]his argument reflects a view of federalism that our cases have rejected."[4] The Chief Justice's opinion, like the joint dissent, extolled the "independent power of the states ... as a check on the power of the Federal Government."[5]

Both opinions read as homages to federalism. But the federalism that the Court embraced was federalism in its bygone, separate-spheres form. The structural choice for Congress in health reform was not, as the Court would have it, "federal legislation versus state legislation?" Rather, the structural question was "federal legislation administered by *whom*?"

Congress answered that question in health reform by including the states as key partners in the implementation of several parts of the statute, including in its Medicaid expansion. Congress did not need to do this, as all nine justices acknowledged: the federal government unquestionably had the constitutional power to implement the Medicaid expansion all by itself. But the Court viewed

Congress's attempt to expand Medicaid in its joint state-federal form as an encroachment on federalism. Specifically, Congress conditioned continued state involvement in Medicaid on a state's acquiescence to Congress's new amendments to the program. The Court viewed this as a coercive trap that violated state sovereignty: given Medicaid's centrality in every state, the Court opined, states had little choice but to go along with Congress's amendments.

I have previously written about the way in which state implementation of national law may, indeed, sometimes be a tool of national encroachment.[6] But one also must consider the alternative, and that is the point of this chapter: in a world of near limitless federal power to spend money for social welfare,[7] and given Congress's proven tendency to legislate incrementally—that is, *through a series of amendments over time*—what good does the Court's opinion do the states, or the cause of federalism? Now that the Court has limited Congress's flexibility to legislate incrementally when it utilizes state partners, perhaps Congress will think twice before including the states at all the next time.

The Court did not acknowledge this possibility, or the possibility that state administration of federal law might sometimes empower, rather than undermine, state players. Instead, the Court may have assumed that erecting barriers to state implementation of federal law would stop Congress from enacting major federal legislation altogether. This is a dubious assumption at best. Every modern president, from President Nixon and the Clean Air Act, to the second President Bush and No Child Left Behind, to President Obama and the ACA, has passed major federal legislation. The New Deal tide will not so easily be turned back.

## 2. Intrastatutory Federalism as the Federalism of the Modern Era

In legal circles, only a handful of commentators have even acknowledged the possibility that federal statutes, in general, might be a source of constitutional interpretation and change.[8] Even among that number, matters of federal statutory design are rarely described as federalism-constituting. Still rarer—because it is so antithetical to the state autonomy typically associated with federalism—is a lawyer's understanding of federalism as a relationship that comes by the *grace of Congress.*

But most major policy initiatives since the New Deal seem to have recognized this possibility. From the early family and old-age assistance laws, to the environmental statutes of the 1970s, to the health reform legislation of 2010, Congress has invoked federalism in giving states the option of serving as the frontline implementers of the most important federal programs. Moreover, Congress often gives states flexibility to do this federal work; for example, by establishing federal floors above which states may innovate or by allowing states to apply for waivers from federal requirements so that they can experiment with ways to accomplish the federal law's goals. In turn, the states have constructed local administrative bureaucracies to implement federal policy and, concomitantly, have become ever more expert in the areas entrusted to their administration. In this fashion, Congress has allowed the states to remain important players in the current policymaking world.[9]

## A. MOTIVATIONS

There are many good and varied reasons why Congress relies on the states to implement federal law.[10] Some of these reasons are pragmatic: the federal government does not have sufficient personnel to administer its programs, and state administrators often are more expert. Some reasons are functional: certain programs may benefit from regional variation (water policy, for example, may look different in the Northeast and the Southwest); or Congress may wish to incentivize state-level experimentation in federal policy administration to generate data for future national policy decisions.

Other motivations may be instrumental. State administration of new federal programs may make federal legislative expansions more politically palatable for those who prefer (at least the appearance of) "small" government. Running controversial federal programs through the states also may diffuse federal accountability. Sometimes, these moves are "nationalist" in nature: a use of the states to increase federal power in a below-the-radar fashion. Other times (or perhaps simultaneously), they may be an effort to effectuate values that we normally associate with "federalism," even as Congress steps in to regulate. For example, a federal law that relies on state implementation might be a way of expressing a preference for experimentation or local control, or respect for areas of traditional state expertise.

The point is not that Congress's reliance on state administration is always "ideal" from state-power perspective or that there is a single model to evaluate. Some statutes delegate power equally to all implementing states; others give certain states leadership roles developing national policy. Some statutes give states much policymaking discretion, while others use states to administer what are essentially uniform national programs. In the ACA alone, we see this type of dizzying variety.[11] The point is that congressional reliance on state implementation is ubiquitous and complex, and that legal doctrine currently offers no tools that assist in evaluating its many forms. The point is also that state implementation, at least some of the time, can offer states a voice in national policymaking.

## B. PERCEPTIONS

Some may contest that this is "federalism" at all. Protesters may offer "decentralization" as a preferred label,[12] precisely because the state presence comes at Congress's pleasure. But more is going on here than the managerial allocation of responsibility. In fact, it seems unmistakable that federalism norms are being expressed in at least some of these statutes.

Consider, as an example, an aspect of the health reform legislation not at issue in the Supreme Court case: the question whether to centralize administration of the law's newly created insurance exchanges (the one-stop-shopping platforms for insurance) in the federal government or whether to give the states the right of first refusal to exercise control over their administration. This was the key question that divided the House and Senate versions of the legislation, with the Senate invoking "federalism" values to insist on the state-leadership default preference that ultimately carried the day. But make note: this federalism was to come in the form of state administration of *federal* law—not in the exclusion of the federal government from the field.

And let's be clear. As a matter of constitutional law, most people agree that the federal government could implement programs like the environmental statutes or health reform all by itself. In the health reform case, what divided the Court was not whether Congress had the constitutional power to expand access to government-provided health insurance but rather *how* Congress did it.

Perhaps the Court would have reached a different answer had it thought about the question in terms of that choice. Consider again, in this light, the health insurance exchanges. As a result of the triumph of the state-led version of those exchanges, individuals and small businesses in those states that accept Congress's invitation to run the exchanges will continue to purchase health insurance through state-governed channels, a result that, at least on the surface, appears consistent with the traditional presumption (itself legislatively established through Congress's discretion in the McCarran-Ferguson Act of 1945) that health-insurance regulation is an area of state control. As a matter of formal constitutional doctrine, of course, an exchange run by the federal government would be no different: federal law—the ACA—will regulate the exchanges no matter who runs them. But as a matter of how individual Americans will experience this regulation, it will be on the local level. And as a matter of what level of government is setting much of the relevant policy, it is *still the states*, precisely because Congress—even though it didn't have to—built state-implementation flexibility into the statute. The same point can be made about the difference between expanding access to health insurance through Medicaid, which puts states at the forefront, as opposed to through Medicare, which doesn't.

The Chief Justice himself began his opinion by writing that traditional feder-alism assures that "the facets of governing that touch on citizens daily lives are normally administered by smaller governments closer to the governed."[13] The Court seemed too quick, however, to conclude that erecting barriers to state implementation of federal law would serve that goal. Fifteen years earlier, in another highly contested case about state administration of federal law, *Printz v. United States*,[14] the dissenting justices (including Justice Breyer, who joined the Chief Justice in the ACA's Medicaid ruling) put the question more realistically. "Why, or how," the dissent asked, "would what the majority sees as a consti-tutional alternative—the creation of a new federal ... law bureaucracy, or the expansion of an existing federal bureaucracy—better promote either state sover-eignty or individual liberty?"[15] The *Printz* dissenters also might have asked how it would better promote administration of law by those governments closest to the people.

It remains a subject for debate whether the kinds of "everyday" experiences with state administration that the state exchanges and Medicaid will offer are federalism in the "constitutional" sense. But it is not clear that the labels really matter.[16] One can argue that the prevalence of these kinds of arrangements has shaped and changed what federalism means as a matter of "constitutional law," or one can argue alternatively that, if constitutional federalism is only about fed-eralism in the sense of autonomy, then that brand of federalism is increasingly irrelevant. But the potential irrelevance of constitutional federalism in its nar-rowest sense does not mean that something often very state-centered has not replaced it.

## 3. The ACA's Tapestry of Federalism

Of course, the reason that the Supreme Court had occasion to address the intra-statutory federalism question at all is because of how the ACA was designed. For the past century, two overarching questions have dominated the health-policy discourse. The first question is that of the health care system's basic normative framework: whether we should have a system that rests on "personal responsi-bility" (every man for himself) or, instead, whether a "solidarity" model (one that emphasizes "mutual aid and support") should govern.[17] The second ques-tion is the structural one that this chapter already has introduced, and asks which level of government, state or federal (or perhaps not government at all), should be responsible for ensuring access to health care for those deemed entitled to receive it.

Congress tackled both questions when it passed the ACA. Or, more accu-rately, it tried to answer the first and declined to answer the second. The ACA offers the strongest federal legislative position thus far on the personal responsibility-versus-solidarity debate. The statute's primary goal is universal access to health care—that is, solidarity—which it accomplishes by making health insurance available to as many Americans as possible.[18] The Medicaid expansion at issue in the litigation was one part of that effort, along with others, including amendments to Medicare, the establishment of the health insurance exchanges, the provision of subsidies for the purchase of insurance, and the imposition of new requirements on insurers to make insurance more accessible. To make the reforms economically viable for insurers, the law expands the pool of insured citizens, requiring almost all individuals to have insurance (or be covered through one of the federal assistance programs), a requirement colloquially referred to as the "individual mandate."

But Congress essentially punted the second, structural, health-policy question. The ACA is a Solomonic and mostly unsatisfying response to the functional question of whether the federal government or the states are best situated to oversee health care, or even to the preliminary question of whether government (any government) should be involved in health care in the first place.

Instead, the ACA offers something for everyone, and does not justify as a functional matter why it divides the world the way it does. The statute includes all of the following structural models: a federal-only model in the statute's Medicare reforms; a cooperative-federalism model in the statute's Medicaid expansion and health insurance exchange provisions; a new "hybrid" federalism model, created in the ACA's implementing regulations, that allows states to take the lead but allows the federal government to perform certain tasks that benefit from centralization or economies of scale across groups of states; and a state-only model that expressly leaves certain functions entirely in state hands. The statute also includes a private-market model in its reliance on employer-provided, private insurance as the default system. (Indeed, the fact that the statute calls the insurance-purchase mandate a "personal responsibility" requirement is likely no coincidence; the label, and the maintenance of the private insurance system, appear to be nods toward those who would prefer a private-market, anti-solidarity model altogether.)

The Court's opinion was essentially a reflection on these two health-policy questions, reframed in legal terms. With respect to the first question, Chief Justice Roberts's opinion and the joint dissent, in discussing both the mandate and the Medicaid expansion, each evinced profound discomfort with Congress's policy preference for the solidarity model, and each repeatedly blanched at the notion of the healthy subsidizing the sick. The link between that normative discomfort and the constitutional-law holdings in the opinions is a fascinating subject, but one beyond the scope of this chapter. The remainder of the chapter focuses on the second, structural question: namely, the ACA's use of intrastatutory federalism and the Court's reaction to it.

## A. THE LINK BETWEEN FEDERALISM AND FEDERAL POLICY INCREMENTALISM

What explains the ACA's structural schizophrenia? It does not appear that any health policy expert has claimed that it was the result of a considered policy decision. Instead, the statute's something-for-everyone approach seems to have been the result of politics (getting to the right number of votes) and path dependence. Specifically, the road to the ACA's structural fragmentation was typical of the *incremental* way that Congress legislates. The Court did not seem to understand this, or at least did not acknowledge it. Nor did the Court recognize that such incrementalism tends to favor the development of federal statutes that include central, albeit sometimes fragmented, roles for the states.

### i. Incrementalism and State Entrenchment

Political scientists have consistently demonstrated that Congress legislates in piecemeal fashion.[19] There are many reasons for the persistence of such policy incrementalism, including the numerous barriers to lawmaking of any sort in Congress and the difficulty of attaining consensus in a polity as diverse as ours. Of particular relevance here, there also is an explicit link between Congress's tendency toward policy incrementalism and the design of federal statutes that rely on state administration. This is largely because what often precedes our incremental federal legislation, especially in the social policy arena, is decades of lawmaking, expertise-building, and institution-entrenching by the states that previously occupied the field.

The historical backdrop of state social policy regulation creates both political and pragmatic incentives for Congress to rely on, rather than to displace, entrenched state administrative apparatus. As a political matter, the same federalism-like concerns about big government and respect for traditional areas of state authority often are cited to support state administration of federal law. Pragmatically, in addition to the lack of sufficient federal personnel, earlier-established state bureaucracies provide ready experts to implement new federal legislation should the states wish to participate. (Since the Court held in *Printz*[20] that Congress cannot commandeer state executive authority, Congress has given the states the choice to administer new federal programs or to "opt out.")

The result can be a policy scheme that is structurally fragmented in multiple ways. The new federal program, like the ACA, may have some aspects designed to be implemented by the states and other aspects designed to be implemented by the federal government. Even with respect to those aspects designed to be implemented by the states, states sometimes opt out, in which case the federal government must step in to operate the program in some states but not in others. The new federal program also rarely occupies the entire field, and so substantial regulatory power often remains, as it historically had been, under exclusive state control.

The 1965 legislation that gave birth to Medicare and Medicaid offers a quintessential example of this type of federal policy development. The health-policy backdrop to the Social Security Act of 1965 was essentially a system of limited charity care provided by the states and localities to the "deserving poor." Conservative Republicans and southern Democrats, both concerned about federal-government aggrandizement, opposed further expansion of the federal government into health care. As a result, during the federal legislative process, nonsouthern Democrats focused on incremental expansion, targeting their efforts at a particularly sympathetic population (the elderly) as beneficiaries of the new federal health insurance program.

The resulting compromise has been described as a "layer cake,"[21] a metaphor that captures its inclusion of, among other things, both federal-led and state-led insurance models. The decision to lodge what became Medicaid in the states was partially the result of the kind of path dependence described above: even though the new program was a federal program, it was *state*-run, and as such was viewed as a mere extension of prior state charity-care efforts, rather than a major reform of them.[22] But making Medicaid state administered was also an effort to prevent further federal encroachment: federalism proponents wished to "put a fence around Medicare,"[23] treating that program as an exceptional federal venture into the health care arena and maintaining state control as the norm. This deserves emphasis: Designing a federal law so that it could be implemented by the states was seen as *protective of federalism*. Completing the fragmentation, the statute left large swaths of regulation entirely in state hands, including the regulation of the private insurance industry.[24]

The same story can be told outside the health care arena. Indeed, one is hard-pressed to come up with any examples of major social policy legislation in which Congress wiped the slate clean of all preexisting state structures and enacted comprehensive, federal-only reform in a single legislative effort. From the near half-century transformation of the state-administered federal food-stamp program—incremental change that occurred through a series of federally authorized state experiments ("demonstration projects") and congressional amendments;[25] to the enactment of the Supplemental Security Income Program as an effort to standardize the state-led Old-Age Assistance and Aid to the Blind programs; to the early federal efforts to fund state environmental efforts that eventually led to the Clean Air and Clean Water Acts;[26] to the 1935 Social Security Act's evolution from an effort to replace state old-age pension programs to its expanded form today,[27] this is the common arc of modern federal policy development.

Moreover, there is a cycle here, one in which state-based federal policy incrementalism continues to perpetuate itself. With each new federal program that relies on state implementation, state administrative bureaucracies are further expanded and become more expert. This, in turn, makes their continuing utilization by the federal government more likely.

The ACA is no exception. Despite the Court's emphasis on the statute's length and scope, the ACA's main components are drawn from preexisting programs (which themselves were the product of an incremental legislative approach). The ACA expands Medicare, Medicaid, and the private insurance system, rather than putting in place the more coherent structure one would expect (and many had hoped for) had Congress been draft from scratch. In so doing, Congress perpetuated, rather than dismantled, the entrenched and fragmented structure of health administration and continued to rely heavily on state bureaucracies.

In this sense, the incremental way in which Congress legislates reinforces the centrality of state administration. Interestingly, the Chief Justice himself recognized this state-entrenchment point in his opinion, noting that "the States have developed intricate statutory and administrative regimes over the course of many decades to implement their objectives under existing Medicaid."[28] But the Chief Justice viewed that pattern as evidence only that states may become trapped in federal programs, rather than also as a potential tool through which states may preserve their centrality in and leverage over future federal legislation.

## ii. Incrementalism and State Experimentation

Federal policy incrementalism also finds its expression in policy *experimentalism*, and this is another way in which the states remain relevant to the development of federal statutory law. The notion that Congress lacks competence to address the complex social problems on its plate is commonplace, as is the notion that this complexity leads Congress to rely on expert federal agencies rather than draft detailed legislative solutions. Less often acknowledged, however, is the way in which intrastatutory federalism serves a similar purpose. Part of what motivates legislative incrementalism is a lack of information about the "best" policy answer,[29] and a related desire to test policies before expanding upon them. State administration of federal law—a modern-era twist on the historical concept of the "states as laboratories"[30]—can allow for more policy experimentation than federal administration alone.

The health reform statute, for instance, appears to have more pilot projects written into the law than any statute in history. These pilot projects are directed at policy questions for which Congress had no definitive answers (such as how to reduce costs without sacrificing quality of care). The ACA also evinces an explicit preference for *state* policy experimentation within the confines of the new federal law. Like countless other cooperative federalism programs, the ACA encourages states to experiment with how they choose to implement the new federal statute. In the context of the ACA's insurance-exchange provisions alone, the statute mentions "state flexibility" six times[31] and explicitly contemplates that the exchanges will look different across the states. Like No Child Left Behind, Medicaid, the Clean Air Act, and many other federal programs, the ACA also has a waiver provision that permits states, with permission, to substitute their own programs to accomplish the federal statute's goal.

As students of federalism well know, the states' role as "laboratories" of experimentation is one of the most frequently touted benefits of state sovereignty.[32] But this mode of experimentation increasingly does not come from sovereignty-emphasizing federalism. In recent years, scholars have noted that states do not conduct experiments at the levels thought ideal by policymakers when states are left to their own devices.[33] The dearth of state-led policy experimentation is due to, among other things, the disincentives for a single state to bear all the costs of innovation and the risk that businesses will leave a state if it is regulating in a more costly manner than others. Federal laws that allow for state experimentation provide an answer to this problem, and, ironically, such federal laws thereby help "federalism" realize its potential. Indeed, some of the most important state policy experiments of the modern era have been conducted in the course of state administration of *federal* law.

There is a long history of federal law developing in reaction to and in dialogue with these state-led federal-policy experiments. In the environmental context, for instance, satisfactory levels of state innovation in the area of air-pollution control did not occur organically, even with the promise of federal funds, until Congress passed the major environmental statutes of the 1970s, which effectively required the states to take the lead or have their air-quality laws preempted by federal statute. And in the Medicaid context, it was the states that first took advantage of that program's flexibility to expand the benefits-eligible population beyond the federal statute's initial target of children and their mothers. These state experiments, supported and incentivized by the federal government, formed the basis of Medicaid's later, national expansions to cover those same populations.

So, too, the philosophy behind the ACA's own Medicaid expansion, that is, eligibility based on an income threshold rather than demographic categories, was first pioneered as a Medicaid state option by a few aggressive states. The Massachusetts health reform law—the law on which much of the ACA was based—was itself made possible by a Medicaid waiver granted by the Bush administration.[34] All of these are examples of experimentalism that derives from intrastatutory federalism, not from federalism in its traditional form.

## 4. The Court's Old-Fashioned Federalism

The way in which federal policy incrementalism perpetuates a central role for the states has obvious salience for the Court's holding in the health reform case. A majority of justices have now erected a barrier to that kind of legislative incrementalism—a barrier that may undermine the very state authority that the Court sought to advance. Seven justices took the position that Congress does not have control over the amendment of its own federal programs when the states are its chosen administrative partners. Instead, the Court held that those state partners are sometimes entitled to reject the statutory amendment and still remain part of the pre-amendment version of the program. Applied to the ACA, the decision means that states are free to reject the ACA's expansion of Medicaid but may continue to participate in the pre-ACA version of Medicaid, even though that is a version that Congress abandoned when it passed the reform bill.

As a matter of structural formalism, there is something bizarre about this holding once one understands this modern federalism as a federalism that essentially is shaped by Congress. So understood, and as elaborated below, one might expect the Court to impose certain hurdles for the legislative process to clear if Congress wishes to utilize state partners. But there is something strange about the Court allowing the states to effectively create and participate in their own version of a federal program—by virtue of refusing to participate in Congress's amended version—when the states had no right to participate in the program in the first place.

On a practical level, moreover, the decision risks creating precisely the wrong kinds of legislative incentives from the standpoint of those who would further state power. To be sure, it is possible that the next time Congress wishes to accomplish an insurance expansion it will enlist the states' help relatively condition-free (for example, using the block grants popular with old-fashioned federalists). Or perhaps it will think twice about legislating at all. The Court itself has noted, in a 1986 case about the incremental expansion of Social Security benefits, that a "constitutional rule that would invalidate Congress' attempts to proceed cautiously in awarding increased benefits might deter Congress from making any increases at all."[35] These sorts of outcomes—namely, stymieing legislation altogether or allowing the states to regulate with few federal strings—are likely the kinds of outcomes that the Court's federalists desire.

But it also is possible that, the next time, Court-watching statutory drafters will still decide to legislate and, to steer clear of the Court's new constitutional obstacle, will do so in a more nationalist manner. This would not be the federalists' desired result. It is true that the Medicaid challenge in the ACA case was brought by some states themselves, but half of the states argued the other side, and no modern federalism proponents today are advocating nationalizing Medicaid. Such an idea (similar to "Medicare for all") has been anathema to federalists at least since Ronald Reagan famously associated that possibility with "socialized medicine."[36]

In fact, it was federalism proponents who supported the creation of the state-led Medicaid program in the first place, as part of the Social Security Act's 1965 legislative compromise, just as it was the more traditionally federalist house of Congress, the Senate, that insisted that the ACA's insurance exchanges be operated by the states instead of the federal government. It also is no coincidence that, now that the Court has upheld the rest of the ACA, some policymakers have invoked "federalism" to try to convince states to establish their own health insurance exchanges rather than letting the federal government operate the exchanges for them. As one governor put it: "[A] federally facilitated exchange is not the ideal approach. Regulating the insurance market is a power best left in the hands of the states."[37] A well-known conservative economist has argued that allowing the federal government to operate the state exchanges would open the door to a nationally-run health care program.[38] Of course, now that the ACA has been upheld, as a formal (constitutional) matter, the federal government is regulating the insurance market regardless. But as these comments reveal, in today's world, both as a practical matter and also as a matter of how a program is understood and experienced, which level of government is doing the implementing of federal law is, indeed, a question about federalism.

The Court's decision also may unproductively incentivize comprehensive, rather than incremental, lawmaking. This is because the decision effectively tells Congress that it may not be able to amend federal programs later if Congress still wishes to use state administrators. Putting aside the political impossibility of such comprehensive lawmaking on a routine basis, it also seems remarkably unwise given the complexity of modern legislative problems. One benefit of incrementalism is its reversibility. State-led federal policy incrementalism, moreover, is particularly reversible because the experimentation often occurs on a smaller scale.[39]

It is something of a mystery why a Supreme Court so concerned with the expansion of federal power would obstruct gradual, state-led federal policy development in this manner. The most plausible explanation is that the Court wished to turn back the tide of major federal legislation altogether; or perhaps the Court simply took particular offense at the policy choices in this statute. As noted, the Chief Justice's opinion and the joint dissent are laced with distaste for the social solidarity model that the ACA embraces, and both condemned the Medicaid expansion for its role in this effort. But even those justices acknowledged that the days of only minor federal-law intrusions into daily American life have long since passed.

## A. NATIONALISM OR STATE LEVERAGE?

Let us now examine the other side of this coin. State administration of federal law does not always work to empower the states. Instead, state administration may offer the federal government a subtle path toward encroachment on state terrain.[40] Relatedly, it may be a way for Congress to obscure its political accountability for particularly unpopular decisions. In such contexts, intrastatutory federalism may have a nationalizing, not federalizing, effect.

The seven justices who voted to strike down the Medicaid expansion focused especially on these arguments about accountability, encroachment, and the diminishment of independent state power. But their specific arguments seemed ill-tailored to the matters at hand. The justices' focus on accountability, for example, translates badly to the doctrinal test that they articulated, which effectively allows Congress to engage in small-scale—and therefore less visible—expansions of cooperative federalist programs but holds that larger changes raise constitutional concerns. If anything, the public is more likely to know where to place blame for major, not minor, changes.

With respect to traditional state functions, the joint dissent emphasized that allowing the Medicaid expansion "would permit Congress to dictate policy in areas traditionally governed primarily at the state or local level."[41] This concern ignores the fact that Congress can use its broad power to tax and spend for the general welfare[42] in areas of traditional state control regardless of whether the states are coequal implementers. Medicare is precisely such an effort.

And with respect to the balance of powers, the Chief Justice emphasized the "independent power of the states … as a check on the power of the Federal government."[43] But the Court seems wrong to invoke state "independence" as a real-world limitation on federal authority. Once one accepts, as the Court did, that Congress has extremely broad power to regulate by itself (if it is willing to use the taxing power), the best chance that the states have to limit or shape the federalization of government functions is via their representation in Congress itself and through their role as implementers of federal law. States must protect their power *through* the national political process, rather than by offering an alternative to it. If anything, the famous "political safeguards of federalism"[44] have special salience here.

The joint dissent did recognize that Congress has become dependent on state implementation. Although the justices did not see political leverage in that dependence, others have. Numerous scholars have described how the states exert formidable political power over the shape of the federal laws they are designated to implement.[45] It was no coincidence that the National Governors Association and the National Association of [state] Insurance Commissioners were active political operators as the ACA was developed and that their efforts had a real effect on how the statute was drafted.

A separate and much more difficult question is who "speaks" for the states in the political process (votes in the Senate? The National Governors' Association? Amicus brief sign-ons? etc.) or whether it even makes sense to think of "the states" as a single unit, with unified interests, when in fact states often take different sides on federalism-related questions (here, too, the ACA is no exception). Some states also may have disproportionate power relative to others.[46] As one particularly famous example of the difficulty of evaluating the question of whether any specific federal statute is state-protective, recall the high-profile federalism case *New York v. United States*, in which the Court invalidated as violative of federalism a federal statutory scheme that was constructed by a coalition of state governors, speaking for the majority of the National Governors' Association, as an effort to preserve state power.[47]

These difficulties, however, are not a reason for the Court to incentivize Congress to leave the states out of its legislative schemes. Instead, they are difficulties related to how legal doctrines should be constructed. They reveal the kinds of questions attendant to understanding and evaluating modern federal-state relations, and the Court's opinion in the ACA case offers no road map for answering them.

The Chief Justice likewise missed the most important point when he disputed Justice Ginsburg's contention that the extent of Congress's constitutional power to expand Medicaid is proven by the fact that Congress could replace the statute altogether. The Chief Justice wrote that "[p]ractical constraints would plainly inhibit, if not preclude, the Federal Government from repealing the existing program and putting every feature of Medicaid on the table for political reconsideration."[48] But what are those "practical constraints" if not the same informal, political—and not constitutional—federalism constraints of the sort that this chapter has emphasized? State-level opposition to a wholesale elimination of Medicaid would be fierce. Such a move, if the federal government then nationalized the program, also would be perceived as a massive federal-government takeover, even though as a formal matter it would be no different, since Medicaid is a federal program in the first place. The predicted political upheaval is what makes the repeal of Medicaid a practical (but not constitutional) impossibility. This is modern federalism at work.

Indeed, the very fact that each of the opinions in the case is full of such "practical" arguments illustrates that we are talking about something other than sovereignty-based federalism. (For another example, consider the dissent's listing of the "practical reasons" preventing the states from declining Medicaid funds, including the political difficulty of levying state taxes to replace the lost federal money.)[49] As proof positive, the Court could not, and in fact explicitly refused to, draw a doctrinal line to demarcate the point at which congressional expansions of state-administered federal programs become coercive. Instead, the

Court articulated a virtually unadministrable rule that recognizes the power of the federal government to amend its state-led programs as it wishes so long as the amendments are not too "dramati[c]."[50] The "we-know-it-when-we-see-it" quality of this doctrine does not fit well with a theory of federalism that depends on hard boundaries.

## 5. Federalism as a Doctrine of Statutory Interpretation

This chapter has focused on the unrealistic assumptions about federalism underlying the Court's opinion. How legal doctrine might evolve to effectuate the different vision of federalism that I have offered requires many more pages and much deeper consideration. But I wish to conclude with one particular point about the direction that such doctrine might take, and that is to emphasize that statutory, not constitutional doctrines, seem a better fit for this context.

The Court has recognized this before: it has created a multitude of statutory interpretation doctrines in the name of "federalism" that are not really about the traditional, hard-boundary federalism that the health care decision tried to resurrect. To take just one of many possible examples, the presumption against preemption is a frequently employed rule of statutory interpretation that requires Congress to be clear when it wishes to legislate over (i.e., preempt) existing state law. The presumption is employed when Congress unquestionably has the authority to preempt and so is not about any constitutional boundary. It is, rather, a statutory interpretation doctrine that acknowledges Congress's discretion to move the line of state-federal regulatory authority, but demands a more public and deliberative federal political process—by requiring Congress to be particularly explicit—when it does so.

The Court has devised similar rules that require Congress to speak extra clearly when it legislates in areas of traditional state authority or wishes to abrogate state sovereign immunity. It is no fluke that each of these doctrines emerged within the last century. Most of our statutory interpretation rules have pedigrees that go back to old England. But these doctrines are the doctrines of the modern regulatory state: they are a direct judicial response to the way that the New Deal changed how federalism works.

The doctrine at issue in health reform's Medicaid expansion was precisely one of these informal, federalism-protective doctrines of statutory interpretation. The so-called *Pennhurst* rule[51] requires Congress to speak clearly when it attaches strings to grants of federal money to the states. Though most often taught in constitutional-law courses, *Pennhurst* also is a statutory-interpretation doctrine. At bottom, the rule is about Congress's intentions and the clarity with which Congress speaks, not about the limits of Congress's authority. *Pennhurst* tells us that Congress has the discretion to attach whatever (legal) conditions it likes to its statutes, as long as it makes those conditions clear.

The Court applied the *Pennhurst* rule in the ACA case, but did not truly follow it. The Court recognized that Congress included the clear statement that *Pennhurst* requires: the Medicaid statute expressly reserves to Congress the "right to alter, amend, or repeal any provision" of the statute.[52] But the Court layered on top of that rule its muddy, "some-changes are-too-much-regardless-of the-warning" doctrine that now makes it impossible for Congress to predict when it will be invoked.

One explanation for the cloudiness of the ACA's new rule may be the Court's reluctance to go further down the road of acknowledging federalism as a creature of Congress's creation. *Pennhurst* suggested that the threat to state sovereignty is eliminated when Congress makes its intentions plain. Perhaps the Court was no longer content to rest with that rule because the Court realized that the *Pennhurst* doctrine is much more about federal statutory design than about state sovereignty in the first place.

Indeed, the entire ACA opinion contains this tension. The Court moved uneasily between recognizing Congress's broad power to legislate today and attempting to protect the historical limits on that power. Consider, for example, how this tension between modern statutory power and traditional constitutional restraints is evident in the Court's decision on the insurance-purchase-mandate question: there, the Court claimed to apply a rule of statutory interpretation, the so-called doctrine of constitutional avoidance, to save the mandate from unconstitutionality by "interpreting" it as a tax.[53] The Court then walked an awkward line by holding that Congress has the power to control the labels that it uses for some purposes, but not for others.[54] Throughout, the Chief Justice invoked the importance of state sovereignty six times.

It is constitutional heresy to suggest that the concept of state sovereignty might be a poor fit, even when we are talking about a federal legislative landscape in which the states play a role only at Congress's discretion. But to press the point, the states are not the only implementers of federal statutes. Congress also routinely relies on nonprofits, quasi-governmental associations, and for-profit entities to implement federal law. No one contends that those players are sovereigns in any sense, even though their role in federal statutory implementation is often quite similar to that of the states.

None of this is to say that the states are not important players in our government structure or that sovereignty is not a relevant concept to describe many other aspects of the states' existence (such as their control of their own government structures). This is an argument about how, realistically, the state policymaking role can remain productive and relevant within the ever-expanding landscape of federal lawmaking.

Of course, not everyone agrees that states should be aggressive national policymakers in the first place, and each context is unique. But even those who generally resist federalism might focus closer attention on state implementation of federal law, and in particular on the parallel between state and private implementation noted above. If one alternative to state-led federal statutory schemes is a bigger federal government, another alternative is more privatization of what previously had been government work. Many scholars have raised accountability, transparency, and democracy concerns associated with this trend toward privatization. One might consider whether state implementation is preferable to privatization; indeed, whether state implementation is a buffer to the withdrawal of government altogether.[55] So understood, state implementation of federal law is a phenomenon that both nationalists and federalists may have interest in preserving.

Consider, in this light, some statutory-law alternatives to sovereignty-focused constitutional-law doctrine. I have argued previously that one of the most important, but often ignored, federalism relationships on the ground is the *intergovernmental administrative* relationship; the relative power of federal administrators over the state administrators concurrently entrusted to implement federal laws.[56] The Constitution has nothing explicit to tell us about how tightly federal agencies can tie their state partners' hands when Congress asks both federal and state administrators to co-regulate. But statutory interpretation doctrine might. We already have statutory interpretation rules that give federal agencies leeway to implement federal laws, and similar rules could be developed that give such deference to state implementers or that even change the balance of power at times between federal and state agencies. My own recent empirical work with Lisa Bressman suggests the possibility that Congress sometimes does intend to give state implementers more policy-implementation discretion than that for which current doctrine allows.[57]

In fact, the ambiguities currently attendant to interagency relationships are precisely what have been cited in the health reform context as the reason for some states' refusal to operate their own insurance exchanges. States claim that they do not have enough information about how much discretion they will have to implement the statute themselves, or what rules the Department of Health and Human Services will impose on them.[58] States have voiced similar concerns with respect to other parts of the statute. None of these concerns stems from arguments about constitutional boundaries—that is, about the federal government's power to regulate in the area in the first place. Rather, these are arguments about how state implementation will be *operationalized* and the respective powers of state and federal agencies, all within a statute that everyone agrees Congress has legitimately enacted. The legal doctrines that we have, however, provide no certainty about these relationships.

In similar vein, Professor Erin Ryan has argued that legal doctrine should oversee the fairness of the political bargaining process—the behind-the-scenes negotiations between state and federal actors—and not the contours of the ultimate result.[59] The Court-created federalism clear-statement-rules already in play and discussed above are of the same order: those rules do not prohibit any particular policy outcome. Rather, they are an effort to *shape the legislative process*; to give additional leverage to federalist voices in how statutes are designed.[60] Those who have raised concerns about asymmetries across the horizontal-federalism landscape might similarly think more about how the statutory design process might be restructured to better equalize power across states.

Admittedly, each of these paths may plunge courts precisely into the kind of political terrain that courts generally eschew. But that discomfort—and the recognition that the political arena is where these boundaries increasingly must be worked out—would seem a reason for courts further to limit their intervention in Congress's statutory work, and not a reason for courts to rely on antiquated constitutional doctrine to provide them with a more familiar, even if inapposite, path to decision.

It also is exceedingly difficult to determine when a particular federal statutory structure is in the "state interest," not only because the states are not always a cohesive unit, but also because what the metric might be is not clear. Federalism is associated with many different kinds of benefits, and different federal statutes generate different packages of those benefits. Some statutes, for example, may encourage more local participation but less experimentation, while others do the opposite. Who is to say which statute is "sufficiently" federalist? In the health reform context, for example, we do not yet have enough information to evaluate the question of how state-protective the health-insurance exchange provisions ultimately will be. What we can say, however, is that thanks to the ACA's intrastatutory federalism, Massachusetts now is operating an insurance exchange through which it can screen and exclude the insurance plans offered, while Utah simultaneously has chosen to operate an open-market model exchange in which all insurers are welcome. That diversity and deference to local governmental preferences likely would not have been possible in a single federal model. There is something that rings of federalism here, but is it "enough" (and enough for what)? Ultimately, our modern federalism may best be understood as existing on a continuum rather than as a feature that is either present or absent from a regulatory scheme.

One final point: if federalism doctrine ultimately does move in this direction, toward rules aimed at how Congress drafts statutes rather than toward constitutional rules that police outcomes, it will be incumbent upon the Court to adhere to the statutory rules that it announces. One of the most important, and unanswered, questions for modern statutory law is the extent to which Congress

and the Court are in dialogue over statutory interpretation; that is, the extent
to which Congress legislates in the shadow of the Court's interpretive doctrines
and the extent to which the Court, in turn, respects Congress's intentions.[61] Any
set of legal rules that aims to make Congress speak more clearly must be heard
and employed by legislative drafters. In the context of the Medicaid expansion,
the Court damaged its own credibility as a reliable partner in that dialectical
relationship by saying "not good enough" when Congress employed precisely
the kind of disclaimer for which the Court previously had asked.

## Conclusion

Traditional federalists embrace state power in the absence, or instead, of federal
authority. It is this traditional federalism that the Court wished to resuscitate in
the ACA litigation. But that option was never on the political table when it came
to designing the health reform statute. The congressional majority that passed
the ACA was determined to legislate. And so Congress proceeded as it typically
does, changing national policy by building on already-existing federal laws that
themselves were the result of incremental federal legislation over a backdrop of
historical state control. The outcome was major federal legislation that, instead
of marginalizing the states, kept them front and center. The Court misread the
ACA as a statute that is fundamentally anti-state, when in fact it is state-empow-
ering in many respects. The statute creates precisely the kinds of partnerships
that maintain the states' relevance in the modern statutory era. The Court's federalists may wish to think twice before again discouraging them.

## Notes

1. The Commerce Clause question is unlikely to arise again because such purchase-mandates
   are rarely necessary and, in any event, Congress now knows to use a different power (such as
   its taxing power) to effectuate the same result.
2. For examples of this robust literature, see FEDERALISM AND HEALTH POLICY (John Holahan
   et al. eds., 2003), *and* HEALTH POLICY, FEDERALISM AND THE AMERICAN STATES (Robert
   F. Rich & William D. White eds., 1996).
3. See THE FRAGMENTATION OF U.S. HEALTH CARE: CAUSES AND SOLUTIONS (Einer
   Elhauge ed. 2010).
4. Nat'l Fed'n of Indep. Bus. v. Sebelius (NFIB), 132 S. Ct. 2642, 2660 (2012) (Scalia, Kennedy,
   Thomas, Alito, JJ., dissenting).
5. *Id.* at 2578.
6. Abbe R. Gluck, *Intrastatutory Federalism and Statutory Interpretation: State Implementation of
   Federal Law in Health Reform and Beyond*, 121 YALE L.J. 534 (2011).
7. This is because Congress can tax and spend as it wishes for the general welfare, see U.S.
   CONST. art. I, § 8, cl. 1, a power that even the conservative wing of the Court agrees gives
   Congress enormous authority over social policy. See, e.g., *NFIB*, 132 S. Ct. at 2643.

8. See BRUCE ACKERMAN, 3 WE THE PEOPLE: THE CIVIL RIGHTS REVOLUTION (forthcoming 2014) (on file with author); WILLIAM N. ESKRIDGE & JOHN FEREJOHN, A REPUBLIC OF STATUTES (2010); Ernest A. Young, *The Constitution Outside the Constitution*, 117 YALE L.J. 408 (2007).

9. Cooperative federalism existed before the New Deal too, but it has become ubiquitous since. See Jerry L. Mashaw, *Reluctant Nationalists: Federal Administration and Administrative Law in the Republican Era, 1801–1829*, 116 YALE L.J. 1636, 1649–1650 (2007) (describing early cooperative federalism in quarantine laws).

10. For elaboration, see Gluck, *supra* note 6.

11. *Id.*

12. MALCOLM M. FEELEY & EDWARD RUBIN, FEDERALISM: POLITICAL IDENTITY AND TRAGIC COMPROMISE (2008).

13. *NFIB*, 132 S. Ct. at 2578.

14. 521 U.S. 898 (1997).

15. *Id.* at 977 (Breyer, J., dissenting) (joined by Justice Stevens); see also *id.* at 959 (Stevens, J., dissenting joined by Justices Souter, Ginsburg and Breyer).

16. The doctrinal relevance of labeling in this context seems to go to the alterability of the doctrines announced. To the extent that one believes that Congress's federal statutory design decisions are creating new constitutional understandings of federalism, then perhaps future congresses, and even courts, have less power to alter those understandings than they would have to interpret and change statutory understandings. This possibility raises a host of other questions, however—including the presumptive unconstitutionality of congressional efforts to bind the hands of future congresses—that require deeper consideration elsewhere (and which also attach to most theories of statutes-as-constitutional-law, not just the one advanced here).

17. Wendy K. Mariner, *Social Solidarity and Personal Responsibility in Health Reform*, 14 CONN. INS. L.J. 199, 205, 207 (2008).

18. The statute is not unequivocal on this point. Some provisions, particularly the so-called "wellness provisions" that allow healthy individuals to reduce their insurance costs, reflect a reluctance to leave the personal responsibility model completely behind. See Tom Baker, *Health Insurance, Risk and Responsibility After the Patient Protection and Affordable Care Act*, 159 U. PA. L. REV. 1577 (2011); Jessica L. Roberts, *Health Law as Disability Rights Law*, MINN. L. REV. (forthcoming 2013).

19. Charles E. Lindblom, The Science of "Muddling Through," 19 PUB. ADMIN. REV. 79, 84 (1959).

20. 521 U.S. 898, 935 (1997).

21. STUART ALTMAN & DAVID SHACTMAN, POWER, POLITICS, AND UNIVERSAL HEALTH CARE 139 (2011).

22. Nicole Huberfeld, *Federalizing Medicaid*, 14 U. PA. J. CONST. L. 431, 445–447 (2011).

23. ALTMAN & SHACTMAN, *supra* note 21, at 141.

24. State control over private insurance essentially continued until the 1974 ERISA statute partially eroded it.

25. The Food Security Act of 1985, Pub. L. No. 99-198; The Hunger Prevention Act of 1988, Pub. L. No. 100-435.

26. The first Federal Clean Air Act, enacted in 1963, provided grants to state and local air pollution control districts. Pub. L. No. 88-206. The first Federal Clean Water Act of 1948 (also known as the Federal Water Pollution Control Act) was "primarily based on state and local efforts." Pub. L. No. 80-845. See ENVTL. PROT. AGENCY, THE CLEAN WATER ACT: PROTECTING AND RESTORING OUR NATION'S WATERS, http://water.epa.gov/action/cleanwater40/cwa101.cfm.

27. NFIB v. Sebelius, 132 S. Ct. 2566, 2639 n.23 (2012) (Ginsburg, J., concurring in part, concurring in judgment in part, and dissenting in part).

28. *Id.* at 2604.

29.  See Allen Rostron, *Incrementalism, Comprehensive Rationality, and the Future of Gun Control*, 67 MD. L. REV. 511, 516 (2008).

30.  New State Ice Co. v. Liebmann, 285 U.S. 262, 311 (1932) (Brandeis, J., dissenting).

31.  Patient Protection and Affordable Care Act, Pub. L. No. 111-148, §§ 1321, 1331, 1412, 124 Stat. 119, 186, 199, 231 (2010), as amended by Health Care and Education Reconciliation Act, Pub. L. No. 111-152, 124 Stat. 1029 (2010) (codified as amended in 42 U.S.C. §§ 18041, 18051, 18082).

32.  The metaphor comes from Justice Brandeis's dissent in New State Ice Co. v. Liebmann. 285 U.S. 262, 311 (1932).

33.  See Susan Rose-Ackerman, *Risk Taking and Reelection: Does Federalism Promote Innovation?* 9 J. LEG. STUD. 593, 594, 610–611 (1980); Edward L. Rubin & Malcolm Feeley, *Federalism: Some Notes on a National Neurosis*, 41 U.C.L.A. L. REV. 903, 925–926 (1994); David A. Super, *Laboratories of Destitution: Democratic Experimentalism and the Failure of Antipoverty Law*, 157 U. PA. L. REV. 541–616 (2008).

34.  Ryan Lizza, *Romney's Dilemma*, THE NEW YORKER, June 6, 2011, *available at* http://www.newyorker.com/reporting/2011/06/06/110606fa_fact_lizza?currentPage=all.

35.  Bowen v. Owens, 470 U.S. 340 348 (1986).

36.  Ronald Reagan, *Ronald Reagan Speaks Out Against Socialized Medicine* (Am. Med. Ass'n. Commc'n Div. 1961), *available at* http://www.youtube.com/watch?v=fRdLpem-AAs.

37.  Elizabeth Crisp, *Federal Government Will Start Setting Up Missouri's Health Exchange*, ST. LOUIS TODAY, Nov. 12, 2012, *available at* http://www.stltoday.com/news/local/govt-and-politics/political-fix/federal-government-will-start-setting-up-missouri-s-health-exchange/article_4bee6ae8-6b8d-5c6c-9ecf-e90dd36234b6.html.

38.  See Douglas Holtlz-Eakin, *Yes to State Exchanges*, NATIONAL REVIEW ONLINE (Dec. 6, 2012, 12:00 PM), http://www.nationalreview.com/articles/334956/yes-state-exchanges-douglas-holtz-eakin.

39.  ROBERT A. DAHL & CHARLES E. LINDBLOM, POLITICS, ECONOMICS, & WELFARE 83 (1953).

40.  For elaboration of these arguments, see Gluck, *supra* note 6.

41.  NFIB v. Sebelius, 132 S. Ct. 2566, 2662 (2012) (Scalia, Kennedy, Thomas, Alito, JJ., dissenting).

42.  U.S. CONST. art. I, § 8, cl. 1.

43.  *NFIB*, 132 S. Ct. at 2578.

44.  Herbert Wechsler argued that that the nature of the political process and the structure of Congress limit national intrusions on state autonomy, making national action "the special rather than the ordinary case." Herbert Wechsler, *The Political Safeguards of Federalism: The Role of the States in the Composition and Selection of the National Government*, 54 COLUM. L. REV. 543 (1954).

45.  See, e.g., JOHN NUGENT, SAFEGUARDING FEDERALISM: HOW STATES PROTECT THEIR INTERESTS IN NATIONAL POLICYMAKING 201 (2009).

46.  See Lynn A. Baker, *Putting the Safeguards Back into the Political Safeguards of Federalism*, 46 VILL. L. REV. 951, 966 (2001).

47.  See New York v. United States, 505 U.S. 144, 150–151 (1992).

48.  *NFIB*, 132 S. Ct. at 2606 n.14.

49.  *Id.* at 2657.

50.  *Id.* at 2606.

51.  Pennhurst State Sch. & Hosp. v. Halderman, 451 U.S. 1, 17 (1981).

52.  42 U.S.C. § 18024 (2010).

53.  In my view, however, the Court did not apply the doctrine properly. The doctrine is best understood as an aid in the interpretation of ambiguous statutory language, not as an aid in choosing among several constitutional hooks for text whose meaning is clear.

54.  Specifically, the Court held that it would respect Congress's decision to call the "tax" a "penalty" for purposes of whether the Anti-Injunction Act's prohibition on preenforcement

challenges applied, but that it would decide for itself whether the mandate was a "tax" for purposes of Congress's power to enact it in the first place.

55. Judith Resnik, Globalization(s), Privatization(s), Constitutionalizations, and Statization: Icons and Experiences of Sovereignty in the 21st Century, 11 INT'L J. CONST. L. 162 (2013).

56. Gluck, *supra* note 6.

57. See Abbe R. Gluck & Lisa Schultz Bressman, Statutory Interpretation from the Inside—An Empirical Study of Congressional Drafting, Delegation and the Canons: Part I, 65 STAN. L. REV. (forthcoming May 2013).

58. See, e.g., Jason Millman, *Chris Christie Nixes State-Run Insurance Exchange*, POLITICO (Dec. 7, 2012, 5:03 AM), http://www.politico.com/story/2012/12/christie-nixes-state-run-insurance-exchange-84718.html.

59. ERIN RYAN, FEDERALISM AND THE TUG OF WAR WITHIN (2012).

60. See also Andrzej Rapaczynski, *From Sovereignty to Process: The Jurisprudence of Federalism After Garcia*, 1985 SUP. CT. REV. 341, 418–419 (suggesting that clear statement rules might be ways for judges to adopt a more deferential stance to Congress while still safeguarding federalism).

61. See Gluck & Bressman, *supra* note 57.

# CHAPTER 17

# Constitutional Uncertainty and the Design of Social Insurance

## REFLECTIONS ON THE ACA CASE

*Michael J. Graetz and Jerry L. Mashaw*

## 1. Introduction

Let us begin this essay with a confession, an observation, and an echo. First, the *confession*: we were surprised that the majority of the Supreme Court found that the individual mandate of the Patient Protection and Affordable Care Act (ACA) exceeded Congress's Commerce Clause powers, including Congress's ability to adopt legislation that is "necessary and proper" to regulate commerce effectively. Writing separately and together, we have argued for mandating—and subsidizing—individual and family health insurance purchases to prevent the unraveling of private health insurance through risk segmentation.[1] While the form of health insurance we recommended varies from that of the ACA, the individual mandate we proposed (as in the ACA) would be coupled with provisions requiring insurers to take all comers, without regard to any preexisting conditions, and to eschew medical underwriting.

As we have argued in detail elsewhere, universal participation is properly a hallmark of social insurance, as is broad distribution of its burdens and benefits. To be sure, an individual mandate—whether to purchase health or automobile insurance, vaccinate your children before sending them to school, or pay taxes—sometimes involves intrusive enforcement and evasion.[2] But as long as our nation continues to provide emergency medicine to all of its citizens and residents regardless of their ability to pay, prudence requires that everyone pay a fair share of the costs of their medical care.

The consequences of inaction here are dramatic. Virtually every American will use the health care system at some point, and people who have no health insurance and are unable to pay for their health care services will receive health care services anyway. This is not true of broccoli, automobiles, or virtually any other product. Health care providers cannot provide their services for free: there are costs involved. Those costs must and will be borne by the people who pay for health care services either directly or indirectly though taxes. Reasonable estimates of the current burden on persons having health insurance of paying for the uncompensated care of the uninsured are roughly $1,000 per year. No one denies that health insurance is interstate commerce. Nor does anyone deny that the cross-subsidies from paying customers to nonpaying customers are very substantial.

The constitutional question is whether the thing that is being regulated substantially affects interstate commerce. Even without relying on the recharacterization of the failure to buy health insurance as a decision to self-insure, failure to buy health insurance clearly does affect interstate commerce. That it is in some sense "inaction" rather than "action" should be a distinction without a difference for Commerce Clause analysis. Imagining a Congress mandating Americans to buy broccoli or to buy automobiles is to leave the real world far, far behind.

When we first made these points in the 1990s and early 2000s, no serious constitutional objection had been advanced against requiring all citizens and residents to purchase some specified minimum level of health insurance. The individual mandate idea had been proposed by the Heritage Foundation, supported by dozens of Senate Republicans, and only at the very last minute removed from the final 1992 health insurance proposals of President George H. W. Bush. Massachusetts enacted such a regime in 2006 and its then-governor, Mitt Romney, subsequently urged it as a model for national legislation.[3] Like virtually everyone else who had thought about it, we believed that the constitutionality of such a mandate had been settled in the legal contests over the New Deal.[4] Indeed, as we discuss further below, one of the objectives of our social insurance analysis and proposals was to liberate state-based unemployment insurance from the archaic structure imposed upon it by long-gone constitutional constraints on the federal government.[5]

Second, an *observation*: like many others writing for this volume, the Court's Commerce Clause analysis is not our only cause for puzzlement in this set of opinions. Take three prominent examples: (1) Justice Roberts's unnecessary dicta telling us that he would strike down the statute on Commerce Clause grounds in an opinion upholding the law under Congress's tax powers; (2) the willingness of the four dissenting justices to abandon the Court's previous jurisprudence and traditions on severability and urge striking down the entire statute, not just the mandate (the only provision which they found constitutionally objectionable), nor just the mandate and its related health insurance requirements of guaranteed coverage and community rating (as the government had urged); and (3) the seven-to-two vote, holding for the first time that a federal-state cooperative program was so coercive as to be constitutionally infirm and doing so long before any federal administrator had exercised her statutory discretion to cut off any state funds. More on the last below.[6]

Third, an *echo*, with an elaboration. We would emphasize, as does Professor Charles Fried,[7] that the gravamen of the constitutional complaint against the individual mandate is its supposed intrusion on personal freedom. But, as Fried points out, "the argument was not made because it would have to be made under the Liberty Clause of the Fifth Amendment, and this would have carried over to the similar clause in the Fourteenth and therefore rendered any such a scheme enacted by a state, as in Massachusetts, similarly invalid."[8] When all was said and done, no one attacked a state government's requirement that individuals must purchase health insurance, nor advanced any constitutional limitation on the states doing so. All we have is a holding that if the federal government wishes to do the same, it must exercise its powers to tax and spend, not its power to regulate. The ACA case then is best understood as a legal attack on the *means* but not the goals of the health care legislation.

This emphasis on means rather than ends and on state over federal powers potentially poses significant risks for the complex institutional arrangements for social insurance that now exist and may imply harmful constraints on how Congress can restructure these programs to better meet the needs of the American people in our twenty-first-century economy. Not coincidentally, the new constitutional framework announced in the ACA decision favors those who want to dismantle rather than strengthen our nation's social insurance protections. We will explain why this is so with regard not only to health insurance, but also unemployment insurance and Social Security. Doing so requires a bit of background.

## 2. The Institutional and Normative Complexity of U.S. Social Insurance

What do we mean by social insurance? The critical risk that social insurance addresses is the risk of inadequate labor income. For some, loss of access to labor income may be complete and permanent, such as when death or permanent disability strikes. Others may lose labor income only episodically and temporarily through unemployment or less severe illnesses or injuries. This risk also occurs as part of the normal progress of the life cycle: both youth and old age put one out of the labor market.

"Private insurance" is a contract to pool common risks so that statistically predictable economic losses will be experienced as small subtractions from all insured persons' wealth rather than as calamities for an unfortunate few. "Social insurance" also pools risks. But social insurance depends on government action, directed at a particular class of risks and designed to pursue societal purposes that could not or would not be achieved through individual contracting in private insurance markets. Social insurance is not merely a variation on private insurance. It is a different product—a social rather than an individual (or group) contract.

Social insurance in the United States is a twentieth-century creation, largely a product of the Great Depression. Before that, economic security was mostly a family responsibility. Children worked beside their parents on the farm or in the family's business after school. Family members who became too old to work were cared for by the next generation; the pastoral image was Grandpa at the fireside waiting to greet his hardworking children and grandchildren as they returned from the fields. (Grandmas never retired from housework and other chores.) Family members who became disabled were cared for within the family. Private philanthropy sometimes provided additional assistance.

Throughout the nineteenth century American governments had taken responsibility only for their military and civilian employees, who were sometimes protected by federal or state pensions and health and disability insurance. (Merchant seamen were a special case having had a compulsory federal health insurance scheme since the 1790s.) A number of states did provide cash assistance for widows and orphans. A few large employers had introduced some pension benefits. Anyone else without an income was supported by relatives or was relegated to the "poorhouse."

President Roosevelt's 1935 Committee on Economic Security proposed a comprehensive scheme of social insurance to provide protections against what were then perceived to be life's major threats to family income: loss of parental income support, old age, death of the family breadwinner, disability, illness, and unemployment. But that scheme was never completed. Over the years, Americans—benefited and burdened by the New Deal legacy—have continued to add and subtract, modify and reaffirm a vision that has been all but lost behind the details and political struggles surrounding particular programs.

The basic purpose of social insurance is income security. To realize that purpose, social insurance must cover common risks to income security across the life cycle of individuals. If it is to fulfill its social purposes effectively, social insurance must be universal in coverage. To provide an adequate level of protection, social insurance must recognize and facilitate two different forms of redistribution— redistribution of resources across the lifetime of individuals and redistribution from families that have not incurred the insured risks to those that have.

In the United States, we provide social insurance through a complex mixture of mandatory and voluntary mechanisms, financed through both public and private budgets, and with a dizzying array of functions allocated between the states and the federal government. This institutional complexity is not only a function of historical and political contingencies, including pre–New Deal constitutional doctrine, but also of conflicting normative commitments. Health insurance alone, for example, reflects commitments to the moral worth of every person's life; to individual and collective responsibilities; to a competitive market for health insurance; to consumer choice; to professional integrity; to individual and physician autonomy; and to budgetary constraints.[9]

Let us briefly review the techniques for providing social insurance now prevalent in the United States. We start with public provision: the government can run a social insurance program and require participation by all workers. This is the current U.S. approach to risks of old age, death (survivorship), disability, and certain medical expenses in old age (OASDHI)—the familiar programs embodied in the Social Security and Medicare Acts. But even these familiar social insurance programs employ more heterogeneous mechanisms than are generally acknowledged.

Medicare Part A (hospital care) and Part B (physician services) are important examples. Part A is a mandatory program financed through a wage tax on employers and employees. Part B is a voluntary program financed through relatively small premiums coupled with large subsidies from general federal revenues. Both programs were designed to ameliorate the threat to family income security that medical costs pose for the retired population. Normal insurance market segmentation in the private health insurance markets would produce high costs for a group like the elderly that, on average, combines high risks with low incomes.

Over time, the Part B subsidies became more and more generous—growing from 50 percent of premiums to 75 percent—so that today Part B coverage is nearly universal. And shifts in medical treatment modalities over time have made out-of-hospital care both medically more important and financially more burdensome. The current scheme may be outmoded, even after the 2003 addition of a complex drug benefit (Part D)—or poorly designed from the beginning— but the point of this example remains. Public provision of insurance coverage need not be of one type, either in its regulatory or its financial arrangements.

Alternatively, insurance coverage can be mandated by law. Some current American social insurance programs use mandates, either to require employer-based coverage or to compel individual participation in a state-run scheme. Workers' compensation offers a ready example of the employer-mandate mode. But mandates can be used as well to require individual purchases of private insurance protection. Automobile liability insurance is a standard U.S. example. Individual mandates are also quite common in the pension and health insurance regimes of other nations. Conservative critics have long urged reforming Social

Security pensions by substituting or including mandatory individual accounts that function somewhat like Individual Retirement Accounts (IRAs).

The IRA suggests yet another common technique for socializing insurance markets: public subsidies. Medicare Part B may be the United States' most conspicuous and successful example of social insurance financed largely by subsidies out of general revenues. But direct subsidies are not the only alternative; much U.S. social insurance protection is subsidized through targeted tax breaks. Tax subsidies for voluntary employment-based regimes have tended to work rather badly, but they are a way for government to "sponsor" and subsidize social insurance without making the size of "government" appear bigger.[10] The tax subsidies for employment-based health insurance and retirement income are now the federal government's largest "tax expenditures," eclipsing the deductibility of home mortgage interest.

Not all subsidies to social insurance are from general revenues. Cross-subsidies within insurance pools are a common response to undesirable private insurance market segmentation. Higher earners can subsidize lower earners through premium or payment arrangements in virtually any social insurance scheme, just as high earners subsidize low earners in the current Social Security pension system. Low-risk elders subsidize those with high risks in the Medicare system. Nor are cross-subsidies limited to public insurance programs. Mandated "community rating," as is common in many states and required under the ACA, for example, can force cross-subsidies within private insurance pools that would otherwise generate differential premiums.

Much social insurance protection for health coverage during Americans' working years and for their retirement income is provided through employer-sponsored, tax-favored health insurance and retirement funds. This coverage is far from universal, turning on the worker's connection to a particular employer. The spotty and inadequate coverage, however, only signals that this kind of social insurance is inadequate; it does not negate its social insurance nature.

Finally, means-tested, noncontributory programs for dependent children and the aged were a part of the original Social Security Act. Indeed, old-age assistance based on need is Title I of the Social Security Act of 1935 and is the part of the Act that had the broadest public support when the statute was enacted. Means-tested support for the blind as well as the totally and permanently disabled became part of the Social Security Act nearly a decade before contributory, earnings-related disability insurance was added. The Earned Income Tax Credit (EITC) has become an increasingly important wage subsidy for low-income families with children. Indeed, what we may now think of as the conventional conception of social insurance through taxing and spending—mandatory, contributory, earnings-related, universal or near universal programs, such as Social Security's OASDI—accounts for less than half of all social insurance transfers in the United States.

In summary, social insurance is a distinctive set of programs designed to moderate the risks of current income loss or inadequacy by providing secure cash or near-cash entitlements on the occurrence of specified risks. Although the general risk to be insured is simply the lack of labor income, the ways that risk materializes are diverse and alter over the lifetimes of individuals and families. Risks also are often different for each individual and family, and they change over time as social and economic conditions evolve.

This diversity of risks requires multiple techniques for providing social insurance. It is impossible to know yet just how the Court's ACA decision may inhibit the federal government's future flexibility in employing these techniques; too much ambiguity remains. But it is not too soon to explore the potential implications of the constitutional limitations embraced by a majority of the Court. We will consider three contexts: (1) health insurance; (2) retirement income security; and (3) unemployment insurance.

## 3. Health Insurance

In the health arena, our institutional arrangements have long been inadequate.[11] No domain of American social insurance has rivaled the incompetence of American health insurance. We have year after year left forty to fifty million persons uninsured and many millions more with inadequate or insecure coverage. Yet the United States spends nearly twice the share of its economic output on health as other industrial nations with little or nothing in measurably improved health outcomes to show for it.

The ACA culminated nearly a century of efforts to reform our nation's system of providing health insurance. Proposals for major change by virtually every president, Democrat or Republican, since FDR were all defeated. Only Lyndon Johnson enjoyed a major success, creating Medicare and Medicaid in 1965, to which George W. Bush managed to add both prescription drug coverage and "Medicare Advantage" on a quite different model. As we have said, Part A, hospital care, is mandatory and financed by payroll taxes. Part B, physician services, is voluntary and subsidized from general revenues. Both Parts A and B are administered by the federal government as insurer, although much of the actual claims processing is contracted out to private insurance companies. Part D, prescription drug coverage, is voluntary and subsidized from general revenues, but provided by highly regulated private insurers, as is Part C, so-called Medicare Advantage, which allows Medicare beneficiaries to opt into a private insurance plan whose premiums are paid by Medicare.

Medicaid is a joint federal-state program for poor persons and certain others who meet specified eligibility criteria. Medicaid coverage is often broader than

Medicare, especially for long-term care. Some poor elderly patients are eligible for both Medicare and Medicaid, but since Medicaid income and assets eligibility tests vary across the states, there is great interstate variation in who qualifies and for what benefits. Because of its income and resources criteria for coverage, Medicaid coverage frequently creates "income cliffs" for low-income workers. A few more dollars of income can mean complete loss of coverage, which means that a good job opportunity, if it does not include adequate health insurance, may be too risky to take. Workers with health insurance coverage rely predominantly on voluntary tax-subsidized employer plans. But these subsidies are distributionally regressive and inadequate to make health insurance affordable for many small businesses or the self-employed. Moreover, both eligibility and coverage vary from state to state under general federal criteria. Complexity reigned long before enactment of the ACA.

Critical examination of the pre-ACA system of American health insurance reveals the limits of private insurance, federal tax subsidies, state financing, and voluntariness when attempting to fulfill the normal social insurance goals of universality and progressivity. Although, as Medicare Part B demonstrates, if everyone's subsidies are large enough and financed by progressive taxation, one can approach universality with some progressivity. Because Medicaid provides coverage for low-income families, the groups generally made worst off in a complex health insurance system like ours are not the poor, but rather those struggling to become or remain middle class.

The U.S. health insurance system has managed to combine large and accelerating medical expenditures with stagnant or decreasing insurance coverage. The ACA endeavors to increase coverage and limit medical inflation while maintaining the vast majority of existing institutional arrangements. New and stronger federal regulatory mechanisms were an essential element of cost control in this context, and the individual mandate was considered necessary to move toward universal coverage in a marketplace of private insurers.

On the Supreme Court's current view, a so-called "single-payer system," like Medicare for all, would not have raised the constitutional objections lodged against the ACA, even though it would have been a far more aggressive federal intervention in the private marketplace. The conventional wisdom, of course, is that no constitutional roadblocks are needed here—insurance industry political muscle and conservative ideological resistance will do the job nicely. In this context a program as comically complex as the ACA begins to look like the only path to universal coverage—and maybe cost control.

There is, of course, no constitutional difficulty with shifting more of the current health insurance responsibilities of the federal government to the states or to private actors (including employers) acting voluntarily. Devolving the purchase and financing of health insurance and medical care to the states and private parties is at the core of conservative proposals for health insurance reform, such as Paul Ryan's premium support plan for individuals to replace Medicare and block grants to the states to replace Medicaid.[12] All U.S. experience suggests that shifting more of these responsibilities to the states and to private parties will serve to increase the gaps and differences in coverage and reduce or eliminate the redistribution of risks.

At stake in the ACA litigation then was an effort to create a constitutional barrier to what had been only a political challenge, not only to the means of providing social insurance, but to its core goals, especially universal coverage. If Medicare for all is barred politically, any improvements in the ACA will some-how have to use the taxing and spending power to further support access to private health insurance. If, for political reasons, taxes cannot be called taxes, one wonders whether legislation can be crafted that is both effective and meets the fragmented Supreme Court's test for recognizing a tax as a tax. At some point—perhaps we have already reached it—Americans will have many health insurance choices and little prospect of understanding either their entitlements, their options, or the adequacy of their coverage. Other key pillars of our nation's social insurance system, such as Social Security and unemployment insurance, face similar challenges in this new constitutional environment.

## 4. Insuring Adequate Retirement Income

Social Security has long been America's most successful social insurance program. Ninety-five percent of working Americans are now covered by the retirement, disability, and survivors' benefits of Social Security (OASDI), and no one doubts the program's success in diminishing poverty among our nation's elderly. But as ongoing demographic changes reduce the ratio of workers to retirees, Social Security's financial challenges have recently come to the fore in our national debates. This, in turn, has created an opportunity for some of Social Security's political opponents—former vice presidential candidate Paul Ryan and President George W. Bush are notable recent examples—to urge substituting private savings accounts, self-protection through thrift, for at least some substantial portion of Social Security's retirement benefits.

Why retirement—a routine and largely predictable event—is not an appropriate occasion for such self-protection through savings does not readily lend itself to a short, simple answer. But its essence lies in the uncertainty about future economic conditions and the risks of longevity; the risks of outliving one's savings.[13] Every Organization for Economic Cooperation and Development (OECD) nation and many others have instituted some form of social insurance to promote retirement security. In the United States, we have relied on what has long been labeled a "three-legged stool," composed of (1) the inflation-adjusted, universally available, defined benefit of Social Security, (2) voluntary, tax-advantaged, employer-based private pensions (which now largely take the form of defined contribution plans), and (3) private savings. The fundamental debate of recent decades has been whether and how to change this mix.

Interestingly, while liberals and conservatives have split over the importance of retaining (and perhaps even strengthening) Social Security's provision of retirement income, Democrats and Republicans have agreed on the importance of strengthening private savings for retirement. Moving toward universal savings accounts has served as a rallying cry for both the Left and the Right. The critical distinction has been that the latter have proposed such accounts in lieu of at least some portion of current Social Security, while the former have pushed for mandatory private accounts on top of existing Social Security protections.

In our prior work, we have urged some specific reforms to put Social Security on a sounder financial footing and, in addition, proposed additional mandatory personal investment accounts.[14] The purposes of the latter proposal were to increase prefunding of retirement income, allow wider participation in the benefits of capital appreciation, and enhance personal responsibility for retirement.[15] (We also have urged using such accounts to reduce the moral hazard of other social insurance protections, such as unemployment insurance; more about that later.) Mandatory personal accounts would provide for all workers a second tier of retirement savings that could fill gaps in current employer-based pension coverage—coverage that now strongly favors higher-paid, better-educated, and older workers, as well as workers employed by large firms.

While some other proponents of individual accounts have urged voluntary rather than mandatory accounts, our nation's experience with IRAs demonstrates that universality can be accomplished only by mandating that each individual have an account. Low-wage workers, of course, would have difficulty funding such accounts if payroll deductions in addition to current Social Security and Medicare taxes are required. Thus, subsidies for such workers funded from general tax revenues would be necessary. As with health insurance, such a program, coupled with voluntary, rather than mandatory, accounts would produce important gaps in coverage and adequacy for middle-class workers and their families.

Along with individual account proponents from both the left and the right, before the ACA litigation we saw no constitutional objections to mandating such accounts. But it is somewhat more difficult to link mandatory personal savings to interstate commerce than the purchase of health insurance. In the wake of the Court's health insurance decision it seems clear that a majority of the current Court would hold that a federal mandate for personal savings accounts could be accomplished only indirectly through the Taxing and Spending Clauses, not by a straightforward requirement that everyone save a specified amount.

The standard technique would be to impose a tax that is completely forgiven by putting an equivalent amount into a savings account for specified purposes. However, Chief Justice Roberts's opinion, which emphasizes the small size of the ACA penalty (the tax) relative to the cost of purchasing the ACA's mandated health insurance coverage, raises the possibility that a larger penalty-to-benefit ratio (even if located in the tax code) might be viewed as a substitute for regulation, and run afoul of the Court's new Commerce Clause limitations.[16]

If it turns out that a direct mandate of savings for specified purposes is now viewed by the Court as beyond the federal government's regulatory powers, but not as overstepping its taxing and spending powers, it would, again, seem that only the means, not the ends, of such a policy have been limited by the Court's ACA decision. But the practical and political limitations implied by the Court's decision may, nevertheless, loom large. It was the allergic reaction of congressmen and senators to the "T" word that caused the ACA "tax" to be presented as a "penalty." If individual accounts can be implemented only through taxation, they may be politically impossible. The potential implications of the Court's decision for modernizing unemployment insurance may be even greater.

## 5. Unemployment Insurance

Unemployment insurance (UI), a centerpiece of the original 1935 Social Security Act, was an essential response to the Great Depression. Ever since, UI has provided crucial support for American workers in recessionary periods. But the Great Recession has surely demonstrated what policy analysts have long understood: our system of UI needs to be modernized. Today, UI undoubtedly should be a national program. In our nation's economy, with its single currency, macroeconomic shocks affect the entire country. But there are very substantial regional variations in an economic downturn's timing and intensity. These variations argue for including the whole nation in the insurance pool; otherwise regional demands will be greatest when regional capacity is weakest.

But unemployment insurance, as it was constructed in the 1930s and as it remains today, is a set of diverse state programs for which the federal government offers a peculiar incentive. The UI program was structured as a national tax on employers who fund their employees' unemployment benefits, modeled— for reasons of both politics and constitutional law—after a federal-state estate tax arrangement that had been upheld by the pre–New Deal Supreme Court. The federal tax is waived for any employer whose state imposes a similar unemployment tax and establishes an UI benefits program that conforms to the broad contours of the federal statute. That every state would act on this incentive was guaranteed by the unnecessarily high rate set for the federal tax. States can virtually always make their employers, or at least some substantial number of them, better off by having a state system of their own.

Franklin Roosevelt understood as well as anyone the difficulties with this design. While governor of New York, he attempted to convince his fellow governors to institute parallel UI systems in every state. As he told them then, unless we all act together, none of us can act at all.[17] Roosevelt's reasoning was unassailable. The inexorable logic of interstate competition for mobile business capital makes it problematic for states to go it alone in a program like unemployment insurance. That same logic also suggests that states will continuously be tempted to improve their "business climate" by reducing the burden of UI on existing and prospective employers. Such a "race to the bottom" tends to undermine both the economic security and the macroeconomic stabilization purposes of the UI program, as well as its effectiveness. States have ended up with remarkably different UI systems. But the general trend over time has been to reduce both coverage and benefits and to fail to respond to changes in labor markets that put more and more low-wage, part-time, and part-year workers outside the system.

The Great Recession and its halting recovery have exposed major flaws in the current structure. Benefits paid to unemployed workers are frequently inadequate to keep their families afloat and to facilitate their search for a new job. Many workers find themselves without any coverage at all.

While state administration of UI is appropriate, there is little or no case to be made for state financing. The current financing structure is a creature of archaic constitutional constraints. And we find nothing in the Court's ACA opinion that would bar federalization of UI financing and eligibility rules. Again, only the techniques for doing so are potentially called into question. Federal repeal and replacement of existing arrangements is not barred. But more incremental—and therefore potentially more politically palatable—changes, such as eliminating the federal credit for state UI taxes unless specified conditions are met, may be questionable. If thought by a majority of justices to cross the vague barrier against "coercion" of the states found applicable to the ACA's changes in Medicaid, they would be barred. The power of the UI program's tax incentive may make it irresistible—and, therefore, on at least one reading of the ACA opinion, unconstitutional. Given the ambiguities of the Court's opinions, it is impossible to know for sure.

In addition to its unique structural defects, UI confronts especially large problems of moral hazard. People are more likely to stop working when the costs of doing so are cushioned by replacement of much of their wages. In addition, private insurance companies suffer in economic downturns just as claims for UI rise. As we have seen recently, insurers can go bankrupt in a deep recession. Hence, even if private insurance could solve the moral hazard problem, private unemployment insurance would be inadequate. Unsurprisingly, private UI is virtually unknown.

To limit the potential for moral hazard, we have suggested combining expanded UI coverage with a system of individual accounts for each worker. In such a system, each employee would be required to contribute, say, 3 percent of wages to her account in order to help fund both periods of unemployment and retirement.[18] If a worker experiences a period of compensated unemployment, his or her account would be reduced by, say, 20 percent of the costs of the unemployment compensation paid. Workers whose accounts are insufficient to fund the required copayment would face a surcharge on their wages when reemployed, which would be paid until such time as the individual's account had an adequate balance. Upon retirement or death, amounts left in the worker's account would be paid in retirement benefits or as a death benefit to the worker's heirs.[19]

The Supreme Court's ACA decision obviously introduces new constitutional uncertainties into this kind of much-needed modernization of our nation's system of unemployment insurance. Changes such as we have suggested here may remain possible, but now apparently must be grounded in Congress's taxing power—the power Congress is most reluctant to use. It is difficult to know why this is a sensible or appropriate reading of the Constitution.

## 6. Conclusion

Health insurance is just one component of a modern system of social insurance—protection of some degree of income security for all Americans in the face of risks common in a dynamic market economy. None of the risks to loss of wage income that we have discussed here—illness, retirement, or unemployment—ever have been or ever will be adequately protected through private insurance alone.[20] Transferring responsibilities from the federal government to state governments or from governmental risk-spreading arrangements to individuals or families inevitably weakens these protections. When states are responsible for financing basic social insurance protections, families' economic security depends on which side of a river they call home. State-based financing also introduces the potential for destructive interstate races to the bottom.

A common feature of the ACA and our proposals for improving retirement security and unemployment insurance is their incremental nature: they largely build on existing institutional arrangements rather than starting anew. The ACA and our retirement security proposals, in particular, fall in the middle between the more radical public provision and privatization proposals advanced in

Washington in recent years. It would be ironic indeed if one consequence of the Supreme Court's ACA decision were to rule out-of-bounds those kinds of incremental changes that are most consonant with the checks and balances at the heart of the democratic structure of our nation's Constitution.

The originalist constitutional vision, embodied in the constitutional challenge to the ACA and found in both Chief Justice Roberts's and the dissenting justices' opinions, ignores the necessity in today's economy of placing both the power and responsibility for social insurance with the federal government. It is a mystery to us why, when it comes to social insurance protections, key politicians seem to believe that state governments always function better than the national government—or, even if not, that our Constitution commits us to a national government of quite limited power and functions in this arena.

To be sure, a majority of the Supreme Court, in refusing to strike down the individual mandate of the ACA, rejected that view. But in doing so, the Court introduced important new uncertainties into the constitutionally permissible *techniques* by which the national government can fulfill its social insurance goals.

Make no mistake: the constitutional challenge to the ACA and the complementary political efforts to devolve social insurance responsibilities to the states and to individuals poses a challenge to the very idea of social insurance. If our individual freedom includes the liberty to opt out of participation in the universal risk-pooling and to evade the intertemporal and interfamily redistribution that sits at the core of our social insurance protections, the very idea of providing social insurance is threatened. Social insurance allows us to thrive in an economic system where only some members of society enjoy financial success because both effort and luck play a crucial role. Social insurance is at base a deeply conservative idea. By protecting family incomes from common risks in a market economy, it simultaneously provides a critical political protection for that same market economy. Why a conservative Court or conservative politicians should want to make the American social insurance system less effective or more difficult to reform is a mystery.

## Acknowledgment

Much of this essay is based on our book Michael J. Graetz & Jerry L. Mashaw, True Security: Rethinking American Social Insurance (1999). See also Jerry L. Mashaw, *Legal, Imagined and Real Worlds: Reflections on the Supreme Court's Decision in* National Federation of Independent Business v. Sebelius, Secretary of Health and Human Services, J. Health Pol'y Pol. & L. (forthcoming 2013).

# Notes

1. See Michael J. Graetz, *Universal Health Coverage Without an Employer Mandate*, 2 DOMESTIC AFFAIRS 79 (1993); MICHAEL J. GRAETZ & JERRY L. MASHAW, TRUE SECURITY: RETHINKING AMERICAN SOCIAL INSURANCE 1–46 (1999).

2. See Graetz & Mashaw, *supra* note 1, at 178.

3. See Mitt Romney, *Mr. President, What's the Rush?* USA TODAY, July 30, 2009, *available at* http://mittromneycentral.com/op-eds/2009-op-eds/mr-president-whats-the-rush/.

4. For further discussion, see Charles Fried's chapter in this volume, The June Surprises: Balls, Strikes, and the Fog of War.

5. See Graetz & Mashaw, *supra* note 1, at 69–91, 188–209.

6. For discussion elsewhere, see chapters 1 through 9 of this volume.

7. See Fried, *supra* note 4.

8. See Fried, *supra* note 4.

9. These conflicts are elaborated in Michael J. Graetz & Jerry L. Mashaw, *Ethics, Institutional Complexity and Health Care Reform: The Struggle for Normative Balance*, 10 J. CONTEMP. HEALTH L. & POL'Y 93 (1994).

10. See Graetz & Mashaw, *supra* note 1, at 61–64, 299–303.

11. Our social insurance conception of health insurance is a "catastrophic" loss, defining catastrophic as income-based.

12. See H. COMM. ON THE BUDGET, THE PATH TO PROSPERITY: A BLUEPRINT FOR AMERICAN RENEWAL (FISCAL YEAR 2013 BUDGET RESOLUTION), *available at* http://paulryan.house. gov/uploadedfiles/pathtoprosperity2013.pdf (last visited August 31, 2012).

13. For more detail, see Graetz & Mashaw, *supra* note 1, at 92–111.

14. *Id.* at 254–263.

15. *Id.* at 263–267.

16. Even mandated savings demonstrates the emptiness of the action vs. nonaction distinction. Savings for retirement (or a period of unemployment) is a deferral of consumption so requiring savings can be viewed as equivalent to limiting current consumption, certainly a constitutionally appropriate use of the taxing power, given the long history of both broad consumption taxes and narrow taxes on the consumption of specific items (such as tobacco and tires).

17. Graetz & Mashaw, *supra* note 1, at 75 (citing DANIEL NELSON, UNEMPLOYMENT INSURANCE: THE AMERICAN EXPERIENCE 1915–1935 (1969)).

18. Graetz & Mashaw, *supra* note 1, at 263–267, 292.

19. *Id.* at 208.

20. Both short- and long-term disability constitute additional examples of the kind of risks at stake here, but we do not discuss those issues here.

# CHAPTER 18

# The Affordable Care Act and the Constitution

## BEYOND *NATIONAL FEDERATION OF INDEPENDENT BUSINESS V. SEBELIUS*

*Timothy Stoltzfus Jost*

In *National Federation of Independent Business v. Sebelius* (NFIB),[1] the Supreme Court concluded that Congress had acted within its constitutional authority in adopting the Affordable Care Act (ACA)'s individual responsibility provision (although as an exercise of its taxing power, not its commerce power) but that the ACA's Medicaid expansion was unconstitutional as written. The chapters in this book address the *NFIB* decision, its history, meaning, and ramifications for the future.

But the ACA and its implementation raise many other constitutional issues not settled by the *NFIB* case; issues that have been and continue to be litigated in the federal courts. While these challenges have not attracted the attention the *NFIB* case garnered, and most have either failed or are likely to fail, they are significant politically. Like the *NFIB* litigation, most of these other cases have been driven by political considerations.[2] They have given support and encouragement to the ACA's enemies, offering state officials politically opposed to the ACA reasons to refuse to cooperate in its implementation and opponents in Congress ammunition to call for its repeal. On the other hand, the tables could have been turned had an administration come to power in Washington opposed to ACA implementation, with the ACA's supporters then resorting to litigation to salvage health reform. This chapter considers a number of constitutional issues presented by the ACA that were not raised in *NFIB*. Some of these issues have been decided by the courts, while others continue to be litigated with no decision yet, and others could have been raised had President Barack Obama not been reelected in November 2012, and might still be relevant as ACA implementation moves forward.

# 1. Issues Already Decided

Nearly thirty cases were filed in the wake of the ACA's enactment challenging the constitutionality of the law.[3] A dozen of these reached the federal appellate courts and certiorari was sought in the Supreme Court in six.[4] Several remain pending as of this writing in the fall of 2012. While most of these cases challenged the constitutional authority of Congress to adopt the ACA's individual responsibility provisions, many raised other constitutional claims as well. These included due process, equal protection, freedom of association, right of privacy, Tenth Amendment commandeering, free exercise, and Establishment Clause issues, as well as constitutional challenges to the process through which the ACA was adopted and the authority of Congress to enact the employer responsibility provisions.

Some of the claims went even further afield, such as the claim in *Baldwin v. Sebelius*[5] that the ACA denied equal protection by creating five offices of women's health but no office of men's health, or the claim in *Shreeve v. Obama*[6] that the defendants had breached "duties contained within their oaths of office to protect and defend the Constitution." One pro se case even raised a "birther" claim, asserting that the ACA was not valid because President Obama was not a citizen.[7] A number of these cases were dismissed because the plaintiff had not alleged an injury sufficient to claim standing or failed to make a plausible claim of violation of a constitutional right.[8]

Some of the claims were taken seriously by the courts, however, and subjected to careful analysis. Judge Moon of the Western District of Virginia devoted several pages of his opinion in *Liberty University v. Geithner* to the plaintiffs' claims that the ACA violates the Establishment and Equal Protection Clauses by creating limited exceptions to the individual mandate for members of certain religious groups and members of health care-sharing ministries, and the Free Exercise Clause and the Religious Freedom Restoration Act by funding abortions.[9] He also took seriously the plaintiffs' claims that Congress lacked the constitutional authority to adopt the employer mandate and violated the Tenth Amendment by requiring the states to establish exchanges, although he seemed somewhat puzzled by the plaintiffs' claim that the ACA violated the Guarantee Clause.[10] He rejected each claim, either finding that the ACA did not do what the plaintiffs claimed it did (for example, fund abortion or require states to establish exchanges), or that the challenged ACA provisions complied with well-established constitutional law. Congress's authority to regulate the terms and conditions of employment, for example, has long been recognized. The religious conscience exemption from the individual responsibility provisions is based on an accommodation in the Social Security Act that has been upheld many times against Establishment Clause challenges.

On appeal, the Fourth Circuit dismissed Liberty University's claims as barred by the Tax Anti-Injunction Act and did not address its other claims (although Judge Davis, in dissent, would have upheld Judge Moon's ruling on these claims).[11] The Supreme Court denied Liberty's petition for certiorari, but Liberty has asked the Court to vacate the Fourth Circuit's judgment and remand the case, as the Supreme Court held in *NFIB* that the Tax Anti-Injunction Act does not apply to the individual responsibility provision. The United States is not opposing this motion, but, presuming the case is remanded to the same Fourth Circuit panel that heard the original case, it seems very unlikely that Liberty will have any more success the second time around.[12]

Similarly, Judge Vinson in the Florida case analyzed at some length the plaintiffs' claims that the ACA unconstitutionally required state employers to insure their employees, commandeered state governments by requiring the states to establish exchanges, and violated substantive due process.[13] Judge Vinson rejected each of these claims, recognizing that under *Garcia v. San Antonio Metropolitan Transit Authority*,[14] Congress can apply "generally applicable" laws to state employers and that the ACA does not require states to establish exchanges. He also rejected the substantive due process claim, though not without wistfully observing that the Supreme Court had "not yet" recognized a fundamental right to "make our own life decisions." These claims were abandoned on appeal.[15]

Judge Kessler in the D.C. district court case fully considered the plaintiffs' claim that the individual responsibility requirement violated the Religious Freedom Restoration Act before rejecting it, concluding that the individual responsibility requirement did not substantially burden the plaintiffs' free exercise of their religion, and in any event, promoted a compelling governmental interest and was the least restrictive means of furthering that interest.[16] The D.C. Circuit on appeal disposed of the claim in a footnote,[17] while the Supreme Court denied certiorari on the claim without comment.[18]

Constitutional claims that have been rejected by the courts may, of course, be raised again in new cases brought by different parties in other courts. But it seems unlikely that, with the Supreme Court having upheld the ACA against the most serious constitutional challenges, courts will entertain broad-based constitutional objections to the ACA as opposed to more targeted claims asserted against specific provisions. Several such targeted cases, however, are currently under way.

## 2. Constitutional Challenges to the ACA Still to Be Decided

A number of constitutional challenges to the ACA survived the *NFIB* decision without final resolution. First, cases remained pending challenging the individual responsibility requirement on individual liberty grounds. Second, the constitutionality of Section 6001 of the ACA, which limits the ability of physician-owned hospitals to bill Medicare for services provided to patients referred by physician owners, remained unresolved. Third, *Coons v. Geithner*, one of the many cases challenging the constitutionality of the individual mandate, also questioned the constitutionality of the Independent Payment Advisory Board. The district court has now dismissed this challenge, but it could be raised again on appeal. Fourth, over two dozen cases have been filed objecting to the requirement that employers cover contraceptive services as a women's preventive service. While these cases rely primarily on the Religious Freedom Restoration Act, they also raise First Amendment challenges. Four of these cases have been dismissed as of this writing, but a preliminary injunction has been entered two others, and the rest remain pending.

## A. INDIVIDUAL LIBERTY CASES

The plaintiffs in *U.S. Citizen's Association v. Sebelius* challenged the authority of Congress to adopt the individual responsibility requirement, but in addition argued that the requirement violated their rights to due process, freedom of expressive and intimate association, and privacy. The district court dismissed these claims as failing to state a plausible claim under recent case law that imposed greater pleading thresholds.[19] The dismissal is on appeal to the Sixth Circuit. In another case, *Walters v. Holder*, Judge Starrett refused initially to dismiss that the ACA violated a right-to-privacy claim, but subsequently entered summary judgment for the defendants.[20] He dismissed the complaint without prejudice on standing and ripeness grounds, however, primarily because it is unclear at this point to what extent disclosure of private financial and medical information will be required under the ACA and how the security of that information will be protected.

Although constitutional privacy, substantive due process, freedom of expression, and intimate association claims were not before the Supreme Court in *NFIB*, it is hard to imagine that the Court, having held that Congress had the authority to adopt the individual responsibility requirement, would invalidate it on these grounds. The individual responsibility provision does not in fact require the disclosure of private medical information, require or prohibit speech, or interfere in intimate relationships. Since insurance will no longer be underwritten medically, insurance companies should have no need for personal medical information; and if insurance is purchased directly from a private insurer, the insurer should not need private financial data. Persons who apply for premium tax credits through the exchanges will need to disclose financial information to establish eligibility, but this information will be subject to strict privacy protections.[21] Moreover, since the Court in *NFIB* interpreted the individual responsibility provision as merely imposing a tax rather than a legal command, individuals can protect their privacy by simply refusing to purchase insurance and paying a tax. This was indeed the position taken by the court in rejecting privacy claims raised by the plaintiffs in *Coons v. Geithner*.[22] Privacy and substantive due process claims may persist or reappear, but are unlikely to prevail.

## B. LIMITS ON MEDICARE PAYMENTS FOR PHYSICIAN-OWNED HOSPITALS

A second issue that survived *NFIB* is the constitutionality of ACA Section 6001, which limits Medicare payments for physician-owned hospitals.[23] Since 1993, Medicare payment for hospital services has been prohibited if the physician who ordered the service had an investment or compensation interest in the hospital.[24] The prohibition was intended to limit conflicts of interest and overutilization of hospital services. It has contained a "whole hospital" exception, however, allowing doctors to admit patients to a hospital if they had an investment interest in the entire hospital rather than in a specific service or department.[25] While this exception was apparently included to permit referrals to small physician-owned rural hospitals, it led to a proliferation of physician-owned specialty hospitals, which raised the same concerns that prompted adoption of the prohibition in the first place.

After several earlier attempts to limit these referrals, Congress finally adopted Section 6001 of the ACA, which prohibits Medicare payment for physician-owned hospital services for patients referred by physician owners for existing hospitals that expand after March 23, 2010 (subject to limited exceptions) or for new hospitals that are not in operation by December 31, 2010. This amendment precludes Medicare payments for a number of physician-owned hospitals that were being planned or under construction but could not meet the deadline, portending a substantial financial loss for investors.

A group of physician-owned hospitals sued, claiming that the law violated their due process and equal protection rights because it was not rationally related to a legitimate purpose and was in fact enacted to win support for health care reform from the general hospitals with which physician-owned hospitals compete.[26] The plaintiffs also claimed that the law took their property in violation of the Takings Clause and was void for vagueness.

District Court Judge Michael Schneider had little trouble finding a legitimate and rational basis for the prohibition.[27] The court also held that the law did not take physical property and that neither its grandfathering provisions nor exceptions were unconstitutionally vague. The court also held that the statute did not cause a regulatory taking. The court recognized that the economic impact of the statute was serious, but also noted that the plaintiffs could not have had a reasonable expectation that the Medicare program would remain unchanged. The hospitals could continue to bill Medicare for services provided to patients referred by nonowner physicians and to bill privately for patients referred by owners. On appeal, the Fifth Circuit vacated the lower-court opinion and dismissed the case because the plaintiffs failed to exhaust their administrative remedies.[28] The issue is not dead, as the plaintiffs could proceed through the Medicare appellate process, but it is unlikely to be decided by the courts for some time, and in the interim Section 6001 remains in effect.

## C. THE INDEPENDENT PAYMENT ADVISORY BOARD

A third case, *Coons v. Geithner*,[29] challenges the constitutionality of the Independent Payment Advisory Board (IPAB) established by Section 3403 of the ACA.[30] The IPAB is a remarkable institution, born out of the perception that Congress is so dominated by special interests that it is impotent to control Medicare cost growth. The IPAB is a fifteen-member board of nationally recognized health care experts tasked with developing detailed proposals to reduce Medicare spending per capita in years, beginning with 2014, when the Centers for Medicare and Medicaid Services (CMS) Actuary projects that spending will exceed statutorily established target levels. The IPAB's proposals are subject to a number of limitations, and specifically may not "ration health care," raise costs to beneficiaries, restrict benefits, or modify eligibility criteria.[31] For each year for which medical costs are projected to exceed the target amounts, the IPAB must submit a proposal to Congress to reduce cost growth. If the IPAB fails to submit a proposal on deadline, the Department of Health and Human Services (HHS) must itself submit a proposal. Congress must consider the proposal under an expedited procedure, and HHS must implement the IPAB proposal unless Congress adopts an equally effective alternative. Congress may not adopt an alternative that does not achieve cost-reduction requirements except by a three-fifths vote of both houses. The HHS secretary's implementation of the recommendation is not subject to judicial review.

The *Coons* complaint raised two constitutional challenges to the IPAB legislation. First, the plaintiffs, who included two members of Congress, claimed that terms of the IPAB statute limited the ability of Congress to eliminate the IPAB, thus "entrenching" the IPAB from repeal. The plaintiffs asserted that this unconstitutionally limited the power of Congress and specifically denied them their First Amendment rights as legislators. In response, the United States denied that the IPAB provision did, or could, limit the authority of Congress to repeal the provision. The plaintiffs dropped this claim after the Supreme Court decided, in a separate case, that the First Amendment did not protect a legislator's vote.[32]

The plaintiffs continued to press their claim, however, that the IPAB represents an unprecedented unconstitutional delegation of legislative authority, noting not only the sweeping power of the IPAB to modify the terms of the Medicare statute, but also claiming that its immunity from judicial review and exemption from administrative rulemaking violates separation-of-power principles. The district court dismissed this delegation claim in a single paragraph, simply holding that Congress has provided "intelligible principles" to guide the discretion of the IPAB. The Obama administration has so far taken no visible steps to implement the IPAB requirements and will likely face stiff opposition in Congress if it attempts to do so; thus a legal challenge to the IPAB may be moot, or at least premature. In any event, given the reluctance of the courts to strike down delegations of authority to administrative agencies, the delegation argument may not have been the plaintiffs' strongest argument.[33] It might have been more fruitful to focus on the extensive authority granted to the IPAB to waive statutory requirements and the limits imposed on judicial review of its decisions, but the court dismissed the case without addressing those issues.[34]

## D. THE CONTRACEPTIVE COVERAGE MANDATE

A fourth issue is the legality of the contraceptive coverage requirement that appears in a regulation implementing the ACA mandate that health plans cover preventive services without cost-sharing. Section 2713 of the Public Health Services Act, added by Section 1001 of the ACA, provides that insurers must cover women's "preventive care and screenings ... as provided for in comprehensive guidelines supported by the Health Resources and Services Administration (HRSA)."[35] Among the preventive services recommended by HRSA are "all Food and Drug Administration approved contraceptive methods, sterilization procedures, and patient education and counseling for all women with reproductive capacity."[36] HRSA's contraceptive services recommendation was based on a consensus report by the Institute of Medicine finding that planned pregnancies provide health benefits for both women and babies.[37] Group plans and health insurers that do not have grandfathered status must implement this coverage for plan or policy years beginning after August 1, 2012.

Insurance coverage of contraceptives is common in the United States. Twenty-eight states have laws requiring health insurers to cover contraceptives.[38] Studies cited in the preamble to the preventive care regulation found that over 80 percent of insurers and large employers already cover contraceptives.[39] Some courts have held that an employer's failure to provide contraceptive coverage violates the Pregnancy Discrimination Act, although others have held that it does not.[40]

Some religious groups, notably the Catholic Church, believe that contraception is morally wrong. These religious groups employ—and provide employee health benefits to—thousands of Americans. But many employers conscientiously opposed to contraception would face significant penalties under the ACA, potentially amounting to millions of dollars, if they dropped health insurance coverage altogether to avoid the mandate. The agencies implementing the ACA have attempted, therefore, to reach an accommodation between the public health objective of increasing access to preventive services and the goal of protecting religious freedom.

The administration initially promulgated a final rule excluding "religious employers" from the contraceptive coverage requirement, but defined this term narrowly to mean churches and their integrated auxiliaries, conventions, and associations, and religious orders that have inculcation of religious values as their purpose, and primarily serve and employ persons who share their religious tenets.[41] Churches and other organizations that fit into this category do not have to provide coverage for contraception at all. Similarly, twenty states exempt at least some religious organizations from their contraceptive coverage mandates, with half of those states limiting the exception to religious organizations that primarily serve religious, as opposed to general charitable, purposes.[42]

The federal exception, like many of the state exemptions, does not extend to religious hospitals, universities, or charities, many of which objected strenuously to providing contraceptive coverage for their employees. In response to this outcry, the administration created a second exception through guidance. This exception establishes a safe harbor for one year (until August 1, 2013) from enforcement of the regulations in order to protect nonprofit organizations with a religious objection to covering contraceptive services.[43] This was followed by an Advance Notice of Proposed Rulemaking announcing the administration's intention to draft rules to accommodate these religious organizations.[44] The Advance Notice proposed various approaches that would allow employees of these religious organizations to secure access to contraception without the organizations having to pay directly for it.

This approach failed to appease the religious organizations. Catholic organizations and others (including seven state governors) have filed about two dozen lawsuits challenging the contraception requirement. Although many of these lawsuits raise First Amendment freedom-of-religion issues, most rely primarily on the Religious Freedom Restoration Act (RFRA).[45] Congress adopted RFRA in 1993 in the wake of the Supreme Court's decision in *Department of Human Resources v. Smith*,[46] which held that the First Amendment did not require governments to demonstrate a compelling governmental interest when defending a "neutral law of general applicability" limiting religious practices in some way. Congress rejected this position in RFRA, prohibiting the federal government from taking any action (including adopting rules of general applicability) that would "substantially burden a person's exercise of religion" unless the law is justified by a compelling governmental interest and is the least restrictive approach to furthering the governmental interest.[47] Although Congress may itself exempt a statute it adopts from the application of RFRA, administrative agencies must comply with RFRA in taking regulatory actions.[48] The Supreme Court has held that RFRA is unconstitutional as applied to state law (since the Court itself, and not Congress, has the authority to interpret the First Amendment),[49] but has applied RFRA in evaluating federal law.[50]

As of this writing, three courts have dismissed cases challenging the contraception mandate, holding that the plaintiffs (including seven state governors in one case) lacked standing because they did not show that the contraception rule actually caused them any injury, and that resolution of the issue is premature while the moratorium still applies and the federal government continues to clarify its approach.[51] The court in one case, *O'Brien v. HHS*, brought by a secular, for-profit, limited liability company dismissed the RFRA claim on the merits.[52] However, in another case, *Newland v. Sebelius*, the court has entered a preliminary injunction blocking the application of the contraception mandate to a private company whose owners refuse to provide coverage for contraceptive services for religious reasons.[53] In yet another case, *Legatus v. Sebelius*, Judge Robert Cleland dismissed the claim of one of the plaintiffs, a religious organization, on ripeness and standing grounds, but entered a preliminary injunction on behalf of the other plaintiffs, a private for-profit corporation and its owners.[54] The private companies in *Newland* and *Legatus* were not covered by any of the safe harbors, and therefore presented live disputes. Other cases involving religious institutions are likely to reach the merits when the current moratorium ends. These cases raise several important questions under RFRA.

The first is whether refusing to provide contraception coverage involves "a person's exercise of religion." Most cases involving free exercise of religion have involved some sort of explicitly religious practice, such as the use of prohibited drugs in religious worship. But some religious freedom cases have also, like the contraception cases, involved employment-related practices, such as required contributions to Social Security or denial of unemployment compensation to employees who lost their jobs because they refused to work on the Sabbath.[55] Therefore, some plaintiffs are likely to prevail on this issue.

More problematic is the question of whether a secular, for-profit corporation can hold a religious belief. In *Newland* and *Legatus*, the courts essentially considered the family-owned corporations as indistinguishable from their owners. But would the situation be different if the corporation was a large, privately held corporation, with thousands of employees, or even a publicly held corporation that espoused certain religious principles in its founding documents? Can any private corporation hold religious beliefs? If a corporation is a person under the Free Speech Clause,[56] is it necessarily a person for the Free Exercise Clause?

Judge Kane in *Newland* left these questions open for later resolution, as did Judge Jackson in dismissing the claim of a secular company in the *O'Brien* case on other grounds, but Judge Cleland accepted the possibility of corporations enjoying protected free exercise rights. Presumably religious organizations not covered by an exception will have standing to challenge the rule, although the highest courts of both New York and California have upheld, against a range of free exercise and establishment claims, state laws similar to the federal rule distinguishing between churches (exempt from the contraception coverage requirement) and other institutions run by religious entities for general charitable purposes (covered by the requirement).[57]

The next question is whether the contraception mandate "substantially burdens" free exercise. Judge Kane simply failed to address this question in the *Newland* case, but Judge Cleland in *Legatus* concluded that the private plaintiffs were likely to be able to show that the contraceptive mandate imposed a substantial burden on their Catholic beliefs. In *O'Brien*, however, Judge Jackson held that any burden on the plaintiffs' free exercise was de minimis. In so holding, Judge Jackson emphasized that the rule does not require the plaintiffs to use contraception, but rather merely to make insurance available to their employees that would allow them to choose independently whether or not to purchase contraception. To excuse the plaintiffs from compliance with the rule would be to assist them in imposing their own religious beliefs on their employees, which is not the purpose of RFRA. Finding no substantial burden, Judge Jackson dismissed the RFRA claim.

Having assumed that the preventive services rule "substantially burdened" the free exercise rights of the Newlands, Judge Kane proceeded to consider whether RFRA's requirements for upholding a federal law burdening religion had been met. Judge Kane held first that the government had not shown a compelling interest supporting the rule. Recognizing that protecting public health is a compelling governmental concern, he held that HHS had undermined its assertion that uniform protection of this interest was compelling by granting broad exceptions for grandfathered plans, small employers (which need not provide any employee coverage), and religious employers. Judge Kane further held that the government had not refuted the plaintiffs' argument that there was a less restrictive alternative for providing contraception—a government program.

Although Judge Kane only ruled on the question of likelihood of success on the merits for a preliminary injunction rather than finally deciding the legal question, his preliminary resolution of these issues raises serious questions. While it is arguable that the widespread exemptions from the preventive services requirement undermine the claim that the requirement is absolutely essential, it surely cannot be the case that the government cannot defend a rule as serving a compelling interest if the rule admits to any exceptions. Leaving aside the question of whether the plaintiffs would willingly pay taxes to finance such a public program covering contraception, the plaintiffs' least restrictive alternative argument would seem to preclude a private sector solution to the problem of health care financing, one of the primary goals of the ACA.

Judge Cleland, in *Legatus*, entertained the government's argument that two compelling interests were at stake—the public's health and gender equality. Although he expressed considerable skepticism about the government's ability to prove the compelling nature of these interests, Judge Cleland nevertheless went on to consider the government's contention that the mandate was the least restrictive means of serving these ends, acknowledging that the creation of a government program to provide contraceptives was probably not practical, but questioning the harm that would be caused by freeing a single employer from the mandate. In the end, Judge Cleland concluded that neither the plaintiffs nor the government had proved likelihood of success on the merits, but entered a preliminary injunction against the enforcement of the mandate because of the seriousness of the threat he perceived to the plaintiff's free exercise rights.

It is unlikely that in the end a free exercise challenge to the contraception rule will prevail, given that the rule would seem to be a neutral law of general applicability.[58] A RFRA claim is closer case. Courts may follow the lead of the *O'Brien* case and find that a contraception coverage mandate is not a substantial burden on religious freedom, but in cases involving self-insured plans, a more direct burden may be found. Even if a court finds a substantial burden, however, it may well find a compelling governmental interest. There is ample precedent for finding protection of the public health or gender equality to be compelling governmental interests.[59] The California Supreme Court, applying California constitutional law that is essentially the same as RFRA, found a governmental interest in combating gender discrimination to be compelling.[60] The same decision found that a public program to provide contraception was not a realistic less restrictive alternative, as it would essentially require public funding to subsidize the plaintiff's religious beliefs. In the end, it is likely, although not certain, that whatever compromise the Obama administration reaches will be upheld.

## 3.  A Future Refusal to Implement the Affordable Care Act

It should be clear from the foregoing that the remaining challenges to the ACA are not insurmountable. Challenges to a few provisions may succeed, but with *NFIB* having generally upheld the law, it faces no existential constitutional challenges. This does not mean, however, that its path to implementation has been without potential roadblocks. The major challenges that ACA implementation has faced are political—resistance from the states, pushback from Congress, political accommodation on the part of the Obama administration that threatens the full and timely implementation of the law, and the potential election of an administration hostile to the ACA.

The campaign website of Governor Mitt Romney, who ran against President Obama in the fall of 2012, stated under the heading, "Health Care," and subheading "Mitt's Plan": "On his first day in office, Mitt Romney will issue an executive order that paves the way for the federal government to issue Obamacare waivers to all fifty states. He will then work with Congress to repeal the full legislation as quickly as possible."[61]

Of course, President Obama was reelected, and the implementation of the ACA can proceed. But would there have been any statutory authority for "Obamacare waivers?" In the absence of statutory authority, would waivers be constitutional? Indeed, If President Obama finds it politically expedient to delay or to refuse to implement parts of the ACA, can he do so constitutionally?

The ACA itself in fact provides for waivers to be granted to states from many of its key provisions, including the individual and employer responsibility provisions, exchange and qualified health plan requirements, and premium tax credit and cost-sharing reduction payment programs.[62] A state granted a waiver may receive the federal funding that otherwise would have gone towards premium tax credits and cost-sharing reduction payments to fund its program. But before a waiver can be granted, a state must meet several conditions: it must adopt a statute establishing its program; meet transparency requirements; demonstrate that its program will provide coverage that is at least as comprehensive and affordable, and covers a comparable number of state residents, as the ACA; and demonstrate that its program does not increase the federal budget deficit. Most importantly, waivers cannot be granted under the ACA until 2017.

The fact that the Obama administration has granted waivers or adjustments from some provisions of the ACA has received a great deal of publicity. Specific sections of the ACA granted authority to HHS to issue waivers from the prohibition on annual dollar coverage limits prior to 2014 if immediate imposition would make coverage unaffordable,[63] and to grant adjustment of the medical loss ratio threshold in states where an immediate move to statutory maximums would destabilize the individual market.[64] But the legal authority for these limited waiver and adjustment programs has now expired. Legislation has been introduced into Congress with bipartisan support and the endorsement of the Obama administration to allow broader waivers as of 2014, but it has stalled in Congress and is very unlikely to be law anytime soon.

In sum, there is no current statutory authority for "Obamacare waivers." In the absence of such authority, such a waiver would be unconstitutional. Under the Constitution's Bicameralism and Presentment Clause, legislation must be passed by both the House and Senate and be signed by the President in order to become law. The President cannot unilaterally amend or repeal a law duly adopted through this constitutional process, even if a statute explicitly authorizes the President to do so. "There is no provision in the Constitution that authorizes the President to enact, to amend, or to repeal statutes."[65] Instead, "Amendment and repeal of statutes, no less than enactment, must conform with" the bicameralism and presentment requirement.[66] A hypothetical President Romney could not have legally granted the states blanket waivers from compliance with the requirements of the ACA, and President Obama lacks authority to grant waivers as well.

What would have happened, however, if Governor Romney had been elected president and simply refused to implement the law, or indeed if President Obama fails to implement some provisions of the law? In fact, analogous issues have often arisen when one president is succeeded by a president from a different party with a different ideology. The most famous such incident occurred with the transition from the Federalist administration of John Adams to the Democratic-Republican administration of Thomas Jefferson. The Federalists, having lost control of Congress and the presidency, created and filled at the last minute a number of judicial offices, hoping to extend the reach of their control. The incoming Jefferson administration refused to deliver a commission to a justice of the peace named William Marbury. Marbury sued for mandamus before the Supreme Court. Chief Justice Marshall, in one of the most famous of all Supreme Court opinions, ruled that the judiciary has the power to order the executive to comply with laws duly adopted by Congress and signed by the President, and could do so at the instance of an individual harmed by the executive's refusal to take action (although the Court also held that the case was not properly before the Supreme Court and did not issue the requested order).[67] *Marbury v. Madison* established not just the principle that the courts have the final authority to say what the law is, but also that the courts can protect the rights of individuals who are illegally deprived of those rights by the executive.[68]

More recently, a federal court enjoined the unilateral attempt by the newly elected President Nixon to terminate the Community Action Agency within the Office of Economic Opportunity; a program that was established by law and funded through an ongoing appropriation.[69] The court ordered President Nixon to reinstate the Community Action Agency. Several other courts nullified President Nixon's attempts to terminate other funded government programs.[70] Presumably, attempts by a president to simply terminate the implementation of the ACA would meet a similar fate.

Many of the provisions of the ACA are already in effect. Some provisions took effect immediately upon the adoption of the statute in March 2010 or soon thereafter, including those establishing the early retiree reinsurance program, the small business premium tax credit, the preexisting condition high-risk pool, and the healthcare.gov website.[71] Others took effect for plan years following the six-month anniversary of the enactment of the ACA, including provisions banning lifetime limits and rescissions except for fraud; requiring insurers and health plans to offer internal and external appeals and coverage to adult children up to age twenty-six; prohibiting preexisting conditions clauses for children; and requiring coverage of preventive care without cost-sharing.[72] Still other provisions have taken effect in 2011 and 2012, including requirements that insurers spend at least 80 percent (85 percent in the large-group market) of their adjusted premium revenue on health care claims and quality-improvement expenses,[73] justify unreasonable premium increases,[74] and provide applicants and enrollees with a uniform summary of benefits and coverage.[75]

All of these provisions have been implemented through final rules, or in some instances, interim final rules. Once promulgated, rules cannot be rescinded except through Administrative Procedure Act rulemaking proceedings. Moreover, the decision to rescind must be subjected to the same level of scrutiny as regulations themselves.[76] If Governor Romney had been elected and had tried to rescind existing rules, he would have had to establish that the decision to rescind was not arbitrary and capricious and was in accordance with the law.

Other provisions of the ACA go into effect on January 1, 2014, including those requiring insurers to guarantee issue and renewal of health insurance coverage and to cease health status underwriting and exclusion of preexisting conditions; establishing the exchanges and risk adjustment, reinsurance, and risk corridor programs; providing premium tax credits and cost-sharing reduction payments; and enforcing the individual and employer responsibility provisions.[77] Some of these provisions are self-executing, that is, if they are not repealed, they will go into effect automatically on January 1, 2014, without the need for any regulatory action. These include the prohibition on health status underwriting and on preexisting conditions exclusions, and the guaranteed renewal requirement.[78] Other provisions explicitly require regulatory action on the part of HHS or the Departments of Treasury or Labor, such as the establishment of age-rating bands or of open enrollment periods.[79] Still other provisions require affirmative action by the federal government, such as the creation of the advance premium tax credit program or the enforcement of the individual or employer responsibility provisions.[80]

Final rules have already been promulgated to implement some of the 2014 ACA requirements and programs. As of late fall of 2012, agencies had not even published notices of proposed rulemaking as to other programs. Even requirements and programs for which final rules have been published still presented unresolved issues that will be subject to further guidance. Finally, some programs, like the federally facilitated exchanges and advance premium tax credit program, are massive programs that must be implemented directly by the federal government. Would a Romney administration have been legally obligated to implement these programs? Can President Obama delay implementation?

The Administrative Procedure Act provides that a court may "compel agency action unlawfully withheld or unreasonably delayed."[81] Courts generally apply a multifactor "rule of reason" test in determining when an agency has "unreasonably delayed" administrative action, considering the type of regulation at issue, the nature of the interests at stake, and agency priorities and resources.[82] When Congress imposes a specific deadline for agency action, however, Congress itself has determined the reasonable time for agency compliance, and an agency that fails to act by the deadline has "unlawfully withheld agency action."[83] A court must simply order compliance with the statutory deadline.[84] If the administration refused to establish federal exchanges or risk adjustment or reinsurance programs in states that do not establish exchanges, a court should order it to do so at the instance of a party with standing to raise the issue. Of course, a court cannot order the impossible, and if litigation were not brought until after the deadline had passed or at a point when timely implementation was simply impossible, a court would have to set a realistic timetable for compliance. As long as a statutory deadline remains in place, however, compliance with clear statutory directives is not optional.

On the other hand, as has already become very clear from the implementation efforts of the Obama administration, there are many provisions of the ACA that are subject to interpretation. Where rulemaking is not clearly required by a set deadline, the courts are unlikely to order that rulemaking proceed.[85] Rules that are promulgated will not be rejected by the courts, unless they are

a. arbitrary, capricious, an abuse of discretion, or otherwise not in accordance with law;
b. contrary to constitutional right, power, privilege, or immunity;
c. in excess of statutory jurisdiction, authority, or limitations, or short of statutory right; [or]
d. without observance of procedure required by law.[86]

A future president will have considerable discretion as to how rules are written.

Moreover, the administration will have considerable discretion in its enforcement of the law. The ACA insurance reforms are federal law, directly binding on private insurers. An insurer that attempted to impose a preexisting conditions clause after 2013 could be sued for enforcing an illegal contract term, either under state law for an insurer in the nongroup market or under the Employee Retirement Income Security Act of 1974 for an insurer in the group market.[87] HHS has authority to enforce the ACA directly against insurers under the Public Health Services Act (PHSA).[88] Primary responsibility to enforce the statute resides in the states, however, and HHS may only enforce the provisions of the ACA that are imposed under the PHSA in a state that "fails substantially to enforce" those requirements.[89] Most of the states are in fact enforcing ACA reforms already in effect.[90] If the administration simply fails to enforce the law, however, it is unlikely the courts would order it to do so.[91] As long as the administration simply drags its feet rather than taking explicit formal action to refuse enforcement, there will probably be little that can be done, at least initially.

Another issue would have arisen if states wanted to move forward with implementation of the ACA under a Romney administration that opposed it. The states have primary responsibility for implementing much of the ACA, with the federal government playing a supportive role.[92] As of this writing in the fall of 2012, fifteen states and the District of Columbia have established state exchanges.[93] As of May 2012, eight states had already expanded Medicaid eligibility to adults, while twenty-nine states had received funding for establishing Medicaid information technology systems to implement the Medicaid expansion.[94] Whether or not an administration opposed to the ACA attempted to implement the federal exchanges or the Medicaid expansion, a state committed to the ACA could decide to proceed with implementation, and could sue the federal government if it refused to provide Medicaid federal financial participation or premium tax credits and cost reduction subsidies.

If, on the other hand, a state decides not to move ahead with exchange establishment or Medicaid expansion, there is little its citizens can do to force implementation. State establishment of an exchange is explicitly optional under the ACA, and the Supreme Court has now made the Medicaid expansion optional as well. There may, however, be some claims enforceable against a state that chooses to take on the responsibility of running an exchange and fails to comply with ACA requirements. A number of the responsibilities of state exchanges seem to be mandatory,[95] and some could be interpreted as creating individual rights. A state exchange that refused to take an application for a federal premium tax credit could, for example, quite possibly be sued for violating a right established by federal law.

One issue that would certainly come up in litigation challenging a refusal to implement all or part of the ACA is standing. As already noted, the self-executing provisions of the ACA are binding on insurers regardless of who is in the White House and could be enforced directly by insurance applicants or enrollees immediately affected by a violation of the law. These provisions would also be enforceable by states whose laws give the Department of Insurance authority to enforce federal requirements. An enrollee in a qualified health plan (QHP) in a state that established an exchange that certified QHPs and enrolled members could presumably claim a premium tax credit on his or her tax return, and proceed through regular IRS appellate procedures and sue in tax court if the tax credit were denied. A state denied certification of its exchange, or federal financial participation for its Medicaid program, would be adversely affected by the administration's action and could sue HHS to enforce the law. Perhaps a resident of a state that refused to establish an exchange could sue to compel the federal government to establish an exchange to obtain access to premium tax credits. But it might be difficult to identify a person with standing to enforce many of the obligations imposed on the federal government under the ACA; for example, provisions requiring the administration to undertake various studies.

Of course, Congress could repeal or amend the ACA, settling the question. With the Democrats holding the Senate, however, this is unlikely to happen unless amendments to the ACA are part of an overarching bargain with the House to address the nation's fiscal difficulties. In the end, the next president cannot simply waive the application of the ACA. Indeed, the next administration will be legally obligated to implement and enforce the ACA unless and until it is repealed by Congress. To what extent the courts can and will enforce this obligation remains to be seen.

## 4. Conclusion

While *NFIB* is certainly the preeminent case in the history of ACA litigation, it is neither the beginning nor the end of that history. Important constitutional issues were decided before *NFIB* and remain to be decided after it. Issues are also likely to arise concerning the implementation of the Supreme Court's decision. The state of Maine, for example, has sued HHS claiming that the Medicaid maintenance of effort provisions of the ACA are unenforceable because they are part of the Medicaid expansion declared unconstitutional by *NFIB*.[96] Its request for a preliminary injunction was refused by the First Circuit, but the claim may be heard on the merits if HHS refuses Maine's request for a state plan amendment cutting back on eligibility, which is now pending.

How has all of this litigation affected the implementation of the ACA? The *NFIB* litigation has likely affected the willingness of the states to cooperate in ACA implementation. As long as the *NFIB* case was pending, many of the plaintiff states were reluctant to take an active part in ACA implementation, both because it would appear inconsistent with their litigation position and because they genuinely hoped that the Court would invalidate the ACA in its entirety. But few opposition states in fact moved ahead with implementation at the conclusion of *NFIB*, either deciding to wait until after the election to commit to implementation or simply refusing to assist in implementation under any circumstances. Indeed, a number of states are continuing to refuse to cooperate with implementation even following President Obama's reelection.

On the other hand, I do not believe that the litigation has had a dramatic effect on federal efforts at implementation, except insofar as it made the states less cooperative. I have been involved continuously in the ACA implementation process over the past two and a half years and have seen no evidence that litigation has dampened federal implementation efforts. Implementation has been, from all appearances, affected by interest group demands (including those of consumer groups), electoral politics, and above all, the sheer practical difficulties of totally reconstructing the nation's health insurance system. But it has not been similarly affected by litigation—except insofar as *NFIB* changed the rules for the Medicaid expansion. Pending litigation directed at particular provisions of the ACA is also unlikely to derail implementation of the ACA as a whole. Whether litigation may stall or block an attempt to stop or roll back ACA implementation in the future remains to be seen. But so far, although ACA litigation has created endless work for lawyers and law professors, it has not, to my mind, dramatically affected federal government efforts to implement the law.

## 5. Epilogue

This chapter was current as of the late fall of 2012. As this book goes to press in the winter of 2013, ACA litigation continues unabated, although many of the issues left open by the *NFIB* decision have been settled. On February 1, 2013, the Sixth Circuit Court of Appeals affirmed the district court's dismissal of the plaintiffs' freedom of intimate and expressive association, freedom to refuse unwanted medical care, and privacy challenges to the ACA in the U.S. Citizens Association case.[97] In a move that surprised some, the Supreme Court vacated its denial of certiorari and the appellate court judgment in the Liberty University case, remanding the case to the Fourth Circuit for reconsideration.[98] The Fourth Circuit, however, has focused its reconsideration in that case on the constitutionality of the employer mandate, an issue on which the plaintiffs would seem to have little chance of success.

Litigation on the religious liberty issues raised by the preventive services contraceptive mandate, on the other hand, continues to expand, with at least forty cases filed on the issue and new court decisions appearing almost weekly. The cases divide between those brought by religious organizations and those brought by secular employers. Most courts have held that the claims brought by religious organizations are premature pending the release of further guidance from the Department of Health and Human Services. Recently released proposed rules that would require insurers to cover contraception but would free religious organizations from having any role in the coverage should satisfy constitutional and RFRA requirements.

The administration, on the other hand, has shown no inclination to accommodate the religious beliefs of secular employers on the contraceptive issue. To date the Seventh[99] and Eighth Circuits[100] have granted preliminary relief pending appeal protecting for-profit employers who object to covering contraceptives, while the Tenth Circuit has denied such relief.[101] The important questions raised by these cases are likely to end up in the Supreme Court.

## Notes

1. 132 S. Ct. 2566 (2012).
2. See Robert N. Weiner, The Potential Impact of the Supreme Court Decision Upholding the Affordable Care Act, in this volume.
3. ACA LITIGATION SPREADSHEET, ACA LITIGATION BLOG (July 3, 2012), http://aca-litigation.wikispaces.com/file/view/ACA+litigation+spreadsheet+%2807.03.12%29.xlsx.
4. Id.
5. Baldwin v. Sebelius, 2010 WL 3418436 (S.D. Cal 2010), aff'd, 654 F.3d 877 (9th Cir. 2011).
6. 2010 WL 4628177 (E.D. Tenn. 2010).
7. Taitz v. Obama, 707 F. Supp. 2d 1 (D.D.C. 2010).
8. Calvey v. Obama, 792 F. Supp. 2d 1262 (W.D. Okla. 2011); Baldwin, 2010 WL 3418436; U.S. Citizens' Ass'n. v. Geithner, 754 F. Supp. 2d 903, 910 (N.D. Ohio 2010).
9. Liberty Univ. v. Geithner, 753 F. Supp. 2d 611 (W.D. Va. 2010), vacated, 671 F.3d 391 (4th Cir. 2011), cert. denied, No. 11-438 (June 29, 2012).
10. Id.
11. Liberty Univ. v. Geithner, 671 F.3d 391 (4th Cir. 2011), cert. denied, No. 11-438 (June 29, 2012).
12. Liberty Univ., 671 F.3d 391.
13. Florida ex rel. McCollum v. U.S. Dep't. of Health & Human Servs., 716 F. Supp. 2d 1120 (N.D. Fla. 2010), rev'd in part on other grds., 648 F.3d 1235 (11th Cir. 2011), aff'd in part, rev'd in part sub nom. NFIB v. Sebelius, 132 S. Ct. 2566 (2012).
14. 469 U.S. 528 (1985).
15. Forest Grove Sch. Dist. v. T.A., 638 F.3d 1234, 1261–1265 (9th Cir. 2011).
16. Mead v. Holder, 766 F. Supp. 2d 16 (D.D.C. 2011), aff'd sub nom. Seven Sky v. Holder, 661 F.3d 1 (D.C. Cir. 2011), cert. denied, No. 11–679 (June 29, 2012).
17. Seven Sky v. Holder, 661 F.3d 1, 5 n.4 (D.C. Cir. 2011), cert denied, No. 11-679 (June 29, 2012).
18. Seven-Sky, No. 11-679 (June 29, 2012), 2012 WL 2470101.
19. U.S. Citizens Ass'n. v. Sebelius, 754 F. Supp. 2d 903 (N.D. Ohio 2010); see Ashcroft v. Iqbal, 556 U.S. 662 (2009); Bell Atl. Corp. v. Twombly, 550 U.S. 544 (2007).
20. Walters v. Holder, 2012 WL 3644816 (S.D. Miss. 2012), motion to dismiss denied sub nom. Bryant v. Holder, 809 F. Supp. 2d 563 (S.D. Miss. 2011).
21. 42 C.F.R § 155.260.
22. Coons v. Geithner, 2012 WL 3778219 (D. Ariz. 2012).
23. Pub. L. No. 111-148, 124 Stat. 199 (codified at 42 U.S.C. § 1395(d)(2),(d)(3), & (i) (2010)).
24. 42 U.S.C. § 1395nn(d)(3).
25. Id.
26. Physician Hosps. of Am. v. Sebelius, 781 F. Supp. 2d 431 (E.D. Texas 2011), vacated and dismissed, 2012 WL 3517362 (5th Cir. 2012).

27. *Id.*

28. The appellate court held exhaustion was required under 42 U.S.C. §§ 405(h), 1395ii, and Shalala v. Ill. Council on Long Term Care, 529 U.S. 1 (2000).

29. *Coons,* 2012 WL 3778219.

30. 42 U.S.C. § 1395kkk.

31. 42 U.S.C. § 1395kkk(c)(2)(A)(ii).

32. Nev. Comm'n on Ethics v. Carrigan, 131 S. Ct. 2343 (2011).

33. Whitman v. Am. Trucking Assocs. Inc., 531 U.S. 457 (2001); Mistretta v. United States, 488 U.S. 361 (1989).

34. See Timothy Jost, *The Real Constitutional Problem with the Affordable Care Act,* 36 J. HEALTH POL. POL'Y & L. 501 (2011).

35. 42 U.S.C. § 300gg–13.

36. WOMEN'S PREVENTIVE SERVICES: REQUIRED HEALTH PLAN COVERAGE GUIDELINES, http://www.hrsa.gov/womensguidelines/ (last visited Dec. 13, 2012).

37. INST. OF MED., CLINICAL PREVENTIVE SERVICES FOR WOMEN: CLOSING THE GAPS (July 2011), http://www.iom.edu/Reports/2011/Clinical-Preventive-Services-for-Women-Closing-the-Gaps.aspx.

38. GUTTMACHER INST., INSURANCE COVERAGE OF CONTRACEPTIVES (Dec. 1, 2012), http://www.guttmacher.org/statecenter/spibs/spib_ICC.pdf.

39. Adam Sonfield et al., *U.S. Insurance Coverage of Contraceptives and the Impact of Contraceptive Coverage Mandates,* 36 PERSPECTIVES ON SEXUAL & REPRODUCTIVE HEALTH 72 (2002); GARY CLAXTON ET AL., EMPLOYER HEALTH BENEFITS: 2010 ANNUAL SURVEY (2010).

40. *Cf.* Union Pac. R.R. Emp't. Practices Litig., 479 F.3d. 936 (8th Cir. 2007) (finding no violation).Stocking v. AT & T Corp., 436 F. Supp. 2d 1014, 1016–1617 (W.D. Mo. 2006); Erickson v. Bartell Drug Co., 141 F. Supp. 2d 1266, 1270–1271 (W.D. Wash. 2001) (finding PDA violation).

41. Dep'ts of Treas., Lab. & HHS, Final Rule, Group Health Plans & Health Ins. Issuers Relating to Coverage of Preventive Servs. Under the Patient Protection and Affordable Care Act, 77 Fed. Reg. 8725 (2012).

42. GUTTMACHER INST., *supra* note 38.

43. CTR. FOR CONSUMER INFO. & INS. OVERSIGHT, GUIDANCE ON THE TEMPORARY ENFORCEMENT SAFE HARBOR FOR CERTAIN EMP'R, GROUP HEALTH PLANS & GROUP HEALTH INS. ISSUERS WITH RESPECT TO THE REQUIREMENT TO COVER CONTRACEPTIVE SERVS. WITHOUT COST SHARING UNDER SECTION 2713 OF THE PUB. HEALTH SERV. ACT, SECTION 715(A)(1) OF THE EMP. RET. INCOME SEC. ACT & SECTION 9815(A)(1) OF THE INTERNAL REVENUE CODE (2012), *available at* http://cciio.cms.gov/resources/files/Files2/02102012/20120210-Preventive-Services-Bulletin.pdf.

44. Dep'ts of Treas., Lab. & HHS, Advance Notice of Proposed Rulemaking, Certain Preventive Servs. Under the Affordable Care Act, 77 Fed. Reg. 16,501 (2012).

45. 42 U.S.C. §§ 2000bb–2000bb-4.

46. 492 U.S. 872 (1990).

47. 42 U.S.C. § 2000bb-1.

48. 42 U.S.C. § 2000bb-3.

49. City of Bourne v. Flores, 521 U.S. 507 (1997).

50. Gonzales v. O Centro Espirita Beneficente Uniao do Vegetal, 546 U.S. 418 (2006).

51. Wheaton Coll. v. Sebelius, 2012 WL 3537162 (D.D.C. 2012); Nebraska v. Dep't of Health & Human Servs., 2012 WL 2913402 (D. Neb. 2012); Belmont Abbey Coll. v. Sebelius, 2012 WL 2914417 (D.D.C. 2012).

52. O'Brien v. Dep't of Health & Human Servs., 2012 WL 4481208 (E.D. Mo. 2012).

53. Newland v. Sebelius, 2012 WL 3069154 (D. Colo. 2012).

54. Legatus v Sebelius, 2012 WL 5359630 (E.D. Mich. 2012).

55. *Gonzales,* 546 U.S. 418 (use of hallucinogens); United States v. Lee, 455 U.S. 252 (1982) (payment of Social Security employer taxes); Sherbert v. Verner, 374 U.S. 398 (1963)

(refusal to work on Sabbath); United States v. Wilgus, 638 F.3d 1274 (10th Cir. 2011) (eagle feathers).

56. Citizens United v. Fed. Election Comm'n, 538 U.S. 310 (2010).

57. Catholic Charities v. Super. Ct., 85 P.3d 67 (Cal. 2004); Catholic Charities v. Serio, 859 N.E.2d 459 (Ct. App. 2006).

58. Emp't Div. v. Smith, 494 U.S. 872 (1990).

59. United States v. Lafley, 656 F.3d 936 (9th Cir. 2011).

60. *Catholic Charities*, 85 P.3d 67.

61. ROMNEY FOR PRESIDENT, http://www.mittromney.com/issues/health-care (last visited Dec. 13, 2012).

62. 42 U.S.C. § 18052.

63. 42 U.S.C § 300gg–11.

64. 42 U.S.C. §300gg–18.

65. Clinton v. City of N.Y., 524 U.S. 417, 438 (1998).

66. INS v. Chadha, 462 U.S. 919, 954 (1983).

67. 5 U.S. 137 (1803).

68. See Mary M. Cheh, *When Congress Commands a Thing to be Done: An Essay on* Marbury v. Madison, *Executive Inaction, and the Duty of the Courts to Enforce the Law*, 72 GEO. WASH. L. REV. 253 (2003).

69. Local 2677, Am. Fed'n of Gov't Emps., 358 F. Supp. 60 (D.D.C. 1973).

70. Gaudamuz v. Ash, 368 F. Supp. 1233 (D.D.C. 1973) (termination of Rural Environmental Assistance program invalidated); Sioux Valley Empire Elec. Ass'n, Inc. v. Butz, 367 F. Supp. 686 (D.S.D. 1973), *aff'd*, 504 F.2d 168 (8th Cir. 1974) (termination of rural electrical cooperative loan program invalidated); see Abner J. Mikva & Michael F. Hertz, *Impoundment of Funds—The Courts, the Congress, and the President: A Constitutional Triangle*, 60 Nw. U. L. REV. 335 (1974).

71. 42 U.S.C. §§ 18001 (preexisting condition high-risk pool); 18002 (early retiree reinsurance programs); 18003 (healthcare.gov), 26 U.S.C. § 45R (small business tax credit).

72. 42 U.S.C. §§ 300gg-11 (no lifetime or annual limits), 300gg-12 (rescission prohibition), 300gg-13 (coverage of preventive services), 300gg-14 (coverage of preventive services), 300gg-19 (appeals), 300gg-19 (patient protection).

73. 42 U.S.C. § 300gg-11.

74. 42 U.S.C. § 300gg-94 (review of unreasonable premium increases).

75. 42 U.S.C. § 300gg.

76. Motor Vehicle Mfr. Ass'n v. State Farm Mut. Auto. Ins. Co., 463 U.S. 29 (1983).

77. 42 U.S.C. §§ 18013, 18031, 18041, 18061, 18062, 18063.

78. 42 U.S.C. §§ 300gg-11 (lifetime limits and annual limits post 2014), 300gg-3 (preexisting condition exclusions prohibited), 300gg-2 (guaranteed renewability), 300gg-4 (prohibiting discrimination based on health status, although regulations are permitted and will be needed with respect to wellness programs), 300gg-5 (nondiscrimination against providers and enrollees), 300gg-6 (limitations on deductibles in group plans), 300gg-7 (prohibition on waiting periods but regulations contemplated), 300gg-8 (access to clinical trials but regulations will probably be needed).

79. 42 U.S.C. §§ 300gg (limiting underwriting factors), 300gg-1 (guaranteed availability, HHS to establish general and special open enrollment periods).

80. 42 U.S.C. §§ 18082 (providing for advance premium tax credits), 18091 (individual responsibility); 26 U.S.C. 4980H (employer responsibility).

81. 5 U.S.C. § 706(1).

82. Telecomm. Research & Action Ctr. v. Fed. Commc'n Comm'n, 750 F.2d 70, 80 (D.C. Cir. 1984).

83. Forest Guardians v. Babbitt, 174 F.3d 1178, 1191 (10th Cir. 1999); *In re* Ctr. for Auto. Safety, 793 F.3d. 1346, 1353 (D.C. Cir. 1986); see also Pub. Citizen v. Mukasey, 2008 WL 4532540 (N.D. Cal. 2008).

84. Biodiversity Legal Found. v. Badgley, 309 F.3d 1166, 1178 (9th Cir. 2002); Inst. for Wildlife Prot. v. U.S. Fish & Wildlife Serv., 2007 WL 4117978 (D. Or. 2007). A defense of impossibility may be raised in a proceeding to order compliance. Cmty. for Better Env't v. Envtl. Prot. Agency, 2008 WL 1994898 (N.D. Cal. 2008). But this defense may be raised appropriately only at the contempt stage. *Forest Guardians*, 174 F.3d at 1193.

85. Norton v. S. UT Wilderness Alliance, 542 U.S. 55 (2004).

86. 5 U.S.C. § 706(2).

87. 29 U.S.C. § 1132(a). The requirements of the ACA are explicitly made part of ERISA. 29 U.S.C. § 1185(d).

88. 42 U.S.C. § 300gg–61.

89. 42 U.S.C. § 300gg–61(a)(2).

90. Katie Keith, Kevin Lucia, & Sabrina Corlette, *Implementing the Affordable Care Act: State Action on the Early Market Reforms*, THE COMMONWEALTH FUND (Mar. 22, 2012), http://www.commonwealthfund.org/Publications/Issue-Briefs/2012/Mar/State-Action.aspx.

91. Heckler v. Chaney, 470 U.S. 821 (1985).

92. 42 U.S.C. §§ 18031 (state exchange requirements), 18041 (federal exchanges if states do not establish exchanges).

93. KAISER FAMILY FOUND., ESTABLISHING HEALTH INSURANCE EXCHANGES: AN OVERVIEW OF STATE EFFORTS (2012) *available at* www.kff.org/healthreform/upload/8213-2.pdf.

94. HENRY J. KAISER FAMILY FOUND., HOW IS THE AFFORDABLE CARE ACT LEADING TO CHANGES IN MEDICAID TODAY? STATE ADOPTION OF FIVE NEW OPTIONS (Nov. 2012), *available at* www.kff.org/healthreform/upload/8213-2.pdf.

95. 42 USC § 18031.

96. Mayhew v. Sebelius, 2012 WL 4762101 (1st Cir. 2012).

97. U.S. Citizens Assoc'n v. Geithner, 2013 WL 380342 (6th Cir. 2013).

98. Liberty Univ. v. Geithner, 133 S. Ct. 679 (2012).

99. Grote v. Sebelius, 2013 WL 362725 (7th Cir, 2013); Korte v. Sebelius, 2012 WL 6757353 (7th Cir. 2012).

100. Annex Medical v. Sebelius, No. 13-1118 (8th Cir., Feb. 1, 2013).

101. Hobby Lobby Stores, Inc. v. Sebelius, 2012 WL 6930302 (10th Cir. 2012).

# CHAPTER 19

# Medicaid's Next Fifty Years

## ALIGNING AN OLD PROGRAM WITH THE NEW NORMAL

*Sara Rosenbaum*

## 1. Introduction

The largest of all means-tested entitlement programs and a long-term survivor of battles over spending and ideology, Medicaid was significantly transformed by the Patient Protection and Affordable Care Act (ACA).[1] But further reforms are needed if Medicaid is to emerge as what Chief Justice John Roberts in *NFIB v. Sebelius* characterized as "an element of a comprehensive national plan to provide universal health insurance coverage."[2] Medicaid figured prominently in the Court's decision; the ruling, which barred the Secretary of Health and Human Services (HHS) from fully enforcing the terms of the mandatory expansion,[3] can be expected to have a significant impact on the rate and scope of state implementation of the Medicaid reforms. Even so, most observers expect states to ultimately implement the expansion, reasoning that the enormous need for insurance coverage for the poor, coupled with the Act's financial advantages, will lead states to move forward. As they do, one would expect that the wheels of legislative innovation would continue to turn, as they have for decades, in order to produce the next generation of legislative amendments essential to retrofitting an established program to a new order. But the question that now confronts Medicaid is whether the reform process will be business as usual or whether a poisonous political environment will impede this effort to ensure that Medicaid indeed is able to more successfully play an expanded role in the American health system.

Continuing the work of redesigning Medicaid is essential for two reasons. First, the success of the ACA's insurance reforms hinges on the new system's ability to enroll millions of previously uninsured young, healthy, working-age adults and their families. Today this population is strikingly poor: more than one-third of all Americans live in families with incomes below twice the federal poverty level,[4] and it is this group that lacks health insurance coverage.[5] Thus, a large proportion of the newly insured will require subsidies if coverage is to be affordable. Because Congress chose to design a subsidy coverage system that spans two distinct markets (Medicaid and state health insurance exchanges), ensuring their harmonious functioning becomes central to the success of health reform. This aim assumes special importance for younger, healthier people, whose tolerance for fractured and inefficient operations—with frequent coverage lapses and loss of access to network physicians—may be minimal.

Second, additional reforms are needed in order to align Medicaid's new mission to insure virtually all poor U.S residents[6] with other program responsibilities. The first responsibility is to finance health care for millions of children and adults with disabilities, for whom conventional health insurance (even if they have it) is not sufficient. The ACA bars insurance companies from imposing preexisting condition exclusions[7] and annual and lifetime dollar limits on most covered care;[8] the law also imposes annual limits on families' out-of-pocket cost exposure.[9] But these reforms offer inadequate protection for conditions that require treatments that lie beyond the outer limits of the commercial insurance coverage design that is the ACA's hallmark in the new insurance market. Historically, Medicaid has played the dominant role in long-term care, not only as a primary insurer, but also as a supplemental insurer for individuals with primary coverage through Medicare or employer-sponsored plans. Aligning Medicaid's historic role in financing care for people with disabilities represents a major challenge left shockingly unaddressed by the ACA, with potentially dangerous results.

The second responsibility is to provide support for the health care safety net; indeed, Medicaid has long served as the economic base on which the safety net rests.[10] That safety net is complex, consisting of health care institutions with a tradition of serving poor and vulnerable patients, as well as entities such as public hospitals and federally funded community health centers[11] that by law must furnish care to all residents of their service areas[12] and that are protected under Medicaid through special payment rules.

The safety net's role will likely only intensify in the wake of reform.[13] Even at full implementation, 27 million people will remain uninsured,[14] and the remaining uninsured can be expected increasingly to shift into safety net settings.[15] Furthermore, persons newly insured under Medicaid will be more likely to reside in medically underserved communities characterized by elevated poverty as well as health risks and reduced access to care, because of the strong association between low income and lack of health insurance.[16] Additionally, millions of lower-income safety net patients who gain coverage as a result of the reforms will nonetheless continue to face significant cost-sharing obligations, both for covered benefits (given that subsidized health insurance plans sold through exchanges will have only a 70 percent actuarial value,[17] and cost-sharing reduction assistance is available but by no means complete) and for uncovered costs such as adult dental care. The safety net can be expected to absorb the immediate surge in health care use following full implementation.

A third responsibility is improving health care for the poor. Continuity is a holy grail of health care quality improvement, one on which deeper health system improvements largely depend. Now that Congress has chosen to create two separate markets for subsidized coverage, the task becomes aligning these markets in ways that enable more stable coverage, foster longer-term relationships between patients and providers, and reduce the potential for gaming. That potential may be substantial in a system that, driven by market forces, may be incentivized to skimp on care, secure in the knowledge that in a matter of months, patients will disappear. Medicaid offers rich and extensive coverage and has proved capable of achieving important health and health care outcomes for the poor.[18] Now the goal is achieving Medicaid's greater integration in to a broader, subsidized market for health care.

The chapter examines Medicaid in the wake of the ACA and prospects for further reform given the political environment that now envelops it.

## 2. The ACA and Medicaid's Five Alignment Challenges

### A. CONTEXT

Uninsured people are the chief immediate beneficiaries of the sweeping reforms made by the ACA. But being uninsured is not a static event, and even before passage of the Act, churning in and out of coverage was a well-documented problem,[19] with over 40 percent of Medicaid-insured adults losing coverage within a year.[20] The problem of coverage churn will persist in the wake of the ACA; its potential magnitude was captured in a 2011 study[21] that simulated the coverage experience of adults with incomes below twice the federal poverty level at the point of full implementation of the Act. The study found that within six months, over 35 percent of American adults with incomes below twice the federal poverty level can be expected to experience a change in income that will shift them from Medicaid (where eligibility ends at 133 percent of the federal poverty level) to coverage through a state health insurance exchange, or the reverse. Within one year, 50 percent—28 million adults—will experience a shift in one direction or the other. Even more striking, 24 percent of this group will have experienced two or more changes in one year; over a two-year period, the number experiencing two or more changes rises to 39 percent. More than 40 percent of these adults are estimated to have children under age nineteen, mean-ing that the problem will affect both millions of children and adults.

The adverse ramifications of churn are great, not only for the families that experience the effects of churn—interrupted coverage, plan switching between two markets, and breaks in the continuity of treatment from a regular provid-er—but also for the broader goal of affordability. The estimated 56 million low-income adults and 35 million children who will experience postreform churn across the Medicaid and exchange markets[22] represent the healthiest risk groups across the two markets. Unlike the millions of older and sicker adults who gain enormous benefits from health reform, this group is in the workforce and in relatively good health. The cause of their cross-market churn is, of course, income fluctuation, which is more likely to occur in working families than for adults who are in poorer health and living on fixed incomes. For these working families, income fluctuates as younger workers enter and leave the job market, add or drop hours of employment, or have children, thereby increasing family size in relation to total household income, which in turn triggers an effective decline in family income in relation to the federal poverty level.

## B. SPECIFIC CHALLENGES

Addressing the problem of constant churning across two distinct insurance mar-kets requires multiple types of market alignment. Entry into the system needs to be conceptualized as a single point of entry, where people can be linked to the proper subsidy source both initially and as circumstances change. Enrollment must be stable so that reevaluation of financial eligibility for subsidies need hap-pen only periodically, in the manner of an annual enrollment period. Benefits and cost sharing need to be aligned so that members become accustomed to what is and is not covered. The same health plans using the same delivery net-works should be sold in the two markets so that, in the event that the source of subsidy needs to change as a result of fluctuation in real or effective income, plan membership and provider continuity will remain stable. Under this scenario, fluctuating income would entail a transactional shift in subsidy source, but no shift in coverage or care.

The question is whether the Medicaid reforms introduced under the Act are sufficient to get the system to this point, even assuming that states fully imple-ment the Medicaid expansion in the wake of *NFIB* and that states' implementa-tion choices are consistent with this vision of market alignment. Unfortunately, the ACA's Medicaid amendments fall short in a number of key respects, as do the provisions establishing state exchanges. Furthermore, early implementation of the Act by the Department of Health and Human Services (HHS) suggests a willingness to tolerate state implementation choices that are at odds with market alignment. Finally, the Act entirely fails to recognize a crucial issue related to Medicaid's long-standing role as a source of supplemental health insurance for children and adults with disabilities.

## 1. Aligning Enrollment

The ACA creates two distinct subsidized health insurance markets: Medicaid for the poorest people; and premium subsidies and cost sharing reduction assistance offered through state exchanges for persons whose incomes fall below the upper limits for this type of affordability assistance, but are too high to qualify for Medicaid.[23] Eligibility for premium subsidies is linked to coverage months,[24] and assistance is barred for any month that an individual is eligible for another form of "minimum essential coverage,"[25] which includes Medicaid.[26] In an effort to avert a "crowd out" effect,[27] the ACA goes to extraordinary lengths to ensure that exchange premium subsidies are exclusively focused on those without another form of coverage. This means that in a fluctuating income environment, enrollment and income evaluation functions between state exchanges and Medicaid agencies must be exquisitely and continually aligned. To this end, the Act requires state exchanges to screen all applicants for potential Medicaid eligibility and to "enroll such individuals in" Medicaid if their "modified adjusted gross income" (MAGI)[28] places them within the Medicaid eligibility range.[29] The Act further requires Medicaid agencies to undertake a series of steps aimed at simplifying the Medicaid enrollment and redetermination process itself[30] and to ensure that individuals who apply for coverage through an exchange and are found eligible for Medicaid will be "enrolled" in Medicaid.[31]

Total alignment of enrollment functions does not cure the problem of having to effectively reevaluate income on a monthly basis. But it certainly helps. However, an already significant alignment problem was worsened by an implementation choice made by the Centers for Medicare and Medicaid Services (CMS), which administers both the ACA's Medicaid and exchange provisions. Despite the ACA's clarity on the issue of alignment through enrollment and reenrollment, final CMS regulations permit exchanges to stop their efforts at the point of eligibility determination and redetermination, and simply transfer files to Medicaid agencies for final determinations and enrollment.[32] The abandonment of alignment through a unified enrollment process is destined to create ongoing problems for individuals, as the evidence shows that the process of losing and gaining income is a dynamic one that can take place multiple times throughout a given year. The absence of a single portal for enrollment, regardless of the source of premium subsidy, virtually ensures breaks in coverage, as the subsidy basis continually changes. This phenomenon is evident even in Massachusetts, where, years after health care reform, lower-income adults continue to experience frequent breaks in coverage.[33]

Two changes might ease this problem. The first is requiring states to fulfill their system integration responsibilities by a set date and barring separate enrollment procedures. In states utilizing federally administered exchanges (and the fact that only thirteen states and the District of Columbia had enacted exchange laws as of May 2012 suggests that many states will do so),[34] such a change would require federal legislation, since by law only a state Medicaid agency can determine eligibility for Medicaid.[35] Either of these methods—state computerized integration of the Medicaid/premium subsidy enrollment function, or direct enrollment of Medicaid-eligible persons in Medicaid by federal exchanges—could lead to greater alignment.[36]

But even if greater alignment were to happen, income fluctuation as a result of a continual flow of life events means that measuring subsidy sources in relation to "coverage months" is hopelessly inefficient. Informing the government of changes in income, family size, and other matters that might affect eligibility will become an all-consuming event. Prior to the ACA, states had the flexibility to ignore minor income fluctuations[37] (although virtually none did so); in the wake of passage, however, this flexibility is eliminated in favor of a uniform MAGI test, which eliminates states' power to disregard income fluctuations.[38]

Where cash welfare is concerned, there might be some limited justification for such a month-to-month approach to government assistance. Where the goal is to stabilize health care, the process is absurd on its face. Far more desirable would be legislation to establish annual enrollment periods with an uninterrupted entitlement to a subsidy source throughout the enrollment period. During periods in which the subsidy is tax-based, the federal government would absorb 100 percent of the costs; when the subsidy is provided through the Medicaid entitlement, states share the cost (after 2016 in the case of newly eligible persons, and beginning in 2014 in the case of traditional eligibility groups, for whom the federal financial contribution remains at pre-ACA levels). Both the federal and state partners would want the other to bear as much cost exposure as possible. But, life being what it is, over a several-year time period the economics of annual enrollment periods would essentially be a wash.

### 2. Aligning Eligibility Policy for Persons with Disabilities

Medicaid plays two basic roles as an insurer. The first is as a primary insurer for millions of children and adults who have no other source of coverage, either through the employer system or any other insuring mechanism. The second is as a supplemental insurer, both for Medicare beneficiaries[39] as well as for individuals who may have other forms of coverage, such as employer-sponsored benefits, and for whom their primary coverage is inadequate. Medicaid's role as a secondary payer dates back to the program's 1965 enactment.[40] Indeed, the ACA strengthens Medicaid's potential role as a secondary payer by requiring states, as a condition of participation, to finance premium assistance as a part of Medicaid coverage, thereby potentially expanding Medicaid's role as a dual insurer.[41] In this respect, Medicaid's role as a supplemental source of coverage predates the policy shift toward exclusivity of coverage under governmental insurance programs, a shift that occurred in response to concerns over the claimed potential of public payers to "crowd out" the private market.[42]

Medicaid's role as a supplemental insurer for persons with disabilities remains central to the program's role in the health care system, particularly in relation to the limitations of commercial insurance, whose design serves as the benchmark for the new subsidized exchange market. Even though the ACA bars exclusion and discrimination on the basis of disability at the point of enrollment, the Act bakes discriminatory insurer practices into coverage design in several ways. The frame of reference for the essential health benefit (EHB) benefit package[43] that lies at the heart of exchange plans is the "typical" employer market.[44] Although the ACA bars the Secretary from introducing benefit designs in essential health benefits that discriminate on the basis of disability,[45] she has, in fact, ceded her authority over benefit design to states, who determine the design of their essential health benefit packages from among their employer-sponsored group markets.[46]

Other than extension of mental health parity to exchange plans,[47] as of fall 2012 there is no federal policy on how states must broadly adjust benefit design to counter discrimination in coverage on the basis of disability. As a result, federal implementing standards do not override the limitations and exclusions commonly used to narrow coverage for persons with disabilities, such as medical necessity limitations that exclude coverage for which "normal" functioning cannot be restored, or exclusions that bar coverage for treatments considered "social" or "educational."[48] These types of limitations have no counterpart in Medicaid, which bars arbitrary limitations based on condition[49] and which provides uncommonly broad coverage of children under twenty-one through the early and periodic screening diagnosis and treatment benefit (EPSDT).[50] For this reason, Medicaid is particularly effective in coverage of supplemental long-term services and supports, such as the services of personal attendants, additional levels of prescription drug coverage beyond that found in a typical employer plan, and additional treatments and services for conditions requiring ongoing interventions. In other words, through its expansive coverage and third-party liability provisions, Medicaid is designed to work alongside other forms of coverage. This has been particularly important for working families with disabled children, as well as for disabled adults who return to work and who, under expanded Medicaid eligibility policies, are permitted to retain Medicaid even while they have primary coverage through an employer.

However, rather than permitting Medicaid to play a supplemental role for persons with exchange coverage, the ACA follows the exclusivity rule and introduces anti-crowd-out restrictions into the law by barring exchange premium subsidies in any coverage month in which individuals are entitled to Medicaid coverage. This means that low- and moderate-income individuals and families entitled to Medicaid on the basis of disability are ineligible to simultaneously receive premium subsidies for exchange coverage. It also means that states are confronted with a choice: either continue higher Medicaid eligibility levels for children and adults with disabilities as permitted under law and forgo the financial offsets that would accrue from their receipt of primary coverage through exchanges; or eliminate more generous Medicaid eligibility standards for disabled children and adults in order to qualify them for fully federally funded exchange subsidies. Furthermore, if, in response to the Medicaid expansion turmoil that the Supreme Court's Medicaid holding in *NFIB* introduced, the administration were to permit states to partially implement the Act's Medicaid expansion provision—say, up to only 100 percent of the poverty line, which in turn triggers entitlement to exchange premium subsidies under the ACA[51]—the termination point for Medicaid eligibility for persons with disabilities could sink even lower.

One solution to this dilemma would be to modify both Medicaid and the ACA's premium assistance and exchange provisions to permit states to continue to furnish Medicaid based on disability to low- and moderate-income persons whose simultaneous entitlement to medical assistance otherwise would be barred by the ACA's anti-crowd-out provisions. In addition, amendments eliminating the anti-crowd-out provisions of the ACA in the case of disability could be paired with amendments that provide enhanced levels of federal funding to states that either retain or establish more generous Medicaid eligibility standards based on disability in order to supplement exchange coverage.

It is too soon to tell what states will do. But the betting is on a massive Medicaid eligibility rollback of enhanced coverage based on disability in order to qualify persons with incomes above the exchange threshold (wherever it is ultimately set) for premium subsidies. In its current form, the ACA simply provides no incentive for states to maintain higher Medicaid eligibility levels for persons with disabilities, nor does it even allow states to do so. Indeed, the incentives ACA creates appear to move state Medicaid policy in precisely the opposite direction, while denying persons with disabilities in more generous Medicaid states the ability to secure primary coverage through a qualified health plan offered through their state exchange. The result is a fundamental disability-based distinction if there ever were one.

### 3. Aligning Coverage Design

As noted, the ACA utilizes the EHB coverage design model for exchange products. The ACA also grafts the EHB design onto the Medicaid coverage standards in the case of the newly eligible adult population.[52] Prior to the ACA's passage, states already had been given the option under the Deficit Reduction Act of 2005[53] to move to a more commercially oriented "benchmark" benefit design in the case of certain low-income adult and child populations. But the benchmark option excluded, among other beneficiary populations, parents receiving Temporary Aid to Needy Families (TANF) benefits and those who would have continue to meet their states' 1996 Aid to Families with Dependent Children (AFDC) eligibility standards.[54] Thus, where the adult population was concerned, the 2006 benchmark option applied only to small groups of low-income adults.[55]

The ACA replaces the 2006 benchmark coverage standard with the more rigorous EHB coverage design.[56] The ACA also preserves the state option to supplement commercial benchmark coverage with additional benefits, such as vision and dental care, which represent coverage options for adults.[57] Finally, the ACA retains the earlier benchmark coverage provision that requires states to supplement benchmark coverage in the case of individuals under age twenty-one with full Medicaid coverage for all early and periodic screening diagnosis and treatment (EPSDT) benefits.[58]

The ACA amendments create an anomalous situation. On the one hand, newly eligible low-income adults receive EHB-level benchmark coverage, including comprehensive preventive services without cost sharing, a wide array of other coverage classes, and full mental health parity. On the other hand, the poorest adult populations (those eligible for TANF or poor enough to still qualify for cash assistance under their state's 1996 AFDC program) receive traditional benefits that do not treat preventive care as a coverage requirement and that lack a mental health parity protection with the exception of beneficiaries enrolled in certain managed-care arrangements.[59] Arguably the EHB benefit design actually is superior to Medicaid's traditional coverage design where low-income adults are concerned, and yet the poorest adults are barred from receiving this level of coverage and remain consigned to Medicaid's traditional coverage design.

One solution would be to allow states to move all low-income adults into the EHB benefit design. As previously discussed, such a move would result in certain limitations in coverage for low-income adults that previously were barred under traditional Medicaid coverage rules, such as the prohibition against arbitrary discrimination on the basis of condition in the case of required services.[60] As noted above, historically this prohibition has prevented state Medicaid programs from adopting certain commercial insurance practices, such as excluding particular conditions from coverage or denying treatments to patients whose conditions require treatments to avert further loss of functioning rather than restore "normal function." But this prohibition against arbitrary coverage rules now is at least partially met through the mental health parity requirements that become applicable to EHB coverage arrangements under the ACA. Furthermore, because

EHB design encompasses not only rehabilitative services but also those that are habilitative in nature, the EHB design limits the degree to which otherwise covered treatments can be excluded because they are prescribed in order to develop or maintain functioning rather than to restore the loss of prior function, a routine form of discrimination found in standard commercial plans.

Moving to the EHB design also would eliminate coverage requirements for certain services directly tied to support of the health care safety net, in particular, Medicaid's "federally qualified health center service" (FQHC) benefit,[61] which treats the services of community health centers as an actual coverage category, not simply a locus of care. At the same time, quite apart from the FQHC benefit mandate, federal Medicaid law also requires states to pay health centers at special enhanced rates for the covered benefits and services they furnish, thereby protecting them from a steep revenue loss for covered services. The FQHC payment rule, which is separate from the coverage rule, spans all health care delivery arrangements, including health plans providing EHB coverage, Medicaid managed-care arrangements, and Medicaid's basic fee-for-service system.[62] Thus, even if the FQHC coverage requirement were eliminated, Medicaid's special payment standard for covered benefits would remain in place, as would Medicaid's special payment rules for hospitals treating a disproportionate number of low-income patients (DSH payments).[63]

### 4. Aligning Coverage Products

Federal Medicaid law provides for program administration, at state option, through managed-care arrangements. Three-quarters of all beneficiaries receive coverage through compulsory managed-care enrollment, akin to enrollment in a qualified health plan in a state exchange. In both cases, the entities that sell these products (e.g., qualified health plans, Medicaid managed-care products) must meet certain conditions of participation. The conditions vary, but not enormously. Indeed, the two sets of conditions of participation parallel one another across most areas, including marketing, access to care, access to emergency care, network adequacy, grievance and appeals rights, independent external review, and safety net payment requirements.[64]

There are differences in requirements, however, the most notable being an insurance licensure requirement that applies only to qualified health plans.[65] In addition, qualified health plans operating in state insurance exchanges must enter into agreements with certain "essential community providers."[66] No similarly comprehensive provider contracting provision applies to Medicaid managed care, but this is because, as a practical matter, Medicaid managed-care networks already are dominated by "essential community providers," treating high volumes of low-income patients. Another difference between the Medicaid managed-care market and the market for qualified health plans through the exchanges involves accreditation: qualified health plans must be accredited,[67] whereas accreditation is not an express Medicaid managed-care requirement. But even here, the differences are not insurmountable; as of 2010, sixteen state Medicaid programs required accreditation, and, as noted, external review is a feature of Medicaid managed care.[68]

Because the conditions of participation applicable to qualified health plans and Medicaid managed-care entities essentially cover the same policy grounds, a logical step to encourage greater alignment is to update the older Medicaid managed-care standards (enacted in 1997) to reflect the ACA's newer expectations. While extending a state licensure requirement to the Medicaid product market would be a major departure from prior practices, states do have the power to establish specific licensure standards for issuers of Medicaid managed-care products. This would thus enable states to accommodate community-based entities that desire to operate in the exchange premium subsidy market but lack the reserves maintained by large issuers. The licensure requirement would likely foster corporate affiliations between these smaller community-based plans and the larger licensed issuers so as to permit the entry of the community-based entities into the large crossover member market as a means of maintaining continuity of care.

Market alignment requires another step, namely addressing Medicaid's historically low provider payment rates (particularly for physician services), which result in a dearth of health care providers willing to participate in the Medicaid provider network. Although the health reform legislation contains a temporary payment boost for Medicaid primary care services, this reform only lasts for two years.[69] One solution might be to require plans operating in the crossover market to use Medicare payments as a floor. Such a requirement would raise Medicaid provider payment rates, while establishing a floor for exchange provider payment levels. Another approach might be the creation of financial incentives in the form of more generous stop-loss levels for plans operating in the crossover market that boost physician payment levels.

## 5. Aligning Federal Financing

The ACA attempts to resolve the age-old problem of the federal government's role in Medicaid financing with an approach that, charitably put, is limited. In essence, states receive a highly enhanced federal contribution toward the Medicaid costs associated with reform, but only for certain populations,[70] who in truth (and contrary to Chief Justice Roberts's characterization in *NFIB*)[71] can barely be distinguished in many cases from traditional Medicaid populations. Indeed, a matter of a few dollars of monthly income would result in the movement of millions of parents from "traditional" to newly eligible categories. Coping with this situation will be extremely difficult, since it will require states to track the slightest income fluctuations of millions of low-income adults, as daily work and family life change. The clear solution is a unified, enhanced federal contribution level covering all Medicaid populations who, depending on income, would qualify for premium subsidies through their state exchanges. Regardless of whether attachment to Medicaid is based on low family income or disability, the group to target for enhanced federal payments is individuals who, based on income, will derive their coverage under either regime. This expanded approach to enhanced coverage (coupled with a new state option to allow Medicaid function as a secondary payer to exchange coverage in the case of persons with disabilities) would blunt the potential for eliminating expanded Medicaid coverage for children and adults with disabilities while simplifying the accounting requirements for calculating federal payments to states. To be sure, this reform would require greater federal outlays on the Medicaid side. But to the extent that moving in this direction reduces states' incentive to eliminate coverage of all optional eligibility groups whose incomes surpass the exchange threshold, the greater federal contribution would likely balance out over time, since the Congressional Budget Office estimates that federal subsidies will be 50 percent higher for exchange coverage than for Medicaid.[72]

## 2. Future Reform Prospects

All legislative reform is evolutionary. The history of legislative health policy is no different—a seminal enactment followed by a succession of amendments aimed at modifying and revising earlier policy decisions or strengthening initial policy choices. Indeed, the ACA itself represents a series of legislative modifications to a host of existing laws in an attempt to make them operate in a more harmonious fashion: the Internal Revenue Code; the Public Health Service Act; the Employee Retirement Income Security Act; Medicare; and Medicaid. In some cases, the legislative foray under the ACA entails the addition of entirely new legislative authority to an underlying law, as in the creation of the health insurance exchanges. More frequently, however, the ACA alters existing provisions of law in order to promote alignment with evolving policy choices.

Under normal circumstances, the types of reforms identified in this chapter would be considered part of the standard course of lawmaking. It took about fifteen years of trying and at least four distinct sets of legislative amendments to create a universal Medicaid entitlement for low-income children and pregnant women, to strengthen their coverage, and to streamline and simplify the enrollment process for these populations. It is hardly surprising, therefore, that the newest generation of Medicaid reforms will require further refinement. Medicaid is a vast program, with total expenditures surpassing $400 billion in fiscal year 2010, and a projected enrollment approaching 80 million people by 2020.[73] It is one of the most complex laws ever enacted by Congress; indeed, no less a judge than Henry Friendly famously termed its provisions "almost unintelligible to the uninitiated."[74] The need for further amendment and refinement thus should hardly come as a surprise.

But, of course, this is no ordinary time for Medicaid. The fury over Medicaid has never been higher, fueled by costs, ideology, and an unprecedented level of political animus. Furthermore *NFIB*, whose undefined reach into the future of federal spending programs is the subject of intense scholarship,[75] casts a cloud over the extent to which one of Medicaid's most fundamental reforms over the past half century ultimately will be implemented. Despite public opinion polls underscoring its popularity with the American public,[76] Medicaid remains exceptionally vulnerable to attack in what is anticipated to be a seminal battle over its future and that of other social welfare entitlements in the wake of the 2012 presidential election.

Following the watershed presidential election of 2012, three possible scenarios await Medicaid. The first—highly unlikely—is that Congress will essentially leave Medicaid alone, making only minor structural modifications in the program. One avenue for minor surgery would be the types of temporary reductions in federal funding that Congress pursued as part of the Omnibus Reconciliation Act of 1981, essentially applying a 3 percent discount to the payments otherwise owed state programs.[77] In 1984, the 1981 payment reductions were eliminated and full federal payments were restored (indeed, in periods of recession, federal Medicaid funding has been increased).[78] States were given certain added flexibility as part of the 1981 reductions, but not such expansive powers that the basic framework of the entitlement to coverage was structurally upended.

The two alternatives to the aforementioned minor surgery are far more invasive. The first is a proposal to "block-grant" Medicaid. The second is a proposal to fundamentally alter Medicaid's open-ended financing structure through the use of per capita caps. In both cases, it is likely that the "baseline" used to estimate the size of the reductions and the impact of the savings will be Medicaid as restructured under the ACA. In other words, the starting point will be a program that assumes elimination of Medicaid's historic barrier against federal funding to cover all low-income people. Whichever pathway Congress chooses, however, states would be expected to achieve the Medicaid reform goals with dramatically less federal financing.

Were Congress to choose what is popularly termed a "block grant"[79] pathway, federal expenditures per state would be subject to annual aggregate caps, with concomitant evisceration of federal legal requirements in order to give states broad leeway in how they absorb the loss of funds. The enormity of the funding loss, as well as the difficulties of apportionment given the differences in states' fiscal starting points under a block grant, have led to repeated abandonment of the proposal.[80]

The latest version of this repeatedly discredited idea shows up in a 2012 proposal issued by the House of Representatives Budget Committee contained in *The Path to Prosperity: A Blueprint for American Renewal*.[81] The proposal, virtually identical to one put forward in 2011, proposes to repeal the ACA Medicaid expansions and to block-grant the remaining program, with growth indexed to inflation and population growth.[82] The committee asserts that this approach would restore state flexibility and autonomy while improving provider payments and consumer choice. The proposal offers no insight as to how states and the federal government will cope with the changes in eligibility, enrollment, benefits and coverage, consumer protections, and administration requirements that the committee favors. The committee estimates that the block grant proposal will reduce federal Medicaid outlays by $810 billion over the FY 2013–2023 time period, not counting the nearly $1 trillion in savings achieved by repealing the ACA Medicaid expansion.[83]

Analysis suggests that the projected $810 billion in losses resulting from placing arbitrary limits on federal Medicaid spending through a block grant would be the least level of impact that states could anticipate. Were state Medicaid costs to rise faster than the proposed growth factor, the level of true loss relative to Medicaid's historic open-ended financing system would be far greater. The losses—which are projected to be about 22 percent over the 2012–2022 time period and a 34 percent loss in 2022 alone[84]—would mask much steeper losses in certain states. The state programs that risk the greatest relative losses are those that stand to gain the most proportionately from the ACA expansions. The impact of the loss would be greatest because these states—such as Texas, Florida, and other southern and southwestern states—have high uninsured populations and thus stand to gain the most from coverage expansion.[85] A prominent analysis determined that under a plan that both repeals the Medicaid expansion and block-grants the program, enrollment would fall by about 35 million persons by 2022.[86] Furthermore, since the federal government would presumably continue to make Medicaid payments only in connection with approved state expenditures, the pattern of federal disallowances and recoveries and constant state disputes that characterizes the program today[87] would likely persist.

In other words, block grant funds would not be free money. If a 2012 congressional flap over whether HHS has the legal authority to permit states to modify the rigid work requirements of the TANF block grant program is any guide,[88] tough federal spending rules, coupled with ongoing and aggressive federal audit practices, will remain core features of any successor program. In short, the desire of federal lawmakers to constrain federal financial support for state programs applies regardless of whether the mechanism for a funds transfer is open-ended or subject to limits. Indeed, were legislation limiting federal funding also to include provisions altering state performance requirements in the areas of eligibility, coverage, payment, and management (as presumably will be the case), federal oversight could become more aggressive given the potential for looser standards to result in less rigorous state spending management and oversight. A race to the bottom does not make the green eyeshades irrelevant.

Furthermore, Medicaid is heavily embedded in state economies as a result of the complex financing arrangements on which the program rests (a combination of general revenues, special taxes, and transfers among units of the different governments that share responsibility for the operation of public health care systems serving Medicaid beneficiaries along with other low-income populations).[89] As a result, a block grant promises to set in motion a great economic unraveling as the losses spread through local public health economies, public health care institutions, school health systems, public health clinics, and public, community-based programs for persons with disabilities. This is where the strong public support for Medicaid is so telling: for millions of families, Medicaid is an essential part of the fabric of daily life.

In view of the enormous consequences flowing from a block grant, the more plausible option, and one being discussed with increasing intensity, is known as a "per capita cap." Under this approach, the federal government would cease to contribute a share of a state's total program spending. Instead, the federal contribution would look more like a defined per capita contribution up to a fixed dollar amount per beneficiary served. While this approach does not as dramatically leave states strapped for resources to provide care for the tens of millions of low-income Medicaid beneficiaries and to support the providers that serve those beneficiaries, it nonetheless raises numerous problems of its own.

The first is the difficulty of fashioning a defined contribution methodology that properly accounts for health risks, given states' limited coverage experience with low-income adults who are not parents of minor children. Many newly eligible persons will be healthy adults, but others will have extensive physical and mental health problems. The lack of cost experience, coupled with the general confusion regarding how to absorb the losses associated with a per capita cap, can be expected to dampen most states' interest in Medicaid expansion, even if expansion with federal funding remains an option.

A second problem with a defined contribution model is the weakness of the methodology in relation to the actual cost of care. A pandemic, an unanticipated public health crisis such as the HIV/AIDS epidemic that swept the nation in the 1980s, a major natural or man-made disaster such as Hurricane Katrina or the World Trade Center attack, all can throw off actuarial projections that reflect normal conditions, as can major technology breakthroughs that create game-changing conditions for the health care system.[90] However, policymakers could fortify the defined contribution model with proper provisions to account for such anomalies.

A third problem is that a per capita cap essentially takes a snapshot of state Medicaid spending as it exists at a specified moment in time (i.e., the baseline). Thus, states that have low per capita spending, either because of low pricing, limited coverage, or both, are in essence locked into artificially depressed caps. States that did not previously cover certain disabled populations but desire to add coverage would have no financial history against which the cap could be measured and so would be exposed to whatever unsupported methodology is proposed. States that experience large annual leaps in per beneficiary costs would have no means of recouping their losses, since the cap would be set to grow at a fixed rate (e.g., inflation plus 1 percent). And quite problematically, once set, the cap could be lowered in the face of budgetary or other constraints. Moreover, in exchange for absorbing the impact of a per capita cap, states would demand far more flexibility in Medicaid than they now enjoy: over eligibility, enrollment, coverage, benefits, payments, and management requirements and safeguards.

The final problem is the reality of Medicaid spending. The great driver of Medicaid spending today is enrollment. Pricing and per capita costs do not factor in as much. Indeed, Medicaid expenditures are so tightly managed that per enrollee growth rates for the coming decade are expected to be at GDP.[91] Viewed through this lens, it becomes evident that a per capita cap essentially saves nothing unless it is held below even the rate of GDP growth. Thus, while it certainly would be possible to embed a number of the reforms outlined in this chapter into a per capita cap approach to federal Medicaid spending, it is also true that states' interest in improving Medicaid's performance might be distinctly dampened by their need to contain costs below even minimal rates of inflation.

## 4. Conclusion

The ACA made seminal Medicaid reforms while triggering a need for further alignment. As the Act has moved toward implementation, the need for additional reform has become clearer, an inevitability in any remarkably complex piece of legislation. Whether Medicaid's next fifty years will witness its ongoing transformation, through continued federal investment, into an effective component of a comprehensive scheme of universal coverage, or instead its decline, ultimately will be an intensely political determination rather than one driven by health policy. The policy argument pleads for continued strengthening; but the enduringly ferocious politics of Medicaid may be moving the program along a far different pathway.

# Acknowledgment

I am extremely grateful to my research assistant, Michal McDowell, for her research help.

# Notes

1. Patient Protection and Affordable Care Act, Pub. L. No. 111-148, 124 Stat. 119 (2010), as amended by the Health Care and Education Reconciliation Act of 2010, Pub. L. 111-152 (2010) (codified as amended in scattered sections of 26 and 42 U.S.C.).
2. NFIB v. Sebelius, 132 S. Ct. 2566, 2606 (2012).
3. For a comprehensive discussion of the ruling, see Nicole Huberfield et al., *Plunging into Endless Difficulties: Medicare and Coercion in the Healthcare Cases*, 93 B.U. L. REV. (forthcoming Jan. 2013). See also Samuel Bagenstos, *The Anti-Leveraging Principle and the Spending Clause after NFIB*, 101 GEO. L.J. (forthcoming 2013).
4. CARMEN DENAVAS WALT ET AL., U.S. CENSUS BUREAU, INCOME, POVERTY, AND HEALTH INSURANCE COVERAGE IN THE UNITED STATES: 2011, at 18 (Sept. 2012), *available at* http://www.census.gov/prod/2012pubs/p60–243.pdf.
5. In 2011, more than three-quarters of uninsured nonelderly Americans had family incomes below 250 percent of the federal poverty level. HENRY J. KAISER FAMILY FOUND., THE UNINSURED AND THE DIFFERENCE HEALTH INSURANCE MAKES 2 (Sept. 2012), *available at* http://www.kff.org/uninsured/upload/1420-14.pdf.
6. Medicaid excludes coverage of otherwise eligible persons not lawfully present in the U.S. Medicaid eligibility for noncitizens is linked to their immigration status, and the law imposes a five-year waiting period on eligibility for legal U.S. residents. See ALLISON SISKIN, CONG. RESEARCH SERV., R41714, TREATMENT OF NON CITIZENS UNDER THE PATIENT PROTECTION AND AFFORDABLE CARE ACT 7–8 (2011), *available at* http://www.nafsa.org/ uploadedFiles/CRS%20analysis%20re%20noncitizens.pdf. Legal residents are covered by the Act's minimum coverage requirements and entitled to use state exchanges. They may obtain subsidized coverage through health insurance exchanges as well as tax subsidies during their five-year waiting period for Medicaid coverage. 26 U.S.C. § 5000A(d)(3) (2010). Persons not lawfully present in the United States are excluded from the minimum coverage requirement, and also are excluded from purchasing health insurance coverage through state exchanges. *Id.* Of the nation's 21.6 million noncitizens, approximately 11.2 million are estimated to be not lawfully present. See Siskin, *supra* note 6, at 2–3. Compared to the general population, undocumented persons are far more likely to be uninsured (47 percent compared to 15 percent). HENRY J. KAISER FAMILY FOUND., SUMMARY: FIVE BASIC FACTS ON IMMIGRANTS AND THEIR HEALTH CARE 1 (Mar. 2008), *available at* http://www.kff.org/ medicaid/upload/7761.pdf.
7. 42 U.S.C. § 300gg-3 (2010).
8. 42 U.S.C. § 300gg-11. The bar on annual and lifetime dollar limits applies only to benefits and services falling within the Act's essential health benefit categories. These classes can be found at 42 U.S.C. § 18022(b) (2010).
9. *Id.* at (c)(1).
10. Medicaid accounts for 35 percent of public hospitals' net revenue and 37 percent of health center funding. See NAT'L ASS'N OF PUB. HOSPS. & HEALTH SYS., IN UNCERTAIN TIMES, SAFETY NET HOSPITALS MAINTAIN COMMITMENT TO SERVE 2 (May 2012), *available at* http://www.naph.org/Main-Menu-Category/Publications/FY2010-NAPH-Characteristics -Report-Executive-Summary.aspx?FT=.pdf; see also PETER SHIN ET AL., HENRY J. KAISER FAMILY FOUND., HEALTH CENTERS: AN OVERVIEW AND ANALYSIS OF THEIR EXPERIENCES

WITH PRIVATE HEALTH INSURANCE (Jan. 2008), *available at* http://www.kff.org/unin-sured/upload/7738.pdf.

11. See Eli Adashi et al., *Health Care Reform and Primary Care—The Growing Importance of the Community Health Center*, 262 NEW ENGL. J. MED. 2047 (2010), for a general discussion of community health centers and the ACA.

12. See THE HEALTH CARE SAFETY NET IN A POST-REFORM WORLD (Mark A. Hall & Sara Rosenbaum eds., 2012), for a discussion of how the PPACA affects safety net institutions and providers. See INST. OF MEDICINE, THE HEALTH CARE SAFETY NET: INTACT BUT ENDANGERED (Marion Ein Lewin & Stuart Altman eds., 2000), for a general discussion of the health care safety net.

13. Sara Rosenbaum, *Reinventing a Classic: Community Health Centers and the Newly Insured, in* THE HEALTH CARE SAFETY NET IN A POST-REFORM WORLD, *supra* note 12, at 67.

14. CONG. BUDGET OFFICE AND JOINT COMM. ON TAXATION, UPDATED ESTIMATES FOR THE INSURANCE COVERAGE PROVISIONS OF THE AFFORDABLE CARE ACT 12 (Mar. 2012), *available at* http://www.cbo.gov/sites/default/files/cbofiles/attachments/03–13-Coverage%20 Estimates.pdf.

15. This is precisely what happened in Massachusetts in the wake of that state's health reform effort; following passage, health centers served an even higher proportion of the state's remaining uninsured population. Leighton Ku et al., *Safety Net Providers After Health Reform: Lessons from Massachusetts*, 171 ARCHIVES INTERNAL MED. 1329 (2011).

16. SARA ROSENBAUM ET AL., NATIONAL HEALTH REFORM: HOW WILL MEDICALLY UNDERSERVED COMMUNITIES FARE? (2009), *available at* http://sphhs.gwu.edu/depart-ments/healthpolicy/dhp_publications/pub_uploads/dhpPublication_5046C2DE-5056-9D20-3D2A570F2CF3F8B0.pdf.

17. The silver plan, the standard health plan linked to premium tax credits in health insurance exchanges, is pegged to 70 percent of the full actuarial value of benefits included under the plan. 26 U.S.C. § 36B(b)(3)(B) (2011).

18. Many studies have shown Medicaid's impact on the health of the poor. See, e.g., KAREN DAVIS & CATHY SCHOEN, HEALTH AND THE WAR ON POVERTY (1978) (discussing reduc-tion in infant mortality); see also Benjamin D. Sommers et al., *Mortality and Access to Care Among Adults After State Medicaid Expansions*, 367 NEW ENG. J. MED. 1025 (2012).

19. See, e.g., Pamela Farley Short & Deborah R. Graefe, *Battery-Powered Health Insurance? Stability in Coverage of the Uninsured*, 22 HEALTH AFFAIRS 244 (2003).

20. Benjamin D. Sommers, *Loss of Health Insurance Among Non-elderly Adults in Medicaid*, 24 J. GEN. INTERNAL MED. 1 (2009).

21. Benjamin D. Sommers & Sara Rosenbaum, *Issues in Health Reform: How Changes in Eligibility May Move Millions Back and Forth Between Medicaid and Insurance Exchanges*, 30 HEALTH AFFAIRS 228 (2011).

22. *Id.* at 232.

23. 26 U.S.C. § 36B(b)(3)(A)(i). The established ranges are from up to 133 percent of the fed-eral poverty level to 400 percent of the federal poverty level.

24. *Id.* at (b)(2).

25. *Id.; Id.* at (c)(2)(B); 26 U.S.C. § 5000A(f)(1)(C).

26. 26 U.S.C. § 5000A(f)(1)(A)(ii).

27. The extent to which government-supported health insurance "crowds out" private sector coverage has been a major, if misplaced, concern in U.S. health reform policy for decades. For an important critique, see Mark Schlesinger, *Crowding Out: Multiple Manifestations, Muddled Meanings*, 37 J. HEALTH POL. POL'Y & L. 851 (2012) (arguing that the concept has deterred government interventions aimed at correcting failures in the health insurance market).

28. The Act establishes a "modified adjusted gross income" methodology for evaluating income for purposes of both Medicaid and exchange affordability assistance. 42 U.S.C. § 1396a(e) (14) (2010).

29. 42 U.S.C. § 18031(d)(4)(F) (2010).

30. 42 U.S.C. § 18083 (2010).
31. *Id.* at (a).
32. Eligibility Standards, 45 C.F.R. § 155.305(b), 155.310(d)(3) (2011).
33. John A. Graves & Katherine Schwartz, *Health Care Reform and the Dynamics of Insurance Coverage—Lessons from Massachusetts,* 367 NEW ENG. J. MED. 1180 (2012).
34. SARA ROSENBAUM ET AL., STATE HEALTH INSURANCE EXCHANGE LAWS: THE FIRST GENERATION (July 2012), *available at* http://www.commonwealthfund.org/~/media/Files/Publications/Issue%20Brief/2012/Jul/1616_Rosenbaum_state_hlt_ins_exchange_laws_ib.pdf.
35. 42 U.S.C. § 1396a(a)(5) (2010).
36. Whether a federal amendment commanding states to accept individuals determined eligible for Medicaid by a federal exchange could succeed politically is another matter.
37. See, e.g., 42 U.S.C. § 1396a(a)(17) (requiring states to set reasonable standards for determining income); 42 C.F.R. § 435.915(c) (2006) (permitting states to establish annual eligibility periods).
38. 42 U.S.C. § 1396a(e).
39. Approximately 9.1 million Medicare beneficiaries also were enrolled in Medicaid in FY 2008 for either partial or full coverage. KATHRYN YOUNG ET AL., HENRY J. KAISER FAMILY FOUND., MEDICAID'S ROLE FOR DUAL ELIGIBLE BENEFICIARIES (Apr. 2012), *available at* http://www.kff.org/medicaid/upload/7846-03.pdf.
40. 42 U.S.C. § 1396a(a)(25).
41. 42 U.S.C. § 1396e-1 (2010).
42. See Schlesinger, *supra* note 27.
43. 42 U.S.C. § 18022.
44. *Id.* at (b)(2)(A).
45. *Id.* at (b)(4)(B). For a discussion of the nondiscrimination in benefit design provision, see Sara Rosenbaum et al., *Crossing the Rubicon: The Impact of the Affordable Care Act on the Content of Insurance Coverage for Persons with Disabilities,* 25 NOTRE DAME J.L. ETHICS & PUB. POL'Y 527 (2011).
46. CTR. FOR CONSUMER INFO. & INS. OVERSIGHT, ESSENTIAL HEALTH BENEFITS BULLETIN (Dec. 16, 2011), *available at* http://cciio.cms.gov/resources/files/Files2/12162011/essential_health_benefits_bulletin.pdf.
47. 42 U.S.C. §18031(j) (2010).
48. See generally, Sara Rosenbaum, *Insurance Discrimination on the Basis of Health Status,* GEORGETOWN UNIV.- O' NEILL INST. (2009), http://www.law.georgetown.edu/oneillinstitute/national-health-law/legal-solutions-in-health-reform/Discrimination.html; see also, Mary Crossley, *Discrimination Against the Unhealthy in Health Insurance,* 54 U. KAN. L. REV. 73 (2005).
49. 45 C.F.R. § 440.230(c) (2010).
50. For a full discussion of the EPSDT benefit in relation to commercial insurance norms, *see* Sara Rosenbaum & Paul Wise, *Crossing the Medicaid-Private Insurance Divide: The Case of EPSDT,* 26 HEALTH AFFAIRS 382 (2007).
51. Whether the Secretary could permit such a result is open to question. See Sara Rosenbaum & Timothy Westmoreland, *The Supreme Court's Surprising Decision On the Medicaid Expansion: How Will The Federal Government And States Proceed?* 31 HEALTH AFFAIRS 1663 (2012).
52. 42 U.S.C. § 1396u-7(b) (2010).
53. Deficit Reduction Act of 2005, Pub. L. No. 109–171, § 6044, 120 Stat. 4 (2006).
54. See 42 U.S.C. § 1396u-7(a)(2)(B) for the excluded Medicaid beneficiary categories.
55. In effect, the only adults whose coverage could be subject to the benchmark standard would be certain narrow optional coverage groups such as eighteen- to twenty-one-year-olds who remained eligible for coverage under their state plan, optional pregnant women, and optional low-income parents.
56. 42 U.S.C. § 1396u-7(b).
57. 42 U.S.C. § 1396u-7(a)(1)(C).

58. *Id.* at (a)(10)(A)(ii). For a discussion of the EPSDT benefit, which has a storied history and has been the subject of extensive litigation, see Sara Rosenbaum & Paul Wise, *supra* note 50.

59. For an explanation of how mental health parity affects managed care arrangements, see CTRS. FOR MEDICARE & MEDICAID SERVS., DEP'T OF HEALTH & HUMAN SERVS., STATE HEALTH OFFICIAL LETTER (Nov. 4, 2009), *available at* http://downloads.cms.gov/cms-gov/archived-downloads/SMDL/downloads/SHO110409.pdf.

60. See text accompanying notes 42–51, *supra*, regarding the interaction of Medicaid coverage standards and disability.

61. 42 U.S.C. § 1396d(a)(2)(C) (2006 & 2010).

62. 42 U.S.C. § 1396bb, § 1396u-7(b)(4), § 1396u-2(h)(2)(C).

63. The fact that revising coverage rules under Medicaid would not alter safety net payment standards is only part of the story, however. The ACA imposes specific reductions on Medicare DSH hospital payments as well as states' Medicaid DSH allocations, which are fixed and subject to annual global limits as a result of amendments enacted to Medicaid in 1991 aimed at halting what was characterized as an abuse of the Medicaid DSH payment system. For a history of federal Medicaid DSH payment reforms, see MEDICAID & CHIP PAYMENT & ACCESS COMM'N, REPORT TO THE CONGRESS ON MEDICAID & CHIP, Ch. 3 (Mar. 2011), *available at* http://healthreform.kff.org/ ~/media/Files/KHS/docfinder/MACPAC_March2011_web.pdf. The ACA's DSH payment reductions were criticized prior to *NFIB* because of their overly optimistic assumption about the extent to which the Act's Medicaid eligibility expansions would reduce the need for supplemental funding for DSH hospitals; the ACA DSH amendments also were criticized for the degree to which the ACA continued to allow states latitude in how they target DSH payments. With the pace of the Medicaid expansion now thrown into uncertainty as a result of the Court's decision, the potential adverse implications of the ACA's DSH payment cuts looms larger. For an overview of the ACA DSH amendments, see *The Estimated Effect of the Affordable Care Act on Medicare and Medicaid Outlays and Total National Health Care Expenditures: Hearing before the H. Comm. on Energy & Commerce, Subcomm. on Health,* 112th Cong. (Mar. 30, 2011) (statement of Richard Foster, Chief CMS Actuary), *available at* http://www.hhs.gov/asl/testify/2011/03/t20110330e.html. For a discussion of the potential implications of the ACA DSH reductions on safety net hospitals without concomitant amendments to strengthen DSH targeting rules, see NAT'L ASS'N OF PUB. HOSPS. & HEALTH SYS., EQUITABLE, SUSTAINABLE, RELIABLE SAFETY NET FINANCING: MEDICAID DSH (May 2012), *available at* http://www.naph.org/Main-Menu-Category/Publications/Safety-Net-Financing/May-2012-Medicaid-DSH-Policy-Brief.aspx?FT=.pdf.

64. Compare standards applicable to state exchanges and qualified health plans (42 U.S.C. §§ 18031, 18022) with standards applicable to Medicaid managed-care plans and states that elect to furnish coverage through managed-care arrangements (42 U.S.C. § 1396u-2). For a comprehensive review of similarities and differences, see DEBORAH BACHRACH ET AL., CTR. FOR HEALTH CARE STRATEGIES, INC., MEDICAID MANAGED CARE: HOW STATES' EXPERIENCE CAN INFORM EXCHANGE QUALIFIED HEALTH PLAN STANDARDS (Nov. 2011), *available at* http://www.chcs.org/usr_doc/Medicaid_Managed_Care_and_QHP_Standards_final.pdf.

65. 42 U.S.C. § 18021(a)(1)(C)(i) (2010).

66. 42 U.S.C. § 18031 (c)(1)(C) (2010). The term is defined to encompass all health care entities qualified to participate in a special prescription drug discount program authorized under the Public Health Service Act for providers furnishing a high volume of care to low-income patients.

67. 42 U.S.C. §13031(c)(1)(D) (2010).

68. BACHRACH ET AL., *supra* note 64, at 9.

69. 42 U.S.C. § 1396a(a)(13)(C).

70. In broad terms (special rules apply to states that already had expanded eligibility for the newly eligible population using the Social Security Act's special demonstration authority, found at 42 U.S.C. § 1315(m)), states receive 100 percent federal funding over the 2014–2016 time

period for medical assistance costs incurred for newly eligible populations (i.e., nonelderly adults ineligible for Medicare and not otherwise entitled to assistance because of their membership in one of the traditional coverage groups). Beginning in 2017, this enhanced funding declines, ultimately remaining at 90 percent in 2020 and for years thereafter. 42 U.S.C. §1395d(y). The normal federal contribution rate remains in place for traditional eligibility groups as well as for costs associated with plan administration.

71. 132 S. Ct. 2566, 2606 (2012).

72. Cong. Budget Office, Estimates for the Insurance Coverage of the Affordable Care Act, Updated for the Supreme Court's Recent Decision (July 24, 2012), *available at* http://www.cbo.gov/sites/default/files/cbofiles/attachments/43472-07-24-2012-CoverageEstimates.pdf (showing $9,000 per capita in the exchange and $6,000 per capita in Medicaid). This difference is commonly attributable to Medicaid's depressed provider payment rates in relation to the private insurance market. Of course, the federal government also would lose the value of state contributions to the cost of Medicaid coverage for previously eligible persons whose coverage was eliminated.

73. Ctrs. for Medicare & Medicaid Servs., Dep't of Health & Human Servs., 2010 Actuarial Report on the Financial Outlook for Medicaid iii–iv (2010), *available at* http://www.cms.gov/Research-Statistics-Data-and-Systems/Research/ActuarialStudies/downloads/MedicaidReport2010.pdf.

74. And this was more than thirty-five years ago, when the program was far simpler. See Friedman v. Berger, 547 F. 2d 724, 727 (2d Cir. 1976).

75. See Huberfield et al., *supra* note 3; Bagenstos, *supra* note 3.

76. See, e.g., Henry J. Kaiser Family Found., Kaiser Health Tracking Poll 1 (May 2011), *available at* http://www.kff.org/kaiserpolls/upload/8190-F.pdf (finding 60 percent public support for preserving Medicaid as an entitlement program and only 13 percent support for major reductions). These figures are not significantly different from public opinion regarding Medicare reforms.

77. Omnibus Budget Reconciliation Act of 1981, Pub. L. 97-35, 95 Stat. 357 (1981).

78. See, e.g., American Adjustment and Recovery Act of 2009, Pub. L. No. 111-5, 123 Stat. 115 (2009).

79. Actually, the term is probably not right. In a block grant, federal payments are made in advance of state expenditures, with limited state accountability for results. My prediction is that federal Medicaid spending would remain an after-the-fact event, with continuing tight federal controls over what is considered a qualifying state expenditure. This type of tight control is not unexpected in a very large program and is the method used in the case of Section 1115 demonstrations, 42 U.S.C.A. § 1315a, that award states flexibility.

80. See Jeanne M. Lambrew, *Making Medicaid a Block Grant Program: An Analysis of the Implications of Past Proposals*, 83 Milbank Q. 41 (2005) (examining the potential effect had block grant legislation passed by Congress but vetoed by President Clinton succeeded). The author estimated as much as a 35 percent decline in federal Medicaid funding, with highly differential effects among the states given differences in underlying economic conditions, health care cost factors, and other considerations.

81. Staff of H. Comm. on the Budget, 112th Cong., The Path to Prosperity: A Blueprint for American Renewal (Comm. print 2012), *available at* http://budget.house.gov/uploadedfiles/pathtoprosperity2013.pdf.

82. *Id.* at 5, 23, 29, 31, 45, 55.

83. See Cong. Budget Office, *supra* note 14.

84. Edwin Park & Matt Broaddus, Ctr. on Budget & Policy Priorities, What if Chairman Ryan's Medicaid Block Grant Had Taken Effect in 2001, at 1 (2012), *available at* http://www.cbpp.org/files/4-20-12health.pdf.

85. See Henry Kaiser Family Found., House Republican Budget Plan: State-by-State Impact of Changes in Medicaid Financing (May 2011), *available at* http://www.kff.org/medicaid/upload/8185.pdf. For example, Florida's ten-year loss reached nearly 44

percent of what it would have received, while Vermont, a more generous state, would experience a 26 percent loss below expected levels. *Id.* at 6.

86. Sara R. Collins et al., Health Care in the 2012 Presidential Election: How the Obama and Romney Plans Stack Up 13 (Oct. 2012), *available at* http://www.commonwealthfund.org/~/media/Files/Publications/Fund%20Report/2012/Oct/1636_Collins_hlt_care_2012_presidential_election_FINAL_CPI_revised_10_02_2012.pdf.

87. States have extensive appeals rights under Medicaid in furtherance of their entitlement interest in payment. 42 C.F.R. § 430.42 (setting forth the procedural requirements for review of federal payment disallowances).

88. See Letter from Lynn H. Gibson, General Counsel, Gov't Accountability Office, to Sen. Orrin Hatch & Rep. Dave Camp regarding congressional power to review the Secretary's decision to permit waivers of the TANF work requirements (Sept. 4, 2012), *available at* http://www.gao.gov/assets/650/647778.pdf. For a sense of the detailed federal oversight procedures used to govern state and tribal TANF spending, see Child Care Bureau, Dep't Health & Human Servs., Tribal TANF and CCDF Guide to Financial Management, Grants Administration, and Program Accountability (Aug. 2004), *available at* http://www.acf.hhs.gov/programs/occ/ta/pubs/tanf-guide/fmgapa14.htm (explaining the types of federal payment disallowances that can be applied to governmental TANF recipients).

89. For a review of federal/state financial relationships and their effect on local health economies, see Medicaid & CHIP Payment & Access Comm'n, *supra* note 63.

90. Edwin Park & Matt Broaddus, Ctr. on Budget & Policy Priorities, Medicaid Per Capita Cap Would Shift Costs to States and Place Low-Income Beneficiaries at Risk 6 (Oct. 2012), *available at* http://www.cbpp.org/files/10-4-12health.pdf.

91. John Holahan & Stacey Morrow, *Medicare and Medicaid Spending Trends and the Deficit Debate*, 367 New Eng. J. Med. 393 (2012).

# CHAPTER 20

# Health Policy Devolution and the Institutional Hydraulics of the Affordable Care Act

*Theodore W. Ruger*

The States are separate and independent sovereigns. Sometimes they have to act like it.[1]

For almost two decades, the Supreme Court has advanced a federalism jurisprudence that evokes Frederick Jackson Turner in its fixation on the distant frontiers of federal authority. Rather than tending to the vast interior spaces where the federal government and states concurrently regulate many fields of activity and jointly administer major social programs, many of the justices on both the Rehnquist and Roberts Courts have chosen to mend fences at the far boundaries of federal power, seeking to delimit the thin sliver of authority that remains "truly local" and thus completely beyond federal attention. In oral arguments in the major Commerce Clause cases from *Lopez* to *NFIB v. Sebelius* (*NFIB*), this has manifested in a parade of questions and hypotheticals to hapless solicitors general searching for some limit, *any* limit, on the scope of federal power. In the context of the Court's Commerce Clause doctrine, this delimiting impulse has led the Court to layer on top of *Wickard's* functional aggregation principle a series of clear-cut but conceptually wobbly categorical distinctions to mark the outer bounds of federal power: first "commercial" and "non-commercial" in *Lopez*, then "economic" and "non-economic" in *Morrison*, and now the kinetic requirement of physical activity as opposed to inactivity laid down in Justice Roberts's controlling opinion in *NFIB*.

A major corollary to this frontier federalism is a certain zero-sum assumption about federalism's sovereignty trade-offs, such that the federal government's gain is portrayed as the states' necessary loss, and vice versa.[2] This binary toggle is far from a realistic depiction of American federalism as it has operated at least since the New Deal, and may have come at a certain doctrinal opportunity cost. By neglecting the large and important spaces of regulatory concurrency and the complex federal-state relationship in some of the nation's most important entitlement programs, the Court has given short shrift to nuanced development of doctrinal areas, such as preemption and rules for conditional spending, which are more important to the realities of state sovereignty as it is exercised today in the capacious spaces of regulatory concurrency.

By upholding the Affordable Care Act (ACA) with its significant role for state policy discretion, and by judicially reworking the terms of the ACA's Medicaid expansion to enable an unburdened choice by the states about whether to accept or reject the generous terms of the expanded coverage, the Supreme Court did as much during the summer of 2012 to foster meaningful state decisional authority as did many of the more formalist decisions of the Rehnquist Court. First, from a doctrinal perspective, the Court's ruling on the federal conditional spending power and the Medicaid expansion gives newfound judicial attention to one of the federalism levers that is functionally of great importance in our current regime of fiscal federalism but had been largely ignored by a generation of judges. Second, and more importantly for the themes of this chapter, by permitting implementation of the major elements of the ACA to move forward in the next few years, the Court has given the go-ahead to an expanded health program that maps onto the existing structures of state policymaking in the field, and invites complex and ongoing strategic interaction between the states and the federal executive on multiple dimensions of health policy going forward.

In this sense the most important conceptual distinction between action and passivity in the Chief Justice's opinion is not the explicit formal test he laid down in his Commerce Clause subsection, but rather his recognition of states as active and potentially sophisticated sovereigns throughout other parts of the opinion. A major thrust of the Rehnquist Court's federalism jurisprudence in prior decades cast the states in a more passive role as the splendid baubles of our constitutional order, possessed of inherent "dignity" but generally helpless (and in need of judicial protection) against creeping federal hegemony. The Court was simultaneously relatively uninterested in protecting state sovereignty in its active forms, as evidenced for instance in its willingness to broadly imply preemption of state law in certain cases.[3] NFIB v. Sebelius sounds a different theme, both doctrinally in its attention to the federal spending power, and in its overall result in upholding a statute that grants the states frontline regulatory primacy. The Chief Justice noted that sometimes the states "have to act like" independent sovereigns, and his opinion both preserves and impels this active conception of state authority in the context of a major decentralized spending program.

This chapter seeks to understand, and tentatively predict, various aspects of the structural interplay between states and the federal government in the early implementation of the ACA, by drawing on lessons from health care federalism in Medicaid and related programs in the recent past. The Court's June 2012 decision, and Barack Obama's November 2012 reelection, together ensure that the many uncertainties inherent in the statute's implementation will now go ahead and play out. States now face major choices about establishing and operating health insurance exchanges and about expanding and reorganizing the delivery of services to their Medicaid populations. The federal executive is already engaged in a flurry of formal rulemaking explicating the breadth of discretion states will have in implementing the ACA's statutory terms, and concurrently in informal negotiations with dozens of states already about particular waivers and other forms of policy variation. What can we predict about the contours of this federalism game from the perspective of the ACA's statutory design and the expected incentives of states and the federal government within that structure?

The answer to this question is informed by the growing attention that legal scholars and others are beginning to pay to the complex dynamics of federalism within the many policy fields where federal and state authority overlap and operate concurrently. An increasing amount of sophisticated work is being done in this broad area, examining the interplay between federal and state authority in the field of preemption,[4] administrative law,[5] complex joint regulatory schemes like immigration and environmental law,[6] and in major spending programs like Medicaid[7] and the Affordable Care Act.[8] Three general insights important for this chapter emerge from this scholarship. First, states are neither passive nor powerless in their interaction with a nominally superior federal sovereignty. As Professors Heather Gerken and Jessica Bulman-Pozen have recently described, in various concurrent regimes states operate strategically, self-interestedly, and often subversively relative to federal authority, and have a number of tools at their disposal for doing so.[9] Second, and relatedly, the federal government's relation to the states in many shared regulatory or spending regimes is not one primarily of hegemonic control but more often one of negotiation and coordination. This has invited a variety of scholarly metaphors for this federal role, from "coach" to "teacher" to "conductor."[10] Third, the vertical hydraulics of federal-state relations may interact in important ways with the horizontal dynamics of separation of authority within the federal government. As described by both Professor Cathy Sharkey in the preemption realm[11] and Professor Bulman-Pozen in the context of joint regulatory schemes,[12] different branches of the federal government may simultaneously hold different postures toward state authority and the need for national uniformity, and states may be able to strategically exploit this interbranch variation. All of these ideas are important for this chapter, although as explained below these dynamics may operate somewhat differently in the context of a major spending program than in other kinds of concurrent policymaking.

With this background in place, the next few paragraphs set forth three major themes about the Affordable Care Act and the federal and state institutional behavior that can be expected to accompany its implementation over the next several years. The remainder of this chapter will elaborate on each of these themes:

First, from a structural perspective the ACA is highly typical of the devolutionary manner in which the United States has framed major social programs over the past century, and thus highly amenable to the strategic interaction between states and the federal government that is of interest here. States are the frontline implementers of two of the statute's three major goals: universal coverage and insurance regulation. (Like all payers in the system, states are also invested in the Act's third major goal—cost control—though that end is more heavily operationalized through federal Medicare payment policy and private delivery system innovation). As to coverage expansions through the state health exchanges and the expanded Medicaid program, the federal government acts primarily as fiscal underwriter and broad standard setter, leaving much discretion and responsibility for implementation to the states. For all of its length, many of the ACA's key statutory provisions on state exchange operation and benefit design are broad and unspecified, and the federal executive has already through rulemaking announced a policy of permitting states "maximum flexibility" in the interpretation of such standards.[13] Moreover, the ACA keeps in place, and expands, the statutory ability for states to receive broad waivers from the statute's rules for both Medicaid and the health exchanges, thus preserving a crucial locus of state policy variation and federal-state negotiation that is explored in more detail below.

A second major theme is that state incentives relative to the federal executive may be weighted somewhat differently in the context of a major cooperative spending program than in a shared regulatory regime. In a jointly administered regime where the primary outputs are conduct-regulating rules or standards, we might expect conflict and lack of cooperation from states when they and the federal government disagree on policy particulars. The story is marginally more complex in a compound program like Medicaid or the state exchanges under the ACA, which entail large budgetary transfers and state cooperation under variable federal standards in the delivery of a social insurance product to expanding numbers of Americans.

I do not mean to overstate this divergence: incentives for cooperation and conflict exist in any joint regulatory or spending scheme where multiple government players are involved. But major streams of federal funding accompanying a federal regulatory initiative will alter state incentives meaningfully. In degree, if not in kind, significant federal funding operates concurrently with state policy preferences, and on this spectrum there is simply no program like Medicaid in terms of the major share of state budgets it occupies. States have pure policy interests they seek to advance in Medicaid program design, to be sure, but often more important are their keen budgetary interests in maximizing federal funding streams and minimizing programmatic costs in delivering the social insurance product. Such fiscal interests have grown steadily more important in the states as Medicaid has occupied an increasing portion of their overall budgets. Thus when states seek to depart from uniform federal oversight rules in program administration, they are seeking favorable fiscal terms (both in terms of incoming revenue streams from the federal government and outlays to health care providers) as well as to optimize policy ends. If they can receive both of these things from a lenient federal executive, as numerous states did successfully under the Clinton and Bush administrations' permissive Medicaid waiver rules (described below), all the better.

This incentive structure in the states for Medicaid policymaking means that in this context, the quintessential "race to the bottom" is often replaced by a kind of "race to the budget," as states vie to cut relatively better deals with the federal underwriter. As recent history has taught, this can generate rather more cooperation with the entity (the federal executive) that holds the levers for doling out such generous financial terms as well as granting permission to depart from uniform national standards in program administration. States in such programs are more likely to engage in strategic bargaining than outright dissent, so long as the federal executive is giving them enough of what they want.

The third theme explored here shifts the focus to the incentives of the federal executive to bargain with states in such a shared spending regime. By and large, the primary federal interest in instituting a new social program is in the broad delivery of the product, and not in the complete specification or control of policy particulars. The federal executive's interests tend to diverge from states and private implementers both temporally and in the level of generality at which they interact with overall program goals. Particularly for major new programs like the ACA (or Medicare and Medicaid before it), the federal interest is in entrenching broad support for the new social program over the longer term rather than in tightly monitoring the subsidiary sovereigns charged with delivering it today. Hence it is often in the executive's interest in seeking to expand and entrench a social program to be extremely tolerant of variation in implementation by the frontline subsidiaries who deliver the product. High-profile examples of this practice include, for instance, Medicare's lenient oversight of private providers in its first two decades, or President Clinton's generous use of state Medicaid policy waivers while seeking to dramatically expand children's health coverage during his second term.

Coupling the foregoing two points suggests that the differential incentives of the states and the federal executive will often align in a manner that is conducive to cooperative arrangements between the two parties, as explored below in the recent history of Medicaid waivers. The federal executive has both the motivation and the tools to give the states some of what they want, and is often willing to sell cheaply policy uniformity and fiscal discipline in return for relative political calm and long-term programmatic entrenchment. The Obama administration has already signaled a willingness to engage in such a strategy during its second term, both in its rulemaking behavior and in its willingness to approve various transitional waivers under the ACA. There are externalities to this game, to be sure, and a crucial issue briefly discussed later in this chapter is the extent to which other institutions—the federal courts, Congress, groups representing providers and program beneficiaries—can and do push back against this often cozy relationship between the executive and the states. The remainder of this chapter treats each of these points in some detail, using Medicaid and other examples of delegated sovereignty as policy examples through which to better understand probable federal-state interaction under the Affordable Care Act.

## I.  The Affordable Care Act and the American Tradition of Delegated Governance

To the dismay of some advocates for more sweeping reform, the Affordable Care Act largely takes the existing structures of health care finance and delivery as it finds them. State governments and private providers will be the frontline implementers of the Act's coverage expansion and cost control goals. In this sense the ACA is highly typical of the American polity's long tradition of channeling the implementation of major social programs through subsidiary sovereignties (states and localities) and private stakeholders.[14] For instance, the Social Security Act of 1934 contained ten social programs, and only one (old-age security) was then or now regarded as primarily nationalized, and even that took on its present centralized form only in the 1970s. A contemporary observer in 1939 characterized the Social Security Act as many today do the ACA: as "a new departure ... as magnitude goes," but in basic implementation structure "simply an enabling act" in which "responsibility both for initiating and administering social security programs is expressly reserved to the states."[15] The 1960s era expansion of poor relief programs generally followed this model, and in the health insurance realm Medicaid was, and is, framed as a highly devolved program where states are the lead implementers and providers of health insurance to a portion of the nation's poor. This recurring reliance on states and localities as frontline implementers has had predictable consequences for public employment in the United States since the middle of the twentieth century: the number of federal employees has remained largely constant while the number of state and local public employees (many of them working to implement federally funded programs) has grown fivefold.[16]

Medicare is an outlier in one respect that proves the more general point about the American tradition of delegated governance in major social entitlements. Rather than leverage state and local implementation, Medicare payment remains nominally centralized at the federal government level. But while bypassing states, the Medicare program has traditionally delegated authority over allocation of health care entirely to private health care providers and fiscal intermediaries with weak central oversight, leading to foreseeable cost inflation over the life of the program. As Robert Ball, one of Medicare's original architects, has stated about the original structural bargain, "There was overwhelming political agreement that Medicare did not have a mission to reform delivery of, or payment for, medical care."[17] In bypassing state authority Medicare is quite different in structure than Medicaid, the Children's Health Insurance Program (CHIP), the ACA, or other federal health programs; in its general reliance on subsidiary institutions for delivery of the entitlement, it is of the same kind.

Unlike in Medicare, the states are clearly front and center in the ACA's approach to delegated governance. Although one of the Act's three major goals—cost control—will be operationalized by private providers under pressure from new payment formulas in Medicare and through various incentive programs for private delivery systems, the states are the primary implementing bodies for the Act's other two main policy goals, universal coverage and insurance regulation. Scholars in this volume (Abbe Gluck, Tim Jost) and others have comprehensively cataloged and assessed the major role that states will play in implementing the ACA. States have a lead role in specifying and enforcing the most popular provisions in the statute, those that limit a host of insurance company practices including preexisting condition exclusions. And states are the primary implementers of the Act's twofold approach to achieving near-universal coverage, by virtue of the Medicaid expansion (already a state-led program) and the creation of state-run health insurance exchanges.[18]

As with any statute, the ACA will not interpret itself, and it is impossible *ex ante* to know precisely how strictly or loosely the states and the various branches of the federal government will interpret its terms. The ACA mirrors other federal statutes that delegate implementation to subsidiary actors in that it contains a bevy of indeterminate federal standards to channel and structure state (and private provider) discretion. Going forward there are two major, and interrelated, questions about the Act's general standards for state implementation of the exchanges, the insurance regulatory mandates, and the Medicaid expansion. The first, a substantive variable, asks how tolerant the federal government will be of variation in the implementation by the states on these dimensions of the ACA's overall scheme. The second question is institutional, asking which branches of the federal government will enforce uniformity on the states and, if multiple federal actors are operating concurrently, how this horizontal struggle between federal branches will play out. We already have a tentative answer to both questions, at least in the earliest days of the ACA's implementation. On the substantive point, in early rulemaking on several sections of the Act the current administration has indicated a policy of "maximum flexibility" to the states on a number of the key implementation points involving the health exchanges and other variables. This is consistent with the general pattern, in the United States and elsewhere, of strategic entrenchment of transformative policy regimes through initial leniency in overseeing implementing stakeholders. On the institutional primacy question, it is unsurprising that the executive branch has taken the lead role in such preimplementation interpretation, but whether in future years congressional oversight or judicial intervention will unsettle this executive posture of policy leniency toward the states is a key question going forward.

## 2. Medicaid Waiver Policy as a Mechanism for Strategic Cooperation between States and the Federal Executive

Medicaid policy in recent decades serves to illustrate the complex dynamic by which states seek to achieve policy goals and maximize fiscal support with a shared federal-state spending program. Medicaid is, and has always been, a federal program in funding and oversight only—its administration remains squarely with the state bureaucracies. The federal executive branch under Presidents Clinton, Bush, and Obama has proven willing to be quite lenient in approving both policy variation and additional program cost in individual state projects. Such leniency may stem from genuine executive support for policy experimentation within a federal system, or more likely from the executive's desire to advance other goals such as overall policy entrenchment or political quiescence, as explored below.

Medicaid "demonstration" waivers are a quantifiable and high-salience manifestation of programmatic variation within Medicaid, and have markedly increased during the past three presidential administrations and generated several significant state experiments in health policy. This is not to say that waivers are the only dimensions of variation within a compound spending program like Medicaid or the ACA. Indeed, given the unspecified standards in the ACA's text on central issues like health insurance exchange design and benefits, and the current administration's stated commitment to "maximum flexibility" on such matters, many states will not need to resort to actual waivers to exercise substantial policy discretion in implementing the Act. Still, the federal executive's management of the waiver approval lever to advance health policy goals and entice state cooperation during both the Clinton and George W. Bush administrations provides tangible (and to an extent quantifiable) evidence of the structural nodes for state-federal bargaining that are embedded, even expanded, in the ACA's statutory text and so will remain important.

The statutory framework for Medicaid contains a provision for express waivers for states from many of the statute's general requirements. Section 1115 of the Social Security Act grants the Secretary of Health and Human Services wide latitude to grant waivers from various federal standards for states implementing Medicaid and other programs under the Act. That section provides that "the Secretary may waive compliance with any of the requirements of [the Act] to the extent and for the period he finds necessary to enable" a state to carry out "any experimental, pilot, or demonstration project which" the Secretary believes is "likely to assist in promoting the objectives" of the Act.[19]

Neither statutory text nor other mechanisms of administrative governance provide much in the way of additional tools to constrain executive discretion in considering and approving Section 1115 waivers. The Secretary's decision to grant or deny an individual state waiver is considered informal adjudication, and thus not subject to the more exacting notice-and-comment procedures governing other forms of administrative governance. And, although the grant or denial of a waiver is potentially subject to judicial oversight, courts have applied an extremely generous standard of review in considering such cases.

Although in the statute from the beginning of the program, the vast expansion in terms of both quantity and scope of such Section 1115 waivers has occurred in the past two decades. From the program's inception through 1993—a period of almost three decades—the federal executive used its Section 1115 power to approve a total of approximately fifty state Medicaid waivers.[20] From 1993 to 2006 the Clinton and Bush administrations granted "a torrent" of such waivers, 149 in all, to a total of forty-six states and the District of Columbia.[21] Such waivers were not merely more numerous under these two administrations but also substantially broader in both scale and in the degree of interstate policy variation—in the 1990s many states sought to place their entire Medicaid population into managed care arrangements, and in more recent years states like Massachusetts used waiver authority to dramatically reform their health insurance systems. As noted below, beginning in the 1990s these waivers were also granted on more favorable financial terms to the states than had been applied in previous decades.

The advent of this increased waiver activity in the 1990s reflects the behavior of a sophisticated federal executive attempting to manage both horizontal and vertical institutional relationships by maintaining control of a key leverage point of fiscal federalism during a period of intense partisan conflict. In 1994, President Clinton had seen his once-popular health reform plan fail, and faced in Congress a disciplined and motivated opposition that had taken control of the House. Then, as now, House Republican leadership decried the growth of federal authority and sought to return power to the states, and then, as now, a favored policy for achieving that end was the "block grant" funding mechanism in which states were given a lump sum, and broad policy latitude, to administer various social programs. In 1995 President Clinton vetoed a bill ("Medigrant") that would have converted Medicaid primarily to the block grant model.

While on the one hand Clinton vetoed the block grant transformation of Medicaid, his administration was simultaneously working to give the states what they wanted in terms of policy devolution through the Section 1115 waiver process, a policy mechanism squarely under executive branch control. Early in his tenure Clinton called the existing waiver process "Byzantine and counterproductive" and promised "relief" for governors in the form of a streamlined and more receptive approval process.[22] The Health Care Financing Administration (HCFA) in 1994 published notice that it intended to streamline the approval process and reduce the time states would wait for Section 1115 approvals. Most importantly, HCFA also announced that it would abandon the strict approach to "budget neutrality" that had sunk many state waiver requests during the Reagan and George H. W. Bush administrations. Rather than prove on a year-by-year basis that their policy innovations would be cost-neutral compared to the existing Medicaid program, states were able to justify their proposals through *ex ante* budget forecasts for the entire five-year life of a waiver program,[23] a methodological change that introduced substantial cost uncertainty and thus dramatically widened the bargaining space within which an agency and a state eager to make a deal could find common ground on the supposed "neutrality" of a waiver request that would be underwritten by federal matching funds. Contemporaneous expert observers such as Comptroller General Charles Bowsher were critical of this change and predicted that under this approach "waivers could lead to a heavier financial burden on the federal government" in funding Medicaid nationally, an assessment that has been borne out by subsequent analyses (in 2002 and 2008) by the General Accounting Office and by other *ex post* studies of the cost impact of specific waiver projects.[24]

These twin elements that were attractive to states—policy devolution and generous financial terms—help explain the success of Clinton's Medicaid waiver strategy across a politically diverse range of states. Through a permissive waiver policy, Clinton was able to outmaneuver congressional Republicans by appropriating the rhetoric and practice of policy decentralization but housing it within a mechanism firmly under his control. And by fudging the requirement of "budget neutrality" for federal matching funding of Medicaid waiver projects, Clinton was able to offer states a better deal than they could get from Congress in the form of block grants, which give policy latitude only in return for a hard (and often reduced) cap on federal funds. As practiced under Clinton and then George W. Bush, waivers offered motivated states the chance to bargain for policy discretion *and* simultaneously obtain a more generous financial deal from the federal underwriter. On these terms one can understand the state inclination to cooperate and strategically bargain with a permissive executive under such conditions. Given the persistence in the ACA of the basic 1115 waiver authority as well as other new statutory waiver provisions (although with more stringent public notice-and-comment procedures attached), and the generous federal funding levels in the statute's Medicaid expansion and exchange subsidy provisions, we might expect to see similar cooperation even while more overt political disagreement remains visible. We can also begin to understand the incentives a sophisticated federal executive might have to employ a lenient waiver process to maximize overall policy entrenchment and political support at the price of short-term policy uniformity, a topic explored in the following paragraphs.

## 3. The Federal Executive: Policy Entrenchment in Thickened Institutional Space

It is clear enough what the states got out of the permissive waiver policies of the Clinton and Bush administrations, and what they might expect to get out of similar behavior from the second Obama administration under the ACA's flexible terms. The question of what motivates the federal executive to be so lenient warrants a bit more discussion. As an initial matter the executive always gains something from blunting direct conflict with the states, particularly in times of intense partisan division. But this in itself is an incomplete explanation—the gains from tamping down political disagreement are potentially attractive across a wide range of policy areas, and yet in some of these fields we see the federal executive working quite hard to enforce national uniformity despite the partisan conflict that such a posture produces. Why might the federal executive tolerate relatively more disuniformity in the administration of major social programs than it does, say, in state participation in enforcing a rule-based regulatory regime?

The answer, I think, lies in the mismatch between the end goals of the national sovereign and the subsidiaries in the context of a devolved social program. By divesting the national executive of frontline implementation responsibility, delegated governance regimes inherently direct the attention of the two sovereigns to different points of concern, pitched at different levels of generality and playing out in different temporal spaces. States care more about Medicaid implementation specifics given their primary role in delivering the product and the keen budget consequences they face every year. The federal executive tends to frame its programmatic goals at a higher level of generality, focusing on more amorphous concepts like "coverage" and overall cost as opposed to the vagaries of implementation details. This interacts with the manner in which presidents seek to secure reputational gains: for instance, after giving away a flood of Section 1115 waivers in the mid-1990s, Bill Clinton in each of in his last three State of the Union addresses claimed credit for "providing health insurance for up to five million children"—unsurprisingly he made no mention of the dramatic departures from national uniformity he permitted in service of that overarching end, or the fact that in part due to such permissive variation access to health care for children in some states lagged behind others.

This conceptual difference in the frame of reference that the federal government and the states prioritize is also supported by a mismatch between temporal frames: state variables of interest in such programs typically are more immediate than the federal concern. Some of this is driven by the hard realities of public finance: the national government is much more capable of countercyclical borrowing to fund deficit spending than are the states, so can take a longer view. Some of this is more functional: states are tasked with the details of delivering a complex insurance product in real time, lining up providers and serving beneficiaries, while the broader federal interests in expanding overall "health security" or "universal coverage" are more vague and thus less immediate. This divergence in primary ends between the two levels of sovereignty creates a bargaining space that can be strategically arbitraged by both parties, as was seen in the Medicaid waiver dynamics of the Clinton and Bush administrations, and might occur again during the first years of the ACA. Cooperation is more likely because, at bottom, the states and the federal government care most dearly about different things.

The incentives of the federal executive to tolerate high levels of variation in implementation specifics may be even heightened the more transformative the major thrust of the new social program is. Political scientist Stephen Skowronek in his important work on presidential authority discusses the manner in which presidents today are hemmed in by a thick accretion of institutions that "mak[e] it possible for other actors to mount more formidable resistance to their will."[25] This resistance applies with particular force for presidents who seek to engage in "reconstructive" politics that transform the American political regime. There is some debate already ongoing about whether Barack Obama, and the Affordable Care Act itself, ought to be regarded as "reconstructive" in Skowronek's typology, but orthogonal to that debate is a more central insight about the ACA in light of Skowronek's concept of institutional thickening. The ACA may be reconstructive in its major aims of providing universal coverage and reforming the national insurance markets, but it is highly conventional in the manner in which it devolves implementation responsibility to states and private actors. Few areas of the American polity are as institutionally "thick" as the health care system, and the ACA's structure treads lightly on this existing regime. We would expect the behavior of the federal executive in implementing such a statute to exercise an equally soft touch relative to other institutional stakeholders like states, in hopes of longer-term entrenchment.

That the long time horizon of those seeking to entrench transformative new social programs lends itself to short-term permissiveness in the early years of the program is shown from experience both here and abroad. The play for the transformative policy sponsor is invariably to the long view of history. No one now remembers the uneven and halting roll out of the unemployment compensation provision of the 1935 Social Security Act: perhaps presaging the disparate readiness of states today to operationalize health insurance exchanges, some states were paying benefits under the new program as early as the middle of 1938, while in other states benefits were not paid out until over a year later.[26] Medicare at its inception, and for much of its life, was famously lax at controlling the private physicians and hospitals who provide services, with ramifications for therapeutic variation and systemic cost increases that persist today. Even the British National Health Service (NHS), now a central tenet of that nation's polity, was on shaky ground in its earliest hour. Enacted without a single Conservative Party vote in 1946, the NHS faced the prospect of failure in early 1948 due to a threatened boycott of the program by the nation's physicians organized by the British Medical Association. Minister of Health Aneurin Bevan cut a last-minute deal with the doctors that increased payment rates in return for their support of the new program—he would later claim that he "stuffed their mouths with gold" to save the fledgling NHS.[27] Bevan's strategy worked in ways he could not have imagined: sixty-five years later the NHS was celebrated in song and dance as one of Britain's greatest national achievements during the opening ceremonies of the 2012 London Olympics (now *that's* policy entrenchment).

The Affordable Care Act will not achieve that sort of bipartisan adulation any time soon, and has no prospect of being feted in patriotic song and dance in the foreseeable future. I suspect the second Obama administration will settle for something much less, namely a dampening of the overt opposition and the strategic co-opting of a centrist majority of states. To paraphrase Bevan, there are two kinds of "gold" at the President's disposal toward this end: the currency of a permissive attitude toward state policy experimentation, and actual revenue transfers flowing from the loose interpretations of budget neutrality pioneered by the Clinton administration. Particularly given the ACA's transformative overall ambition, the federal executive will have strong incentives to purchase policy entrenchment and political quiescence by sacrificing programmatic and fiscal discipline in the short term.

## 4. Uncertain Oversight by Alternative Institutions

If the above story of incentive alignment between the executive branch and the states seems too good to be true, it is—at least without mentioning the clear and predictable consequences of such permissive bargaining over health program variation. First and foremost, there is strong risk that the intended beneficiaries of the Medicaid expansions and the state insurance exchange regimes of the Affordable Care Act may be disserved by overly lax federal oversight, and there is no shortage of scholarly evidence that this has occurred in the past with particular waiver projects. The strong incentives states have to use waivers to limit or reduce their own budget outlays have led many observers to suggest that more federal uniformity is needed in the provision of basic benefits.[28] Second, overall budget discipline and cost control is another substantive end that is clearly harmed by the lax posture toward budget neutrality that administrations have employed since the 1990s.

There is also an important institutional imbalance in the story told here—Congress and the federal courts remain largely on the sidelines. It is unlikely this is a stable status quo, although experience shows that both of these other branches are limited in their ability and/or willingness to intervene to force greater uniformity and adherence to standards. Most members of Congress have state clients themselves, and during the Clinton and Bush Medicaid waiver proliferation were as likely to intervene in favor of more lenient and quicker waiver approvals as they were to exercise concern over the lack of uniform standards or budget neutrality in waiver projects generally. This tendency toward home-state patronage of members of Congress in the Medicaid waiver area is underscored by the few extant empirical studies of the practice—one such study found that an important predictor of the speed with which the Department of Health and Human Services (HHS) granted state waivers was the relevant state's representation on one of several key congressional oversight committees.[29] In the divided Congress following the fall 2012 elections it is possible the House Republicans might aim to complicate the Obama administration's implementation of the Act by closely monitoring executive branch waiver activity, but the past suggests little concerted congressional will to do so.

The federal judiciary's oversight role presents a more interesting case. On the one hand, relatively recent policy history gives a prominent example of federal judicial superintendence of national uniformity in the Medicaid program that was much more rigorous than the oversight provided by the federal executive. This history involves the enactment and subsequent repeal of the Boren Amendment, offering an interesting snapshot of institutional choice in the oversight of state discretion in Medicaid. Congress enacted the Boren Amendment in 1980 to free states from perceived federal executive branch micromanagement in the area of Medicaid reimbursement rates from nursing home facilities.[30] Ironically, given what actually happened under the amendment, the states felt that HHS was too rigorous in its oversight and thought the Boren Amendment's ambiguous standard (state rates were required to be "reasonable and adequate" to meet efficient operating standards by nursing homes) would provide them more regulatory flexibility. In actuality the federal courts during the Boren Amendment years became a much more rigorous overseer of state policy than HHS ever had been, entertaining dozens of lawsuits by nursing homes and other providers who were able to successfully challenge state rate-setting. State Medicaid officials discovered that the federal courts were a less tolerant institutional monitor than the executive branch had been, and after years of complaint finally achieved the repeal of the amendment in 1997.[31]

The history of litigation under the Boren Amendment illustrates the institutional potential for the federal courts to become de facto enforcers of programmatic uniformity in the Medicaid area, by giving substantive content to the capacious and unspecified language of key statutory terms. Still, the amendment's demise in the late 1990s correlates with related doctrinal shifts emerging from the federal judiciary itself that make it much more difficult for Medicaid beneficiaries or providers to redress their grievances in court. Beginning with the landmark case of *Gonzaga University v. Doe*,[32] the Supreme Court and the circuit courts have made it progressively more difficult for program beneficiaries to use Section 1983 as the foundation for a private right of action to enforce the terms of Medicaid and related statutes. The *Gonzaga* Court held that "unless Congress speaks with a clear voice, and manifests an unambiguous intent to confer individual rights, federal funding provisions provide no basis for private enforcement by Section 1983."[33] Since *Gonzaga*, the federal circuit courts have held almost uniformly that Medicaid's equal access provision and other statutory terms do not contain the sufficient rights-creating language to provide a foundation for private enforcement. In light of this new obstacle to Section 1983 enforcement, certain beneficiaries and providers have sought to challenge Medicaid policies on Supremacy Clause grounds, an alternative theory that the Supreme Court considered (but did not decide) in a 2012 case but that faces similar barriers to judicial endorsement.[34]

The Affordable Care Act looks likely to only accelerate this dynamic. The Act itself contains no language conferring a private right of action, a drafting choice that—since made in light of *Gonzaga's* clear statement rule—may be regarded by subsequent reviewing courts as even more freighted with negative implication by Congress regarding a private right of action. What's more, the ACA vests various decisions in the Secretary of HHS in a manner that expressly disables administrative or judicial review. The statutory text of the ACA thus endorses and accelerates, rather than dampens, the Supreme Court's hostility to private enforcement of the terms of federal benefit programs. This statutory language, coupled with preexisting doctrinal trends, makes it extremely unlikely that the federal courts will reverse course and prove more receptive to private actions by beneficiaries or providers over the terms of future federal-state negotiation over the ACA's implementation. And this institutional reluctance to intervene will only further leverage the bargaining space that states and the federal executive can be expected to exploit in the first decade of the ACA's existence.

## 5. Conclusion

The Supreme Court's decision on the Affordable Care Act in June 2012, like the November 2012 reelection of Barack Obama, cleared away potential obstacles for commencing the difficult and uncertain process of implementing the ACA. This in turn opens up space for the complex dynamics of modern American federalism to operate in myriad ways, as states and the federal executive bargain and bicker over various ways to implement the state exchanges and the Medicaid expansion. Experience suggests that this will entail substantial state sovereign choice exercised in an active capacity under the relatively lenient superintendence of a federal executive more interested in long-term policy entrenchment.

## Notes

1. Nat'l Fed. Ind. Bus. v. Sebelius, 132 S. Ct. 2566, 2603 (2012).
2. Such a mutually exclusive conception of state and national power was held by many in the Framing generation, and remains important in other federal systems where the national sovereign's entry into a given regulatory field presumptively displaces subsidiary authority. For a discussion of early American views on this subject, see Stephen Gardbaum, *The Nature of Preemption*, 97 CORNELL L. REV. 767 (1994); see also Theodore W. Ruger, *Preempting the People: The Judicial Role in Regulatory Concurrency and Its Implications for Popular Lawmaking*, 81 CHI.-KENT L. REV. 1029 (2006).
3. See, e.g., Geier v. Am. Honda Co., 529 U.S. 861 (2000).
4. See Catherine M. Sharkey, *Preemption by Preamble: Federal Agencies and the Federalization of Tort Law*, 56 DEPAUL L. REV. 227 (2007).
5. See Gillian E. Metzger, *Administrative Law as the New Federalism*, 57 DUKE L.J. 2023 (2008).
6. See Heather K. Gerken & Jessica Bulman-Pozen, *Uncooperative Federalism*, 118 YALE L.J. 1256 (2009).
7. See Nicole Huberfeld, *Bizarre Love Triangle: The Spending Clause, Section 1983, and Medicaid Entitlements*, 42 U.C. DAVIS L. REV. 413 (2008); Abigail R. Moncrieff, *The Supreme Court's*

*Assault on Litigation: Why (and How) It Might Be Good for Health Law*, 90 B.U. L. REV. 2323 (2010).

8. See Abbe R. Gluck, *Intrastatutory Federalism and Statutory Interpretation: State Implementation of Federal Law in Health Reform and Beyond*, 121 YALE L.J. 534 (2011).

9. See Gerken & Bulman-Pozen, *supra* note 6.

10. See, e.g., Michael S. Sparer, *Leading the Health Policy Orchestra: The Need for an Intergovernmental Partnership*, 28 J. HEALTH POL. POL'Y & L. 245 (2003).

11. Catherine M. Sharkey, *Preemption as a Judicial End-Run Around the Administrative Process*, 122 YALE L.J. ONLINE 1 (2012).

12. Jessica Bulman-Pozen, *Federalism as a Safeguard of the Separation of Powers*, 112 COLUM. L. REV. 459 (2012).

13. See Patient Protection and Affordable Care Act: Establishment of Exchanges and Qualified Health Plans, 76 Fed. Reg. 41,866 (proposed Jul. 15, 2011) (to be codified at 45 C.F.R. pt. 155 & 156).

14. For a long view of the development of this model in the American context, see KIMBERLY J. MORGAN & ANDREA LOUISE CAMPBELL, THE DELEGATED WELFARE STATE: MEDICARE, MARKETS, AND THE GOVERNANCE OF SOCIAL POLICY (2012).

15. Frank Bane, *The Social Security Board and State Organizations*, 202 ANNALS AM. ACAD. POL. & SOC. SCI. 137, 137 (1939).

16. See Thomas Gais & James Fossett, *Federalism and the Executive Branch*, in INSTITUTIONS OF AMERICAN DEMOCRACY: THE EXECUTIVE BRANCH 503, Table 2 (Joel Aberbach & Mark Peterson eds., 2005).

17. Robert M. Ball & Arthur E. Hess, *Dialogue on Implementing Medicare, Jan. 31, 1992, in REFLECTIONS ON IMPLEMENTING MEDICARE* 2 (M. G. Gluck & V. Reno eds., 2001).

18. I note the possibility under the statute that the federal government may impose a federal-operated exchange in those states that do not have an exchange up and running by 2014. In keeping with the theme here about strategic leniency by the federal executive, I would expect both that (*a*) HHS will be permissive about granting timing extensions to states who are behind schedule in structuring their own exchanges; and (*b*) solicitous of local preferences and local stakeholders in setting up and running "federal" exchanges in those states that do opt for the federal model.

19. Social Security Act § 1115(a)(1), 42 U.S.C. § 1315 (2006).

20. See Bruce Vladeck, *Medicaid 1115 Demonstration Waivers: Progress Through Partnership*, 14 HEALTH AFFAIRS 217, 218 (1995).

21. Frank J. Thompson & Courtney Burke, *Executive Federalism and Medicaid Demonstration Waivers: Implications for Policy and Democratic Process*, 32 J. HEALTH POL. POL'Y & L. 971, 977–978 (2007).

22. Thomas L. Friedman, *President Allows States Flexibility on Medicaid Funds*, N.Y. TIMES, Feb. 2, 1993, *available at* http://www.nytimes.com/1993/02/02/us/president-allows-states-fle xibility-on-medicaid-funds.html.

23. See Thompson & Burke, *supra* note 21, at 976.

24. See GENERAL ACCOUNTING OFFICE, GAO-02-817, MEDICAID AND SCHIP: RECENT HHS APPROVAL OF DEMONSTRATION PROJECTS RAISE CONCERNS (2002); GENERAL ACCOUNTING OFFICE, GAO-08-87, MEDICAID DEMONSTRATION WAIVERS: RECENT HHS APPROVALS CONTINUE TO RAISE COST AND OVERSIGHT CONCERNS (2008).

25. STEPHEN SKOWRONEK, THE POLITICS PRESIDENTS MAKE 31 (1993).

26. Bane, *supra* note 15, at 139.

27. See David Mechanic, *The Managed Care Backlash: Perceptions and Rhetoric in Health Care Policy and the Potential for Health Care Reform*, 79 MILBANK Q. 35, 48 (2001).

28. See, e.g., GENERAL ACCOUNTING OFFICE, MEDICAID AND SCHIP, *supra* note 24; but see Thompson & Burke, *supra* note 21, at 999 (examining over a hundred waivers and conclud-ing that "Medicaid 1115 waivers have not been a major force for subterranean program ero-sion through the implementation process").

29. See Eric Helland, *The Waiver Pork Barrel: Committee Membership and the Approval Time of Medicaid Waivers*, 17 CONTEMP. ECON. POL'Y 401 (1999).

30. See generally Edward Alan Miller, *Federal Administrative and Judicial Oversight of Medicaid: Policy Legacies and Tandem Institutions under the Boren Amendment*, 38 PUBLIUS 315 (2007).

31. See *id.* at 328.

32. 536 U.S. 273 (2002).

33. *Id.* at 280.

34. Douglas v. Ind. Living Ctr. of S. CA, 132 S. Ct. 1204 (2012).

# INDEX

CPSIA information can be obtained at www.ICGtesting.com
Printed in the USA
BVOW04s1335271113

337514BV00004B/250/P